HARD CLIMB UP THE LADDER

The Story of the First Black Fire Chief of a Major New England City

CHIEF JOHN B. STEWART JR. (RET.)

And the Founding of the International Association of Black Professional Fire Fighters (IABPFF)

WITH RUBIN TENDAI

Chief John B. Stewart Jr., who rose up in rank to become one of Hartford's greatest fire chiefs and later a city councilman, has been and continues to be an inspiration and mentor and role model encouraging our youth, particularly African American young men and women, to be the best of who they are. His lifetime of dedication and activism for civil rights, justice and equality, inspired me as an elected official, and he continues to be a valued friend. The fire station in Hartford named in his honor will be a lasting memorial to his life of dedication, inspiration, and commitment to his family, our community and our residents.

Thirman L. Milner—Former Connecticut State Senator
and Mayor of Hartford, Connecticut

Make no mistake, when you say 'The Chief' in the City of Hartford, only one man comes to mind—John B. Stewart Jr. His influence in diversifying the Hartford Fire Department, particularly its leadership ranks, is unquestioned. As a fire fighter, city councilman and real estate agent, the Chief touched many who lived in the capital city.

Stan Simpson—Host, *The Stan Simpson Show*, FOX CT.
Columnist, *Hartford Courant*

HARD CLIMB UP THE LADDER

The Story of the First Black Fire Chief of a Major New England City

And the Founding of the International Association of Black Professional Fire Fighters (IABPFF)

Hartford Courant articles used by permission.
Hartford Public Access conversation used by permission.
Thanks to Stacey Close for permission to quote
from *Fire in My Bones*

For Gladys, my wife and loving companion,
and for my children and grandchildren.

And to the memory of
Fire Fighter William Henry Jacklyn

William Henry Jacklyn was the first Black to join the Hartford Fire Department. He was hired in 1898 as a substitute fire fighter. In 1908 he was told he could become full-time, but would not be allowed to sleep in the same quarters with White fire fighters. A proud man, Jacklyn refused, but remained a volunteer. He was reported to have distinguished himself as a fire fighter during the Great Hartford Railroad Station Fire of February 1914.

Acknowledgments

I am indebted to the Phoenix Society, an organization of Black professional fire fighters in the Hartford County area, and to the members of the International Association of Black Professional Fire Fighters (IABPFF). Special thanks go to: the "Father" of the IABPFF Captain Vincent W. Julius (Ret.); the late New York City Fire Commissioner Robert O. Lowery, the first Black to head a major fire department; Chief Ronald C. Lewis (Ret.), the first Black fire chief in Richmond, Virginia; the late Chief Samuel Golden, the first Black fire chief in Oakland, California; Chief Claude Harris (Ret.), the first Black fire chief in Seattle, Washington; Chief Larry Bonnafon (Ret.), the first Black fire chief in Louisville, Kentucky; and Chief Edward Wilson (Ret.), the first Black fire chief in Kansas City, Missouri.

I also owe my success to, and give thanks for, the founding members of the Phoenix Society, especially Chief Nelson K. Carter Sr. (Ret.), Fire Marshal Carl G. Booker (Ret.), Lieutenant Frank Carter Sr., and Lieutenant Cecil W. Alston (Ret.). Nelson and Cecil were *there for me* during the formative years of the Phoenix Society, and from the beginning of my career in the fire service to my rise to chief of the Hartford Fire Department.

In addition, I owe my success to the department's first Hispanic and female recruits, my executive officer, Lieutenant Thomas Jacobucci (Ret.), Chief's Aide Lieutenant Rudy Saccoccio, Lieutenant Arnold Goldstein, Lieutenant Patrick Leonard, and Chief's Aide James E. Lewis.

The Fire Chaplain Corps was a key element to my success as fire chief. It was the first fully integrated Fire Chaplain Corps in New England, and was established by me in October 1980, two months after my appointment to the office of chief of the Hartford Fire Department. The members of the corps at that time were Rabbi Hans

Bodenheimer, Father Stephen Foley, the Rev. Charles E. Blake, and the Rev. Dr. Joseph Zezzo.

Highest of honors and blessings go to the late Woodrow Wilson Gaitor, Hartford's first Black city manager, who made my appointment. Blessings and honors go to the Rev. Dr. Rubin Tendai, the former senior minister at Faith Congregational United Church of Christ, who encouraged me to share my story. I am forever grateful for the time he spent wading through boxes of memorabilia and organizing material for this memoir. Last and most assuredly not least, I give thanks God for the opportunity to tell my story, which I hope will be an inspiration to others.

Chief John Bradley Stewart Jr. (Ret.)

CONTENTS

FOREWORD

The pioneers of the Stewart family left North Carolina in 1898 and settled in Glastonbury, Connecticut. In all, thirteen children of the Faust clan left the South. This was the family into which my grandfather, John Lewis Stewart married in 1895. In 2007 one of them, Emma Faust Tillman, became the world's oldest living person at age 114. This is recorded in the *Guinness Book of World Records*. Another notable fact is that four other Faust family members lived beyond the age 100. Ava lived 102 years, Antoinette lived 102 years, Eugene lived to be 108, and Ada reached the age 105. The Faust family made it into the *Guinness World Book of Records* for having the most siblings who lived beyond the age 100.

I have no memory of my mother Mattie Baker Stewart. She died in 1932 when I was just two years old. My foster parents, Walter and Ella Murray, with whom I spent most of my childhood and adolescent years, are largely responsible for shaping the values I carried into adulthood. The Murrays moved to Hartford from Virginia in the 1920s. In addition to owning a grocery store, they owned two three-family houses from which they received rental income. The Murrays, who had no children of their own, took me in and raised me as their son.

Like many who grew up before the 1960s, I attribute the stability of family life to the strong influence of the church. In 1944, when I was fourteen years old, I joined Talcott Street Congregational Church. This was the church where my grandmother and my aunts held membership. Talcott Street Church merged with Mother Bethel African Methodist Episcopal Church in 1954 to become Faith Congregational Church. My membership in this church continues to this day. I credit my professional success to my religious upbringing, my public school teachers, to the many positive community influences, my social and professional affiliations, and to my family within the fire service. This family extends beyond the city of Hartford to many parts of the nation and to other countries.

HARD CLIMB UP THE LADDER

The Story of Hartford, Connecticut's First Black Fire Chief

And the Founding of the International Association of Black Professional Fire Fighters (IABPFF)

Circa 1953, Rookie fire fighter John B. Stewart Jr.
at top of ladder participates in fire fighting exercise.

Tribute to a Black Fire Fighter

I heard the engines' clanging gongs,
A block or two away.
And then I saw the raging fire,
Dark smoke and waters' spray
I saw the shiny ladder
As it reached up to the wall.
And then I saw him climbing,
Climbing upward, toward the call.

His black hands gripped the ladder,
Which he climbed with sured pace.
The smoke engulfed his body,
Flames danced about his face.
"I can't hold on! Please help me!"
A youthful voice, a pleading cry.
"Hold on! I'm coming!"
Was his firm assured reply

The roof began to crumble,
The building's end was near.
Those below began to scatter
At the sound which filled their ears.
His dark face was gripped with horror,
His mind was seized by fear.
As he reached the fiery window
He heard—"Swing the ladder clear!"
In the next heroic moment
As I closed my eyes to pray,
A black hand grasped the child
And lifted him away.

There atop the ladder,
Clearly seen by every age,
Were fireman and child
Dark silhouettes against the sky.
He was grimy, hot and haggard,
As he stepped down to the ground
A cheer arose—he smiled,
But he never turned around.
When a reporter asked his name,
I heard him quietly say—"No name please.
Compared to bigotry and other barriers I've overcome,
This was an easy day."

By James Overton Rogers

Written and dedicated to John B. Stewart Jr., on the occasion of his promotion to lieutenant in in March 1966. Later it was rededicated to honor all Black fire fighters.

PROLOGUE

HARD CLIMB UP THE LADDER

I am a Connecticut Yankee. A Nutmegger down to my core. I am from Connecticut and of Connecticut. I was born, educated, married, and raised a family in Connecticut, and have lived and worked in Connecticut all of my life. There were two generations of Stewarts in Connecticut before me, and there are three more generations behind me. There were times when I considered leaving Connecticut after retirement and moving south as some of my close friends and colleagues have done. Like them, my wife, Gladys, and I would trade in the cold snowy winters of Connecticut for the warm sunshine of Georgia or Florida. But I am nearing my eighty-fourth birthday, and I'm still here. It's most likely I will die here, and be buried in Yankee soil.

Like my late father, John Bradley Stewart Sr., after whom I was named, I am somewhat of a local historian. The roots and branches of Black families in Connecticut's capitol city of Hartford, and the events that helped shape and define our lives, have long been of interest to me. Of greater interest, however, has been our local politics, which I continue to watch with great fascination and try to make sense of.

I know that Yankee culture has not always been kind to its people of color. The treatment of Native Americans and Blacks in Connecticut's early days is not something I can point to with pride. A look into this chapter of Connecticut's history is to see cruelty committed against a people who by their culture and color were looked upon as inferior. Long before the White settlers arrived, Native Americans were living and raising their families in the territory they called "Quonehtacut," which meant "the long river." These people were hunters-gatherers and farmers. The northeast section of Quonehtacut was occupied by the Nipmuc tribe, while in the southeast were the Mohegan and Mashantucket Pequot tribes.

When the Dutch and then the English newcomers encountered these native inhabitants, their immediate thoughts were to conquer and confiscate the land. Bows and arrows and tomahawks proved no match for well-aimed musket balls. The Pequot war in 1637 killed hundreds of Native American men, women, and children. Many of those not killed were sold into slavery in the West Indies, while others were not allowed to return to their villages or to use their tribal names. The Europeans also brought with them a disease unknown to Native Americans. An epidemic of smallpox brought death to thousands of Native Americans resulting in the near decimation of their culture. While many of the colonists were killed during years of fighting, it was the Native Americans who became subject to the White settlers. "Quonehtacut" had become "Connecticut."

Black slaves were reported in Hartford as early as 1639. In 1730 officials reported there were about seven hundred Blacks in the state, a number that grew to nearly three thousand by 1750. Most had been brought to Connecticut as a result of trade in rum, molasses, and slaves, which linked New England, West Africa, and the Caribbean. The larger number of these slaves worked on farms in and around New London and Fairfield counties. By 1756 many of the influential doctors, lawyers, ministers, and public officials in Hartford and New Haven owned at least one or two slaves. In 1730 Connecticut enacted the Black Code, which required that runaway slaves be returned to their masters, and that a slave caught outdoors after nine at night without an order from his master could receive up to ten lashes. The code stated that a Black, mulatto, or Native American servant found wandering outside the boundaries of the town to which he belonged after nine, without a pass from his owner or a magistrate, could be seized and returned to his master, who had to pay any costs. It further stated that if a slave spoke words for which a free person could be found liable, that slave should receive not more than forty lashes.

While the Connecticut colony was more severe in its discrimination than any of the other New England colonies, it did pass the Gradual Emancipation Act in 1748. This Act stated that a manumitted slave born after March 1 of that year had to serve as an indentured servant until age twenty-five, after which he would be free. The act also stated that slaves who fought in the American Revolution became free persons after their service. Although slavery had been woven deeply into Puritan society, Connecticut did outlaw the evil institution in 1844, the last of the New England states to do so.

While not as overt, only the naive would believe that racism no longer exists in Connecticut. In the 1920s Connecticut was a center of Ku Klux Klan activity with as many as twenty-three chapters and eighteen thousand members. As late as 1996, the Connecticut Supreme Court, stated in its ruling in *Sheff V. O'Neill* that students in Hartford's public schools were racially, ethnically, and economically isolated.

While there are shameful chapters in Connecticut's history, new and more progressive chapters have been written. The election of Thirman L. Milner as Hartford's first Black mayor in 1981; the election of Carrie Saxon Perry as Hartford's first Black female mayor in 1987; the appointment of Howard Brown Jr. as Connecticut's first Black banking commissioner in 1985; the election of Francisco L. Borges as the first Black state treasurer in 1986; as well the election of a Hispanic mayor and appointment of a Hispanic fire chief in Hartford—all these, and more, attest to the new and progressive chapters that have been written in Connecticut's relationship with its people of color. My story is an additional chapter.

I was born at the beginning of the Great Depression to a twenty-year-old mother and a twenty-three-year-old father. At the time of my birth, we were one of the more fortunate Black families in Hartford because my father had a steady job. In those days Hartford was populated mainly by Italians, Irish, Jews, and Blacks. While many of the

Blacks were part of the Great Migration from the South, there were many who, like me, were native to Connecticut. In the 1940s there was an influx of Jamaicans into Hartford, looking for work in the wartime industries. In the 1950s there came a steady stream of Puerto Ricans. It was after World War II that a number of college-educated Black men began to make their presence felt in Hartford. Men like Dr. Frank T. Simpson, the first Black to head Connecticut's Human Rights Commission; Boce Barlow, Connecticut's first Black state senator and judge; and John C. Clark Jr., Hartford's first Black city councilman. These men along with others began opening doors in the areas of employment, politics and law that had been shut to Blacks.

I was a career fire fighter in Hartford's fire department. As a boy I remember standing wide-eyed when a shiny red fire engine roared by with its bell clanging and siren wailing. I even imagined myself riding atop the fire engine. But as I watched the fire engines race by it looked as though you had to be White in order to be a fireman. Years later I learned that Hartford did have a Black fire fighter in 1898. His name was William Henry Jacklyn. When he left the department in 1914, it would be another forty years before the color bar would again be lifted and Blacks allowed to join the city's fire department. It would be another eighteen years before a Black person would be elevated to the officer's rank in the department. It would take fourteen more years for a Black person to make chief. Being named Hartford's first Black fire chief in 1980, and later having a firehouse bear my name was nothing I envisioned when I joined the Hartford Fire Department in 1952.

When I was a boy people clapped and they cheered when a fire engine sped by on its way to fight a fire, or to rescue a person from a burning building. This was not the reality in Hartford from 1967 to 1970, as the city experienced four consecutive summers of racial violence. Fires were set, stores were looted, and the police became targets of rooftop snipers. When fire fighters arrived at the scene of a fire, we were viewed as intruders and pelted with bricks, bottles, and stones. We didn't want to see city blocks burn to the ground, but neither did we want to be hit by flying objects. The worst violence took place in the North End, where the majority of low-income Blacks and Puerto Ricans lived. In an effort to stop fires from being set, and to end the attacks on fire fighters, the fire department created a new unit called Special Services, of which I was placed in charge. I was instructed by the fire chief to work with the people in the community and help ease the strained relationship. So I became the liaison between the minority community and Hartford's fire department.

Four other fire fighters were assigned to work along with me in Special Services. We were all put on detached duty, meaning we no longer went out to fight fires. We worked out of small satellite offices set up in ethnically diverse neighborhoods. Each of these offices functioned like a branch of city hall. As members of Special Services, we had the important task of closing the gap of distrust and misunderstanding that separated the minority community and the city's fire department. The police department already had a similar type unit in place, but its members were viewed with suspicion by many of the young people in the community. My hope was that those of us in Special Services would be viewed as friends, and not outsiders.

When I became Hartford's first Black fire chief I was under the close scrutiny of city administrators, elected officials and union leaders, as well as the watchful eyes of city residents. Some thought that running an organization as large and as complicated as the fire department was beyond my ability. Some just plain hoped I would fail. Others wished me well, or prayed for my success. As fire chief I encountered both racist attitudes and behaviors within and outside the department. The leadership of the fire fighter's union challenged my every action. As a result I was called to testify before the State Labor Relations Board more times than I can or care to remember. I also received racist phone calls at home. This made me more determined to do the job as well, if not better, than the fire chiefs who preceded me.

In the spring of 1992, after forty years of government service, I retired from the fire department. Upon leaving I announced that I would spend my time working to bring economic development to the city's distressed North End. During my time with the fire department, I had been called twice to serve as assistant to two different city managers. This allowed me to work closely with government and elected officials, and to see how services were delivered to city residents. Often I found myself drawn into the stressful machinations of city politics. At age sixty-two I reasoned that I was young enough and in good enough health, and had citywide name recognition, that if I decided to run for political office I had a good chance of winning.

Before retiring from the fire department, I had set my sight on the city's top job, that of city manager. Hartford had a weak mayoral form of government, so the city manager was responsible for the day-to-day operation of the city. I felt that my administrative experience, my knowledge of how city government worked, and my skill at getting things done positioned me well to make for an effective city manager. The city manager was an appointed position, with the selection of the appointee being made by the mayor and the city council. The city was without a manager at the time, so I submitted my resume and cover letter. I reasoned that a nationwide search was unnecessary. It was after the job was offered to someone else that I submitted my retirement papers.

Against the advice of my wife Gladys, in the spring of 1995 I began my campaign for a seat on Hartford's City Council. I was out of the house day and night making campaign stops, giving speeches, participating in debates, meeting with supporters, and planning strategy. On election day in November 1995, I received more votes than any other candidate on the Democratic slate. As the top vote getter, I became the city council majority leader. I served two terms in this position, from 1995 to 1999. I could have served more, but at the end of my second term and approaching my seventieth birthday, I said my good-byes and went home to be with Gladys.

During my career of public service I received many awards and experienced many special and memorable moments. One such moment was being honored as the 2004 recipient of the Thomas Hooker Award. I was only the seventeenth recipient of this rather prestigious award. During the presentation ceremony I was humbled when Ken Johnson, president of the Ancient Burying Ground Association, Inc. said of me:

> I am pleased to present the award to Hartford native and outstanding citizen John Bradley Stewart Jr. Throughout his life, John Stewart has opened doors and created opportunities. His leadership while Chief of the Hartford Fire Department, and as the first African American to hold that post in New England, has inspired many to excellence. Hartford's Fire Department is one of the busiest, and one of the very select few in the country to receive the top rating, achieved during Chief Stewart's tenure from 1980 to 1992, and maintained by our current Chief Charles Teale, who spoke of being motivated as a young man by John Stewart's leadership.
>
> After retirement as Chief, John Stewart served on the Court of Common Council of the City of Hartford from 1995 to 1999, during which he was majority leader. He has been active with many local organizations, including the Urban League of Greater Hartford, the Salvation Army, the Blue Hills Neighborhood Revitalization Zone, and the Dr. John E. Rogers Cultural Center...

Another award that gave me a tremendous amount of pride was the President's Award presented by the Greater Hartford Branch of the NAACP. I had been retired for ten years when I was honored with this award on September 30, 2011, at their Ninety-Fourth Annual Membership and Freedom Fund Dinner. The theme for the evening was "Putting the People of Greater Hartford First." I was humbled when described as a person who had sought in my lifetime to do precisely that.

Although being the first Black person in Hartford to achieve a particular position was quite unintentional on my part, this distinction is part of my story. I was the first Black person to operate a lathe machine at Hartford Machine Screw Company; one of the first two Black cashiers in the New England A&P Supermarket chain; one of three persons hired as the city's first Black Yellow Cab drivers; the first Black person to become an officer in the Hartford Fire Department; and Hartford's first Black fire chief.

It can be said that I belong to what a Washington Post writer has called "a diverse group where membership requirements are universal and rigid." If you're persistent enough to overturn 200 years of history and courageous enough to surmount stereotypes, you might have what it takes to become the first African American to achieve a position, he states. If you manage it here, he says, is what might await: threats, media scrutiny, jealousy, and the pressure of representing an entire race. At first you experience much of this alone, he concludes.

Climbing from the bottom rung of the ladder, a rung deeply embedded in racial bigotry, to the very top in the Hartford Fire Department was a hard climb fraught with challenges that needed to be overcome. Remaining at the top of the ladder proved equally as hard. This was mainly due to my acrimonious relationship with union officials.

When people ask how I was able to overcome, I tell them it was with the love of family and friends, and by the grace of the Good Lord.

GROWING UP

I couldn't believe my eyes. Slender and lanky for my fourteen years, I folded my knees to my chest and sat down at the curb. As I stared up at the black plumes of smoke billowing into the sky, the realization hit me. My father would be worried and come looking for me. Jumping to my feet, I ran as fast as I could to my house only a few blocks away on Barbour Street, in Hartford's North End. .

It was Thursday, July 6, 1944, two days after Hartford's annual Independence Day fireworks celebration in Bushnell Park. Ringling Bros. and Barnum & Bailey Circus had pitched the big top in the vacant lot running along Barbour, Hampton, and Kensington Streets and Cleveland Avenue, in the city's North End. Just as they did every summer when the circus came to town, people from Hartford and the surrounding towns poured onto the grounds for a day of excitement and fun. Inside the big top, over six thousand people, many of them women and children whose husbands and fathers were away fighting in the war overseas, were enjoying the two o'clock matinee performance. The antics of the clowns, the Flying Wallendas on the high wire, and the sweet sugary taste of cotton candy melting in their mouths offered the spectators a wonderful break from their usual routines.

Many of the Black kids who lived on the nearby streets were away at Camp Bennett, a camp for colored children in nearby Glastonbury. Because we were not allowed in the downtown YMCA, a group of concerned Black men in Hartford had purchased fifteen acres of land and started the camp. These men believed that Black kids in Hartford needed to swim and participate in outdoor recreational activities during the summer, just as the White kids did. I wasn't at Camp Bennett because I had planned to earn some money by working in a nearby tobacco field. It was only when I was offered the job of watering the circus elephants, the same job I had the summer before, that my plans changed. So I was carrying buckets of water back and forth from the water hydrant to where the elephants were kept. For me, the fun of being at the circus was not diminished by not being inside the big top watching the show. Seeing the performers coming and going, the animals in their cages, and hearing the joyful music of the band all added to an air of excitement. Besides, with the six tickets I was to receive as my payment, I would enjoy a later show with some of my closest friends.

On one of my trips I was balancing a water bucket in each hand when the sound of screaming caused me to stop in my tracks. "Fire! Fire! Fire!" people were screaming. The screams were coming from inside the big top. "Fire! Fire! Help! Fire!" I stood there frozen and wide-eyed as people with frightened looks on their faces began scrambling and pushing their way out of the big top. Then I saw smoke, dark and thick. I saw a path of fire begin to spread its way up one side of the big top. Men, women and children running, pushing and being pushed, shoving, falling down and getting up. There was fright on the faces of women with babies in their arms; women leading and pushing little children out of the big top. In what seemed a matter of only seconds flames were spreading their way around the huge tent. I watched in disbelief. Was I dreaming this? It was all so surreal, like a movie at the Daly Theatre over on Albany Avenue.

Then I heard the sound of fire engines off in the distance, and in what seemed like no time at all several fire trucks pulled onto the circus grounds. Grim-faced fire fighters began unraveling hoses and shouting orders. "Get the people out!" "Unblock that entrance!" "Attach the hose!" "Get the water over there!" Police officers and fire fighters were evacuating people from inside the big top and directing them to safe areas. "Clear a path!" they yelled. Fire fighters began pouring water on the blaze. More fire engines pulled onto the grounds. From a safe area where I had been directed with hundreds of others, I watched as the fire ripped through the big top. It was now fully engulfed. People were fainting and falling as fire fighters and police carried motionless people on stretchers to waiting ambulances. Medical attendants in white jackets administered emergency treatment. Some people were using their cars to take injured family members and friends to the hospital. After a while the fire fighters had the fire under control, and then water from their hoses extinguished the last burning embers. From the curb I saw the once-huge big top with multicolored streamers rippling in the breeze, now a smoldering heap of twisted metal and black ash under a rising canopy of dark smoke.

After leaping from the curb to my feet and running home, I told my father and stepmother all that had happened. Later that evening, I watched from my bedroom window as a steady stream of ambulances passed by my house on their way to the hospital, or to the morgue. The next morning the newspaper headline announced the fire's grim toll. "167 Bodies Recovered From Circus Fire, Most Were Children," it read. What a shock it was to learn that one of the children who died was my little neighbor Billy Dineen. Billy was only eight years old and lived only a few houses from me when I lived on Martin Street. My mind went back to the many times I had seen Billy playing on the street and walking home from school. In the days that followed, whenever I saw Billy's father I remembered my little friend who died in the circus fire.

Fire investigators learned that many of those who died or were injured had trouble escaping the big top because of the steel railings that had been placed in front of the bleachers. Others had trouble getting out a main exit that was blocked by an animal chute. Fire inspectors also discovered that the dark acrid smoke that made it so difficult for people to see and breathe was the result of a mixture of gasoline and paraffin that had been applied to the tent. Not realizing how dangerous a mixture this was, circus workers had used it to waterproof the big top. Besides those who died, 487 people had been injured, most of them women and children. In the years to come, this terrible tragedy would be known as the Great Circus Fire.

On a warm summer afternoon in July of 2004, I stood at the scene of the Great Circus Fire with a group of city officials for the dedication of a memorial plaque. Now seventy-four years old and retired, I listened as Hartford Mayor Eddie Perez called it the deadliest fire disaster in the history of Hartford. He spoke of the heroism of the fire fighters that day and the safety regulations now in place to prevent anything like this tragedy from ever happening again. My mind drifted back to that day sixty years earlier, and I again saw the fright on the faces of the people trying to escape the deadly flames. I remembered that the newspaper had called it "the day that the clowns cried."

From past interviews it was widely known that I had been present at the circus fire. So when the ceremony was over a reporter walked over to me. "Chief, was it this fire that inspired you to become a fire fighter?" I had been asked this question a number of times. "No, I can't say that it did," I told him. Most of the time, those asking the question hoped my answer would be yes, making for a more interesting story. But thinking back, there may have been a time or two when I claimed the circus fire as my inspiration for becoming fire fighter.

The truth be told, more than anything else, I was inspired to become a fire fighter one afternoon in 1949. I was nineteen years old and relaxing on my front porch when I saw my cousin Frank Davis strolling up the street. He was one of six Black fire fighters hired a year earlier by the Hartford Fire Department. As he neared my house, I could see that he was wearing his fireman's uniform. I noticed the sun reflecting off the shiny gold buttons and badge on his dark-blue jacket making them sparkle. A blue cap with a black brim and shiny gold insignia sat squarely on his head. When he stopped in front of my house, I noticed the sharp creases of his trousers and his shiny black patent-leather shoes.

"You sure are looking good in that uniform, Cousin Frank," I said. He gave me a prideful nod and then a smile lit up his face. "How do you like being a fireman?" I asked. "Oh, I like it just fine," he answered. Then he told me about the good pay and all the benefits he was getting. I listened with interest, not realizing at the time that this chance meeting was destined to be a defining moment in my life. Two years later I took and passed the fire fighter's exam. Seeing my cousin Frank in uniform that day set a course for my life that at the time I could never have imagined.

I was born on Friday, May 16, 1930. It was a time when millions of people in this country were out of work. Men who could not make house payments or feed their families were desperate to find employment. By the hundreds of thousands, they roamed the country looking for jobs that did not exist. Hungry people stood in bread and soup lines and scrounged in garbage cans for morsels of food. States looking for help from the federal government found none. Believing that the individual states should provide for their own people, the Hoover administration had thus far developed no relief programs.

This was the time of the Great Depression. In Hartford nearly seven-thousand people were jobless. The unemployed looked to the state government for financial relief that did not come. People in Connecticut, beaten down by the Depression, felt that Governor John Trumbull and his Republican Party looked upon their desperate situation with indifference. In response, voters in Hartford voted Trumbull out of office in favor of Democrat Wilber Cross. One sign of the times was that White men in Hartford and the surrounding communities were forced to accept the most menial jobs usually left to Blacks, and White women were cleaning their own homes.

My birth took place at McCook Hospital in Hartford's North End. In those days the neighborhood surrounding the hospital was Jewish, but it was expected that Mattie Stewart's baby would be delivered there. This was the hospital that served most of Hartford's Black population. At the time of my birth, my father, John, was twenty-three, and my mother, Mattie, was twenty. My father was fortunate enough to have a full-time job. While he had not yet finished high school (he would later), he was viewed in the Black community as a deep thinker. He especially enjoyed reading Black history and committed to memory many facts he deemed important. In later years he would hold court, sharing with his audience little-known facts and events about Black life in Hartford. In later years Hartford would honor him for his contribution to the city's cultural life.

Tall, dark, and ruggedly good-looking, my father knew how to turn on the charm when in the presence of a lady. When he met Mattie Baker, he wooed and courted her and eventually won over her heart. At this time she was still a student at Weaver High School. Two years after her graduation, they were married. Mattie received several college scholarships, but instead of college she went to work as a maid for Bill and Mary Savitt, who lived on Canterbury Street. These were the same people who had employed Mattie as a babysitter while she was a high school student. Even today I remember with fondness the Savitts' presence at my own graduation from Weaver High. They owned a jewelry store downtown and in honor of my mother, presented me with my class ring. Just as they had encouraged my mother two decades earlier, they encouraged me to get a college education.

When Mattie brought me home from the hospital, it was to her mother's small house on Bellevue Street in the city's North End. A large area that ran north of Albany Avenue to the borders of the Bloomfield and Windsor suburbs, the North End was where most of Hartford's Blacks lived. This area would be transformed over time from majority Jewish to majority Black and Hispanic. When I was two years old, my mother died. She was just twenty-two years old. To this day I have no memory of her. I do have a faded black-and-white photo showing my mother to be a slim, attractive, brown-skinned woman. The realization that I did not know where my mother was born came to me after reading her death certificate some years later. She was born in a small town in southwest Georgia called Shellman. The death certificate also stated the cause of her death. It was then that I realized why every year until I was eighteen my father took me to the doctor for a physical examination. He wanted to know if the tuberculosis that took my mother's life had been passed down to me.

My father was the personal chauffeur to the Holstein brothers, owners of a rubber manufacturing business. Because his job kept him on the road driving them around the country, my grandmother, Lela Baker, Mattie's mother, was left to care for me. She and her brother, the Reverend Toby Jones, were well-respected charter members of Mount Calvary Baptist Church, a prominent church in the North End. When I was three, my father took me from my grandmother's house to the home of Walter and Ella Murray. To my father's way of thinking, the Murrays were the perfect couple and their well-kept house on Martin Street the perfect environment for his son. Martin Street was quieter and better kept than Bellevue Street. Most of the people on Martin Street, which included several White families, owned their homes and took pride in keeping their property up. The Murrays had migrated to Hartford from Virginia, and my father was impressed by the fact that both had college degrees.

It also helped that unlike my father, the Murrays were churchgoing people. She was a member of Metropolitan AME Zion on North Main Street, and he was a member of Shiloh Baptist Church on Albany Avenue. Besides being a staff member at Camp Bennett, Mr. Murray had what was considered in the Black community to be a very good job. Dressed in a suit and tie, he sat outside the governor's office door at the State Capitol Building. If the governor or a member of his staff needed a message delivered or an errand run, Mr. Murray would deliver it and run it. The Murrays had once owned a neighborhood grocery store, but lost it during the Depression. Still, they owned several multi-family dwellings from which monthly rental income was received. The Murrays had no children of their own, so when asked by my father, they readily agreed to take me in and raise me as if I were their own son.

In September 1935, two months after Jesse Owens won four medals at the Summer Olympics in Germany, and four months after my fifth birthday, Ella Murray enrolled me in the predominantly Jewish Brackett Elementary School. My memories of this school on Westland Street in the city's North End are good ones. I cannot remember ever having any problems there on account of race. In fact, I became friends with many of my Jewish classmates. Besides my normal studies, my extracurricular activities at Brackett included violin lessons and membership in the Audubon Club. The violin lessons were at the insistence of my father, who wanted to expose me to "some of the finer things of life." I graduated from Brackett in 1941, when I was eleven-years-old. Ella Murray then enrolled me in Northeast Junior High School. It was during my first year at Northeast that President Roosevelt announced the Japanese had bombed Pearl Harbor and country was at war. But Japan and Pearl Harbor seemed very faraway places and this had no impact on me at the time. Like Brackett, the student body at Northeast was predominantly Jewish, and there too I can recall no problems on account of race.

One day in 1942, on one of his visits to the Murray household, my father brought with him a woman. "This is Dorothy Stewart, my wife," he told us. "Because John now has a stepmother he can come and live with us." This was a cause of much sadness for both the Murrays and for me. None of us had any idea my father was contemplating marriage, and that I would soon go live with him. I had been with the Murray's for nine of my twelve years. These were my formative years, and they were the parents I knew. But I had no choice but to go live with my father and his new wife at their house on Barbour Street. Over time I came to like my stepmother very much. She was soft-spoken and very nice to me. She told me she had grown up as Dorothy Kellums in the nearby town of Rockville. She worked at Stieger's Department Store downtown, but didn't tell what she did there. She said her father was Black and her mother was White. This explained why she was so fair-skinned with wavy dark brown hair. She said her father and mother had moved from Philadelphia to Connecticut when she was a baby to escape those who frowned on their interracial marriage.

Back on Barbour Street, my father didn't allow me to associate with the boys who hung out on the block. Some of them were more than likely headed for trouble, he would say. "I want you to do more with your life." He encouraged me to study hard, set goals, and amount to something in a country where Whites considered Blacks to be inferior. My stepmother agreed with my father. She was so pleased that I was taking violin lessons that she presented me with an original copy of a Stradivarius violin. She had received this rather valuable violin from her mother. Her mother's father, who was a German American, had inherited the violin from his father. So now I was the only kid on my block, and maybe even the only Black kid in Hartford, with a Stradivarius. Sometimes while walking home through Keney Park with my violin, the neighborhood kids would tease me.

"What's that you got there John, your vi-yoo-lin?" they said, as they feigned playing a violin, and fell to the ground rolling in laughter. I just ignored their teasing and continued on my way. My father also encouraged me to join the marching band at nearby St. Michael's Catholic Church. And being the obedient son, I was soon playing a bugle at St. Michael's. It didn't bother me that I was the only Black kid in the marching band. I made friends with the other band members and rather enjoyed the attention we received when we marched in parades dressed in our brown khaki uniforms.

Sadly, after five years, the marriage between my father and stepmother came to an end. In 1947 she packed her suitcase, gave me a big hug, kissed me on the cheek, and walked of the house for good. I was real sorry to see her go. Now, like the Murray's, Dorothy Kellums was no longer an everyday presence in my life. One problem that contributed to the breakup of their marriage was that my father was hardly ever at home. He was now working as a salesman for a big liquor company down in Bridgeport. This job kept him on the road most of the time. Also contributing to the breakup was the fact that on most weekends when my father was at home, he and a group of friends drank liquor and gambled at our kitchen table into the early hours of the morning. To keep the card game from being raided and the gamblers from being hustled off to jail, my father paid the neighborhood cop. Turning a blind eye to this infraction of the law, the White police officer gladly pocketed the payoff.

With all the cussing and drinking and smoking and card playing and my father's long absences, my stepmother finally had enough. She would have left sooner, I overheard her tell my father, but she stayed because of her concern for me. After leaving she petitioned the courts to have me moved out of the Barbour Street house and back to Martin Street with the Murrays. It was for my own good, she stated in the petition. The truth was I actually wanted to go back and live with the Murrays, but my father was adamant that I remain with him. At the time, I was attending Talcott Street Congregational Church with my father's mother and sisters. So my stepmother asked the minister there, the Reverend James Wright, to accompany her to court on my behalf. Believing this action was to my benefit, Reverend Wright agreed.

After the judge heard from my stepmother about my father's actions and absences, and then heard from Reverend Wright and from me, I was ordered back to the Murrays. This ruling angered my father, because he wanted to personally see me through high school and into college. But he had no choice but to abide by the judge's order. Now that I was back with the Murrays, my stepmother began divorce proceedings. She would remarry several years later and move to Rocky Mount, North Carolina. I was seventeen and the plan was that I would remain with the Murrays until I finished high school. Then I would go off to college. As it happened, instead of spending one year, I would stay with the Murrays for three more years.

2

LIKE FATHER, LIKE SON

It is a rare occasion when a man experiences the very last moments of his life on the same day of the week and on the same date in the same month that he experienced the very first moments of his life. But my father, John Bradley Stewart Sr., was a rare man. The eighty-nine years that separated his birth on Sunday, March 31, 1907, and his death on Sunday, March 31, 1996, chronicled the life and times of a man, who in my estimation, stood apart from ordinary men. The fact that the span of his life was bound on either side by the Lord's Day, with his birth being on Easter Sunday, I would like to believe had something to do with his helping to resurrect the lives of so many people who were down and out. As the personal chauffeur to the owners of a local rubber manufacturing company for over twenty years, my father was able to travel most of this country, visiting interesting places and encountering interesting people. Though his formal education was limited, in conversation he was as much at ease with PhD's as he was with those, as they say, "who had no Ds." My father was the keeper of Black history, a salesman extraordinaire, a community activist, and an advocate for the downtrodden. Many of his experiences in life he chronicled in several Black newspapers. Some of these experiences my father shared with me in conversation, some I observed firsthand, and others I read about in his writings.

My father was born to John Lewis Stewart and Ava Catherine Faust Stewart. I unfortunately know nothing of my grandfather's early history. What I know of my Grandmother Ava's history was told to me by her, and by my father and his sisters. Ava's parents, Alphonsa and

Martha Faust, were born into slavery. Alphonsa was born on March 8, 1860, to Cain Faust and Lethe Smith Faust, both of whom were slaves. Cain took the surname "Faust" from his White owner. Martha was born on October 22, 1862, to Alfred Gibson and Eliza Hoffman Gibson, they too were slaves. They were freed by the Emancipation Proclamation, but could not claim their freedom until the end of the Civil War. Nineteen-year-old Alphonsa Faust and seventeen-year-old Martha Gibson were married on November 6, 1879, and took-up sharecropping on a plantation near Gibsonville, North Carolina. My grandmother Ava, was born on January 29, 1881, one of twenty-three children born to the couple. In 1898, Alphonsa and Martha were among the approximately 15,000 Southern Blacks who migrated to Connecticut by the year 1900.

My grandparents, John and Ava, who were married in 1895, settled in Hartford, where she gave birth to five children, including my father. In 1910 they moved to the town of Glastonbury. Ava's father, Alphonsa, worked in the Glastonbury tobacco fields and her mother, Martha, picked and sold berries. After living in Glastonbury for five years, during which time Ava gave birth to two more children, my grandparents moved to East Hartford. They moved with my grandfather's younger brother Reuben and his family into a two-family house on Latimer Street. Back then Blacks were not allowed to buy a house in East Hartford, so the nearby St. John's Episcopal Church bought the house for them. My grandfather and his brother made monthly payments to the church, and the church later transferred ownership of the house to them.

It was in the Latimer Street house that my grandmother Ava gave birth to three more children, bringing the total to ten. Their children were Lucille, born on March 14, 1904; Lillian on April 13, 1906; John on March 31, 1907, Helen on December 5, 1908; William on August 5, 1910; Dolly on April 23, 1912; Raymond on January 3, 1914; Shirley on May 24, 1917; Margaret on June 4, 1919; and Gertrude on April 9, 1921. The Latimer Street house would remain the Stewart homestead until the last Stewart moved out in 1979. While I have no memory of my grandfather John, I came to know my grandmother Ava quite well. As a little boy, my father sent me to Talcott Street Congregational Church with her, and later in life, I would visit with her at the home of her daughters, my aunts Lucille and Lillian on Garden Street. My grandmother Ava was 102 when she died on March 14, 1983.

My father has written that it was his father's expectation that each one of his ten children would take on work outside the house as soon as each of them was old enough to do so. While a student at Union and Second North Grammar Schools in East Hartford, my father took on his first job before he had reached his tenth birthday. For several summers he picked strawberries, earning two cents for every basket he picked. His next job, also before he was ten-years-old, was cleaning a meat and grocery market where he was paid one-dollar and twenty-five cents a week. About this my father has written:

> We children were taught to hand it all in, so I gave my pay to my father and he gave me back a nickel to keep for myself. When I was ten years old I got a job as an assistant newsboy selling Sunday papers. I sold many of my papers to colored employees of the railroad who lived in abandoned, outdated railway coaches. Most of them couldn't read the newspapers, but were attracted to the comics and the colorful Sunday supplement. These were immigrant men from the South who worked in the section gangs laying tracks and replacing tiers. They got salt pork and molasses along with their wages. The men came up alone first and only sent for their families when they had a place to live and had set something aside. We thought that was no way to live so our first impression was negative.

> During the summer, while World War I was going on, I was the water boy on the Shade Tobacco Plantation of A. & S.

Hartman. I earned fifteen dollars a week and my two older sisters, Lucille and Lillian, earned twenty-five dollars a week picking leaves, and sewing tobacco leaves together. After a few years of working on this plantation, I found summer employment with my Uncle Kane who raised tobacco in Glastonbury. I harvested tobacco plants in the hot sun after the plants had been cut down and had wilted in the sun. As I grew older and larger I was given other duties, such as loading wagons with lathes of the tobacco—five or six plants strung on a wooden lathe. Later I became the "hanger" in the tobacco shed. This meant I would stand on a 4-by-4 beam holding onto another beam with the left hand, while reaching down to get a lathe of tobacco, and placing it on the cross beams approximately eight inches apart.

When I was fifteen I left East Hartford High School to go to work full-time. At the time I was halfway through my third year. Eventually I would finish by taking evening classes at East Hartford High and Hartford High. After leaving school, I found work learning to vulcanize tires and I worked at this job from 1923 to 1925. When my employer closed the shop down I applied for a job as a "vulcanizer" with Jack the Tire Experts. The tire shop was located in Hartford and was the largest of its kind in Connecticut. I was given a tryout and it was determined that I could do the work. Because most of the white men working on that job as vulcanizers who were from the South didn't see me as equal, they wouldn't work with me. So I had to give up the trade.

My next employment was with Mr. Ely Austin, who operated an International Harvester Agency selling farm machinery. The foreman was an Australian, who taught me to read blueprints and assemble farm machinery. After learning this I delivered equipment to farms and taught farmers how to operate the equipment. I read information about all of the career possibilities with International Harvester in their catalogues, thinking that when they spoke of career it meant for everyone. However, since it was evident that the Depression was coming, I was one of the first to be laid off. I had worked for them for six months. I next worked briefly as chauffeur for a middle-aged lady who ran an inn. She would come to the pool hall in Hartford, where I sometimes shot pool, to replace the chauffeurs who for some reason did not remain long in her employ. I left that job running from a shotgun and ran across the river to Windsor Locks and asked the constable to get my pay.

My father's interest in Hartford politics began at a relatively young age. When he was twenty-one, he and a group of men came together and organized Hartford's first Black independent political club. The year was 1928. The political club claimed allegiance to neither Democrats nor Republicans, but to the party that was most helpful to Blacks living in Hartford. This was the beginning of over sixty years of community and political activism on my father's part. He has written:

My community involvement began at the age of twenty-one. I became a member of an independent political party that was started in the Henry Williams's barber shop located at 1978 Main Street near the corner of Pavilion Street. We started the club after listening to a political speech by Walter Batterson given at the Arsenal School. Batterson was the Republican mayor of Hartford at the time. The Batterson family was associated with the Travelers Insurance Company. The mayor's grandfather had built the State Capitol. Walter Batterson told us that we had enough black voters in the Third Ward to control it, if we learned how to vote together. He pointed out that if he sent one thousand dollars to us and five hundred dollars to each political party, that he could keep us divided. As a result of listening to that plain talk, and his speech having "awakened us up," thirty men came together and formed an independent political club. Besides myself, the organizers of this independent club, which was the first of its kind in the city, included John E. Rogers Sr., Edward Swett, Connie Nappier Sr., the brothers, Henry, Ozie, and Homer Williams, Henry "Pee-Wee" Thomas, Lonnie Ferris, and James Johnson. We let it become known that we would support the party that supported our principles, including the hiring of black post office clerks, and the passage of a stronger equal rights bill.

Vincent Dennis, a protégé of John Bailey, approached our political club and asked us to help him defeat Alice Merritt, the State Representative for this District in which the Third Ward was located. Representative Merritt, a Republican, was supported by a number of black Republican leaders, including Green Lee, a professional bondsman and owner of a food market on Russell Street and grandfather of Carrie Perry, also Boce Barlow Sr., Minnie Glover, Charles Jones, James Patterson, and Sidney Johnson the Undertaker. Boce Barlow had a disagreement with Green Lee, and joined us in the Independent Political Club.

We rang door bells, knocked on those doors that had no bells, spoke on street corners, at Elks clubs, pool halls, gambling clubs, barber shops and churches. Vincent Dennis defeated Alice Merritt by 332 votes. Because of our support Dennis introduced and got passed legislation creating a stronger equal rights bill. This resulted in one of our members, a former Olympic champion, becoming the first black clerk of the court. Sidney Johnson, Charles Jones and James Patterson Sr. were hired as police messengers. Also as a result, eight black clerks were hired by the post office. John E. Rogers Sr., who became the first black superintendent of a post office branch, was one of those hired. Another was Ed Swett, who became the first black assistant postmaster of the Hartford Post Office. Only Swett's untimely death in a car accident kept him from becoming Postmaster.

For seventeen years, from 1928 to 1943, my father was executive chauffeur for the Holstein Rubber Company. The Holstein brothers manufactured ceiling and wall tiles, kneelers, and other products mostly for Catholic churches, convents, hospitals, and colleges. Dressed in a black suit, white shirt and tie, and black shoes and socks, and seated behind the wheel of a new shiny black Chrysler, my father drove the two brothers around the county. As the brothers sold and sought out new buyers for their products, my father drove them to every state except Utah. He was never allowed to stay at the same hotel with the Holsteins. My father would always have to seek out a Black family willing to let him spend the night in their home. Often he would spend the night curled up in the back seat of the car, using his jacket for a pillow. All during this time, my father carried in his wallet an Associated Negro Press Card. Whenever he came upon an interesting story or event, he would write an article and mail it to several Black newspapers. The newspapers that published his articles were the *Chicago Defender*, the *Indianapolis Recorder*, the *Pittsburgh Courier*, and the *Hartford Chronicle*. Just a few weeks before I was born, my father was at the 1930 Kentucky Derby, about which he wrote an article. Three years later he wrote an article about the 1933 Chicago

World's Fair. About this and other interesting events he attended my
father writes:

It was at the Chicago World's Fair that I met Hartford
native, Frederick H. Robb. He was a graduate of Howard
University, Northwestern University Law School, and had
a Doctorate from the University of London. He had a two
year grant to put together something significant relating
to black contribution to civilization. One of his classmates
at the University of London was Kwesi Kuntu, a wealthy
African from the Gold Coast. He brought members of his
tribe to the World's Fair where they performed a series
of dances. In one of their dances, which was narrated by
Ripley, of "Ripley's Believe It Or Not," they danced on broken glass with no shoes and without injuring their feet.

In the summer of 1936 I went to the Memphis Cotton
Carnival. I was one of the "King and Queen" escorts.
However, this affair did not impress me due to the absence
of any significant exhibition of black progress. It was all a
carnival atmosphere.

My next important stop was Dallas, Texas and the 1936
Texas Centennial. While there, I renewed my acquaintance
with Alonzo Aden, curator of the Howard University Art
Museum. The state of Texas hired Dr. Aden to create a
Hall of Negro Life for the Centennial. So he took a two-
year sabbatical from Howard University. A large building,
it was 400 feet by 200 feet, had been erected to house Dr.
Aden's collection. He had put together the most complete
collection of black contributions to the world at that time.
The walls were lined with murals of just about everything
the Negro had invented or created. This collection came to

be known as the Barnett-Aden Collection and was eventually housed at Howard University.

Rachel Taylor Milton, a Hartford native and one of the Urban League of Hartford founders, started her career after college. At a YMCA in Pittsburg she was secretary to Henry Craft, the executive secretary at the Center Avenue YMCA. Then she became the girl's activities secretary at the YWCA. In 1929 she was assigned to Omaha, Nebraska where she created a YWCA branch. Then she went to Nashville and then to Chicago where she completed her YWCA career and returned to Hartford. Wherever Rachel Taylor Milton served the YWCA as a builder of branches, I managed to turn up inasmuch as my firm's business was nationwide. Through my knowing her I made many valuable connections with many prominent black business and professional people in Omaha, Nashville and Chicago.

When the Urban League idea started here in Hartford, Rachel naturally enlisted me, a community activist, in helping the League get started. I served on various committees, especially Project Star, a group of people circulating citywide making residents familiar with the various programs of the Urban League. After my retirement in the early seventies I became very active with the Urban League of Greater Hartford. In 1939 I was at the New York World's Fair and at the San Francisco Exhibition. While they had nothing to compare with some of the others, however, I felt fortunate to attend both.

In his travels around the country, my father was often subjected to the humiliating realities of American racism, even in places where he was not expecting it. Once while "up North" in York, Pennsylvania, he was denied a meal in a restaurant because they didn't serve Blacks. Not being one to take racial bigotry lightly, my father told the proprietor, "My family fought for this country and as slaves helped to build this country. Now you tell me I can't be served." While the proprietor was somewhat taken aback by my father's bluntness, my father still was not permitted to eat in the restaurant. My father did, however, gain some measure of satisfaction in having gotten his point across. In 1943 my father's travels around the country with the Holstein brothers came to an end. The resources needed by the United States during World War II made it necessary to ration gasoline and this made it impossible to take long road trips. My father has written:

> So I took a job as shop foreman for the Holstein Rubber Company. After four years in this job I took a leave of absence and went to work for Pratt & Whitney Aircraft. I was the first black man to sit at a machine in that plant. However, I had to resign after eight months because of the dusty work atmosphere. By the time I resigned they had hired more blacks. So I went to work for Plunkett Chemical Company as an inspector of services. For a year, I traveled throughout Massachusetts instructing janitors how to keep rest rooms germ free through the use of chemicals. At the same time I was working as associate editor and advertising manager for the *Hartford Chronicle*, the city's only black newspaper at the time.

My father's outgoing and friendly nature suited him perfectly for his next job. He became a liquor salesman. This job called for someone who was a "people person." Employing a Black salesman was a first for this company. My father has written:

> I was the first Negro ever employed as a liquor salesman in Connecticut, according to an announcement by Hartley &

Parker, Limited, Inc., located on Front Street in Bridgeport. This company was one of Connecticut's largest wholesale liquor distributors. They wanted me to serve their extensive clientele in populous Negro areas. In recognition of my work Julius Rosenberg, one of the owners wrote, "Stewart has proven himself a successful salesman. His commendable sales record is due to the interest and understanding he projects toward his accounts' problems, his courteous and unassuming manner and his knowledge of the products he sells."

All during this time as a salesman and in various other positions held over the years, my father continued his work as a community activist. He was drawn particularly to people and organizations that rendered assistance to Blacks living in Hartford. He writes:

I also worked with the Citizens Committee of the North End. This committee was headed by Dr. George Goodman, who was the founder of the Urban League in Boston and in Washington, DC, along with Ella Brown. Goodman and I had worked together for the *Hartford Chronicle* in the early 1950s. I was associate editor and advertising manager, and Goodman was editor. In 1953 Goodman left Hartford to become Dean of Men at Fisk University in Nashville, Tennessee. He later relocated to New York City to head the Harlem Neighborhood Association and helped establish New York's black radio station WLIB. Goodman retired and relocated back to Hartford to write editorials for the *Hartford Times*. The Committee's work resulted in the building of Parker Memorial Center.

After eight years in this profession, I resigned as a liquor salesman to become an *Encyclopedia Britannica* salesman.

I spent twelve years as part-time sales representative for this company, and in 1966 I was made a member of their Britannica Salesmasters Club, and was awarded a Master Sales Degree.

In 1962, while selling encyclopedias part-time, my father went to work for the Community Renewal Team (CRT), an organization that provided resources and programs for underserved Hartford residents. As a CRT employee, he helped the unemployed and those who were in need of some type of assistance. He reached out to people in pool-rooms, on street corners, and anywhere people would gather to let them know what city services were available to assist them, and how they could get educational and vocational training. This was the work that was closes to my father's heart. My father writes:

> For a year-and-a-half, I delivered total supportive service due to the fact that very few unemployed are job ready. There were many who could not find employment and many who needed help in just knowing where to seek assistance from the many funded human service delivery programs. Many of the programs overlapped each other and actually competed instead of complementing each other. When Wilson Gaitor directed the city of Hartford Northside Field Office, located on the corner of Barbour and Westland Streets, he summoned all who delivered human services from the many state, city and Federal programs to meet monthly so as to become familiar with each other's services.

> As a para-professional, I was told that after a period of two years I might qualify for a job with the state employment service. Working for the Community Renewal Team did eventually lead to me being hired by the State Labor Department as a job developer. After a year-and-a-half I

recruited over one-hundred-fifty people. I made certain that they could make it to a payday by obtaining carfare, welfare assistance, and clothing, and also provided transportation to job interviews, assistance in making out job applications, and last but not least, if the applicant was an ex-offender I used the Connecticut Prison Association services. I was told to apply for an interviewer job with the State Employment Service. I passed the examination and shortly after I was hired as an interviewer.

Working as an interviewer for Employment Service, a state agency, allowed my father to perform a service that he was very passionate about. He was now helping former prison inmates reenter the community and become productive citizens. My father writes:

A. Ray Petty, who was director of the Prison Association, persuaded my employer to assign me to his office to deliver total supportive services to those with arrest record histories. I became permanently assigned to the Prison Association offices at the Department of Corrections on Capitol Avenue. The program I developed became an immediate success, and after three years, and with a heavy caseload, my program was expanded and became The Crisis Intervention Program for Parolees. I became coordinator of this program.

I had to overcome opposition from some para-professionals who wanted to establish a bureaucracy by actually slowing down procedures, by taking three to five weeks to process applicants who could not wait that long for assistance. This was met by a suggestion that I submitted to the state that actually reduced the time it took to process a released inmate, who while incarcerated had taken advantage of the educational and vocational training available, by up to nine weeks.

In the mid 1960s, as the civil rights movement was underway, my father assembled a small group of Black men to discuss local and national issues of concern. They met precisely at twelve noon at the Carpe Diem House on North Main Street. With my father serving as facilitator, they engaged in a spirited discussion and debate around issues of city services, local and national politics and elected officials, business, crime, unemployment, and other issues they deemed important. At the end of this initial meeting, the group of men agreed to meet again the following week, at the very same hour, to take up their discussion where they left off. After several weeks of meetings, and discussions, debating, and taking one side of an argument or the other, the men decided they would meet every week on the same day, at twelve noon. Because these meetings were always held the same day and at the same time, the meetings took the name "High Noon."

As word of the High Noon gathering spread around Hartford, the attendance steadily grew. Elected officials, government workers, business people, and community leaders, men and women, Black, White, Hispanic, and anyone interested, would bring their lunch and participate in High Noon. Concerns were expressed, issues were argued, actions defended, positions were taken, and solutions offered. The facilitator of High Noon rotated, and at a High Noon gathering in 1972 I was the facilitator. Until High Noon ended in the early 1980s, it played an important role in fostering understanding and better relations between the different ethnic groups, the minority community and city government. It was because of my father's initiative that for nearly twenty years people would gather at High Noon at Carpe Diem House and "seize the day."

My father's knowledge of the history of Blacks in Hartford prompted him to begin writing what he called a "Black Achiever's

Journal." In the journal he began chronicling the lives of the city's prominent Black families. He felt this would be an important contribution to the history of Blacks in Hartford. Two entries in his journal included the following:

> Dr. Patrick Henry Clay Arms was Hartford's first black doctor. Dr. Arms was poor when he arrived in Hartford in 1906 and did not have the means to advertise his presence. So he went to the newspaper and announced that he was going to run for mayor of Hartford. He made the headlines and suddenly everyone knew there was a black doctor in Hartford. He got a million dollars worth of publicity for free. That was a very good scheme.

> There was Howard Drew who was considered the first black lawyer in Hartford—although Harvey Wood started before him. But, when Harvey Wood returned to Hartford from college with his law degree, someone said, "Hi, Harvey." And he replied, "It's Mister Wood." That killed him.

At this same time, my father also envisioned and spoke of a Hartford Black History Project. He had in mind a large collection of pictures, artifacts, collectables, and other memorabilia that would tell the story of the history of the Black presence in Connecticut. To accomplish this he worked with the Connecticut Historical Society, providing largely unknown information that would help in the completion of this project. Unfortunately my father was unable to complete his Black Achievers Journal. While working on the journal he lost his battle with prostate cancer and died in March 1996.

"Hartford has lost another of its great elders...a community father," wrote *Hartford Courant* columnist Stan Simpson. "But Greater Hartford, and beyond has gained much from the life that he shared with us and for us. An ebullient storyteller, his stories were not fiction but the result of his uncommon knowledge of the histories of many of Hartford's prominent Black families," Simpson continued. "He could go back a hundred years and recount an event that was heretofore unknown to his listeners." Former State Senator and Hartford Mayor Thirman L. Milner wrote of my father, "A behind-the-scenes force in the rise of Black politicians in the city…a very, very strong unsung hero. He was one who acted as the conscience of the community."

The Hartford Black History Project opened to the public in 1997, a year after my father's death. It was housed at the Pavilion near the Old State House and contained more than three hundred pictures and other memorabilia. It included the shackles worn by a slave in Connecticut, a picture taken in 1914 of Hartford's first-known Black farmer, a listing of "firsts" for African Americans in Hartford, and a genealogy from Thirman L. Milner's family tree. It also contained an African-Native American wedding dress with its medicine pouch and wampum, as well as many other objects of historical interest. The Black History Project continues to this day to celebrate the contribution of Blacks to Hartford's and to Connecticut's history.

My father expected much of me, and I tried in my lifetime to live up to his expectations. We were father and son, but our relationship extended beyond that. We were friends and confidants, and no one understood my father as I did. There were things we talked about that we would talk about with no other. There were times when we did not see eye-to-eye, but we were cut from the same cloth.

"You are just like your father," Gladys would sometimes tell me. Sometimes it was in reference to my father's stubbornness, and at other times, it was in reference to his willingness to drop whatever he was doing to help someone who approached him with a need. This was an observation I gladly accepted. After all, I was his son and his namesake. And as the saying goes, "like father, like son."

3

LOOKING FOR A CALL

In 1947 Weaver High School was located on Ridgefield Street, where today the same majestic red-brick building has been renamed Martin Luther King Elementary School. In the fall of that year I was a seventeen-year-old student at Weaver, about to enter the eleventh grade. This was the same year that Jackie Robinson signed with the Brooklyn Dodgers. Some White players refused to play with him, and some fans jeered and booed when he took the field. Still, Robinson maintained a sense of dignity, which in my mind made him a better person than the racists who taunted him. Standing over six feet tall, I had some athletic skills myself and was a member of both the football and track team at Weaver High.

I was one of forty-one Black students, comprising less than 5 percent of Weaver's total student body. A number of Black students who entered Weaver the same year that I did had already dropped out. They reasoned that there was no connection between a high school diploma and the menial job they would eventually have to accept. "Why get a diploma when the only job a Black person can get is operating an elevator or doing menial work in some factory," one student told me. "You don't need a high school diploma to do that."

There were a small number of Irish and Italian students, while nearly 90 percent of Weaver's student body was Jewish. In the late forties, college was something that many students were not geared for, and a number of White students also dropped out. They, however, were finding employment in the public sector, including jobs in public works, the water bureau, the fire department, and some were hired by the insurance companies as janitors. At "Kosher Tech," as we sometimes jokingly called Weaver, I was one of a few Black students in the academic track, or the college track, as it was known. I was also involved in a number of extracurricular school activities, where I became friends with many of my Jewish and White classmates. On one occasion we went on a senior class trip to New York City and toured the United Nations building. Even though I was the only Black student to go on the trip, I can remember having lots of fun laughing, talking and joking with my fellow classmates. I was also one of the founding members of Delta Sigma Phi, an interracial high school fraternity, and helped plan the Annual Senior Spring Dance held at the Bond Hotel in downtown Hartford.

I can recall very vividly one rather disturbing incident I was involved in at Weaver that had racial overtones. But this incident had nothing to do with any of my classmates. My father was the instigator. At my father's insistence, I was playing the violin in the school orchestra. I decided one day that the bass fiddle was a more masculine instrument, so I switched from violin to the bass. When my father learned that I was playing the bass, he was outraged. He hurried to the school to confront the orchestra director, who he believed had switched me from violin to bass.

"I got my son that violin because that's what I want him to play!" he shouted loudly into the director's face. "You don't think Negros should play the violin, so you put them on an instrument you think is more suited to a Negro!" I felt sorry for the director who didn't know what to expect next from the tall angry Black man standing only a few inches from him. By this time my father's ranting and raving had attracted a rather large crowd of students, both Black and White. "Don't let White teachers do things to you out of their ignorant stereotypes about Negros!" my father said, looking at the Black students. He then turned abruptly and left the building. I stood there embarrassed that my father had raised such a ruckus in front of the students. At the next orchestra rehearsal, I was seated back in the violin section.

At my graduation ceremony in June 1948, along with my high diploma I was awarded two athletic scholarships. A number of colleges in Connecticut were giving scholarships to Black graduates in an attempt to increase the presence of Blacks on their campus. While I was a good athlete, I did not considered myself exceptional. In fact, it was because I was so unexceptional at catching the football that Weaver's coach played me at the defensive end position. I was one of three Blacks on Weaver's varsity football team, and probably the least athletically talented. Arthur Green was a running back, and Henry Crouch played on both the offense and defensive units. Both these players had better skills than I had. I later played on an all-Black semi-pro football team, made up of players who lived mostly in the North End. We played against other Black teams in the state, and sometimes against teams made up of convicts from state prisons. In one game I made the stupid decision to keep on playing, even though I had hurt my knee pretty bad. I played the rest of the game in a lot of pain. Today when the weather's cold or it's raining, my painful knee is a reminder of the stupid decision I made all those years earlier.

In September 1948, I began my freshman year at the University of Connecticut. I had been accepted into its school of agriculture. The decision to study agriculture was one I made while listening to some friends at Weaver talk about farming and food production, and their plans to enter this field of study. However, just two weeks into the semester I dropped out. That's how long it took for me to discover I was not suited for a career in agriculture. I just couldn't get interested in how the food on my dinner plate was grown. Just over three months later, in January 1949 I began classes again, this time at New Britain Teachers College. But I again dropped out before the semester ended. It was not that I didn't want to continue my college education, or because I saw very few Blacks on the campus. The issue was, I had turned nineteen, I was seriously dating Gladys Strong, and I was feeling the stress that came with having a girl friend and no money in my pocket. I needed to find a job.

While taking classes at New Britain Teachers College, I applied for a job at a small tool company. When I got a call from the owner offering me the job at Hartford Machine Screw, I took it. I left school with the thought that one day I would return and complete my college education. The day after receiving the job offer, I reported for work at the tool company as a stock chaser and counter. The work was simple enough. When one of the machine operators needed a tool, I was sent to the stockroom to get it. When screws carved out on the machines were deemed unusable and thrown to the floor, I would pick them up. After accumulating a certain amount of discarded screws I would dump them into a pan, place the pan on a large scale and weigh them. I would then record the weight of the discarded screws on a sheet of paper. This repetitive duty, and sweeping up the place, encompassed the scope of my responsibilities.

Often as I walked around the shop fetching tools and picking up screws, I thought about what one of the Black students who dropped out of Weaver High had said to me: "For the menial job I'll get in some factory, I don't need a high school diploma." Was I now working at one of those menial jobs? A voice inside my head answered, "uh huh." Well, the good thing was that I had a few dollars in my pocket.

"Once you get to know the shop layout, I'll let you begin training as a machinist apprentice," the shop manager told me one day. True to his word, two months later I began training on a lathe machine. "You're the first Negro to work on one of these machines," he told me. I wasn't sure how to respond. Was I suppose to be glad? I nodded my head in acknowledgement. Standing at my machine, my job now was to grind out metal spindles. At the end of my first week, I had produced more scrap metal than I had usable spindles. Well, it only took me this long to realize that working in this machine shop was not my calling. A few weeks later, I gave the shop manager my notice and quit.

When my father told me that not having a job increased my chances of being drafted into the army, I knew I had to find a job right away. I wanted no part of the army. I knew that nearly a million Blacks had fought for this country in World War II, only to return home to a country that continued to discriminate against them. For helping to defeat Hitler, Black soldiers were regarded in Europe as heroes, but returning home they still had to sit in the back of the bus. Now there was talk of the United States sending soldiers to Korea to help stop the spread of Communism. It didn't matter to me that President Truman had desegregated the army two years earlier; I wanted no part in such hypocrisy. So to avoid being drafted, I enlisted in the navy reserves. I called it good fortune smiling upon me when I was assigned to a navy reserve unit based in Hartford. I would remain a naval reservist for the next six years. Except for a two-week cruise to Nova Scotia, all of my reserve duty was done at the naval station in my hometown.

In what was now a hurried search to find a job, in September 1949 I went downtown to see Mrs. Martha Shaw at the G. Fox Department Store. I was told that she might give me a job at the store. I knew her personally, having grown up with her children. Martha Shaw was a middle-aged woman, active in community affairs and from a well-respected family in the North End. She was employed at Hartford's largest department store screening Black job applicants. G. Fox was one of the first stores in the city to hire Black employees for positions that allowed for advancement. Martha Shaw worked in the personnel office, and a few other Blacks worked on the sales floor. G. Fox was said to be the largest and finest department store in all of southern New England. There were eleven floors of clothing, jewelry, and furniture. There was also a large hair salon, a pharmacy, a medical clinic with registered nurses on duty, a large restaurant called the Connecticut Room, and a whole floor of offices. In all, the store had over two thousand full- and part-time employees.

I was directed to the personnel office, where Martha Shaw stood up and walked from behind her desk to greet me. I was impressed by how nicely dressed she was and that she had a desk. This is the kind of job you get when you have a college education, I thought. Martha Shaw told me that the store was in need of a part-time stock boy. I could have the job, she said, pending approval by Mrs. Auerbach. No one, I was told, could work at the department store without first standing before Beatrice Fox Auerbach, the "matriarch of G. Fox," as she was called. She always had the last word about who would be an employee at G. Fox. Martha Shaw then sent me to Mrs. Auerbach's eleventh floor office, admonishing me to "make a good impression."

While sitting in her secretary's office and waiting nervously to be called, I wondered what Mrs. Auerbach was like. I would learn years later something of her background. Beatrice Fox Auerbach was the granddaughter of Gerston Fox, a German-Jewish immigrant, who along with his brother Isaac founded I & G Fox Company in Hartford in 1847. Later, they built a five-story building and named the store G. Fox & Company. In 1917 the building burned to the ground. Moses Fox, who took over operations after his father, Gerston, died, built an eleven-story building that opened in 1918. Beatrice Fox Auerbach was Moses's daughter. When Moses died in 1938, Beatrice Auerback took control of the store. Under her guidance the business grew tenfold. She remodeled the store, adding elegant art deco and grand interior details. She had the store's signature marquee placed above every display window and above each entrance on Main Street. Through her efforts the store was transformed into the most dominant retail store in southern New England, and she became one of the most prominent executives in retailing. She was respected in Hartford for her civic and philanthropic efforts, and she demanded fierce loyalty from her employees.

After about ten minutes of waiting, I was summoned into Mrs. Auerbach's office. Sitting behind her desk in a large and nicely decorated office, she appeared rather small in stature. She had brown hair, a slender face, and a jutting chin. I estimated her to be in her fifties or sixties. She greeted me with a smile, and told me to have a seat. I sat down in an upholstered chair. I could feel her eyes looking me over. I always took particular care about my appearance, so I knew I had nothing to worry about on that score. "So John Stewart, you'd like to work here at G. Fox Department Store?" she asked. "Yes ma'am," I answered. She then asked me about my family and my education. She seemed pleased that I had earned my high school diploma and had plans of returning to college. She wanted to know what my future goals were, and what I knew about the G. Fox Department Store. The interview lasted around ten minutes, and I was pleased about the way I had answered her questions showing as much confidence and self-assurance as I could. Then I was sent back down to Martha Shaw's office.

When I entered Martha's Shaw office her smile told me I had the job. I was now an employee of G. Fox Department Store. The busy Christmas shopping season was approaching, so I was assigned to work in the Toyland stockroom. I was responsible for keeping track of all the toys that came in and went out of the stockroom. Because I was such a good and dependable worker, and also because of my ability to add and keep track of stock with little use of pencil and paper, after several months I was promoted to the position of head stock boy. The stockroom manager, a White man who I sensed had not spent much time around Black people, was amazed that I was able to do math so effortlessly. It amused me that he had difficulty accepting the fact that I was better at math than he was. Working at the G. Fox Department Store was much more interesting than operating a lathe machine at Hartford Screw, but after mastering the stockroom job, I again began to experience feelings of not being satisfied. So without a word to anyone, I was on the lookout for a new job.

There are defining moments in the life of every person. These are those moments, or a moment in time, when life and circumstances come together and the course of one's life is changed. Three o'clock in the afternoon on Saturday, January 27, 1950, was such a defining moment in my life. It was at that moment, as I stood beside Gladys Leona Strong, that Reverend James Wright pronounced us husband and wife. In that moment I became a married man. Gladys and I had known each other most of our lives. We grew up in the same neighborhood and attended the same church. As children and later as teenagers, much of our time together was spent participating in church related activities, including singing in the youth choir. I continue all these many years later to have such wonderful memories of the two of us lined up with other choir members in front of the congregation and singing.

There's a church in the valley by the wildwood,
No lovelier spot in the dale.
No place is so dear to my childhood,
As the little brown church in the vale.

Come to church in the wildwood,
Oh come to the church in the dale.
No spot is so dear to my childhood,
As the little brown church in the vale.

How sweet on a clear Sabbath morning,
To listen to the clear ringing bells.
Its tones, so sweetly are calling,
Oh, come to the church in the vale.

Although we had been friends since childhood, it was as teenagers that Gladys and I began dating. By the time I was a junior in high school and she was a freshman, our relationship had grown more serious. Gladys was the daughter of Otis and Florence Strong. Besides Gladys they had fourteen other children, four boys and ten girls. The Strong family was a widely known and highly respected family in Hartford. Though he was born in Bridgeport, Connecticut, Otis Strong's roots went back to the Portuguese. For some unknown reason Otis Strong never spoke of his childhood or his parents, and Gladys and her siblings learned that that was a subject not to be broached. Florence Strong could trace her roots back to Connecticut's Pequot and Mohican Indians. Her grandfather was a full-blooded Native American, and her grandmother was Irish. Gladys' long black silky hair, olive complexion, and high cheekbones testified to her Native American heritage. When she was a baby, Gladys had puffy cheeks that reminded her older sister Florence, whom everyone called Tootie, of the cartoon character Tweety Bird. The name stuck, and Gladys was thereafter known as Tweet.

Two months before our wedding I had stood beside Tweet in her living room and asked her mother for her daughter's hand in marriage. Gladys' father had died two years earlier of bleeding ulcers. Tweet's mother liked me well enough, and she also knew that her daughter was in a family way. So with her mother's blessing, Gladys and I announced to friends and family that we were getting married. One of Gladys's brothers worked in a jewelry store downtown and wanted to do something special for his little sister. I guess you could say that the owners of the jewelry store sold their jewelry and Gladys's brother sold his. He presented us with two gold wedding rings, which we accepted with no questions asked.

Our wedding took place in Gladys' mother's living room. It was supposed to be a small quiet wedding with just family and a few friends attending. But on the day of our wedding, the house was full to over-flowing with people squeezed into just about every nook and cranny.

"I don't know how they all found out. If I had known it was going to be like this, I would have had it at the church," Gladys whispered in my ear.

"You may now kiss your bride," Reverend Wright said after we had taken our vows. To loud applause and cheers, I kissed Gladys fully on her lips. We were now husband and wife. I was nineteen, and Gladys was seventeen. When the reception ended later that evening, I took Gladys to her new home, Walter and Ella Murray's house on Martin Street. Then next day we were all smiles as were being driven around Central Park in a horse-drawn carriage. This was our honeymoon weekend in Manhattan, and the sign attached to the carriage read "Just Married."

The following Sunday, Gladys and I went to church. People greeted us with smiles and words of congratulations. My grandmother, Ava

Stewart, and my aunts Lucille, Lillian, and Margaret smiled and nodded approvingly, as did Gladys's mother and sisters. Our lives still revolved around activities at Talcott Street Congregational Church. Gladys and her family were lifelong members, and my grandmother and aunts were longtime members. I started out worshiping at Metropolitan AME Zion with Mrs. Murray, but my father pulled me out when I was a little boy and sent me to worship with his mother and sisters at the Talcott Street church.

Talcott Street Congregational Church had the distinction of being the oldest Black church in the city of Hartford. It was founded in 1819 by a group of Blacks who were tired of worshiping in the "Negro pews" of a White church. So they began holding their own worship services in the conference room of the First Church of Christ. The following year, 1820, they moved into a building on State Street and secured the services of a Black minister. Under the supervision of the Hartford Sunday School Union, they organized a Sunday school for Black children. Six years later, in 1826, they took the name African Religious Society. They elected officers and voted to erect a house of worship. Their building committee was made up of four Blacks and three Whites. These men were extremely effective in securing subscriptions and managed to have the new church built and paid for in just one year. The new stone and brick church stood on the corner of Talcott and Market Streets, an area of the city called "the Bottom."

After moving into the new church, two issues arose that would eventually cause a split in the congregation. The issues were, one, what would be the style of worship, and two, what type of minister would be hired. Some members wanted "intelligent preaching" and "helpful progressive forms of worship and work." They understood this to be the "congregational way." Other members were opposed, contending that "an educated minister had no religion." They preferred a worship service with "loud exhorting, singing, shouting, jumping and exaggerated emotion." Without this, they argued, "the worship was dead, with no spirit and no power."

A vote by church members found that the majority favored the congregational style of worship and order. Aided by several White Congregational ministers, the Hartford Colored Congregational Church was formed in 1833. The church hired Reverend J.A. Hempstead, a White Congregational minister, as their supply preacher. Membership in the church included some of Hartford's most prominent Black citizens. James Mars, a church deacon, had been brought up in slavery in Connecticut. He was set free when he became an adult, and now was a member of the executive committee of the largely White Connecticut Anti-Slavery Society. Henry Foster, another church member, had chaired the organizing meetings of the state's Black temperance society, and Talcott member Ann Plato was a respected writer, author, and teacher.

The church members who were opposed to becoming part of the Congregational church and voted against it remained members of the African Religious Society, but met in a separate worship service in the same church building. These members finally left in 1936 after erecting their own church building on Elm Street. Under the leadership of Elder Hosea Easton, they became the Metropolitan AME Zion Church.

The members of the Hartford Colored Congregational Church had a strong social consciousness, and opened a school for Black children in 1833. They hired nineteen-year-old Amos Beman as the teacher. Young Beman was destined to one day become a widely known Congregational minister, orator, and writer. His father was the Reverend Jehiel Beman, pastor of the Cross Street African Methodist Episcopal Church in Middletown. Reverend Jehiel Beman was a former slave who changed his surname to "Be Man," to celebrate his freedom and humanity. Be Man eventually became Beman. In 1833 his son Amos applied for admittance to Wesleyan University, but because the school had already admitted Charles Ray as its first Black student in 1832, a resolution by trustees banned other Blacks from admittance.

A sympathetic White student began tutoring Amos on campus, but that ended when Amos received threatening letters from angry White students who resented his presence. So Amos walked the twenty miles to Hartford and applied for the teaching position at the school started by the Hartford Colored Congregational Church. Amos had been teaching at the school for about two years when in 1835 he witnessed a group of White men harassing Blacks who were leaving the church. One of the Black parishioners went home and came back with his gun. Aiming and then firing his gun he wounded one of the White agitators. The following day there was general rioting between Blacks and Whites in the area around the church. Several buildings where Blacks lived were burned to the ground.

Five years later, on July 16, 1840, the Hartford Colored Congregational Church installed the abolitionist minister James W.C. Pennington as its first pastor. A brilliant scholar, author, and orator, the thirty-three-year-old Pennington had escaped from slavery in Maryland fourteen years earlier. Mostly self-taught, he had been allowed to listen to the lectures from the back of the classroom at Yale Divinity School, but was prohibited from speaking. Under Pennington's leadership the church became a center for abolitionist and social activity. Speakers at the church included Arnold Buffman, a former president of the New England Anti-slavery Society, and abolitionist Reverend Henry Highland Garnet. Pennington remained pastor of the church until 1848. A succession of ministers then followed, and in the year 1860 the Hartford Colored Congregational Church was renamed the Talcott Street Congregational Church.

The minister who officiated at our wedding was the very dignified Reverend Dr. James A. Wright, who was called to be the pastor of Talcott Street Congregational Church in 1916. Highly educated, he had degrees from Howard University, Andover Newton Theological School, and Harvard University. Reverend Wright stood well over six feet tall, and his booming voice and distinguished presence commanded attention and respect from those with whom he came in contact. He took great pride in being both a Harvard and an Alpha man. In 1940, along with a number of his Alpha brothers in Hartford, they founded the local Beta Sigma Lambda Chapter of Alpha Phi Alpha Fraternity. Now, as I sat in church next to my new bride, I listened with pride as Reverend Wright announced our marriage from the pulpit.. Looking at him I remembered how proud I was when he told me he was my godfather. It didn't bother me at all that he also bestowed his godfather status upon all the other young people in the church.

The next day I was back working in the Toyland stockroom at G. Fox. Five months later Gladys gave birth to a baby girl. With the birth of Wendy Elaine Stewart, I experienced another of those life-defining moments. I was now a father. When Wendy was christened a few months later at Talcott Street Church, I promised the Lord that I would be the best father that I could be. The following year, 1951, a job for which I had been recommended by Dr. Frank T. Simpson, a member of Talcott Street Church, came through. He had told several church members that he was looking for a high school graduate to fill a position at a local supermarket. In my father's estimation, Dr. Simpson fit the bill as the kind of person I should look to as a role model. Like Reverend Wright, Dr. Simpson was an Alpha man. He had moved to Hartford in 1929 after graduating from Tougaloo College, a school in Mississippi started for Blacks by the American Missionary Association. Dr. Simpson had established a social work agency to help underprivileged Blacks in the North End better themselves. When the Connecticut Inter-Racial Commission was established in 1944, he was selected by state officials to serve as its only employee. This was one of the first civil rights organizations in the United States and eventually became the Connecticut Commission on Human Rights and Opportunities. Dr. Simpson became the commission's executive secretary.

While working to end racial discrimination in employment, Dr. Simpson had submitted my name for a job as cashier at the A&P Supermarket. I was interviewed and told I would have to go to Springfield, Massachusetts, for two weeks of training. So, much to Martha Shaw's disappointment, I resigned my job at G. Fox Department Store.

Along with Alfred Pitman, a Weaver classmate and friend, I went to Springfield for training to be a cashier. Besides learning to use the cash register, the training was also to help strengthen our skills in math, as well as develop our skills in customer relations. After completing the training, I became a clerk/cashier trainee at the Hartford A&P Supermarket. I was on probation for the first six months, doing various jobs in the supermarket, but not that of cashier. When my probationary period was over, I was placed at a cash register. One day after I had finished ringing up a customer, the store manager said something to me that left me wide-eyed.

"John, if you can spend about twenty years as a cashier, it just might lead you into management." I'm sure he thought that I should have been grateful for such a lifetime opportunity. But at twenty-one years old, I couldn't see myself standing at that cash register until I was forty-one. What had already angered me was that while I was not allowed to operate a cash register until my six-month probationary period was over, young White high school part-timers were put on the registers immediately after being hired. As grateful as I was to Dr. Simpson for getting me the job, I eventually came to the realization that being a cashier was not my life's calling.

While working at the A&P Supermarket, I became acquainted with a customer who worked as a training officer for the Hartford Fire Department. Every time he came into the store, he would tell me of the great benefits of being a professional fire fighter, and he would encourage me to take the test. I filed this information away in my mind, not sure whether I would act on it or not. It was several weeks later that I saw my cousin Frank Davis proudly strolling down my street in his fire department dress uniform. After seeing and talking with him, my mind was made up. I would take the exam.

After telling a number of people that I planned to take the exam to become a fire fighter, some suggested that I also take the police test just in case. So I took both exams with the intention of accepting whichever job was offered first. Today I thank the good Lord that the first job offer came from the Hartford Fire Department. I didn't like being around guns, and probably would not have been a career police officer. The fire department instructed me to report in a week to the training school for a physical examination. This was to determine if I was physically fit to be a fire fighter. After passing the physical, I was assigned to the next training class. As I waited for the class to begin, I grew more and more excited about the prospect of becoming a fire fighter. When the class began I was introduced to fire fighting apparatus, tools, and other fire service equipment. I was taught fire fighting principles and techniques, including how to react quickly and calmly in emergency conditions, and how to perform strenuous work under adverse conditions. After completing six weeks of training, I graduated with a certificate of completion, a fire fighter's badge, turnout gear, a dress uniform, and the title "fire fighter." It was 1952. I was twenty-two years old, married with a two-year-old daughter, and earning $48.50 a week. Just maybe, I thought with a sigh of satisfaction, I had found my calling at last.

JIM CROW IS IN THE FIREHOUSE

Jim Crow laws were a series of laws enacted by Southern states and local authorities after the Civil War, meant to segregate public facilities and services according to race. Even though racial discrimination and segregation in employment was outlawed by statute in Connecticut, when I became only the seventh Black fire fighter in the 150-year history of Hartford's fire department, I discovered that Jim Crow was alive and well. I was assigned to the firehouse at the corner of Main and Belden Streets in the city's North End. The two-story red-brick building that stood guard over the mostly poor Black and Hispanic neighborhood housed Engine Company 2 and Ladder Company 3. Over the years I had walked by this firehouse many times, never imagining that I would one day work there. I was assigned to the ladder company because I had the physical attributes needed for the strenuous work involved. I was over six feet tall, young, strong, and in good physical condition. If I had to carry a man on my back while descending a ladder, I was physically able to do so. Ladder Company 3 consisted of one fire truck with an assortment of ladders and forced entry tools, an officer, a driver, and five fire fighters. Engine Company 2, which occupied the other side of the firehouse, consisted of a single fire engine, an officer, a driver, and four fire fighters. There was also a deputy chief in the firehouse and his aide.

In Hartford firehouses the fire fighters lived together, just as they do in firehouses throughout the country. They eat meals together, laugh, and joke with one another, and commiserate together. The firehouse is their home away from home. They spend so much time together, they become like a second family to one another. When I reported to the firehouse at Main and Belden as a rookie fire fighter, what I found housed there was not one family of fire fighters, but two—one White, the other Black. White fire fighters passed the time playing cards with White fire fighters; Black fire fighters played cards with Black fire fighters. White and Black fire fighters did not sit together when watching television, nor did they share personal experiences. When I reported to the firehouse, the White officer in charge told me I was to sleep in an area reserved for Blacks. In this area of the firehouse, they kept what were called the black beds. I looked and saw several beds set off in a separate area. The black beds were located on the north side of the firehouse. This was the side of the firehouse where men assigned to the engine company slept. The beds for the White fire fighters who slept on this side were in a different area from the black beds. In pointing out the sleeping arrangements, the officer was letting me know that the White fire fighters did not want to be near me while they slept. I was assigned to the ladder company, which was on the south side of the firehouse, so when the alarm sounded, I had to run from the north side of the firehouse to the south side where the ladder truck was parked.

"Don't worry about being the last one to the ladder truck," the officer in charge told me. "We won't leave you."

Since there were only seven of us Black fire fighters, not every firehouse had black beds. The unwritten policy in the fire department was that firehouses without black beds were not assigned Black fire fighters. The only other firehouse in the city with black beds was located downtown at Market and Temple Street. The black beds there were occupied by Harry Ashe, John Kitchens, and Ray Thomas. Because fire fighters spent so many hours on duty, each firehouse had a kitchen where meals were cooked and eaten. If the White fire fighters didn't want to sleep near Black fire fighters, you can be sure they weren't going to sit down and eat with us. Nor would they eat from dishes we had eaten from, or use utensils we had held in our Black hands. So the kitchens in the firehouses were segregated. Black and White fire fighters ate at different times and used designated plates, knives, forks, spoons, glasses, and cups. If a Black fire fighter used a plate or utensils other than those designated, the White fire fighters would break the plate and throw the utensils in the trash. There was no breaking of bread together.

As far as the White fire fighters were concerned, brotherhood and loyalty in the firehouse extended only to those of like skin color. The only time a mixing of the races occurred was when we were out fighting a fire. I decided quickly that I would focus only on doing my job and receiving my pay. As a twenty-two-year-old rookie fire fighter, I had no thought of climbing a promotional ladder. In those days there were no Black role models in the fire department—no Black drivers, no Black aides, and no Black officers. Blacks were excluded from these positions. The six other Black fire fighters, who had joined the department back in 1948, had advanced no higher than the position I now held.

What I encountered in 1952 as a rookie in the Hartford Fire Department was a deep-seated institutional racism. The culture of racism was so entrenched, it had become a matter of simple routine. In the firehouse where I was assigned, I was confronted by racist attitudes and behaviors on a daily basis. I recall one evening when I was detailed to do an overnight shift at Ladder Company 5 on South Whitney Street. This was unusual in that Black fire fighters were not detailed to other firehouses. The local fire fighters union, however, had taken the position that not to detail Black fire fighters placed an unfair burden on White fire fighters. The union wanted Black fire fighters to be detailed as well. But opportunities to detail Black fire fighters were limited in that only two firehouses had black beds.

Every ladder company had to have at least six men on duty at all times. On this particular night, my company had seven men on duty, while Ladder Company 5 on Whitney Street was a man short. So I was detailed there for the night. When I reported to the firehouse, my presence posed a serious problem for the officer on duty. This fire-house had no black beds.

"I don't know where to put you," the lieutenant said with a worried look on his face. "I can't let you sleep in the same area with the rest of the men."

The other fire fighters looked at me with a *what's he doing here* look.

I stood there wanting to say, "What am I to do, sleep on the floor in a corner?" But I was silent. Sure, I was pissed. Why should I be made to feel as though there was a stigma attached to my Black skin? I wanted to tell him where he could shove the black beds, but I said nothing. The lieutenant then remembered that the captain in charge of the firehouse had the night off. Not only was his bed open, but it was also somewhat removed from the White fire fighters. Reluctantly, but not knowing what else to do, he told me to sleep in the captain's bed. So I crawled into the captain's bed and went to sleep.

When the captain learned the next morning that I had spent the night in his bed, he was pissed with the lieutenant, and called him into his office. To my surprise he chewed the lieutenant out for not treating me as equal to the others, and for not assigning me to the empty bed in the same area as the White fire fighters. I was pleasantly surprised to encounter this captain who did not appear to be prejudiced toward Blacks. He told the White fire fighters that if any of them had a problem with my presence, they could go home. He was one of many White fire fighters in the department I would come to know who were not racial bigots.

Because we were treated unequally and humiliated almost daily, I wanted to go to the local branch of the NAACP and have it take up our cause. Another Black fire fighter wanted to sue the Hartford Fire Department in court for violating the state's equal employment laws. But we decided to take the advice of Ben Laury, one of the six Blacks who had broken the fire department's color line in 1948.

"I don't like it as much as you," he told us. "Just hold on. I can assure you that things will change." I had developed a great respect for

Ben. He was only seven years my senior, but he showed a wisdom and maturity well beyond his age. I was impressed that he came to work every day with a copy of the *New York Times,* which he read with great interest. Like the rest of us, he disliked the way we were treated, but he was positive that a day of reckoning would come. When I complained to my father about the racism in the fire department and how intolerable it was, he responded in a way that was similar to Laury.

"Stick it out," he told me, "one day things will have to change."

In 1954, two years after becoming a fire fighter, the city undertook a reorganization of the fire department's personnel operations. One change welcomed by Blacks was that promotions would now be awarded on the basis of test scores. This new open test policy would supposedly end the traditional practice of promotions by the buddy system, or White only. While the personnel changes allowed Blacks to take tests for promotion, we were warned by some White fire fighters not to take any tests. They believed we posed a threat to White fire fighters who didn't have the educational background to compete successfully against us. The mere thought of Blacks being promoted over them was a cause for great concern. To have to answer to a Black person was an alarming prospect. This personnel change happened in 1954, just after the US Supreme Court declared in its *Brown v Board of Education* decision that segregation was a violation of the Equal Protection Clause of the Fourteenth Amendment to the Constitution. This ruling, however, had no effect on the segregated black beds and kitchen in Hartford's firehouses. Later that year, when the first promotion test was announced, and the city personnel department made it clear that Black fire fighters were eligible, I chose not to take the test. This decision I later came to regret, and I promised myself I would never ignore another test for promotion.

I can state unequivocally that skin color did not matter when it came to looking out for the safety of a fellow fire fighter when fighting a fire. Every fire fighter seemed equally dedicated to that objective. Just as I had done on many other occasions, when the alarm sounded one October evening in 1954, I leaped from my bunk, climbed into my turnout gear, raced across the floor, and was on the engine speeding to a fire. This fire was in a section of the city called South Meadows. When we arrived at the scene, we discovered the fire was in a building that housed the Hartford Electric Light Company. This was the site that supplied the city with two-thirds of its electric power. The impending threat was that a large portion of the city could be thrown into darkness. None of us wanted that outcome, so we began working together as a team to keep this from happening.

Our aggressive teamwork made it seem like the fire was out in no time at all. By working together the loss of electrical service to the city was prevented. Back at the firehouse, I thought about how we had all worked together as a team. How we were all now equally exhausted, and how we all just wanted to go to sleep. As the White fire fighters settled down in their beds, I settled down in my bed, separated from the others and on the opposite side of the firehouse. And so it went.

One night in December 1956, I was shaken out of my bed by the loud ringing of the fire alarm. In a matter of seconds, I was in my turnout gear and standing on the fire truck. The fire was at the historic St. Patrick's Catholic Church on the corner of Church and Ann Streets. This was one of the city's major churches, where many of the Irish Catholics in Greater Hartford worshiped. The church also had the misfortune of having experienced two previous fires that badly damaged the building. Arriving at the scene, I rushed into the church and found most of the interior walls of the sanctuary on fire. I began doing the "grunt work" of forcing open doors and removing obstacles that could feed the fire. Other fire fighters unraveled hoses and began pouring water on the fire as it spread from the walls to the roof.

Two more alarms sounded as the intense heat caused the stained-glass windows to shatter. It took about an hour for us to contain the fire. When the fire was finally out, most of St. Patrick's roof had been destroyed and the interior heavily damaged. As I stood at the curb of the ice-crusted street, I was tired, wet, and shivering cold. I climbed on the engine, and we went back to the firehouse to clean up. At that time we worked fifty-six hours a week, rotating days and evenings. When you worked days, you worked three days, with one-and-a-half days off. When you worked evenings, you worked three evenings, with two full days off. I was currently working the day shift, so when the fire fighters on the evening shift reported for duty, I went home.

That evening, when Mass ended at the Cathedral of St. Joseph on Farmington Avenue, the church's engineer went to check the boilers in the basement before locking up and going home. He had heard about the fire earlier that day at St. Patrick's, so as a precautionary measure, he decided to give the boilers at the Cathedral one more look. Seeing that all was in order, he went home. At five o'clock the next morning, the engineer was back at the Cathedral of St. Joseph to fire up the boilers that heated the huge edifice.

At seven o'clock Father Francis O'Neill entered the Cathedral to prepare for the early-morning Mass. After being inside a few minutes, Father O'Neill thought he smelled smoke. After searching and finding no fire, he determined it was the smell of the recently ignited boilers. As the Mass was in progress, several worshipers told Father O'Neill that they smelled smoke. As a precaution Father O'Neill had his secretary call the fire department. The alarm sounded at the firehouse on Sigourney and Niles Streets, which housed Company 5. In a matter of seconds, fire trucks were speeding to the Cathedral. When the fire fighters arrived, they began searching for the source of the smoke. Finding nothing amiss in the basement, they searched the main floor. Several minutes passed before they discovered the source of the smoke. A fire was burning inside the sanctuary walls.

I was back on duty, and when the second alarm sounded at the firehouse, I was in my turnout gear and on the ladder truck in a matter of seconds. Arriving at the Cathedral, several of us were sent to fight the fire from inside the sanctuary. Upon entering I saw flames shooting up into the ornate ceiling supported by pine timbers. I made my way up to the chancel area and onto a ledge above the pulpit. Using my

Halligan tool, a long bar with a hook at one end and a claw at the other, I began pulling down wooden timbers to prevent them from feeding the fire. This was very hazardous because the fire was burning just a few feet from where I was working.

After a few minutes, I heard someone shouting. "Mayday! Mayday!" It was Fire Chief Henry Thomas rushing into the building and ordering us out. With the ceiling and slate roof now almost entirely engulfed in flames and windows being blown out from the heat, Chief Thomas felt that in a matter of minutes the roof could collapse. Our lives were in danger. I made it out of the building just minutes before the roof collapsed down onto the spot where I had been working.

A third alarm was sounded. This alarm was a call for off-duty fire fighters to report to their firehouses. The flames were now shooting up at least a hundred feet into the sky. A general alarm was sounded, bringing more than 125 fire fighters to battle the out-of-control fire. As we fought the blaze, three fire fighters were overcome by the smoke and collapsed. For more than five hours, we poured water on the fire before it was brought under control and then put out. After extinguishing hot spots, we removed debris so that the smoldering remains could be ventilated. All that remained of the once-magnificent mother church of the Archdiocese of Hartford was a charred ice-encrusted ruin, its stone walls standing erect against the gray sky.

Because the two church fires happened within a time span of only thirty-six hours, City Manager Carleton Sharpe was not sure whether an arsonist was at work. So he ordered the police to be posted inside and outside churches and synagogues around the city. For a brief while the next day, a police car was parked in front of Faith Congregational Church.

Since our marriage six years earlier, Gladys and I had managed to triple the size of our family. Our daughter Wendy now had a little brother Gregory, born in 1951; a little brother Donald, born in 1952; and a little brother John, born in 1954.

Money in our household was tight, so to supplement my fire fighter's pay, I was now working a part-time job. The way my salary at the fire department was structured was that I earned one dollar an hour. I worked fifty-six hours a week and received $56 in pay. During the summer months, I could get overtime because many of the fire fighters took vacation. But we were allowed only two overtime shifts. So I was working a part-time job unloading freight cars at a local warehouse. The warehouse was owned by Sisson Drugs, a large wholesale drug distributer. I had originally started working part-time for Sisson Drugs when I was a student at Weaver High. One of Gladys's brothers got a job there when he was discharged from the army, and he managed to get me hired part-time during the summer months.

Back in those days, there seemed to be a drug store on almost every corner. Most were owned by Jews, but the large drug company Eli Lilly wouldn't sell to them. So the Jewish druggists in the area bought their drugs wholesale from Sisson Drugs. Since my connection with Sisson Drugs extended back nearly fifteen years, I had keys to their warehouse and was working there a couple of days a week. Ben Laury also worked there part-time and had keys. Because I had been there the longest, the owners put me in charge. When the freight trains came in, we unloaded hundreds of boxes and huge drums weighing close to seven-hundred-pounds each. We also made deliveries to stores around the Hartford area, and twice a week we drove a truck to New London and Norwich to make deliveries. Sometimes, in order to make ends meet at home, I sold a few cases of tissues, toilet paper, and paper towels to relatives and friends. I knew what to take and what not to take, and my boss never asked any questions. I knew it wasn't right, but times back then were very hard and feeding and clothing a family of six was even harder. That's why every summer I would climb into my 1951 Buick, a green "deuce and a quarter" (green was my favorite color), and with three other fire fighters, drive to East Hartford, East Windsor, or Broadbrook to cut tobacco leaves.

At the time, we were living in a three-bedroom apartment in Bowles Park, a housing community in the city's North End. But with four children, we needed more space. In 1958 I purchased our first home, a nine-room house on Enfield Street. The next year we were blessed with another addition to our family, a son we named Jeffrey. He was number five. What can I say, we just enjoyed having children around the house.

One evening in September 1959, what was unthinkable for a fire fighter happened. I was stretched out on my bunk at the firehouse when the alarm sounded. When I heard the dispatcher say over the speaker that the fire was at a church, the location 2030 Main Street, my whole body shook. That was my church! I knew some church members had been meeting there earlier that evening. In fact, if I had not been scheduled to work, I would have attended the meeting myself. This was also the evening that the choir rehearsed.

I would later learn that choir member Ozella Beckford smelled smoke. She called her husband, Ken, who told her to call the fire department. As the alarm continued ringing, I jumped into my turnout gear, slid down the pole, and was on the fire truck as it sped down Main Street. When the fire engine came to a stop in front of the church, I saw that the front doors of the church were wide open. Looking in, I could see smoke in the sanctuary. Without giving it any thought, I ran into the church and up the center aisle of the sanctuary to where the Communion table sat just below the pulpit. I could see that the smoke was coming from behind the large organ that sat high up in the choir loft.

I grabbed the large Bible and cross from the Communion table. Both these items had been presented to the church by Gladys' family when the church moved into its present location. They had been blessed and dedicated by Reverend Wright and had special meaning to our family. I knew I had to save them. Once I had the Bible and cross secured safely outside, I went back into the church to help fight the fire. The fire had now spread beyond the organ and into the walls, across the ceiling and into the rooms behind the sanctuary. Second and third alarms were sounded, and fire fighters from other firehouses were arriving at the scene. Using water hoses and our axes, we were able to cut the fire off from spreading throughout the entire church. This meant breaking through walls, tearing down sections of the ceiling, and pouring hundreds of gallons of water onto the fire. For me this was heartbreaking work.

After about an hour, the fire was under control and soon after it was out. We had managed to save the sanctuary, but the roof, along with the rear of the church, the parish hall, kitchen, parlor, Sunday school room, and the minister's office, were all lost. As I looked at the damage, I was devastated. The front of the church, the narthex, and sanctuary were waterlogged, the back of the church was smoldering wood and ash. I felt numb. I couldn't believe this had happened to the church that was so much a part of my family's life.

Then I saw Reverend Wright standing off to the side. I suspected that the glassy look in his eyes had come from tears. Moving the church from "the Bottom," where every time it rained, the church would be flooded, to this present location had been the major work and dream of his adult life. After years of prayers, the congregation was finally able to move when G. Fox Department Store purchased the church building on Talcott Street for one hundred thousand dollars. In 1954 Reverend Wright oversaw the church's move into its new home, which had become vacant when the Windsor Avenue Congregational Church merged with the Vine Street Congregational Church and became the Horace Bushnell Congregational Church. My church, the Talcott Street Church, had merged with Mother Bethel Methodist Church in 1953, and together as one congregation, they moved into their new home on North Main Street, renaming it Faith Congregational Church.

With Reverend Wright as the senior pastor, the Reverend Samuel Gilbeau, pastor of Mother Bethel, became the associate pastor. Now, with the extensive damage caused by the fire, the congregation would have to find someplace else to hold worship. Several months after the fire, Reverend Wright suffered a heart attack and was rushed to the hospital. He was allowed to go home after a few weeks, but never fully recovered and remained in a weakened condition. Shortly thereafter

Reverend Wright died, and a pastorate of forty-three years came to an end. I believe to this day that it was the shock of seeing his dream going up in smoke that led to his untimely death. In Reverend Wright's memory, the members of Faith Congregational Church vowed to rebuild.

I had now been a fire fighter for over seven years and was no longer considered a rookie. I had participated in hundreds of fire drills behind the firehouse. These drills included ascending and descending an aerial ladder without stopping, sometimes carrying a person on my shoulder. In hundreds of fires, I had used my ax, plaster hook, and Hallagan tool, doing the necessary grunt work, like knocking holes through roofs, knocking down doors, pulling down walls, breaking out windows, and removing obstacles. I had led adults to safety, and carried badly burned children from houses. I had been taken to the hospital with the children for fear that pulling away my gloves would pull away burnt and blistering skin as well. On occasion I had been overcome by smoke.

Over these seven years, I had also come to understand the concept of "traditionalism" that was in play at the fire department. This was the long-standing tradition of giving promotions to relatives and friends. The fact that all the relatives and friends being promoted were White was a problem for Black fire fighters. Even with the open test policy in place and Blacks taking tests for promotion, Whites still were the only ones being promoted. What we were unaware of at the time was that prior to each test, the White fire fighters had in their hands the books from which the test questions were formulated. They would pass these books back and forth among themselves in preparation for taking a test. Because Black fire fighters had no knowledge of these books or where the test questions originated, we were placed at a disadvantage. There was a ray of hope when my cousin Frank Davis passed a test in 1955 and was promoted to driver-pump operator. He was the first Black in the history of the department to hold this position. Instead of doing the hard grunt work at fires, he now drove the fire engine and maintained the water pressure in the hose line when fighting a fire. It also meant he received a pay raise.

I had taken my first test for promotion back in 1956. There were fourteen pump operator positions that needed to be filled. I passed the test and was number eight on the promotion list. However, when the department added five veterans' points to those who had passed the test (ten points if the veteran had been wounded in either World War II or the Korean Conflict), I dropped down to number eighteen. Being a naval reservist for six years didn't qualify me for veteran's points.

In 1959, the same year Faith Church suffered the devastating fire, I passed the pump operator's test, placing seventh on the promotion list. After veterans' points were applied, I dropped down to number seventeen, and out of the running for one of the fourteen available positions. Later that same year, I passed the aerial ladder driver test. There were five positions to be filled, and I placed number four on the list. If promoted to this position, I would drive the fire engine with the aerial ladder and be responsible for elevating, rotating, and extending the aerial ladder at the scene of a fire. However, I was again undone by veterans' points. When veterans' points were added, I dropped from number four to number eleven.

Up until this time, answering the test questions was a hit-or-miss proposition for Black fire fighters. It was not until 1960 that we learned that White fire fighters were using books to prepare for the tests. So in preparation for the lieutenant's test, I ordered some fire fighting books from a publishing house in New York City. There were fourteen positions, and I passed the test and was number fourteen on the list. Again, I became a victim of veterans' points, dropping down to number twenty-six. Needless to say, this was all very demoralizing to those of us who were nonveterans, especially the practice of giving veterans' points to the same person every time he took a test. So we began fighting this practice and eventually won with the implementation of a new policy stating a person could use his veterans' points only once.

I also began lending my books to other Blacks in the department who were preparing for tests. Soon they too were purchasing their own books. I was thirty-years old and had been a fire fighter for eight years, had taken and passed four tests, and had yet to receive a promotion. I knew that climbing the promotion ladder would be hard, but I was now determined to climb it.

BURNING ISSUES ALONG THE WAY

The decade of the sixties began with an American spy plane being shot down by the Soviet Union, and John F. Kennedy being elected president. In 1960 the average life-span of a Black person was seven years less than it was for a White person. Black children had only half the chance of Whites of completing high school, and only a third of a chance of completing college. In Hartford, just as it was in other Northern cities, Blacks were still second-class citizens who suffered humiliation, insults, embarrassment, and discrimination.

I credit the decade of the 60s with helping me to come to a better understanding of who I was as a Black man living in America. I saw the extraordinary lengths to which Black people would go to achieve their freedom and dignity. They were putting their lives on the line as they registered to vote, marched and sat-in, rallied and protested, and took freedom rides. And I witnessed the lengths to which some Whites would go to deny Blacks the same freedom and dignity they enjoyed. Out of a deep-seated hatred, they cursed, beat, arrested, jailed, and murdered Black men, women, children, and their White and Jewish sympathizers. Though I felt a deep empathy for the statement these people were making with their bodies, during these early days of the civil rights movement I was one who watched from the sidelines.

One day in early 1960, I went with fellow fire fighter Frank Carter to the Yellow Cab office on Farmington Avenue. I knew that a few of the White fire fighters were earning extra money driving taxicabs part-time, and we wanted to see if we could get hired. The man who did the hiring was named Bobby Landin. When we walked in, he looked up from his desk.

"We're fire fighters," I said. "We're from Hartford, and we know the city, and we're hoping you will hire us part-time."

Landin stared at us for a few seconds with a look of contemplation on his face and then said, "Why not? I got White fire fighters, why not let Blacks drive. You guys want to start, then start." We were somewhat surprised that becoming cab drivers was that easy. Because we were part-time drivers, we had to buy our own uniforms, consisting of a black cap with a black shiny bib, and a black waist-length jacket. Horace Caffee was the first Black full-time Yellow Cab driver in Hartford, and Frank Carter and I became the first Black part-time drivers. I drove the cab during my off-duty hours at the fire station. I drove around the North End where I knew it was hard sometimes for people to get a cab. I also waited for fares outside the downtown hotels and at the train station. Some Whites were hesitant about getting into my cab, and both Blacks and Whites would often do double-takes when they saw me sitting behind the wheel with my taxi driver jacket and cap and flashing a smile. After a while I became a familiar sight and people just climbed right in.

I was always very courteous, opening and closing the door and helping people with their packages. Friday and Saturday nights were especially good nights for tips, but I never worked late on Saturdays because I had to get up early the next morning for church. I was still working at the Sisson Drug warehouse and had grown weary of handling those heavy drums. So a few weeks after becoming a cab driver, I quit working at Sisson Drugs. This worked out fine for me, because I made more money as a cab driver.

In January 1961 Mayor Dominic DeLucco was calling for Hartford residents to celebrate the one-hundredth anniversary of the Civil War. He urged churches, schools, libraries, museums, colleges, and communications media to take an active part in what was to be a four-year observance of the War Between the States. As far as I was concerned, the North had won and that was that.

Three months later, in May 1961, as Alan Shepherd became the first American to fly in space, I was observing my ninth year as a fire fighter. I had received no promotion, was still doing the hard grunt work at Ladder Company 3, and I was still driving a cab. Things went on about the same and then in December the city experienced its deadliest fire since the circus fire of 1944. A flash fire in a rubbish chute had reached a hallway at Hartford Hospital. When the alarm sounded at Engine Company 1 and Ladder Company 6 on Main and Park Streets, fire fighters rushed to the scene. When they arrived at the fire they saw a fire fighter's worst nightmare. Looking up from the sidewalk they saw people hanging out of windows screaming for help. In the mind of a fire fighter, our foremost thought is saving lives. We willingly put our own lives in danger in an effort to save the lives of others.

The fire fighters quickly raised their hundred-foot ladder and placed it against the side of the building. One fire fighter scrambled up the ladder and into an open window on the ninth floor. The dense smoke made it hard for him to see what was in front of him, but he could see that the ceiling and the walls were on fire. As he made his way down the corridor he shouted instructions to the patients inside their rooms. "Run water! Wet some towels and rags and line them around the door!" Frightened patients rushed to comply with his instructions. Patients too sick or weak remained helpless in their beds. The fire fighters knew that evacuating the patients could only begin after they put out the fire.

A large two-and-a-half-inch fire hose was pulled up the outside the building and through the window, while other fire fighters raced up the inside stairwell with a hose and irons. The smoke made it hard to breathe, and the fire fighters were calling for gas masks. However, none were available. At the time there was no requirement for each fire fighter to carry a gas mask. So the fire fighters could only go into the smoke-filled ward for a few seconds before having to come out to get fresh air. A third alarm sounded in my firehouse. I had been off duty when the fire broke out, but was called back and remained on standby.

With the sound of the alarm I was on my way to help fight the fire. The fire was still out of control, and frightened people were still trapped in their rooms when my ladder company arrived on the scene. We had two major concerns. One was saving lives, and the other was preventing the fire from spreading to other parts of the hospital.

I rushed into the hospital and made my way up the stairs to the ninth floor. My job was to clear away anything the fire could feed on. It took awhile, but finally we had the fire was under control and shortly after the fire was completely out. Then the evacuation of people trapped in their rooms began. Those who couldn't walk, we carried to safety. As I walked along the darkened, charred, and water-soaked ward, I knew this was the type of fire and location that had the potential for loss of life. After our job was done, we went back to the firehouse. The news came later that sixteen people had died. Seven were hospital patients, and four were employees, including a nurse and doctor. Five people who were visiting patients had also lost their lives. While we were thankful that more lives had not been lost, for a fire fighter any loss of life makes it a bad day.

In January 1962 I was nearing my tenth year as a fire fighter. Still no promotion had come. In February Astronaut John Glenn circled the earth in a space capsule called *Friendship 7*. The Civil Rights Bill was being debated in Congress, and Martin Luther King Jr. was scheduled to speak in Hartford at a Freedom Day Rally at Metropolitan AME Zion Church. On the day of the rally, word came that King could not leave Albany, Georgia. Things were not going well for protesters there trying to end segregation, so King had to stay in Albany and lead a march. A minister and civil rights leader from Brooklyn, New York, spoke in King's place. Over a thousand people were crowded into the church on North Main Street.

During his speech the speaker took Connecticut Governor John Dempsey to task, claiming he had not done enough to end bias and discrimination in the state. This angered many Blacks in the audience who supported the Democratic governor. While I had not been in attendance, like many others Blacks in Connecticut, I felt that Governor Dempsey favored civil rights. In fact, the governor had called the General Assembly into a special session to strengthen Connecticut's fair housing laws.

Dr. King did make to Hartford on two later occasions in 1962, and at one of them I got to shake his hand. Several months after the rally at Metropolitan AME Church, King spoke at Mount Olive Baptist Church. Because of the large crowd expected at the church, I was one of several fire fighters assigned there to make sure there were no fire hazards. As Dr. King was leaving the church and making his way through the overflow of people out on the street, I extended my hand and he shook it. Then, near the end of October, at what was called a Festival for Faith and Freedom, King spoke to more than two-thousand people at the Bushnell Auditorium. Before King was introduced by the Reverend Robert E. Moody, pastor of Shiloh Baptist Church, another prominent Hartford Minister, the Reverend Richard A. Battles Jr., pastor of Mount Olive Baptist Church, introduced gospel singer Mahalia Jackson. Rev. Battles presented her with an award, and during the program praised Tom Parrish, Walter "Sonny" Fredericks, Justina McDonald, Mary-Ellen Lumpkin, Curley Ross, Wilbur Smith, Ivor High, William Mortensen, and the Boscos Club, for their help in organizing the program.

Rev. Richard A. Battles with Dr. King presents award to Mahalia Jackson at Festival of Faith and Freedom.

Much to my delight, in June of 1963, I received my first promotion. I had taken and passed both the written and the performance tests for three vacant positions. One was ladder truck driver, another was pump operator/driver, and the third was deputy chief's aide. The deputy chief's aide was the position I was hoping for, but the pump operator/driver position was the one offered. I accepted my new job gladly. It meant a few more dollars in my paycheck, and an end to the hard grunt work that I had been doing for the past eleven years. In my new job, I drove a thousand-gallon pressure water pumper truck. I was responsible for making sure the truck, the equipment, the fire fighters, and any other apparatus that might be needed arrived both speedily and safely at the scene of a fire. Once at the scene, I initiated the fire pump operations. This included securing a water supply, operating the pump, and maintaining the water discharge pressure.

This promotion also meant that I had to move out of the firehouse at Main and Belden that had been my home away from home for the past eleven years. So I packed my belongings and moved to the firehouse on Huyshope Avenue, which housed Engine Company 6. By now the black beds had become a thing of the past. Reporting to my new duty station, I just claimed an empty bunk, not giving any thought to who was sleeping nearby.

As happy as I was over my promotion, something happened that same day that brought me even greater happiness. I was working the 8:00 a.m. to 6:00 p.m. shift when I received a call informing me that Gladys was in labor at Mount Sinai Hospital. I had arranged with another fire fighter that if I was on-duty when Gladys went into labor, he would cover my shift. When I arrived at the maternity ward, I learned that Gladys had just given birth to a baby girl. We had been married thirteen years, and now added to our four boys and one girl, was another girl. When we brought baby Holly Ann home, Gladys and I promised each other that six was enough.

About the time I was promoted and Holly Ann was born, an organization called North End Community Action Program was holding demonstrations and calling for White businesses in Hartford to hire more Blacks. One of the tactics of the young activists in NECAP was to hold kneel-ins at various business establishments around the city. Two establishments where I knew a kneel-in was taking place were Terry Square Diner and Carville's Restaurant. At the same time these kneel-ins were taking place, A.D. King, the younger brother of Martin Luther King, was in Hartford raising money for a March on Washington, planned for August. While speaking to NECAP members, A.D. King reportedly said, "Don't get mad at Blacks in Hartford who do not support you, feel sorry for them." This statement only further divided NECAP members and those not supporting their tactics. On Wednesday, August 28, 1963, over one hundred people from Hartford and some of the surrounding communities held a rally at Hartford's Union Station. They then boarded a train for Washington, DC, and the March on Washington. Governor John Dempsey declared it Freedom Day in Connecticut.

It was a "March for Jobs and Freedom." Over 300,000 people crowded onto the National Mall in front of the Lincoln Memorial. Sitting in my living room, I watched as Dr. King delivered his "I Have A Dream" speech. His deep sonorous voice held me in rapt attention, and when he finished, I knew I had heard one of the greatest speeches of all time. A month later King was in the pulpit of Ebenezer Baptist Church in Atlanta when word came that a bomb had exploded in the Sixteen Street Baptist Church in Birmingham killing four little Black girls. King's response was, "Oh my God, why?"

With the murder of the little girls, I thought I had now seen it all. But a few months later, I witnessed something that angered me just as much. I saw fire fighters in that city advance on Black schoolchildren with high-powered water hoses. "You're going to get wet," a city official told the marchers as they gathered outside the same church where the four girls were killed. When the order was given, the White fire fighters willingly complied. Their fire hoses were fixed with special monitor guns that forced the flow of water from two hoses into one.

The children were hit with water pressure of one thousand pounds per square inch. The water was so powerful, it knocked the bark off trees and bricks loose from mortar. Children ducked behind trees and poles, while others were knocked to the ground, leaving some unconscious. I couldn't believe what I was seeing. One reporter at the scene gave this shocking report:

> Four fire engines arrived at the intersections and set themselves up for business. Each disgorged its high-pressure hoses and nozzle-mounts were set up in the street. I was to learn the reason for the mounts later, when I watched the powerful water stripping bark off of trees and tearing bricks from the walls as the firemen knocked Negroes down.
>
> The hoses were directed at everyone with a black skin, demonstrators, and non-demonstrators. A stream of water slammed the Rev. Fred Shuttlesworth against the church wall, causing internal injuries. Mrs. Colia LaFayette, a twenty-five-year-old SNCC field secretary from Selma, Alabama, was knocked down and two hoses were brought to bear on her to wash her along the sidewalk. A youth ran toward the firemen screaming oaths to direct their attention from the sprawling women. All while the streets were being soaked and black people flung hither and thither by propulsion of water.

As a professional fire fighter, I was trained to use a water hose to protect and save lives. But here were professional fire fighters using their hoses to harm defenseless men, women, and children. After watching those women and children being attacked with high-pressured fire hoses, Black fire fighters in Hartford wanted to do something about it. But at the time, we just didn't know what.

On November 23, 1963, six months after the fire hose attacks on Blacks in Birmingham, I watched in disbelief as a somber Walter Cronkite announced that President John F. Kennedy had been shot and killed by an assassin. As the reports of the shooting came in from Dallas, Texas, my mine drifted back to Kennedy's visit to Hartford three years earlier. What made it memorable was that he had brought his presidential campaign to the Black community. His rally took place at Tom Parrish's gas station on the corner of Main and Pavilion in the North End. This was a popular gathering spot where people passed the time of day. One brisk October afternoon in 1960, Kennedy stood on a makeshift platform in front of the gas station and gave his campaign speech to a predominantly Black audience. He had come seeking our votes in order to beat Richard Nixon and win the presidency. Many Blacks viewed Kennedy as a supporter of civil rights, recalling that he had said in an earlier speech that "discrimination was a stain on America." Hundreds of North End residents cheered him on that day. He was very popular among Black Americans, and when the 1960 presidential election was held, Kennedy received 72-percent of the Black votes. Mine included.

Sworn-in aboard Air Force One, Lyndon Baines Johnson was now the country's President. Like many Blacks, I didn't know what to expect from this Texan with a deep Southern drawl. I had never heard LBJ, as he was known, say anything in support of civil rights. Three months after becoming President, Johnson introduced his War on Poverty program. The goal of this program was to help the nation's underprivileged obtain jobs and educational opportunities. It was May 1964, and I was trying to establish a middle-class lifestyle for my family. At the time we were one of the small numbers of Black families living in the suburbs. Five years earlier, in 1959, I had purchased a detached house in Bloomfield. My reason for moving the family out of Hartford and into a house on the quiet tree- lined Cottage Grove Road was to enroll our children in a better school system.

To go along with our suburban lifestyle, I took the family on afternoon drives through the countryside in our station wagon. On these outings we would delight in the colorful New England foliage and occasionally stop at Dairy Queen or a restaurant. On occasion Gladys and I would host social gatherings in our home with music, drinks, and some of our closest friends. With the children enrolled in Bloomfield's public schools, we became active in the Parent Teacher Association as well as other school-related programs. We also got involved in a number of community programs. I joined the Bloomfield Town Committee and was appointed chairman of the Blue Hills Renovation Committee. I also organized a Little League baseball team. I did this after I was unable to get two of my sons on one of Bloomfield's predominantly White teams.

I went to a meat-packing house in Bloomfield called Copaco and asked the owners if they would sponsor the team. They thought it would be good publicity to have their names displayed on the player's shirts, so they agreed. I became the manager of the Copaco Little League Team, and Gladys was the assistant manager. There were eleven kids on the team, Blacks, Whites, and one Jewish kid. Two friends on the fire department were also assistant managers. To be honest, neither Gladys nor I knew the first thing about managing a baseball team, so we "BS'd" our way through it. Once, when I had to work on a game day and Gladys was managing the team, she did something that left me shaking my head in disbelief. Our team was behind by a couple of runs. It was the last inning, and we had the bases loaded. Our son John had a lot of natural talent, and was the team's best player. So I would have put him up to bat as a pinch hitter. Instead, Gladys put in our somewhat less athletically talented son Donald. But to the surprise of everyone on the team, except maybe Gladys, Donald knocked the ball over the fence for a grand-slam home run and won the game for us. When Gladys told me about it, all I could say was, "Well, I'll be darn."

In October 1964, a story in the morning newspaper reported that Reverend Richard A. Battles, pastor of Mount Olive Baptist

Church, and regional director of the Southern Christian Leadership Conference, had accompanied Martin Luther King to Oslo, Norway where King was to receive the Nobel Peace Prize. I had great respect for "Dick" Battles, as he was known to friends. He had only been in Hartford since January of 1961, but had already made a huge impact on Hartford's Black community. He would later help found Hartford's Congress of Racial Equality and serve on the board of education.

I made history in the Hartford Fire Department the following month. After successfully passing the test, I was promoted to the position of deputy chief's aide. This was my second promotion. This time it was to a position that no Black fire fighter had ever held, so I was breaking new ground. I soon found some aspects of my new job to be especially to my liking. For instance, I was now passing down orders from the deputy fire chief to White company officers. "You are to report here"…or…"You are to go there"…or…"You are not to do this… or that." I especially liked it when I knew I was talking to a White officer who didn't like a Black person telling him what to do, or not to do. On a few occasions, I gave an order in the name of the deputy chief that actually originated with me. I figured this was payback for some of the grief I had been made to endure.

The year ended with Lyndon Johnson beating Barry Goldwater for the presidency, the "Great Society" not being realized, and the Black community listening to Sam Cooke singing "It's been a long time coming, but I know a change is going to come."

Three months after my promotion, the big news story in the North End was the assassination of Malcolm X, and who was to blame. The fiery Muslim minister had been shot to death by several Black men on Sunday, February 21, 1965, while giving a speech in a Harlem ballroom. Some were speculating that his killing was on the order of Elijah Muhammad, leader of the Nation of Islam. The first visit of Malcolm X to Hartford may have been back in 1955, when he helped establish the Nation of Islam Temple 14. Back then he told Minister Thomas J. X, the Temple leader, and the other Black Muslims in attendance that "the only people in this country who are asked to be nonviolent are Black people." His last visit to Hartford had been in November 1963, when he spoke to an audience of about eight-hundred people at the Bushnell Auditorium. In that speech he accused the Whites in the audience of wanting to keep Blacks dependent and referred to Black Christian ministers as "Uncle Toms."

In March, one month after Malcolm X's assassination, several hundred people gathered on the Capitol grounds in Hartford for a rally in support of Martin Luther King. King, his wife, Coretta, Andy Young, and John Lewis, were leading a march from Selma to Montgomery. The march was a continuation of a voter's rights march that had been stopped by state police two weeks earlier. Many of the six-hundred people in that march had been beaten with billy-clubs as they walked across the Edmund Pettis Bridge. That day became known as "Bloody Sunday." Now Martin Luther King and over three thousand others, both Black and White, were nearing completion of the five-day march, where over twenty-five thousand enthusiastic people awaited them in Montgomery.

Five days earlier, on Thursday, March 18, Reverend Richard Battles and a delegation of ninety had boarded a chartered plan at Bradley Airport and flew to Montgomery. About one hundred others from Hartford and several surrounding communities had planned to join in the march on the last day, but were unable to make travel arrangements that would get them to Montgomery in time. So now, led by the Reverend Herbert Smith, director of Inner-City Exchange, they gathered in Hartford and marched the half mile from the Old State House to the State Capitol Building for a rally. Speakers at the rally included Ella Grasso, Connecticut's secretary of state; Wilbur Smith, president of the Hartford Branch of the NAACP; and Rachel Milton, secretary of the Hartford Urban League of Greater Hartford.

"The purpose of this demonstration is to answer the question asked by Connecticans who went to Selma," Reverend Smith told reporters. "The question is, 'What are we going to do for civil rights when we get back to Connecticut?'"

Over five hundred people crowded into the auditorium at the Travelers Insurance Company's headquarters in Hartford. It was March 1966, and they were there to hear Dr. Martin Luther King Jr. Most of those in the auditorium were members of Hartford's business community, city politicians, and community leaders. During his speech the thirty-six-year-old Dr. King warned his listeners that trouble could come to northern cities if the economic plight of Black people was not immediately dealt with. He most likely was alluding to the possibility of racial violence in a city like Hartford, similar to what had occurred the previous year in the Watts section of Los Angeles. At the time no one foresaw something like that happening in Hartford.

In November, eight months after Dr. King's visit, I made history in Hartford. Remaining true to the vow I had made to take every test that was posted, I successfully passed the test for lieutenant. When Fire Chief Edward Curtin pinned the lieutenant's badge on my jacket, I became the first Black person promoted into the officer's rank in the history of the Hartford Fire Department. In recognition the *Hartford Times* wrote the following article:

> Promotion in any municipal department ordinarily is of interest mainly to the individual, his family and friends. However, the promotion of John B. Stewart Jr. to be a lieutenant in the Hartford Fire Department is of special significance because he is a Negro. Lieutenant Stewart is the first of his race to become an officer in the local department, which he joined in 1952. Two years ago he was named as aide to the deputy chief.
>
> A native of Hartford, Lieutenant Stewart was graduated from the Weaver High School in 1948. He has had an outstanding record in the Department. Fire Chief Curtin has noted that the promotion examination on which his

appointment was based was the third he has passed successfully since becoming a fireman.

It is indeed gratifying that our Negro citizens are winning places in the upper grades of city departments on the basis of their abilities. There are a half dozen Negroes in the officer ranks of the Police Department where they are serving ably and effectively. The steady erosion of the color barrier is a satisfying development. The faster the barrier disappears, the better it will be for Hartford.

After reading the editorial, I couldn't help thinking about the six Black fire fighters who were hired by the fire department in 1948, four years before I was hired. They were the ones who broke the color line. Harry Ashe, Frank Davis, George Hayes, Joseph Kitchens, Benjamin Laury, and James Lewis were the first Blacks to be hired since Henry Jacklyn left the department in 1914. They had endured the racist behavior longer than I had. Shouldn't one of them have moved up the promotion ladder before me? They were the real trailblazers. But as far as I knew, none of them had taken the officer's test. Maybe they were just turned off because the racism was so entrenched. I remembered hearing that Frank Davis had been warned by a White officer not to take any test for a promotion. But after Davis ignored the warning and took a test anyway, he was reassigned to Company 16 up on Blue Hills Avenue. Back in those days, that was like being exiled to the far country. Being buried and forgotten up there was his punishment for seeking to be promoted. Racism had placed the ladder of opportunity out of his reach. He got discouraged and just waited out his time. When he had put in enough time, he walked away from the department and never looked back.

With this promotion I was now a "line lieutenant." I was assigned to a ladder company with the responsibility for the day-to-day operations on my shift. I also supervised my company when I was the senior officer at the scene of a fire. This meant I had to know what needed to be done, and when to do it. I could never forget that I was responsible for the safety of the men under my command. Any wrong decisions on my part could put their lives in danger. When the deputy chief arrived at the scene, he would take over command.

In celebration of my promotion, more than three hundred guests gathered for dinner on a Friday evening in March 1967 at Valle's Steak House. Dressed in a rented tuxedo with a flower in my lapel, I sat at the head table next to Gladys. Fire Chief Edward Curtin; Don Perkins, a professional NFL football player; New York Fire Commissioner Robert O. Lowery; and a number of other guests were seated at the table with us. When everyone raised their glasses and a toast was made in my honor, a feeling came over me that is still hard to describe, I can only say that it was a very good feeling.

6

THE RACIAL DISTURBANCE OF 1967 AND 1968

By July of 1967, I had pretty much adjusted to my new leadership responsibilities. After fifteen years with the fire department, I knew how things worked and had no problem being in charge of the people on my shift. Although I'm sure some of them had a problem with me. I not only knew how to handle myself, but I also knew how to handle things on a working fire line. While racial tension within the department seemed to be easing a bit, I had no way of knowing about the clash that was soon to take place between the fire department and segments of Hartford's minority community.

The events leading up to the clash began on the afternoon of Wednesday, July 12, when a young Black man in the North End was arrested, handcuffed, and taken off to jail. The complaint lodged against him was that he was being disorderly and had used vulgar language while ordering a hot dog from the waitress at Battles Luncheonette. A number of people objected to the way the White policemen treated the young man when arresting him. Around eleven o'clock that night, a crowd of about fifty people protesting the arrest gathered at the corner of Main and Pavilion Streets. Meanwhile, State Representative Leonard Frazier had paid the young man's bail and brought him back to the angry crowd.

"Here's your boy," he told them. "It's all over. You can go home." But the crowd was in an irritable mood and wouldn't leave the corner. A short while later, the fire alarm sounded at Engine Company 7 on nearby Clark Street. Someone had set a fire at the Westbar Super Market. Fire fighters rushed to the scene. At the same time this alarm was sounding, groups of young people were running through several streets throwing rocks and bricks through windows. At the Meat Mart on Westland Street, at Ben's Package Store, and at Battles Luncheonette, windows were smashed. At Family Chef on Main Street, owner Ken Beckford saw a group of young men assembled nearby, so he quickly shutdown his restaurant and went home. Just minutes after leaving, the men broke out the windows and looted his restaurant, stripping it of everything not bolted down. Automobiles passing by were pelted with rocks as frightened drivers tried to find routes of escape.

When police cars began converging on the area, they too were met with a barrage of rocks, bottles, and bricks. Patrol car windows were shattered, and several police officers were injured. Several more buildings were set on fire, and as fire fighters arrived on the scene, they were bombarded by flying objects. Police estimated about two hundred young people were in the streets taking part in the disturbance. When I arrived at one of the fires with my ladder company, we were harassed by people throwing objects. The attacks continued as we worked to put out one fire after another. We needed police protection, so the police began setting up lines of protection around us. More patrol cars and police wagons arrived at trouble spots, and blue helmeted police in riot gear poured out onto the streets .

Albany Avenue looked like a war zone as the police stood shoulder to shoulder with riot sticks at the ready as they faced an angry crowd. As the police line advanced, many of the young people dispersed onto side streets. The police began subduing and arresting the young men who seemed to be the main instigators of the violence. After about three hours, calm was restored as police in patrol wagons and armored cars cordoned off approximately a one-mile area. I watched in shock and disbelief. Could this be happening in Hartford?

Early the next morning, Thursday, July 13, Hartford Mayor George "Pete" Kinsella, and City Manager Elisha Freedman summoned their advisors, elected officials, Fire Chief Ed Curtain, and Police Chief John Kerrigan to an emergency meeting at city hall. They sat around a table and recounted the events of the previous night, and discussed what their course of action should be to prevent further violence. After the meeting they drove around the North End to view the damage. The police were still on alert and out in full force on the streets. Community leaders and local clergy from the Ministerial Alliance of Greater Hartford were walking the streets, attempting to the cool tempers of young people milling about.

On my way to the firehouse that morning, I drove through the area to see for myself the extent of the damage. It looked like I was driving through a battlefield. Burnt-out buildings, shattered store windows, litter-strewn streets, and overturned automobiles told the story of the violence the night before. I spent most of that day at the firehouse on full alert. When night came, crowds of Black youths again began gathering on Albany Avenue and other nearby North End streets. Several hundred city and state police in riot gear stood anxiously watching as the crowds grew larger and louder. An unofficial count by police numbered the youth on the streets in a one-mile area at around three hundred.

Then from the crowd rocks and bricks began flying into store windows, shattering them on impact. Meanwhile, the violence was spreading beyond the North End to a neighborhood across town called South Green. Fire alarm bells sent fire fighters to this low-income, predominantly Puerto Rican area where supermarkets, drug stores, bakeries and other shops were hit with firebombs. Like Blacks, Puerto Ricans in South Green were expressing their anger and discontent over poor housing, police brutality, lack of jobs, government neglect, and other concerns. As soon as we put one fire down, we went immediately to fight another. Even as we encountered stones and rocks being hurled at us, as fire fighters we couldn't just stand there and let buildings burn without trying to save them. At a meeting earlier in the day, City Manager Freedman had discussed with police and fire officials how the police would protect the fire fighters. As we responded to each alarm, many of which turned out to be false, the police were on hand to back the crowds away. Mayor Kinsella, angry and frustrated over this second night of violence, consented to a police request to use tear gas.

The next morning, Friday, July 14, after two nights of rioting, dozens of police were on patrol in the North End and the South Green neighborhoods. All days off had been canceled, and the entire city police force was standing by on twelve-hour shifts. At an emergency city council session that afternoon, the mayor, after being questioned about the use of tear gas on North End residents, raised his voice in anger.

"Police officers and fire fighters were being injured by bricks and bottles!" he said, looking at those who questioned this tactic. "The tear gas helped to keep property damage down before any of the riot controls were put in effect. The state of emergency now in effect is a technical move allowed by city charter!" he continued. "This step is necessary to protect lives and property in the area!" The mayor then tried to quash what he thought was a mistaken belief that the two nights of disturbance were racial.

"This is not a racial thing, it's a local internal disturbance," he said. Collin Bennett, the city's only Black council member agreed, but only in part. He then offered his own perspective on the disturbance.

"The root of the whole trouble is the feeling of maltreatment," said Bennett. "If a man's got a police record, he can't get a job. Some Blacks without a police record can't get one. And the White shopkeepers to whom these people give their dollars overcharge and give them abuse in return." It was true that Whites owned the majority of businesses in the North End and were reluctant to hire more than one token Black.

Also in attendance at this specially called city council session was Hartford's first Black state senator, fifty-two-year-old Boce W. Barlow Jr. If you were asked to list the names of the most respected Blacks in Hartford, State Senator Barlow's name would probably be at the top of nearly every list. As one writer put it, Barlow had "earned the respect of his colleagues by sheer force of intellect and humanity." This was indeed true. Having moved to Hartford with his parents from Americus, Georgia, when he was just a year old, Barlow had come to know firsthand the city's capacity for racial discrimination. After graduating from Hartford Public High School in 1933, he enrolled in Howard University in Washington, DC. While majoring in political science at Howard, he distinguished himself as class president and by earning his degree cum laude. He was then drafted into the army during World War II and served with an all-Black unit in the South Pacific.

After his discharge with the rank of sergeant, he enrolled in Harvard University Law School and after graduating was admitted to the Connecticut Bar in 1949. After being turned down for employment by several Hartford law firms because he was Black, Barlow established his own law practice. During this time he served as a hearing examiner for the State Civil Rights Commission, and later as a prosecutor for the Hartford Police Court. It was while serving as a prosecutor that Connecticut Governor Abraham Ribicoff noted Barlow's superior ability and appointed him a judge in 1957. With this appointment Barlow became Connecticut's first Black judge. After two years on the bench, Barlow stepped down due to the mounting pressures of his one-man law office. Then, in 1966 he challenged the endorsed Democratic slate and became the first Black elected to the Connecticut State Senate. Now as rioting was destroying his community, Senator Barlow wanted to make clear the cause of the rioting.

"It's not a Black and White issue," he told them. "The violence appeared to be directed at one store, where the first firebombing and rock throwing occurred Wednesday night." The North End residents at the emergency council session knew the Senator's reference was to the Black-owned luncheonette where the young disorderly man was arrested.

City Manager Freedman's main concern at the council session was not whether or not the disturbance was racial. He wanted those who had committed crimes arrested and jailed.

"The first job of the city is to apprehend the persons responsible for the disturbances and make this city a safe place again," he intoned.

"Nine people were arrested Thursday night, mostly in a two-block area where the violence was centered," Chief Kerrigan said in response. "The nine were charged with breach of the peace or resisting arrest." Kerrigan also reported that eleven policemen had been injured, mostly by thrown objects including flying glass. Several community leaders at the meeting blamed outsiders for the second night of violence near the corners of Wooster and Pavilion Streets.

"After learning of the first night of violence, young militants from other cities came to Hartford to keep it going," they contended. They also cited ill feelings toward both Black and White merchants as a primary motivator for the initial violence. Many in the community believed the merchants overcharged them for their goods. The emergency council session ended with some still questioning the causes of the disturbance. It was resolved, however, that the police and fire departments would remain on high alert. Even though it appeared tensions were easing, both the fire and police departments relaxed only slightly through the rest of the summer.

Labor Day came, and summer became autumn. At the fire department, we were back working our regular shifts. We still had not gotten over the experience of being attacked and were hoping it was just a one-time occurrence. Then in September police and fire fighters were back on full alert. This alert was the result of an incident that took place on the morning of Monday, September 18. History Professor Stacey Close provided some of the details here. About 150 people, mostly young Blacks and Puerto Ricans, and a few Whites, had gathered in the North End and were preparing to set out on a march for open housing. The march had been organized by an organization called the Black Caucus, under the leadership of John Barber. He planned to lead the three-mile march to the predominantly Italian South End, and once there to hold a peaceful rally demanding that Hartford city government enforce Connecticut's open housing law.

Apparently, some young men among the marchers were taking a more militant stance. One of them jumped onto a bench and shouted, "Black people should divorce themselves from the White power structure because of past transgressions against Black people and continued harm!" Several young men in the crowd who agreed with him picked up bottles and threw them into the street.

Barber then jumped onto the bench where the young man had been standing and yelled, "All this is not the Black Caucus," referring to the militant rhetoric and the bottle throwing. "We want a peaceful demonstration! Cool it, everybody! These bottles don't prove nothing! We gathered here to go to the South End, so let's go!"

Then someone in the crowd shouted, "We didn't come here for speeches!" After the march got underway, they had covered a distance of about one mile and were nearing the city's downtown area when someone threw a bottle over the viaduct and onto the I-84 expressway. At this point Police Captain Benjamin Goldstein and the approximately 250 police officers with him, many of them in riot gear walking alongside the marchers, stopped the march.

"The march must be orderly," Goldstein told Barber. But Barber's efforts to calm the militants in the crowd came up empty. Using a loudspeaker, Captain Goldstein then told the marchers, "All right, gentlemen, we're going to ask you to disperse! Your intentions aren't peaceful! You have five minutes to disperse! Those who remain will be arrested!" As Captain Goldstein was speaking, the police with tear gas ready drove cruisers and paddy wagons up to block off Main Street so that the marchers could not advance any farther. Ignoring the Captain's demands and the police presence, some of the marchers rushed forward and were quickly arrested.

Meanwhile, waiting in the city's South End was a crowd of over three hundred Whites who considered the marchers to be invaders. Father Robert Doyle, a Catholic priest, stood among the angry crowd and urged them to "remain calm and to react like disciples of Christ."

When word reached the crowd that the marchers had been dispersed, they broke out in loud cheers and applause.

"They've got no right to come down here and make trouble for us," a man in the crowd told a reporter.

"There might have been serious difficulty if the two groups had met," a relieved Police Chief Kerrigan told City Manager Freedman. It had been reported that some in the crowd were armed with bricks and bats, and maybe even a pistol or two. "While there were no serious injuries, windows were broken and about twenty-five of the marchers had been arrested," the chief told the city manager. In the North End later that night, several groups of teenagers, who were angry over the failed march and arrests, began throwing rocks and bottles at store windows and passing cars. Chief Kerrigan rushed nearly three hundred patrolmen in riot gear to the neighborhood where the disturbance was taking place. When the police arrived, they were greeted by the protestors with rocks and bottles. To protect motorists from injury, the police blocked off the streets leading into the North End. After a while the crowds dispersed, and fortunately no fires were set.

The next day, Tuesday, September 19, as those arrested at the march were being arraigned at the courthouse, sporadic rock throwing erupted, and a pharmacy on North Main Street was broken into and looted. At the arraignment those who stood watching noted that all of those arrested were young and a few were White.

"The governor says I can get a house down there in the South End!" a man watching the proceeding yelled out. "He ought to go with me when I try!" Racial discrimination in nearly every type of housing had been outlawed in the state. Still, Blacks in Hartford complained that discrimination in housing continued. That night groups of Black youth again gathered in the North End, throwing rocks and bottles at passing cars. Again the police used tear gas to disperse groups, and thirty-six people were arrested.

"It's unbelievable," remarked a frustrated Mayor Kinsella to a reporter, both of whom were observing the crowd from a distance. "These kids are running through the streets yelling for blood."

The next day, Wednesday, September 20, city officials and community leaders gathered at city hall in an attempt to determine what had caused the latest unrest. They also wanted to identify what needed to be done to prevent such disturbances from happening again. At the time approximately 26,000 people, mostly Black, lived in the blighted, poverty-stricken North End of Hartford. My feelings were that the city needed to do a number of things to make life better for these people. Recreational facilities were needed for the youth and young people, job training programs for the unemployed and better housing. There was also a need for improved communication between Black and White city residents. By the end of September, tensions between the minority community and the police seemed to have eased considerably. Those of us in the fire department were trying to put the events of the summer of 1967 behind us.

Meanwhile I had completed the real estate course I had been taking at Morse College in downtown Hartford. I had passed the state examination and had been granted my license to sell real estate. Whites at the time controlled the local real estate market in the Greater Hartford Area. So I went to work part-time for Hurwit & Simons, one of the largest real estate companies in the area. The owners wanted to make some inroads into the Black community and were looking for Black agents. They persuaded me to cut back my hours of driving a cab, and to spend more time selling real estate. I would later go out on my own after spending two years with Hurwit & Simons. I would establish my own real estate company called *Stewart & Associates*.

In November 1967 a tragic accident occurred within the department that caused me a great deal of sadness. On the way to a fire, a fire truck collided with a car at an intersection. A fire fighter was thrown from the truck, and struck his head on the concrete pavement. For days he lay in a coma at St. Francis Hospital. This young fire fighter knew I was selling real estate as a sideline, and had asked me to be his agent for a house he wanted to buy in Bloomfield. He was the first White person to seek me out, and after closing on his house I felt I could be a successful real estate agent. After he moved into his house I remained friends with him and his wife. For seven weeks he lay in a comma, never to regain consciousness. One of my saddest days was the day I served as pallbearer at his funeral. This was a tragic reminder of the danger that comes with being a professional fire fighter: when you leave the firehouse to fight a fire, there's no guarantee you will return.

The following month, December 1967, the first woman ever to be elected mayor of Hartford was sworn into office. She was forty-five-year-old Antonina P. Uccello. She further distinguished herself by being Hartford's first Republican mayor in twenty years. The new mayor was well-known in the city, having served two terms as the city council's only female member. Four years earlier, while working as an executive at G. Fox Department Store, Uccello had asked, and received permission from the department store owner, Beatrice Fox Auebach, to run for city council. This was the same Beatrice Fox Auebach before whom I had sat almost twenty years earlier seeking her approval to work at the department store. Since the council met on Mondays, and G. Fox was closed on Mondays, Auebach gave Uccello her approval. It was while a council member that Uccello won national recognition following the racial disturbances the previous July. She had called for an "Info-Mobile" to travel the poverty-stricken areas of the city to assist the poor with job information, available city services, and other needs. When put into effect, the program proved to be extremely effective, benefiting many underserved people in Hartford.

Then in September she shook up the city's Democratic establishment by coming in ahead of her six opponents, including the incumbent Mayor George Kinsella in the primary. Despite a cold, snowy election day, voters gave Uccello an upset victory. Disappointed and still unwilling to accept defeat, Mayor Kinsella called for a recount, but still came up 165 votes short.

I actually liked Mayor Kinsella. I thought his heart was in the right place, and he wanted to do more for the Black community. In this way he was somewhat like his father, who had served two terms as Hartford's mayor in the 1920s. In 1919 he had signed a petition urging Congress to begin a nationwide investigation of lynching and mob violence against Blacks. Like the father, the son was looked upon by some Whites in the city as being too favorable toward Blacks. This prompted someone in the early-morning hours of October 1966 to wrap newspaper around a rock, set it on fire, and throw it through Mayor Kinsella's living-room window. The sound of breaking glass woke the sleeping mayor, and he quickly extinguished the fire. He told police the incident may have been related to an anonymous anti-Black letter sent to the Hartford Human Relations Commission in which bomb threats were made against his home, against the *Hartford Times*, and against buses carrying Black children to suburban schools in Project Concern.

In January 1968, Antonina Uccello officially began her duties as mayor. Several months passed with nothing out of the ordinary happening in the city. Then, on the evening of Thursday, April 4, a news bulletin came over the television that Martin Luther King Jr. had been shot and killed in Memphis. I wanted to believe that what I was hearing could not be true. But how could I not believe Walter Cronkite? As news of King's murder spread through the North End of the city, people began leaving their homes and gathering in the streets. As a precaution stores closed down and boarded up their windows.

It didn't take long for nearly a hundred young people to crowd the streets around Tom Parrish's filling station at Main and Pavilion Streets. Some pumped angry fists into the air with shouts aimed at the police in riot gear. "You killed Martin Luther King! You killed Martin Luther King!" Others took up the chant. "You killed Martin Luther King! You killed Martin Luther King!" When their rage had reached the boiling point, some began an angry rampage through the streets of the North End. Buildings on North Main Street were set on fire. Windows were smashed and stores looted. A group broke into Ben's Package Store at Main Street and Mahl Avenue. Parked cars were overturned.

In the firehouses in the North End, alarms were sounding. Rocks and bottles smashed into police cruisers that now had plastic screens in place to protect their windows. Bar and restaurant owners were told by police to close down their establishments. According to Denton Watson, a Black reporter for the *Hartford Courant*, as one woman, apparently shaken by Dr. King's murder, was leaving a restaurant, she said angrily, "He was our Black messiah. Now who we got as a leader… Stokely Carmichael and H. Rap Brown?"

Theodore Napper, a Black police lieutenant, and Reverend J. Blanton Shields, pastor of Bethel AME Church, rode in a sound truck, calling for calm. But bottles were hurled in their direction. As the angry crowd continued its rampage, the police responded with tear gas. This caused the crowd to break into smaller groups onto Barbour, Canton and Windsor Streets, where they continued to mill around and shout defiantly at the police. When fire fighters rushed to a fire at Andy's Market at Wooster and Pavilion Streets, they were greeted with rocks and bottles. The police rushed to protect them as they worked to put out the fires, while young people on rooftops showered them with a barrage of rocks and bottles. We spent the entire night putting out fires, one right after the other. The tough conditions made it difficult to fight the fires, and many of us were operating on pure adrenalin alone.

Around one o'clock in the morning and against the urging and the insistence of police, Mayor Uccello went into the riot area for a first-hand look. Wearing a protective helmet, she was escorted by police through the streets where disturbances had taken place. As she walked she pleaded with some of the young people still on the streets for calm.

"You have a lot of nerve," a man reportedly told the mayor. "Somebody might throw a brick and hit you." In the morning the mayor met with advisors and elected officials. Her immediate concerns were to ease tensions and prevent further unrest. Meanwhile, community leaders and clergy from the local ministerial alliance were walking the streets, pleading with the young people to stop the violence. I was also talking to young people, trying to make them understand that burning and looting White-owned businesses in our community wasn't in their best interest.

"Who are you going to work for now?" I asked. "We don't have the money to open a business in our community." Even today, more than forty years later, the scars of this riot are still visible in the North End. Businesses that burned to the ground became vacant lots, and stores that closed were boarded up and never reopened.

A few days later, in what a local newspaper called a "summit," Mayor Uccello met with dashiki-clad John Barber at police headquarters. This was the same John Barber who had planned the derailed open housing march to the South End the previous September. Now the Yale graduate was serving as spokesperson for the city's disaffected Black youth. Besides the anger over Dr. King's murder, Barber told Uccello that the unrest was also a result of longstanding issues in the Black community.

"Decent housing, police brutality, and lack of jobs, these are sore points that had to be addressed," he told her. Many in the Black community believed these issues had not been addressed by the previous mayor because he did not want to alienate his White power base in the city's South End. He was putting politics before his mayoral duty.

Within days city officials began a cleanup campaign, sending crews and trucks to pick up the debris in vacant lots and demolition sites in the North End. Street sweep-downs and extra refuse collections began happening in the run-down housing projects and other areas. In June, two months after the disturbances caused by the murder of Martin Luther King, Fire Chief Curtin called me to his office. He wanted to discuss how the fire service could respond to the rioting and the anger in the Black community. He told me he wanted to establish a new unit within the fire department called Special Services. This new unit, he said, would address the poor relations that existed between the Black community and the fire service.

Chief Curtin told me that he hadn't thought through completely just how the new unit would operate. But as the fire department's sole Black officer, he wanted me to head it. As head of Special Services, he said, I would be released from my current duties and put on special detached duty. After the rioters had attacked fire fighters with bricks and bottles, I knew some action had to be taken to stop this from ever happening again. When I left the chief's office, I began to think about the value of such a unit for the fire service and for the Black community. Sure it would be a real challenge, I thought, but it needed to be done. I began thinking about how this new unit would operate, and I started to feel good about being asked to head it.

My feeling was that this new assignment would not only benefit the city's minority population, but it also would add another dimension to my life's experience. At thirty-eight I was a lieutenant in the fire department and a member of the Police and Fireman's Association; I was the founding president of the Phoenix Society, and a Thirty-Second Degree Mason, Prince Hall Affiliation. I was also a husband, father of six, and living a middle-class life in the suburbs, where I served the local government as a member of the Citizen's Committee. I had come a long way since those days when I spent monotonous hours picking up discarded screws from the floor at Hartford Machine Screw.

7

UP FROM THE ASHES

The Founding of the Phoenix Society

Historically, Blacks have been involved in professional fire fighting in this county for over 150 years. In 1826 there was an Ax and Bucket Brigade and an engine company in Savannah, Georgia, comprised solely of Black slaves. It was said of these men that they were unequaled in their efficiency and management when putting out fires, and were the pride of the county. In New Orleans in 1833, there were two fire companies made up of "two squads of Negroes," including Lafayette No. 3 and Washington No. 4. In 1858 the fire department in Charleston, South Carolina, had ten of their engines "manned by Negroes." In 1882 Topeka, Kansas, had an all-Black fire station.

Initially Topeka's White fire chief doubted the wisdom of an all-Black fire station, but changed his mind when he saw the men in action. He acknowledged that their work at fires proved them to be very capable fire fighters. In Danville, Illinois, there was an all-Black fire company in 1898. A White fire fighter wrote the following about this company: "They were some of the best damn fire fighters this city ever had." The fire department in Washington, DC had included several Black fire fighters since 1868. In 1919 the fire department in that city established Engine Company No. 4 as an all-Black company under the command of Charles E. Gibson. Yet despite this long history of professional fire fighting, in 1965 Black fire fighters in many cities still struggled for full acceptance by their White peers.

Black fire fighters in Hartford's fire department were aware in 1965 that Black fire fighters in New York City had come together thirty-years earlier to form the Vulcan Society. In their struggle to overcome prejudicial attitudes in the fire department, Black fire fighters in that city found strength in unity. They point to the experience of Wesley Williams, and said no longer would a Black fire fighter in that department have to go it alone. When Williams was hired by the New York City Fire Department in 1919, on the day he reported for duty, the captain took the morning roll call, thanked his men for their loyal support over the years, and walked out of the firehouse, never acknowledging Williams. Not wanting the stigma of having a Black man in his company, the captain retired that very day. Neither did any of the other White fire fighters in Engine Company 55 want to serve beside Williams. That day every man in the company requested a transfer. This forced fire department officials to impose a one-year moratorium on all transfers.

Having no choice but to remain in that firehouse, the White fire fighters refused to speak to Williams. On one occasion he was told, "We will only talk to you if you sleep in the cellar." Williams refused. When he went upstairs to the sleeping quarters, the White fire fighters moved their bunks downstairs. Not one to back down when challenged, Williams on many occasions proved himself by showing how tough he was at fighting "and whipping butt." His determination to stand up against racism and his ability to fight fires led to his advancement in the New York City Fire Department. In 1938, after nineteen years as a fire fighter, Williams was appointed to the rank of battalion chief. This made him the highest ranking Black fire officer in the country.

Besides our knowledge of the Vulcan Society in New York, we were also aware of the Club Valiants, an organization of Black fire fighters in Philadelphia. Black fire fighters in the City of Brotherly Love had organized in 1962 to advocate for equal opportunity within the department. Both the Vulcan Society and Club Valiants were also involved in civic and charitable work in the Black community. We knew that the situation in Hartford's minority community and in our own fire department demanded some action on our part. Some of us wanted to organize as the Black fire fighters in these other cities had done.

In October 1965 five of us met in the basement of Nelson Carter's aunt's house on Eastford Street to talk about how we should proceed. Besides Carter and me, the others present included Frank Carter, Carl Booker, and Cecil Alston. Even as we met, we knew there would be a negative reaction from some White fire fighters when they learned we were planning to organize. We were also unsure of Chief Curtin's reaction. Still, we agreed that organizing was necessary if traditional patterns of advancement in the Hartford Fire Department were to be interrupted. The only thing we needed to know was the proper steps to be taken in forming our own organization.

In December we wrote a letter to Lieutenant Vincent W. Julius, president of the Vulcan Society, asking for his assistance. We wanted his thoughts about what we should take into consideration as we began to organize. Julius responded, providing us with helpful information about their experiences when organizing the Vulcan Society. He told us he was ready to offer any other advice, support, and guidance we might need. He also invited us to come and observe one of their meetings. So in March 1966, the five of us drove to New York City. Upon arriving at their meeting hall, we were warmly greeted as brother fire fighters. We listened and observed, and we were impressed with their sense of unity and purpose. We were also impressed to see New York City's Black Fire Commissioner Robert O. Lowery present at the meeting, and to learn that he was a founding member. Returning to Hartford, we were eager to get started and to have our own organization up and running.

**Nelson Carter, Frank Carter, Comm. Robert Lowery,
John Stewart, Carl Booker, and Cecil Alston.**

We began holding what we called "organizing meetings." One of the first questions to be answered was what we would call our new organization. Carl Booker suggested the name Phoenix Society. He explained that the Phoenix was a mythical Egyptian firebird. At the end of its five-hundred-year life-span, the bird consumed itself in fire, only to rise up majestically and spread wide its wings. We all liked the name and what it symbolized. Blacks in the fire service had been down, but like the Phoenix we would rise up to new heights. The vote to adopt the name was unanimous, and in May 1966 the Phoenix Society was born.

We then began to draft the goals and purposes of the Phoenix Society. We agreed the Phoenix Society would be an organization dedicated to helping brother fire fighters as we strived to achieve equality in promotional opportunities within the Hartford Fire Department. We would help brother fire fighters overcome obstacles in the promotion process. Obstacles such as being interviewed by an all-White oral examination board, and not knowing in advance what to study for on the tests. We would settle for nothing less than equal treatment. The Phoenix Society also would raise funds for needy persons and charitable organizations in the city's Black community, and we would establish a scholarship fund for the children of fire fighters. Through the Phoenix Society, we would recruit Blacks into the Hartford Fire Department, and create a feeling of fraternity among all brother fire fighters.

I had been a member of the Hartford Fire Department for fourteen years, and had what I considered a good understanding of the department's inner workings. I wanted to be sure that young Blacks coming into the department were aware of certain realities. One of these realities was that the majority of fire fighters were either Irish or Italian, and that fire fighting for them was a family tradition. It was a career passed on from father to son, and promotions were based on family relations and friendships. That was the way it was done in Hartford down through the generations.

Another reality was that rookies, both Black and White, traditionally got the most difficult and unpleasant assignments, and were often the butt of practical jokes. To be sure, there was racial discrimination in the department, but I wanted Black recruits to understand that traditionalism, however unfair, did not necessarily mean intentional racial abuse. Not every objectionable action in the department was based on racial prejudice. The Phoenix Society would be a vehicle for helping Black rookies to understand this reality, while at the same time advocating for equality in hiring and promotions.

Having voted to name our organization the Phoenix Society, the next order of business was to fill the various offices. I accepted the nomination when my name was put forth and became the Phoenix Society's first president. Carl G. Booker Sr. was elected first vice president; Frank Carter Sr., second vice president; Nelson K. Carter Sr., secretary; George Hayes, treasurer; Cecil Alston, chaplain; and William Butler, chairman of the trustee board. The day after we elected our officers, I reported these actions to Chief Curtin. Needless to say, I was pleased when he endorsed our efforts. Carl Booker later designed the Phoenix Society's official emblem. It was a large black Phoenix with widespread wings, centered within a circle. Above the bird were the words "Phoenix Society." Beneath it were the words "Fire Fighters State of Connecticut."

All of the Phoenix Society's founding members had strong ties to Hartford's Black community, and this strengthened our determination to forge a close bond between this community and the fire department. We voted to give a Phoenix Society Award each year to an outstanding member of the community, one whose unselfish efforts and dedication were helping to bring people in the community closer together. At our First Annual Phoenix Society Community Awards Banquet in 1967, we presented our first award to Don Perkins, a professional NFL football player who was admired by the young people in the community. We especially liked the fact that he would always encourage them to believe in themselves. Our second award was the William Henry Jacklyn Award, which would go to a fire fighter whose actions best reflected the high standards of the profession, and who constantly sought to update and promote change in the fire service. Actually, two Jacklyn Awards were presented that evening; one was given to Chief Curtin and the other to me. In January 1968 I completed my two-year term as president of the Phoenix Society. Nelson Carter was sworn in as my successor. The Phoenix Society was up and running and now had close to fifty members.

In October 1969 the Phoenix Society received an urgent message from the Vulcan Society requesting our presence at a two-day conference in New York City. Besides the Phoenix Society, this same urgent message was sent to Club Valiants of Philadelphia; the Vulcan Pioneers of Newark, New Jersey, the Vulcan Pioneers of Hudson County, New Jersey; and to Black fire fighters in various cities around the country. The meeting was to be held at the Commodore Hotel in Lower Manhattan.

Because we were eager to meet with Black fire fighters from other cities and discuss our mutual concerns, five of us from the Phoenix Society went to New York to attend the meeting. As we gathered at the hotel, there was an immediate feeling of camaraderie among the approximately fifty Black fire fighters present. We had come from Boston, Hartford, New York, Newark, Jersey City, Philadelphia, Cleveland, St. Louis, Los Angeles, New Orleans, Washington, DC, Baltimore, Chicago and Detroit. The conference was chaired by Lieutenant Vincent Julius, president of the Vulcan Society. Julius, who appeared to be in his early thirties, explained that the racial climate in the country, the urban rioting, the attacks on fire fighters, and the discrimination within the fire service had prompted his call for the conference. To address these issues, Julius wanted to discuss the formation of a national Black professional fire fighter's organization. He felt that such an organization was not only needed, but could also be used as a vehicle for change, and could make a difference in the fire service and in Black communities.

"The time has come for Black fire fighters to organize on a national level," he said. The possibility of such an organization sparked excitement among everyone present. For two days we discussed and debated such issues as minority hiring practices and national trends in the fire service, the state of Black urban America, the value of a national Black fire fighter's organization, and how such an organization could become a reality.

The lasting importance of this groundbreaking conference was that we agreed to hold a national convention of Black professional fire fighters with the purpose of organizing nationally to combat racism in the fire service. This national convention, which at my request would be held in Hartford, would take place for three days in October 1970. The purpose of this national convention would be unite brother fire fighters throughout the country, who working together would develop within the fire service a more professional attitude toward minorities. Further, we believed that sharing positive experiences of Black fire fighters on a national level would help Black recruitment and advancement within the professional fire fighting service.

Our stated goal was to have a Black man who was searching for a profession feel that he could confidently walk into a fire station anywhere in the country and be accepted on his merits. Only when this was achieved could Black fire fighters say that our American dream was at last nearing realization. With this national convention now to convene in just one year, there was much to be done. So we formed a committee made up of members from each of the five sponsoring organizations; these included the Vulcan Society, the Phoenix Society, Club Valiants, the Vulcan Pioneers of Newark, New Jersey, and the Vulcan Pioneers of Hudson County, New Jersey. As a member of the committee, I was excited and eager to begin planning this first of a kind event.

On January 7, 1970, pump operator Cecil Alston, an eleven-year veteran of the Hartford Fire Department was sworn in as president of the Phoenix Society. This same year our wives came together and organized the Phoenix Society Women's Auxiliary. Our wives not only wanted to get to know one another, but they wanted to help the Phoenix Society in its civic work, as well as providing fund-raising assistance.

As the host organization, the Phoenix Society welcomed Black fire fighters from around the country when the National Convention of Black Professional Fire Fighters convened in Hartford in October 1970. It was out of this historic gathering that the International Association of Black Professional Fire Fighters (IABPFF) was born. (The events surrounding this three-day gathering are detailed later in this memoir.) Of course, the Phoenix Society was pleased that it could play such a vital role in the establishment of this international organization. In 1972, Richard Epps was elected president of the Phoenix Society. In 1973, we could count seventy-one Black fire fighters in the Hartford Fire Department, though all had not become Phoenix Society members. Over the next few years, the number of Blacks in both the fire department and the Phoenix Society gradually increased. We were aware, however, that there was not a single Hispanic fire fighter in the Hartford Fire Department.

The Phoenix Society did give public support to local Puerto Rican leaders who in 1979 were demanding that changes be made in the Hartford Fire Department. Their demand stemmed from the accidental death of twelve-year-old Julio Lozado. The boy had been playing in an abandoned garage in the North End when the roof collapsed, burying him under the debris. When fire fighters arrived at the scene, frantic bystanders tried to tell them where to look for the boy. But none of the fire fighters understood or spoke Spanish. Unable to find him in the rubble and believing he was not there, the fire fighters left. It seemed to the boy's family members that the fire fighters had ignored their frantic pleas. When the fire fighters and police were summoned back by angry residents, they located the boy beneath the debris.

Tragically, Lazado died on the way to the hospital. The Hispanic community was outraged. They charged that the boy could have been saved if the fire fighters had not allowed so much time to elapse. They filed a lawsuit against the city demanding that fire fighters be given sensitivity training, as well as hiring Hispanic fire fighters. At the time I was head of a unit in the fire department called Special Services, and was the department's community liaison. I was trying to resolve the friction between the fire department and the Hispanic community by advocating the hiring of Hispanic fire fighters.

The following year, 1980, both the city and La Casa de Puerto Rico, a local social agency that aided Hispanics, were spearheading a drive to recruit Hispanics into the fire department. In an attempt to prevent the recruiting drive from taking place, lawyers for the local fire fighters union filed suit. They claimed they were representing eight fire fighters on the existing fire department's hiring eligibility list. The union believed the city was going to allow the existing list to lapse, so the suit asked the court not to let that happen. As a result, the court ordered the city to put the recruitment drive on hold until it could rule on the matter.

Meanwhile, Phoenix Society President Walter McKenney announced publicly that the Phoenix Society supported the drive. "The Phoenix Society will support any attempt to place more Spanish-speaking persons in the department," said McKenney. "We are not in agreement with the fire fighter's union's 220 to 218 vote not to participate in the drive." The issue of recruiting Hispanics into the fire department was still being hotly debated when the Phoenix Society hosted its annual awards banquet in 1980. During his keynote address, William J. Brown, the executive director of the Greater Hartford Urban League, took the city and the fire department to task.

"The city must shift its priorities and return the fire department to full strength," he said. "Sooner or later some lives are going to be lost. City politicians have their priorities mixed up, and they haven't seen fit to bring the fire department up to strength."

Two Historic Conversations

In 2012, forty-five years after the founding of the Phoenix Society, Hartford Public Access Executive Director Billie Scruse gathered together some of its founding, and later members, for two historic conversations about their experiences as Hartford firefighters. They included Captain Steven Harris, Assistant Chief Aaron West, Lieutenant Cecil Aston, Chief Nelson Carter, Audabon Hill, Fire Marshal Carl G. Booker, Robert Farmer, Bill Butler, Raymond Tyson, and Chief John B. Stewart Jr. Portions of these conversations are presented here.

Harris: I needed a good paying job. I was employed at Pratt and Whitney. The pay was okay but there were no benefits. I had a young family and I needed a job that offered benefits. That's the one thing the Hartford Fire Department had at the time. They didn't pay you much but they had good benefits. That was my reason for coming on the job.

West: I joined the fire department after getting out of the service. My good friend Chief Carter kept pushing me, saying, "Why don't you join the fire department?" I was also looking for a job with benefits—long paying benefits. That's my reason.

Alston: I joined the fire department basically for the same reason as Steve. I had six-and-a-half years at Pratt & Whitney but I couldn't see any future there. I had two children and another one on the way. And looking at the benefits of the fire department, I saw that I had more opportunity for advancement. At Pratt and Whitney I didn't see that advancement there. So that's why I joined the fire department.

Carter: I think all of us joined the fire department looking for job security and the benefits. And the benefits for the fire department, and for city employment at that time were pretty good. The money was low, but the benefits were good. Having young families, we knew that we had job security. I think that was the major reason we all joined. And knowing some of the fire fighters who had been employed a few years before, they were instrumental in talking with us and convincing us to give it a try.

Hill   I joined for the same reason, but mainly I was looking for a good job with a retirement plan. The first job I had I was working downtown at a department store. I had a friend and he was working downtown part-time at a bank, and he also worked at the fire department. That was Frank Davis, one of the first Black professional fire fighters in the Hartford Fire Department. He was always encouraging me to come on into the fire department. But I lived in Bloomfield. At that time, you had to be a Hartford resident. I owned a house in Bloomfield and was not ready to give up my house to try and get on the fire department. But one night as I was in my car traveling from Winsor Locks, I had the radio on and an announcement came on saying the Hartford Fire Department is looking for fire fighters nationwide. I came off the highway, went down by the firehouse where he worked. I got an application, put it in and the rest is history.

Booker: Well, I had a small family, and it was job security. Where I was working at the time things weren't going that well. And I was informed that the fire department was hiring. So I went down and took the test, fortunately I managed to pass, and then entered the fire department.

Farmer: I was looking for a better job. I wasn't making much at Hartford Hospital at the time. My brother was working at the post office and I took the test for the post office, the fire department and the police department. I was on all three lists. The fire department called me first, and the police department called me a week later. So I accepted the job on the fire department. There was no particular reason, just that it was a better job than the one I had. I knew nothing about the fire department. I took the job, because I was looking for a better job.

Carter: In 1948 we had the "Fabulous Five" come on the department. That was Ben Laury, George Hayes, Frank Davis, Harry Ashe, and George Hayes. And they were all at Engine Company 2. They were the pride of the community; we had Black fire fighters finally on Hartford's Fire Department. We were young at the time, but when we did come on those gentlemen were still fighting fires, and they were instrumental. They had so much wisdom and they imparted it to us down through the years. And they were a great part of the reason why the Phoenix Society began.

Harris. I credit John Abrams with being the force that got me into the fire department. He sat me down and he said, "Listen man, the fire department is a steady job. It doesn't pay much, but it has the benefits." He went on to talk about those benefits. And I saw that the benefits were good, the pay I figured would eventually catch up. Because you have to realize in 1970 at Pratt I was making two hundred dollars and fifty cent a week. And I left two hundred dollars and fifty cent a week, to go to work for one hundred forty-seven and fifty cent a week. When I passed that test I went home and told my mother I was going to the fire department she said, "I know I didn't raise no fool." She said, "Why in the world would you leave a job making two hundred dollars and fifty cent a week for a job making one hundred and forty-seven dollars a week, and run into a burning building?"

Alston: I came onto the fire department on April 1, 1959. I was the last Black man hired by Chief Henry G. Thomas. And I'll never forget, one night I went down for my interview. And near his office there was a hallway—a waiting area. And I'm sitting there and I thought perhaps there was a waiting room inside. So I opened the door and walked in and he was sitting at his desk. And he looked up and said, "Who are you?" And I told him my name was Cecil Alston, and I came down for an interview. "So you just walk in without being invited?" I told him I thought it was a waiting room. "You thought! Why didn't you just ask someone if this was a waiting room?" So after he finished chewing me out he says to me, "If I hire you when can you start?" At the time I was working at Pratt and Whitney. And I left Pratt and Whitney. I had two children and another one on the way. I was bringing home seventy-six dollars a week. I came on the fire department; believe it or not, I was now bringing home seventy-two dollars a week. And they couldn't understand why I was leaving a job that was paying me more than the job I was going to. But I could not see the benefits or the security at the Pratt and Whitney. And all factories had too many layoffs for me.

Booker: Well, after I passed the test I was informed that I was a quarter of an inch too short. You see, at the time you had to be five seven, and I was five six and three quarters. They had informed me, even though I had passed, that I was too short. Of course, I went to my minister and I informed him of that. And he said, "Okay, that's okay." But to make a long story short, when I finally got on the job I saw men there shorter than me. I mean, guys like five feet tall. And that's when I began to develop some hostilities, but still I could understand. It was explained to me that in those days they had what was called commissioners. And with commissioners there was a whole lot of nepotism and politics being played. So it wasn't a matter of your height or your weight, it was a matter of who you were. And that was the first obstacle I had to overcome. I was already looked at as a minority and not equal to the guys that I was going to be working with.

Farmer: The thing that bothered me the most about going on the job, after serving three and a half years in the military as a good soldier. I mean as a real good soldier. When I came up here I thought the streets were paved with gold. I thought there was no way I wouldn't be treated equal up here. When I went on the fire department I found a lot of things just the opposite. The racism on the fire department that I saw—people not wanting to sleep in the same bed that I slept in.

Second Conversation

Stewart: In the early years it was very hard for me to get adjusted to the black beds. When I came on the department, they basically were taking the bigger persons—five foot ten, six feet, and they would put you on a ladder company because the ladders weighed as much as 350 pounds. And it took two or three strong people to lift it. So the feeling was that for the ladder company they would take the bigger ones. When I was assigned they didn't know what to do with me, because we had two houses that had separate beds. That was Engine Company 3 on Market Street, and Engine Company 2 and Ladder 3 on Main and Belden. Those were the only places that had separate beds. There were three shifts. On one shift Ben Laury, George Hayes, and Fred Turner Jr. shared a bed on their respective turns. On the other side was Engine Company 2, and I was assigned to Ladder 3. That meant two of us African Americans, me and Ben Laury, were on the same ladder company, which was something that we couldn't figure out. We thought they would transfer Ben over to the engine company, but there was resistance because Ben was a good ladder man. So they told me I had to sleep in the engine company side of the firehouse. In other words, the north side of the house was where the engine company slept, and on the south side of the house is where the ladder company slept. It was hard for me to imagine that I've got to run across the floor and go over to the ladder company, but I was assured by the officer that they wouldn't leave me. But that was what I faced, and I didn't understand it. But Ben Laury explained to me that you have to live with it, and in due time it'll catch up.

Farmer: I was the second Black fireman to work in the firehouse up on Fairfield and New Britain Avenue. And it was back during the start of the riots, and the movement for equal rights. And that's when I really saw the racism come out. I felt a lot of it was directed toward me. And I even became bitter about it. But I will have to say there were some guys on the fire department back then who really took me under their wings. These were guys that had been in the army, in World War II. One guy was in a concentration camp. And one guy was a prisoner of war. They really took me under their wings. Because I had a tough time adjusting, I did some things that made me look like I was a very militant person—which I guess I was. But I wasn't going to take anything. When I went on the job, I was a man, and I said I been a man and I'm not going to give up my manhood for any reason or for anything. And I didn't.

West: The name Phoenix Society was originated by Carl Booker. In fact, he designed the original patch. We all thought we needed to join an organization for the camaraderie, for brotherhood, and for protection, because we faced all kinds of little insinuations every day. We felt that if we formed an organization, we could look out for each other, discuss our problems with each other, and study together. This helped us tremendously all through our careers because we would sit up three or four nights a week, until three or four in the morning studying to advance ourselves. Because we weren't going to just sit back on the truck and let these people who really didn't know the job tell us how to run a fire department.

Harris: Well, not only that, but I think for me, being the youngest guy at the table, I think if it hadn't been for Frank Carter, I wouldn't be sitting here today talking about my experiences in the fire department, because I was picked on. And I was hot-tempered. I was militant and I just didn't take crap from anybody. And this guy, he was Italian, saw that and he didn't want me on the job. He kept saying, "I'm going to keep after this kid until I make him do something." At the time they were building Fox Middle School across the street. And one morning I came in and he started picking on me. I said, "I don't need this." I walked across the street and picked up a two-by-four. As I was coming back across Blue Hills Avenue, Frank Carter was in the upstairs room and saw me pick up the two-by-four and come back across the street. Frank ran down the steps and met me and asked me what was wrong. I said, "I'm going in there and kill this guy and I'm going home." I was that angry. I had had enough of him. And Frank Carter said to me, "Son, you don't want to do that. You worked too hard, and you've come too far to blow it like that." And he cooled me off. He took me into the officer's room and told the officer, "You better do something. Tell him to get off of this kid." That's when I knew that the best thing that happened to me was to meet these guys right here, because if it hadn't been for them, I wouldn't be sitting here. God only knows where I would be sitting right now.

Alston: When the Phoenix Society was formed, we used to meet in Chief Carter's mother and father's house in the basement. That's where we formed, over on Eastwick Street in Hartford.

Harris: The Underground Railroad.

Alston: Chief Stewart was the one that had the idea of forming a fraternal organization. Carl Booker was the former fire marshal, and he's the one who came up with the patch for the Phoenix Society. The Phoenix Bird that lived five hundred years, consumed itself in fire, and then rose again. That was our patch. And once we formed and started going around the country meeting with other departments, we found out that we had similar problems. We formed the International Association of Black Professional Firefighters in 1970 in Hartford. And I was president of the Phoenix Society at the time. Word got around that the Blacks were forming an organization, and were going to form their own union, and break away from the union of the fire department, but that was not the case. Chief Curtin called me down to his office and threatened to fire me and have me locked up, because I was going against the union for the city of Hartford Fire Department. This happened because of an erroneous word that we were forming our own union to break away from the white union. All we were trying to do was form our own organization with the other cities around the country.

West: Let me piggyback on something the Chief said about the International. Hartford's Phoenix Society is one of the five original founding members of the International. We hosted the first convention here in Hartford. That's when Cecil was going to jail, and we did say to Cecil, "If you go we go too. We're all going to stick together as one—as brothers." There was a write-up in the paper that said the national president of the International Association of Black Professional Fire Fighters took the oath of office with a clenched black fist. That's a part of the International emblem. Each one of the five organizations had a particular responsibility at the convention from chairing a panel to serving as convention chair. I was fortunate enough to chair the name committee. And each organization had to bring a list of names for the whole convention to vote on. I'm very proud of the fact that I was one the original members that named the International Association of Black Professional Fire Fighters. The reason I picked that name was that I foresaw—in my wisdom I guess—the International not only being the United States.

Hill: The Phoenix Society created a much better dialogue between the citizens of the city of Hartford and the fire department.

Harris: I think I can speak for all of these guys. If you ask what our greatest satisfaction was, I think we could all say that it was the day that City Manager Wilson Gaitor pinned the badge of the Chief of the department on John B. Stewart Jr. It was the proudest day of my life.

Stewart: It was August 2, 1980, at 1:32 in the afternoon. It was unbelievable. It was like a dream come true. Our City Manager Woodrow Wilson Gaitor, who was the first African American city manager, said to me, "I'm not appointing you because we know each other. I'm appointing you because I believe you have the skills and the knowledge to surround yourself with the best, and for you to turn the Hartford Fire Department around." I thank God for Wilson Gaitor. I took the examination for the chief's position and they told me that I didn't finish in the top three. Wilson Gaitor showed me the final paperwork that showed that I finished number one. And all Gaitor did was eliminate the out-of-towners, and he chose the Chief from within the department. And for those who thought that Wilson Gaitor appointed me because I was his friend are wrong. He appointed me because he had faith in me, and because I had come out number one on the test. That was the reason I got the appointment and the rest is history.

Hill: You have to be different to be a fire fighter. Because everybody else is running out of a burning building and you're running in. So you're different. You're special as a fireman. So definitely stay involved in the fire service, because you're needed. You're always going to be needed.

Alston: I came onto the fire department in April 1959. And I thank Chief Stewart for the inroads he made in the fire department. I now have a son on the job with twenty-three years. I don't know what he would be doing today if he wasn't a fire fighter. So I appreciate Chief Stewart and the inroads he made.

Butler: I came on the job in 1959. I'd like to say that Chief Stewart has always been an inspiration for me and for many other people on this job. And my hat is off to him always.

Tyson: I came on the job in August 1963. I came on because I saw African American firemen taking the bus or walking to work. And I liked to see the uniform on people, and I decided that's what I wanted to do. When I came on, Chief Stewart was deputy chief's aide. But it was a great day and a memorable day when he made Chief. I retired in 1991.

West: Without Chief Stewart I would never have risen to the rank of assistant chief before I retired. Every day, whenever I would see him, he would tell me to stay in the books, get in the books. I've been proud to have known such a compassionate man, and I think one of the top fire fighter persons in the whole United States.

Harris: I came on the job in 1970. And the one thing I can say about Chief Stewart is that he was a mentor and role model to me. He taught me the importance of community service. He taught me to understand the politics of the community that we lived in. The proudest day of my career was the day they pinned the gold badge on the chest of my mentor, my friend, retired Chief John B. Stewart Jr.

Stewart: I would like to think that the Phoenix Society members kept me together. It wasn't easy, but they kept me straight somehow. I have to thank them, and say God bless them all. We also have to thank our families because they stuck with us, especially our wives. There were a lot of things going on in the department that we didn't understand, and they helped us when we came home and encouraged us to keep going. We also have to thank the community, the churches, the NAACP, the Urban League, the sororities and fraternities. It took all of these organizations to keep us going and to keep me on top.

**

It was the tenor of the times in May 1966 that compelled five Black Hartford fire fighters to meet together in secret to form the Phoenix Society. Once organized, the Phoenix Society joined with the Vulcan Society, Club Valiants, the Vulcan Pioneers of Newark, New Jersey and the Vulcan Pioneers of Hudson County, New Jersey in taking the lead to establish the International Association of Black Professional Fire Fighters. Now, forty-seven years later, a new generation of fire fighters have assumed the leadership of the Phoenix Society. Captain Patrick D. Jones, the son of a retired fire fighter, currently serves as president. At the Phoenix Society website (www.phoenixsocietyinc.org) Jones makes the following promise: "As president of this organization I will continue to promote the values of our founding fathers, as well as develop new ideas, creating new relationships, and making the Phoenix Society highly visible in our neighborhoods."

And indeed, President Jones and the Phoenix Society continue to honor those promises. Following its obligation to promote education within the community Black students need only go to the Phoenix Society website to obtain a Phoenix Society Scholarship Application. It is our intent, it says on the application, to invest in future leaders within the community we serve.

In June 2012, at the 46th Anniversary Awards Recognition Dinner and Dance, the Phoenix Society celebrated thirty years of African American women in the Hartford Fire Department. The society also awarded scholarships to high school students, and it recognized community leaders.

"Tonight we will honor the first woman in this profession who broke the barrier of a male-dominated fire department, and recognize her accomplishments as well as the achievements of the women who have followed behind her," stated Phoenix Society President Patrick Jones. His reference was to Captain Zandra Watley as she received the William Henry Jacklyn Award. "Tonight is Ladies Night!" he proclaimed.

Fire Chief Edward Casares Jr., who was appointed Hartford's first Hispanic fire chief in 2010, also spoke. "I am committed to continue diversifying the department with highly qualified and competent individuals. This passion was taught to me by retired Fire Chief and Councilman John B. Stewart Jr. Chief Stewart laid a strong foundation for future chiefs in the country to build upon." During the program fire fighters who had advanced in the promotional ranks were recognized. "The Phoenix Society looks forward to your continued support in the future. Keep the fires burning for justice," President Jones stated. "It's not a challenge; it's a step toward a higher level."

Phoenix Society Presidents

1969–1970	John B. Stewart Jr.
1969–1969	Nelson K. Carter Sr.
1969–1970	Cecil W. Alston
1970–1971	Richard A. Epps
1971–1972	Leonard E. Wallace
1972–1974	Walter McKenney
1974–1976	Carl G. Booker Sr.
1976–1978	Steven M. Harris
1978–1980	Carl G. Booker Sr.
1980–1982	Jeff Powell
1982–1984	Steven M. Harris
1984–1988	Aaron O. West
1988–1992	Bradley G. Jones
1992–1994	Billy Smith
1994–1996	Charles A. Teale Sr.
1996–2000	Darren Hudson
2000–2002	Phillip McCalla
2002–2008	Duane Milner
2008–	Patrick Jones

Phoenix Society Inc. Honorary Members

Edward M. Curtin Jr.	Paul Littman
James O. Rogers	Alfred Rogers
Don Perkins	Author Dixon
Stanley Huckabey	Allyn A. Martin
Collin B. Bennett Sr.	Woodrow Wilson Gaitor
Herman Milton	Charles Smith
Edward Perry	Raymond Hooks Sr.
Keith Gill	Roger Copes
Patrick D. Jones	James Jackson

Phoenix Society Inc. Members

Levine Albert	Michael Alston	Rodney Barco	Donald Brown
Rodney Barco	Clifton J. Cooper	Tyrell Cox	James Eaton
Robert Farmer Jr.	Kerry Foster	Gregory Gentry	Steven M. Harris
Anothony Healis Sr.	Vincent Hooks	Darren Hudson	Robert James
Corey D. Johns	Martin Jones	Patrick D. Jones	Terry Jones
Curtis Lewis	Henry Mann	Ralph Martin Jr.	Nicole Mercado
Tony Milledge	Matthew Miller	Anthony Milner	Duane Milner
Lamar Mitchell	Robert Mitchell	Ramon Morgan	Peter Murphy
Michael Patterson	Jerry Robinson	Carlyle Saunders Jr.	Cinque Scott
Ewan Sheriff	Gregory Simon	Michelle Simon	Kevin Singleton
Gerald Sisco Jr.	Michael Smith	Anthony Taylor	Charles A. Teale Sr.
Lionel Thompson Jr.	Frederick Turner	Jason Wallace	Anthony Williams
Shelly Wilson-Tolliver			

Retired Members

Alfred Allison	Cecil Alston	Lumis Arnold	Willie Barrows
William Butler	Kenneth Bryant	Nelson K. Carter Sr.	Frank Carter Jr.
Tommy Dixon	Robert Dobson	Norman Ellis	Michael Eady
Lewis Fortson	Richard Epps	Robert Farmer Sr.	Marblin Fitzpatrick
John Fortson	Charles Garner	Walter Hodges	Steven M. Harris
Audabon Hil	Don Hill	Cassel Ingraham	Billie Jackson
Bradley G. Jones	Donald Lambert	David Mathis	Cornell Murray
Anthony Napoleon	Robert Richardson	Freddy Smith	Billy Smith
John B. Stewart Jr.	Willie Tate	Raymond Tyson	Leonard Wallace
Zandra Watley	Aaron O. West	Clyde Wilson	Richard Woods Jr.
Michael Thomas			

Past Recipients
William Henry Jacklyn Award

To the outstanding fire fighter in the community who best reflects the high standards of the profession and constantly seeks to update and project the complex changes facing the fire service in this ever-changing world.

1966	Chief Edward M. Curtin Jr.	Frank Davis Jr.
	Lt. John B. Stewart Jr.	George B. Hayes
1967	John T. Kelly	Joseph Kitchens
		Benjamin Laury
1968	Lt. Frank Burnes	James Lewis
		1988 Charles H. Green
1969	Lt. Richard A. Epps	1989 Chief Ronald Lewis
1970	Not Awarded	Dep. Chief Nelson K.
1971	Chief Edward F. Fennely	Carter Sr.
	Assistant, Chief Henry G.	1990 Vulcan Society Inc.,
	Thomas Jr.	NY City
1972	Not Awarded	1991 Chief Earl D. Geyer Sr.
1973	Not Awarded	1992 Aaron O. West
1974	George Sweeney	1993 Chief Nelson K. Carter Sr.
1975	Lt. Carl G. Booker Sr.	1994 Gloria Stokes
1976	Lt. Charles Parrish	1995 Robert E. Dobson
1977	Lt. David Floyd	1996 Deputy Fire Marshal
1978	Not Awarded	Capt. Willie
1979	Jeff Powell	Barrows
1980	Chief John B. Stewart Jr.	1997 Anthony R. Milner
1981	Fire Marshal Carl G. .	1998 Not Awarded
1982	Steven M. Harris	1999 Charles A. Teale Sr.
1983	Zandra M. Clay	2000 Cecil W. Alston
1984	Frank Carter Sr.	2001 Lt. Clifton J. Cooper
1985	Charles Hendricks	2002 Lt. Anthony
1986	Phoenix Society Inc.	Napoleon
1987	Harry Ashe Sr.	2012 Capt. Zandra Watley

Past Recipients
Phoenix Society Award

To the outstanding person in the community who through unselfish efforts and dedication has helped to bring a closer-knit community for all people

1967	Don Perkins	1987	Lucy Summers
1968	Marshal Slakin		Dr. Frederick G. Adams
	(awarded posthumously)	1988	Carrie S. Perry
1969	Author Dixon		Fred Ware
1970	Stanley Hucaabey	1989	Sheila H. Perry
1971	Woodrow Wilson Gaitor	1990	Cathalee Johnson
1972	Walter "Doc" Hurley	1991	Bernadine Silvers
1973	Barbara Henderson	1992	Jim Jamison
1974	Conelia Johnson	1993	Charles Christie
1975	Alice Ellison	1994	Elizabeth Horton-Sheff
1976	Raymond Montiero	1995	Deveria A. Berry
1977	Ida McKenny	1996	Patrica E.Larson
1978	Joel Gordon	1997	Richard Barton
1979	John B. Stewart Sr.	1998	Ozzie McKinnon
	Author L. Johnson	1999	Linnet E. Carty
	James G. Harris Jr.	2000	Rev. Brian K. Sinclair
	William J. Brown	2001	Kimberly A. Bridger
1980	Adrianne Baughns		
1981	Robert Nichols Jr.		
1982	Thirman L. Milner		
1983	Edward M. Strong		
1984	Woodson Wilson Gator		
1985	Evelyn Horn		
1986	Fredrica Gray		
	John J. Brittain		

Deceased Phoenix Society Members

Drvr. Harry Ashe

Drvr. Frank Davis

Fire George Hayes

Joseph Kitchens

James Lewis

Benjamin Laury

(photo unavailable)

(photo unavailable)

(photo unavailable)

The Fire Fighters Thereafter 1949–1973

Lt. John B. Steward

Lt. Carl G. Booker

Lt. Nelson Carter

Drvr. Cecil Alston

Lt. Alfert Allison

Lt. Richard Epps

Lt. Robert Easterling

Lt. Leonard Wallace

Drvr. Frank
Carter

William Butler
Rev.

Drvr. Willie
Barrow

FF. Grady
Sullivan

Insp. Clyde
Wilson

Drvr. Raymond
Tyson

Dep. Chief's Aide
Robert Farmer

Lt. Alferd
Allison

Drvr. Audabon
Hill

Drvr. Aaron
West

Drvr. Bradley
Jones

Drvr. Freddie
Smith

Drvr. John
Abrams

Drvr. John Joiner

Drvr. Walter
McKenny

FF. Marblin
Fitzpatrick

FF. Loomis
Arnold

FF. Troy Jones

FF. John Sykes

Drvr. Ray Woods

FF. Grady
Sullivan

FF. Victor Solis

FF. Wilie Tate

FF. Cornel
Murray

FF. Norman Ellis

FF. Billie Jackson

FF. Steve Harris

FF. Leroy Wilson

FF. Richard
Woods

FF. Don Hill

FF. Lewis Fortson

FF. Mike Blue

FF. Leroy
Johnson

FF. Ollie Little

FF. Willie Lay

FF. Billie Smith

FF. Leroy Becker

FF. James
Murphy

FF. Walter
Hodges

FF. Richard
Slappy

116

First Hartford Fire Department Female Fire Fighter (1982)

Lt. Zandra (Clay)
Watley

Phoenix Society Inc.—1996

D/C Charles Teale

Lt. Terry Waller

FF. Kenneth
Bryant

LT. Darren
Hudson

Capt. Steven
Harris

Lt. Cornel
Murray

FF. Donald
Lambert

L/D Duine
Milner

Chief John B.
Stewart

Lt. Frank
Carter Sr.

F/M Carl G.
Booker

Chief Nelson
Carter Jr.

D/C Aaron West   Lt. Alferd Allison   Lt. Cecil Alston   P/O Bradley Jones

D/M Willie Barrows   P/O Freddie Smith   P/O Ray Tyson   Capt. Audie Hill

FF. Don Hill   Chief Robert Dobson   D/C Leonard Wallace   Capt. Robert Richardson

Lt. David Mathis   Lt. Anthony Milner   P/O John Fortson   Mech. Mike Smith

Lt. Frank Carter Jr.   P/O Lewis Fotson   P/O Walter Hodges   P/O Ray Woods

118

FF. Lavine Albert   FF. Michael Alston   FF. Lumis Arnold   FF. Rodney Barco

FF. Robert James   FF. Brainard Carter   FF. Clifton Cooper   FF. Kerry Foster

FF. Lomont Freeman   FF. Charles Garner   FF. Henry Mann   FF. Philip McCalla

FF. Peter Murphy   FF. Anthony Napoleon   FF. Lionel Thompson   FF. Anthony Williams

FF. Tyrone Williams   FF. Anthony Healis   FF. Martin Jones   FF. Patrick Jones

FF. Curtis Simon   FF. Gregory Simon   FF. Anthony Taylor

Photos Courtesy of
Michael A. Thomas, Entrepreneur, Retired Member Phoenix Society

Black Professional Fire Fighter Organizations in the United States

Afro American Firefighter League
Chicago, IL

Black United Firefighters (BUFF)
Camden, NJ

Brothers Combined
Atlanta, GA

Brothers United
San Diego, CA

Club Valiants Inc.
Philadelphia, PA

COFFEE
Plainfield, NJ

Firefighters Institute For Racial Equality
St. Louis, Mo.

Phoenix
Detroit, MI

Phoenix Society, Inc.
Hartford, CT

Progressive Firefighters Association
Washington, DC

United Black Firefighters
Atlantic City, NJ

Vulcan Pioneers of New Jersey Inc.
Newark, NJ

Vulcan Pioneers of Hudson County
Jersey City, NJ

Vulcan Society Inc
New York City, NY

Santorian
Los Angeles County, FD CA

Vanguards
Baltimore, MD

The Firebird Society
New Haven, CT

The Firebird Society
New Haven, CT

Vulcans of Massachusetts
Boston, MA

8

A CALL TO SPECIAL SERVICES

In June 1968, as the nation observed a day of mourning following the assassination of Robert F. Kennedy, I was also grieving was over a city that appeared tired and in the throes of death. Despair hung over the city of Hartford like the blanket of smoke after the more than 120 fires set following the murder of Martin Luther King Jr. After two consecutive years of rioting, city taxpayers, both Black and White, were fleeing to the tranquility of the suburbs. This latest disturbance had left charred and burnt-out remains not only in the city's North End, but also in the Dutch Point, Charter Oak Terrace, and Rice Heights sections. Tensions in these poorer neighborhoods remained high, but I was hoping we could get through the coming summer without a similar disturbance.

Not even my recent elevation to the newly created position of administrative lieutenant and the community organizing I was now doing lessened my anxiety. As a result of this promotion, I was now in charge of a new unit within the fire department called Special Services. Chief Curtin had called me to his office to talk about how the fire service might be able to establish better relations with the Black community. The reaction within the fire department to the attacks on fire fighters was one of bewilderment more than anger. Fire fighters, who put their lives in danger to save the lives and property of others, couldn't understand why they were not viewed as friends. Unlike the Black fire fighters, Chief Curtin and the others had failed to make the connection between the action of Black rioters and what they had witnessed White fire fighters doing to Black protesters in Birmingham,

Alabama. Blacks in Hartford had watched on their televisions as White fire fighters turned high-powered water hoses on Black men, women, and little children. When White fire fighters came into Hartford's Black community to fight the fires, the rioters saw only the color of their skin. Throwing bricks and bottles at them was payback.

Chief Curtin was a fair man who had earned my respect. He had gone out on a limb to make me the first Black officer in the history of the Hartford Fire Department. A few Whites in the department still harbored ill feelings toward him for elevating a Black man over them. But that seemed not to bother Curtin. Like me, Curtin was a Hartford native. He grew up in the city's South End. After graduating from Bulkeley High School, he studied accounting in college. He worked several years as an accountant before being drafted into the army during World War II. After two years of service he was discharged in 1944 with the rank of lieutenant. He then followed his father's footsteps into the Hartford Fire Department.

Once in the department Curtin rose quickly through the ranks. He made lieutenant in 1950, captain in 1953, administrative deputy chief in 1960, and chief in 1965. He was the youngest person ever to make chief. I also considered Curtin to be a man of principle. I knew he believed in full integration of the fire department. He once said to me in private, "Before I close my eyes, I want to see you bring Black and Hispanics into the department." I had pondered that statement for some time. That is, the part about me bringing Blacks and Hispanics into the department.

Now, as we talked, he was showing his sensitivity toward the reasons for the disturbances in the Black community. He not only wanted to end the rioting and the attacks on firemen, but he also wanted to do something about the underlying causes. He wanted a program that would end the resentment and build a sound harmonious relationship. Besides these obvious reasons, he confided that this needed to happen so the fire service could answer critics who claimed the fire department wasn't doing anything to solve the existing problems. Curtin wanted to tell those critics that he had taken measures that he believed would prove effective.

It may have been that Curtin had read the report issued several weeks earlier by President Lyndon Johnson's Commission on Race Relations. Because the type of program he envisioned was exactly what the commission said was needed in urban areas. The report had stated that "Inner-city police and firemen are perceived by inner-city Blacks as outsiders and not part of the community. Police and firemen need to come out of their buildings and into the streets and get to know the people living around them. They need to become part of the community and not continue to be viewed as the enemy." This was exactly what Chief Curtin was hoping to achieve with this new unit.

The first large city to establish such a community relations unit was New York. Relations between Blacks and the fire service in some parts of that city were so bad that neighborhood Blacks were not even allowed to enter the fire stations to use the water fountain. Los Angeles was the second city to establish a similar community relations unit. Once our unit was implemented, Hartford would become the third. Following Hartford's first disturbance in the summer of 1967, the city manager and police officials were quick to establish a police community relations division. It was patterned after those that had sprung up quickly in other cities that had experienced racial unrest. Now Chief Curtin and City Manager Freeman wanted me to head the new unit they had in mind.

I agreed that I was probably the logical choice. I was the department's only Black officer, and I had strong ties to the Black community. Curtin believed I could gain quick acceptance and help the people understand that the fire service was truly concerned about their plight.

"Let's not call it community relations," Chief Curtin suggested. "People have heard that. Let's call it Special Services." I nodded in agreement. As we continued discussing the program, which we both viewed as adventurous, some cautionary thoughts entered my mind.

Would I be able to gain the respect of the young people who seemed bent on acts of violence? In three years I would be forty. Wouldn't a younger person be better able to identify with them? Would our efforts be looked upon by the Black community as just one more token gesture? Well, the answers to these questions would come soon enough, I thought. When our discussion ended, I left Chief Curtin's office with the task of developing a new unit called Special Services. The even greater task was changing the minds, if not the hearts, of people in the Black and Hispanic communities who presently had no faith in city government.

As head of Special Services, I was placed on detached duty. This meant no more fighting fires; I would spend all my time in the streets talking with community people. In order to be successful and achieve the goals Chief Curtin was hoping for, I knew I would have to gain an even better feel for the community and the lives of the people who lived there. I especially needed to begin a meaningful dialogue with those young Black and Hispanic youth who were involved in the disturbances. The bottom line was that the setting of fires and the harassment and attacks on fire fighters had to stop. I knew this was a tall order. It meant the fire department would have to do more than just put out fires and leave people on the street homeless and without shelter. We would have to make sure that people who lost their homes to fire had someplace to go, and had some semblance of order in their lives. We would have to establish educational programs and take these programs to churches, schools, and community centers. We had to let people know about the range of services provided by the fire department for their benefit. Special Services would also perform a task that would mark a major turn in the direction of the Hartford Fire Department; I would actively recruit Blacks and Hispanics. In other words I had to show the people in the community that we in the fire service truly cared about them.

I spent the next several days walking the streets and talking with people about what they felt were the root causes of the disturbances, and also getting their thoughts about the fire department. Much of what they said, I had already suspected, but I wanted to hear it first-hand, and gauge the level of their emotions. Wearing my uniform, I went from neighborhood to neighborhood talking with people. I was welcomed in some neighborhoods and looked upon with suspicion in others. Several days later I wrote the following report for Chief Curtin:

Many of the youth and young adults have little or no understanding of the good work fire fighters perform in their community. They identify fire fighters as enemies in their neighborhoods. They stone and swear at fire fighters even as they perform life-saving duties. In the poorer sections of the city including the North End, the Tunnel area, South Park, and Charter Oak Terrace, the Blacks and the Spanish-speaking people see the firehouses, and the nearly all white men inside, as intruders in their neighborhoods.

The people in these neighborhoods feel they live in a society controlled by whites, and are frequently discriminated against. They are alienated and disrespectful of traditional authorities. The people in these neighborhoods generally lacked the opportunity to improve their conditions. They have found out quite pragmatically that making trouble is a way to force the governing white society to recognize their needs. They are not afraid to make trouble, no matter what the costs to them personally. It is simply a matter of not having anything to lose.

At this point almost anything would be better than the hostility now evident. My intent is to develop a program that removes the hostility, and builds the sound and harmonious community relations needed for efficient and effective fire prevention throughout the city. We need to have a relationship with schools, churches, hospitals, and other groups in the community so we can deliver the message that fire fighters are here to protect the community. We need to deliver a message that emphasizes the importance of cleaning up litter, keeping covers on barrels and not ringing false alarms.

After reading my report, Curtin agreed there was important work to be done by Special Services. The question now was, how would I work through what seemed like a deep-seated hostility, and build a harmonious relationship between the fire department and the minority community? I knew that a White man coming into the Black community would generally be ignored, because many in the Black community wouldn't identify with White men delivering messages. I was hopeful that the people would receive me as one of their own.

What Chief Curtin did next was of great help. In preparation for my new assignment, he made an appointment for me to meet with New York City Fire Commissioner Robert O. Lowery, and to observe that city's community relations bureau in action.

"Select someone to accompany you on the trip," he told me. So I selected pump operator Cecil Alston. I had worked closely with Alston while we were organizing the Phoenix Society, of which he was now president. Alston had moved to Hartford from North Carolina after his discharge from the army. For a while he worked at the Pratt & Whitney aircraft plant in East Hartford, but quit in 1959 to become a fire fighter. When Curtin asked who was going with me, I told him Cecil Alston. "Why did you choose Alston?" Curtin inquired.

"Because we're the same age, and the two of us think alike," I answered. Then Curtin gave me some advice that to this day I have never forgotten.

"Never pick someone to go with you on an important mission who thinks the same as you," he told me. "If you're in a battle, selecting someone who thinks exactly the way you do could get you killed." I knew the chief was speaking from his experience of being in action during World War II. He went on: "Always pick someone who thinks differently than you do. Choose someone who will ask the questions that you wouldn't, and would question your actions if he felt the need to. Remember that if you ever become chief of the fire department."

His advice made good sense. I also took note that it was not too farfetched for him to envision me as fire chief one day. When I later became chief, I always welcomed a variety of viewpoints when analyzing a situation. Curtin's advice caused me to change my mind and take Richard Epps with me to New York instead of Alston. Epps, a driver, had joined the department in 1962. He was a few years younger than me, but was born and raised in Hartford. And I knew from previous conversations that we did not always think alike. We spent five days in New York, from June 23 to 27, 1968. We gained valuable information as we talked with fire fighters and studied every aspect of their community relations operation. We even had the opportunity to discuss community relations procedures with New York's Mayor John Lindsay. We returned to Hartford with a lot of ideas, and I was eager to get our own program up and running. After briefing Curtin I selected three men to work with me in Special Services: Richard Epps, Nelson Carter, and Cecil Alston.

First on my agenda was to take a look at some local organizations that were already doing the things in the community that Special Services wanted to do. So I arranged a meeting with the director of the Police Community Relations Bureau, and a second meeting with the director of the Hartford Human Relations Commission. At each meeting I told them about the fire department's new Special Services unit, and what we hoped to achieve. I asked them to tell me about their operations and about both their positive and negative experiences in the community. From my talks with community people, I was aware that the police were especially disliked by many young Blacks and Hispanics. For them, police shootings and being stopped without cause made police the enemy. At the time Hartford had only a handful of Black police officers, and a lesser number of Hispanic officers.

At my meeting with the police community relations director, I was informed that they were having a difficult time identifying new minority recruits. Like the fire department, they too had an image problem that needed changing. Fostering better relations between the minority community and public and private organizations was the goal of the Hartford Human Relations Commission. It advocated on behalf of minorities, taught them better work habits, and sought to eliminate discrimination in the workplace. Since we were all trying to help the same group of people, I enquired at these meetings as to whether there were areas where we could work together. They agreed to be available to Special Services if ever the need should arise. Next on my agenda was to meet with public school and housing authority officials, tenant relations advisors, local political leaders, and people who ran neighborhood recreation centers, as well as various civil groups. After two weeks of one meeting after another, I prepared a report for Chief Curtin, sharing the information I had gathered. I explained in my report how I thought this information could benefit our work in Special Services.

In mid-July 1968, with most of the summer in front of us, large numbers of young people began gathering nightly on the streets in some neighborhoods. When they became unruly, the police fired tear gas into the crowd to disperse them. One night over a hundred young people at the intersection of Main and Kennedy Streets were scattered by tear gas, with a number arrested for unlawful acts. The next weekend some teenagers returning from a dance at the Fred D. Wish School in the North End tore down protective gratings and looted at least six stores. Tear gas was also used at Barbour and Kensington Streets, where three liquor stores were being looted. Fortunately no fires were set during these incidences.

Meanwhile, I was hoping to have Special Services in operation before the end of July. If fire fighters were needed, I wanted to make sure they were welcomed because their only purpose was to serve the people of Hartford. I decided to get our message out through the media, direct mail, fliers, and brochures. We would also make direct contact with both the young and the old at community centers, schools, churches, senior centers, and other places where people gathered. And we would develop and support recreational and educational programs for young people. I was confident that through our efforts, people would eventually realize that the fire service was their friend.

Once I developed a community relations program on paper, laying out program goals, objectives, and strategies, I shared them with Chief Curtin. Some aspects of the program we had already put into operation. I told him that members of my Special Services team were already out walking the streets, meeting and getting to know people in the community. The reaction from many people was one of surprise. They had never before seen uniformed firemen walking the streets, talking, listening, and spending time standing on the sidewalks. This caused some people to just stand and watch out of curiosity. Others welcomed us to the community and voiced their support of what we were attempting to do.

Initially, Chief Curtin's thinking was that the Special Services unit would remain in operation only until we had achieved our goals. Once achieved, the unit would disband. But Chief Curtin was so impressed with what we were doing that he issued an official bulletin on August 5, 1968, making Special Services a permanent unit within the fire department. In the bulletin Curtin explained the need for and the role of Special Services, and told all fire fighters to be supportive of its mission.

"The purpose of the Special Services unit is to quietly and effectively overcome what must clearly be a misunderstanding and distortion of this department's responsibility to the general public, which has always been to render the best service possible to all, regardless of the situation or circumstances," he told a *Hartford Courant* reporter.

Special Services was now a permanent unit within the fire department, with the responsibility for all aspects of community relations. This included getting to know community leaders and participating in community activities; supporting programs for youth and educating them about the dangers of illegally opening fire hydrants, turning in false alarms, and setting fires in Dumpsters; and recruiting minorities into the fire department. Special Services would also function as liaison with other city agencies, as well as state and federal community relations divisions. We were responsible for handling community complaints and any related concerns as they presented themselves.

Toward the end of August, we opened a Special Services satellite office in the North End. This allowed us to have a real presence in the community where people could see us coming and going every day. It also meant people knew where to find us if need be.

During this time I was monitoring a debate in the city council over the merits of the Model City Program. I could envision how a massive physical and social renewal of run-down neighborhoods in the North End would make the people who lived here feel better about themselves. This would certainly make my work a lot easier. Also, what was happening in Chicago at this very time helped me put Hartford's past disturbances in perspective. In the "Windy City" fifteen thousand protesters were battling police for the control of the streets during the Democratic National Convention.

In November 1968, as President-elect Richard Nixon was pledging to end the war in Vietnam, criticizing those involved in the student protests, and promising to restore racial peace and social harmony, Special Services was working to maintain the peace in Hartford's Black and Puerto Rican communities. Many of the young people who harassed and pelted fire fighters with rocks lived in the Stowe Village projects. One evening while I was walking through Stowe Village, a man came over and introduced himself to me.

"My name is Darrell Garner," he said. "I live here in Stowe Village. I know what you're trying to do here. I spend my off hours working with the young boys and girls in these projects who don't seem to have any direction. If you want, I can arrange for you to meet with a gang of kids here who call themselves the Hustlers."

I introduced myself and thanked him for his help. "Can you set the meeting for tomorrow evening at six o'clock?" I asked him.

"Sure, I can," he told me. I thanked him again, and we shook hands. At six o'clock the next evening, Garner and about twenty-five boys were waiting for me when I walked into the Stowe Village community room. Some of the boys looked to be as young as ten or eleven. I was not too surprised that kids this young, disadvantaged and living in the projects would see themselves as Hustlers. The older kids in the group appeared to be eighteen or nineteen. I introduced myself and told them I knew how things were in the North End, because I was born and raised there.

"My interest now," I said, "is helping the young people living in the community where I was born." I was wearing my uniform and explained that the fire department was their friend and cared about young people. While talking with them and listening to what they had to say, I realized how much they were in need of something constructive to do with their free time. Several of them spoke of their interest in organizing a boy's club and a football team. I told them that a boy's club and football team would be good programs for Special Services to sponsor. Before ending the meeting we set a date to meet again the following week, and I thanked Darrell Green for assembling the boys. This would not be my last meeting with Green, who would become a well-known community organizer, and who in 1970 would be named Man of the Month by Connecticut Mutual Life Insurance Company.

After meeting with the kids at Stowe Village, I went to the Betty Knox Foundation the next day to see if organizing a boy's club and football team qualified for a grant. I thought it might because the foundation was named after a woman who had dedicated herself to making life better for people living in Hartford. Betty Knox had died two years earlier, but left a couple of million dollars to start a charitable foundation. It was because of her desire to help low-income people, especially those living in public housing that I felt we had a good chance of getting a grant.

I went next to the Boy's Club of America to see if they would assist Special Services in this effort. I knew of their expertise in working with young people. After a meeting with Hartford Housing Authority officials, I was able to secure space in the basement of a building where the young people could hold their meetings. I also managed to get a few adult volunteers to help supervise their activities. It was a great day for all involved when the Stowe Village Boy's Club opened its doors in the spring of 1969. My hope was that this activity would keep the boys focused and moving in the right direction. When I was asked to serve on the club's board of directors, I agreed without hesitation.

In late April the work of Special Services was recognized by the Greater Hartford Urban League. League Director William Brown issued the following press release:

> We are always seeking representation from all kinds of outstanding people in the community. Lieutenant John Stewart is one such person. Therefore we are naming him today to the Urban League Board of Directors.

I could not have been more pleased that my work in the community was being recognized by such a well-respected organization. I recalled that it was back in 1961 that Norris O'Neill and members of the Concerned Citizens of the North End invited Urban League President Whitney Young to Hartford. Young gave a speech at Aetna Life and Casualty Insurance to local bank presidents and business leaders, raising thousands of dollars for the Hartford Urban League. O'Neill became league president, and Brown, a former dean of men at Talladega College in Alabama, became its executive director.

Even with all the effort Special Services was putting into the community, I was troubled by the high number of false alarms the department was experiencing. We told the students when we visited the schools how false alarms tied up equipment and men that might be needed to fight a real fire. Still, from January through April, I calculated that there had been 487 false alarms, with ninety-nine in the month of April alone. In the past twelve months 2,868 false alarms had been sounded. On one occasion I was staked out with another fire fighter in an unmarked car near an alarm box on Blue Hills Avenue. This box had been pulled thirteen times over the past weekend. We wanted to talk to the kids who were responsible. As we watched, two girls who looked like teenagers walked up to the alarm box and pulled the handle. What they did was against the law, so after apprehending them, we had to turn them over to the police.

As the summer of 1969 approached, Special Services was busy at work in the community. Other organizations, including the recently opened Hartford Chapter of the Black Panther Party, were also at work in the community. Under the direction of Charles "Butch" Lewis, the Black Panthers had established a free breakfast program for public schoolchildren. A decorated Vietnam veteran, Lewis had also established a "street academy" that offered alternative educational programs to high school students who were struggling in public schools. All of us who were working in the community were hoping for a trouble-free summer. We continued our efforts in Stowe Village, organizing a Midget and a Pony Team for the younger boys there. We entered both teams in the Charter Oak Midget and Pony Football Leagues. Several insurance companies that had experienced financial losses because of the riots helped us by purchasing uniforms and football equipment. In June we gave brand-new football uniforms to the teams we named the "Fire Fighters."

This success boosted our hopes, which were now extremely high. We wanted our efforts to make a real difference in the lives of these under-privileged young people. With the youth programs now a reality in Stowe Village, we set our sights on the nearby Bellevue Square Housing Project. Many of the young people who attacked fire fighters lived in this sprawling complex of over three hundred apartments. We were aware of a group of boys in Bellevue Square who called themselves the Emperors. We were successful in setting up a meeting with these boys and their parents to talk about how we could channel their

energy into positive activities. This meeting led to several more meetings, and overtime we felt the attitude these boys had toward the fire
department was beginning to change for the better. We also joined
with a group of concerned men in Bellevue Square who were trying
to change the negative image of their community. We were happy to
work with these men, and eventually they made Richard Epps and me
honorary members of the Bellevue Square Men's Club.

To help people better understand the good work we were doing at
the fire department, Special Services developed an easy-to-read information pamphlet. This pamphlet turned out to be an effective tool for
telling our story to the public. It also went a long way toward helping
to improve relations between the community and the fire service. We
recruited some kids from a community service project called Project
Co-op to help distribute the pamphlets. Project Co-op had been founded
in memory of Dr. Martin Luther King Jr. to help direct the energy of
twelve- to fifteen-year-old kids in positive ways. The youngsters were
organized in groups with adult group leaders and did beautification and
community relations work. The kids also worked with other organizations, including the Inner City Exchange and the Human Relations
Commission, as well as city government. They earned ten dollars a
week, but were given only two dollars to spend. The remaining eight
dollars was held for them until the end of the summer.

On an afternoon in June 1969, I stood at the corner of Suffield
and Main Streets with Arthur Johnson, a longtime Hartford activist and head of the Human Relations Commission, and with Police
Lieutenant Theodore Napper, head of police community relations.
We were watching these young people pass out the pamphlets. Both
Johnson and Napper were enthusiastic supporters of the work Special
Services was doing in the community. As we watched the kids pass out
our pamphlets, we talked about the importance of citizen cooperation
with the fire department. We had high hopes that our efforts together
would bring an end to the summer disturbances. Little did we know at
the time, that our high hopes were about to be shattered.

THE RACIAL DISTURBANCE
OF 1969 AND 1970

The following month, July 1969, a White policeman shot and killed a Black teenager in North End. After no charges were brought against the police officer, sporadic disturbances broke out but ended quickly. The atmosphere, however, remained tense. During the second week of August, a group of Puerto Ricans in the North End were complaining that police were not making a serious attempt to find the person who had severely beaten a Puerto Rican man. As the group grew larger and more boisterous the police used tear gas to disperse them. When two of the four Puerto Ricans on the Hartford Police Department complained that the tear gas was not necessary, they were cited for insubordination.

At this time, Hartford's Puerto Rican community numbered 15,000 to 20,000, or approximately 10 percent of the city's 160,000 population. A large number of Puerto Ricans lived in the North End, and many lived in the decaying South Green and Clay Hill neighborhoods, having replaced the Italians and Polish who had moved away. The majority of the housing in the area was considered slum housing, for which they paid exorbitant rents. A major complaint of Puerto Rican residents was poor, overpriced housing. It was not unusual for them to be charged $130 a month for a four-room apartment in a dilapidated tenement. Many of the Puerto Ricans worked in the nearby tobacco fields for minimum wage. Some who had skills and learned English did manage to find industry jobs that paid a little more.

In 1969 approximately 3,000 of the city's 63,000 registered voters were Puerto Ricans, the majority of them in the Democratic Party. Still, there were no Puerto Ricans among high city government officials or sitting on the city council. Like Blacks, many Puerto Ricans in Hartford viewed themselves as victims of discrimination and police brutality. Their concerns prompted members of the Puerto Rican community to gather at the South Park Methodist Church in August 1969. Louis Rivera, a college student fed up with police brutality, expressed his concern.

"The issue here is about a small gang that uses tactics like beating people with clubs and turning animals upon them to chew them!"

This prompted James Frazier, treasurer for the local NAACP chapter, to stand and speak. "You need to understand that you are considered people of color! And you need to join a civil rights group!" he told the gathering. "If you don't think you're colored like me, you've got something to learn!"

That weekend the first of a three-part series on the condition of Puerto Ricans living in South Greene appeared in the *Hartford Times*. In the Sunday, August 31, 1969, article, an unidentified Hartford fireman was quoted as saying that all Puerto Ricans were "pigs." The next day, Labor Day, a group of Puerto Rican youths stormed the fire station at Main and Belden Streets, apparently in response to the article. Hearing the radio call, I hurried to the firehouse, finding that things had been thrown around, but no fire fighter had been injured. The same roving band of angry Puerto Rican youths was later joined by a group of Black youths. What followed would be three days of Hartford's worst rioting. It began with Black and Puerto Rican youth fire bombings and looting in the North End. The violence then spread to the South Green neighborhood.

Fire fighters rushed from one fire to another, being greeted at each fire with rocks, bottles, bricks, and pieces of pavement. A reporter called these objects "curbside ammunition." Helmeted police with batons rushed to each fire and formed a line of protection between the fire fighters and the jeering crowd. Several blocks away on Barbour Street, Jaiven's Drug Store, the only drugstore in the neighborhood, burned to the ground. The police field commander had already called for backup to help disperse the crowd. Seven families living in the apartments above the store now had no place to live. When I arrived at the scene, I had Special Services transport the now homeless families by police vans to Red Cross headquarters on Farmington Avenue. I knew the Red Cross would place them in temporary hotel rooms provided by the city.

Thankfully, no rock-throwing incidents occurred at this fire. This, I believed, was out of sympathy for distraught families on the sidewalk who had lost everything. Two fire fighters were transported to St. Francis Hospital, one overcome by smoke and the other cut by broken glass. About seven in the evening, the police began ordering people off the streets, threatening to arrest those not complying. Ignoring the police, the crowds of young people grew larger and more boisterous. A sniper from somewhere in the crowd wounded a police officer. To my knowledge, this was the first incidence of a gun being fired by a protester. In response, police returned fire, wounding four people. At the outbreak of this disturbance, Mayor Uccello was vacationing in Maine. Upon being notified she rushed back to Hartford. Around midnight a visibly distraught mayor was seen walking the streets of the North End with police and city officials, calling for calm. Gradually, as things were brought under control, police estimated that sixty stores and business places, including restaurants, package stores, grocery stores, a drugstore, and a pool hall, were either burned or looted in the Albany Avenue and North Main Street areas.

People in Hartford woke up on Tuesday morning, the day after Labor Day, to find the city under a state of emergency. This meant that no large crowds were allowed to assemble in the streets, and a 10:30 p.m. curfew was in effect. This was the second curfew to be implemented in the history of Hartford. Police were on twelve-hour shifts, and at least one hundred Connecticut State Troopers patrolled streets.

Governor John Dempsey put ten units of Connecticut's National Guard on "practice alert." Walking the streets of the North End in the daylight, Mayor Uccello saw garbage burning in the middle of Windsor Street, and a huge blaze near Center Street and Albany Avenue.

"The North End looks like a city under siege," a reporter accompanying the mayor remarked.

"The damage appears to be worse than it was in June," the mayor responded, looking over a street that resembled a war zone. "But we are prepared to meet the situation with state police, National Guard, or any necessary force." After a tour of the North End, the mayor went to police headquarters to get an update from the police chief.

"We will not terminate the state of emergency or cut the curfew until we're confident the situation is completely under control," the mayor told Police Chief John Kerrigan. "I want people to know that we are not going to stand for this kind of violence." But even the increased number of police and the presence of state troopers were not enough to deter the most determined of the rioters. Late that afternoon firebombs were thrown into several North End buildings and onto the middle of north Main Street. About six o'clock that evening, Bob's Furniture Warehouse on Westland Street was firebombed. It took fire fighters over two hours to put this fire out. Before the fire was out, the call went out that the public library at Main and Belden had been firebombed. Not far from the library, the police were crouched behind an overturned car to protect themselves from a hidden sniper.

Sniping and firebombing also spread to Puerto Rican neighborhoods on the city's south side. By eleven that night, the police felt they had the situation on the streets under control. The next day, Wednesday, there were sporadic acts of violence. The unofficial count of those arrested was over five hundred, both Black and Puerto Rican. Some were arrested for breaking and entering and others for violating the citywide curfew. The jail in Hartford was so crowded that those arrested were being taken to the jail in the nearby town of Haddam.

To process the large number of people, the courts were holding night sessions.

You cannot imagine my total devastation. I was positive that the work of Special Services over the past year had not been in vain. Many of the young people we had been working with in the community were now involved in constructive activities. But the rioting, the nearly two hundred fires, and especially the attacks on fire fighters told me there was much more work to be done, and many more minds to be changed. I knew that after years of unequal treatment, the anger and frustration of Hartford's disadvantaged poor would not be appeased by mere talk alone. Decent affordable housing and jobs were needed to improve their quality of life. But city government would have to see to that.

I began walking the streets and talking with frustrated community leaders and angry citizens. When I spoke with young people, I let them know I understood why they were angry, but destruction of their own community just made no sense. At a meeting with government officials, community leaders, and reporters, an incensed Mayor Uccello blamed the violence and destruction on power-seeking hoodlums.

"Poor housing conditions or uncomplimentary newspaper articles are no excuse for criminal action, and those who say they are do a disservice to the total community and to the people whose condition they wish to improve," she told them. "This violence was organized, instigated by hoodlums looking for an opportunity to loot and burn, who would steal no matter the social condition. They were joined by irresponsible young people lacking parental control and who were influenced and egged on by those hoodlums and swept into a carnival of violence and destruction that was soon beyond their capacity to control, let alone understand."

Learning of the mayor's words, Theodore Pryor, head of the Ebony League, a local Black businessmen's association, gave a cynical response. "Sure it was organized," he said. "They were organized by the ghetto in one hundred years of oppression."

Over the next few days an uneasy peace hung over the North End, South Green, Charter Oak, and other minority neighborhoods as tempers began to cool off. City and state police were still out on the streets in large numbers. Many of the young people were reacting negatively to their presence, feeling as though their neighborhood had been taken over by an occupying force. A number of community meetings were being held to discuss the causes of the disturbances. At one meeting, sponsored by the Hartford Chapter of the Black Panther Party, people wanted to talk about the behavior of the police. A woman angrily complained that police unleashed dogs that went into a crowd and bit people.

"It's not right," she said, shaking her head.

A young man shared his experience. "I was downtown eating at a restaurant and a policeman came in. And another White man asked him what he was doing with his dogs. He said, 'I've got the best nigger chasers going.' Now that makes me want to throw a brick. And I'm a college-educated intelligent Black. That makes me want to throw a brick. There's only so much people can take."

While I spent most of my time working in the community, I did manage to involved myself in the activities of the Phoenix Society. In October 1969 the Phoenix Society was contacted by the Vulcan Society. They asked that we attend an urgent meeting in New York City to discuss the disturbances in the inner cities, the attacks on fire fighters, and racism within the fire service. Since Hartford had now experienced its third consecutive summer of racial disturbances, I was eager to participate in such a meeting. On the last day of October 1969, I traveled with several other Phoenix Society members to New York City for a two-day conference. Besides the Vulcan Society and the Phoenix Society, members of the Valiants of Philadelphia, the Vulcan Pioneers of Hudson County New Jersey, and the Vulcan Pioneers of Newark, New Jersey, were also in attendance. Fire fighters were also present from a number of other cities.

It was at this conference that the five organizations voted to reach out nationally to Black fire fighters, and invite them to a national convention in Hartford the following October. I left that conference excited because we had voted to do something that would be historic in the fire fighting profession. Our next meeting was just over three months later, in February 1970, when Phoenix Society members traveled to Brooklyn for a meeting at Vulcan Society headquarters on Eastern Parkway. This was a meeting of representatives of five Black fire fighters' organizations that comprised the National Convention Planning Committee, of which I was asked to serve as chair. The purpose of this meeting was to discuss the steps that needed to be taken in advance of a national convention.

At the same time, I was still focused on my work with Special Services. With the arrival of spring, police and fire fighters, elected officials, and community leaders were all hoping for a peaceful summer. Naturally we were anxious, given the disturbances of the past three summers. In April, 1970, while the country was hoping for the safe return to earth of the three endangered astronauts aboard the *Apollo 13* space capsule, a policeman stopped a car on a Hartford street driven by a nineteen-year-old Puerto Rican. What transpired between the two remains unclear, but as a result the young man was shot and killed. The family of the dead youth, Abraham Rodriguez, and the Puerto Rican community were outraged. They called the shooting unprovoked and demanded the White police officer be charged with murder. The police officer claimed Rodriguez came at him with a screwdriver.

Several days later, as national attention was now focused on the four students killed at Kent State by the Ohio National Guard, the county coroner in Hartford found the police officer criminally responsible for Rodriguez's death. He was dismissed from the police force and charged with manslaughter. The last week of July, the police officer went on trial. During the trial young people with seemingly nothing else to do, stood in clusters on a number of North End and south side streets. This caused the mayor to issue a nine o'clock curfew for youth under eighteen, and to increase police patrols in these

areas. Still, sporadic fires were being set. At his trial the police officer received strong support from the police rank and file, and from
many of Hartford's White residents. This, along with the speed of the
trial and a not-guilty verdict, left a bitter taste in the mouths of many
Puerto Ricans and Blacks.

On Friday, July 31, the day after the not-guilty verdict, a Molotov
cocktail was thrown through a side window of the firehouse at Main and
Sanford Street. Patrol cars were ordered to park outside each firehouse
in the North End. Over the next several days, isolated acts of vandal-
ism occurred in the North End, and in the mainly Puerto Rican areas of
Charter Oak Terrace and South Green. That night the firebombing and
looting began in earnest. The curfew was being ignored by roving bands
of youths, who seemed to have no purpose other than to create trouble.
Hundreds of police in riot gear and carrying bully clubs, rifles, and tear
gas faced off a large crowd in the North End's Arsenal area. Only when the
police were ordered by their commander to back off was calm restored.

That night, just before nine o'clock, Efraira Gonzales, a twenty-eight-
year-old Puerto Rican man, was shot and killed. Witnesses and police at
the scene gave differing accounts of what happened. The brothers of the
man who was killed, Juan and Estevan Gonzales, said two policemen
approached them as they walked along Syms Street in the North End.
One of the policemen, they said, fired tear gas at them while the other
knelt and fired a shotgun from about 200 feet away. The police maintained they had only birdshot in their weapons, and that Efraira had
been shot by a sniper. This account was backed up by a hospital report
the next day, which stated that Efraira had two bullet wounds, one in his
shoulder and one in his chest. Mayor Uccello announced that as a result
of the sniper fire, the curfew would now be for all residents of the North
End, regardless of age. Just before the curfew went into effect, police did
shoot and wound two men as they were looting a liquor store.

The next day a meeting convened at city hall to determine the
cause of this latest disturbance. "It was the not-guilty verdict," one
person contended, while others agreed.

"The police should have learned from the previous riots how to develop police-minority relationships that lead to respect," said another. "But the police have failed to do that, and until they do that, we'll have trouble every summer." One council member noted that with 45,000 Blacks and 15,000 Puerto Ricans living in the city, there were only fifty-five Blacks and four Puerto Ricans on the nearly five-hundred-member police department. Chief Curtin noted that within a five-day period, the fire department had responded to 290 alarms, with 80 percent of them directly related to the rioting.

"My hope is that community-minded citizens in the North End would come forward and help restore law and order to the streets," Chief Curtin added.

Responding to Chief Curtin, a North End community leader remarked, "You come to us and want our help when there's trouble, but where are you when we need you?" Still, it was agreed that citizens would be asked to patrol the streets as a way of heading off trouble. At the beginning of August, at least seventy-five civilian volunteers were out on the streets in the North End. They encouraged young people to obey the curfew, and they attempted to cool down those with hot tempers. Their presence also helped to reduce the number of false alarms. Special Services compiled a roster of these volunteers, hoping we could call upon them again if needed. I continued to walk the streets engaging people in conversation. We talked about issues underlying the disturbances, and how burning and looting stores was putting our community at a great disadvantage. To this day I believe the reason why Blacks didn't know for the longest time how to properly run community drugstores or other types of stores was because the Whites and the Jews who were trying to teach us were scared off. In the streets, it bothered me when I heard some young Blacks jokingly call the disturbances the "illegal shopping season for minorities."

Before the end of her second term, Mayor Uccello resigned to run for a seat in the US House of Representatives. She had planned to run for governor, or a seat in the US Senate. Instead, she ran as a Republican in the heavily Democratic First Congressional District, after being urged to do so in personal phone calls from President Richard Nixon and Vice President Spiro Agnew. Uccello had attended Nixon's inauguration, and after a private meeting with him was successful in having Hartford become one of the first cities to receive funding for its Model Cities Program. However, she lost her congressional bid by just over one thousand votes. Interestingly, after both Nixon and Agnew left office in disgrace, one because of the Watergate break-in and the other on charges of tax evasion, Uccello was later appointed to a high post in the Transportation Department by President Gerald Ford.

KEEP THE FIRE
OF JUSTICE BURNING
(FROM BPFF TO IABPFF)

From National Black Professional Fire Fighters to the
International Association of Black Professional Fire Fighters

"In July 1969, race relations in the firehouses were on razor's edge, but rocks fell like rain on Black and White fire fighters alike," observed Vulcan Society member John Ruffins. He made this observation after reading an article in the current *Newsweek* magazine titled "The Fireman Under Fire." The article described the harassment of fire fighters in minority communities across the country as approaching a guerrilla war. Rocks and bottles are commonplace; Molotov cocktails had been thrown at fire trucks; windshields had been shattered by snipers' bullets, the article read. "In the previous year," it continued, "there were 947 attacks on fire fighters in New York, with 125 of them being injured. The open fire trucks in New York were being covered with makeshift plywood panels to protect the White fire fighters from flying objects thrown from roof tops and vacant lots."

Troubled by what he had read, Ruffins cited the *Newsweek* article during a Monday night meeting of Black fire fighters at Vulcan Hall in Brooklyn. He then moved that the Vulcan Society sponsor a national conference of Black fire fighters to discuss their common problems in the firehouse and in the minority communities. After some discussion,

Ruffins's motion was approved by those in attendance. Vulcan Society President Dave Jackson appointed Ruffins and Vincent Julius as co-chairs with the responsibility of planning the conference. The following month, Ruffins and Julius sent out nearly 250 letters to fire chiefs around the country, asking for the names of Black fire fighters in their departments. The Vulcan Society was sounding the alarm. It was a call to Black fire fighters in this country to come to New York for an urgent conference. In October 1969 five of us from the Phoenix Society drove from Hartford to New York to attend the conference. The one thought in the forefront of our minds was the historic nature of this conference.

On Friday, October 31, 1969, the two-day conference of Black fire fighters convened at the Commodore Hotel in Lower Manhattan. Over a hundred Black fire fighters from cities around the country had come in response to the call. They came from firehouses in Boston, Newark, Jersey City, Philadelphia, Cleveland, St. Louis, Los Angeles, New Orleans, Washington, DC, Baltimore, Chicago, Detroit and Hartford. We were warmly welcomed by conference co-chairs John Ruffins and Vincent Julius, and everyone present introduced himself to others. Citing the *Newsweek* article, Ruffins then explained why they felt this conference was both urgent and necessary. As we listened, Ruffins shared with us four problem areas that he and Vincent Julius said would be the focus of the conference. These included the harassment of firemen; fire prevention in minority communities; recruitment and promotion of Black fire fighters; and the internal relations between Black and White fire fighters.

Over the next two days Ruffins and Julius led us in discussions around these issues. It seemed that everyone in attendance had a story to tell or a personal experience to share that related to all four of the problem areas. We discussed the need to establish better relations between the Black community and the fire service, and what we could do to ease the tension in inner-city neighborhoods. Some of the brothers shared what they were already doing in their communities and the problems they were encountering, as well as their successes. I spoke about racial disturbances in Hartford over the pass three summers, the attacks on fire fighters, and the efforts of Special Services in the minority community. Robert O. Lowery, New York City's first Black fire commissioner, talked about the social climate in America in which we as Blacks lived and worked. The gravity of his remarks hit home for those of us who had confronted angry young Blacks in our communities. Lowery talked about the need for us to educate these young people about the importance of the fire service, and the need to recruit more Blacks into the fire-fighting profession. He talked about promotional concerns, educational opportunities, and other issues in the fire service.

Without question our most significant action at this conference was the unanimous vote to hold a national convention, with the goal of establishing a national association of Black professional fire fighters. With so many issues before us, we agreed that we would find strength in numbers. So we would seek to bring together Black fire fighters from around the country into a single organization. We decided that the national convention would be held the following year, in 1970. We agreed the purpose and aim of the national convention would be three-fold: 1) to pool together the experiences of Black fire fighters from different sections of the country; 2) to hold workshops to formulate solutions to the problems of harassment of fire fighters and the high rate of fires and deaths in inner-city neighborhoods; and 3) to help implement the findings of the convention in the areas where these problems exist.

In our discussion about the steps necessary to make this national convention happen, it was decided that the Vulcan Society of New York City, the Phoenix Society of Hartford, the Vulcan Pioneers Inc. of Newark, the Vulcan Pioneers of Hudson County in Jersey City, and Club Valiants of Philadelphia would take the lead responsibility. Operating under the name Black Professional Fire Fighters (BPFF), the five organizations would plan this historic national convention. After two days the conference ended with great exuberance and excitement over what we had accomplished and the work that lay ahead. As I drove back to Hartford with the other Phoenix Society members, I had the feeling this was the beginning of a new movement for justice and equality in this country, and I was part of it. I was no longer watching from the sidelines; this was a movement of Black professional fire fighters.

Three months later, in February 1970, members of the five sponsoring organizations charged with planning the national convention gathered at Vulcan Hall in Brooklyn for our first meeting. Besides me, the members of the Phoenix Society at the meeting were Cecil Alston, Otis Haywood, Leonard Wallace, Aaron West, Frank Carter, Richard Epps, Nelson Carter, and Audabon Hill. Vulcan Society members included Vincent Julius, Charlie Burgess, Jim Lee, Dave Jackson, Dave Floyd, and Aiden Spooner. There was Bob Slaughter and Alex Mills from the Vulcan Pioneers of Newark. There was Thomas Taylor, John Sterling, Joe Tinsley, and W. Harris from the Vulcan Pioneers of Hudson County, New Jersey; also Donald Brown, Howard Rhone, Charlie Hendricks, Ron Lewis, and Ken Babb from Club Valiants of Philadelphia. In all, twenty-seven Black professional firefighters had gathered for this initial meeting.

Our first order of business was to select someone to chair the meeting. I was nominated and voted in as chair. It was also decided that for future meetings, we would function under the name National Convention Planning Committee. Next we had to identify a location for the national convention. I told the group that the Phoenix Society would be honored to host the national convention in Hartford. I told them that I had already done some preliminary work and that several insurance companies in Hartford were interested in giving support to the convention. One insurance company had promised to make space available in its twenty-two-story building. I also reported that the downtown Hilton Hotel would let us have rooms at reduced rates. Those in attendance all viewed Hartford as a good choice, and we voted unanimously to hold the national convention there.

Then we began a discussion on how we would finance the national convention. Each of the five co-sponsoring organizations agreed to place one hundred dollars into an account for the use of the host organization. These funds would be used for making preliminary convention arrangements. We voted that the presidents of the five co-sponsoring organizations would serve as the convention governing body. At the time the presidents were Cecil Alston of the Phoenix Society, Joseph Tinsley of the Vulcan Pioneers of Hudson County, David Jackson of the Vulcan Society, Howard Rhone of Club Valiants, and Robert Slaughter of the Vulcan Pioneers of Newark. We agreed that at our next meeting, we would elect officers, assign duties, and begin work on the national convention agenda.

Three weeks later, on February 28, we gathered for our second planning meeting, this time in Hartford. The meeting began with a discussion on procedural matters, in preparation for electing our committee officers. Following the discussion names were placed in nomination. When my name was placed in nomination, I accepted and was elected to the office of interim national chair of the convention committee. Vulcan Society member David Floyd was elected to the office of vice chair. Donald Brown was elected interim national secretary, and Howard Rhone was elected interim national corresponding secretary. Both Brown and Rhone were members of Club Valiants of Philadelphia. Phoenix Society member Nelson Carter was elected interim national treasurer. Those of us who were now the officers of the convention committee had primary responsibility for the success of the upcoming national convention.

Taking my place as chair, I called upon the brothers to offer suggestions for an official name for our national convention. After some discussion we decided on the name "The National Convention of Black Professional Fire Fighters." Since we had already selected the national convention site, we next had to select a date. After some discussion we agreed the convention would begin on Thursday, October 1, 1970, and end on Saturday, October 3, 1970. It was already February, so this meant we had just seven months to complete all our work. We then began a discussion about the workshops to be held during convention. We eventually voted to hold the following five panels: (1) convention purposes and aims, (2) name and structure, (3) membership and dues, (4) By-laws, and (5) constitution. We also set the days and times for panel workshops, plenary sessions, and the banquet. When this meeting ended, we felt we were well on our way to making the national convention a reality.

Six weeks later, on April 18, 1970, the convention committee held its third meeting in Newark, New Jersey. I reported that the Phoenix Society, as the host organization, had finalized arrangements for the national convention to be held at the downtown Hilton Hotel and at the Hartford Insurance Plaza. Corresponding Secretary Donald Brown reported letters announcing the National Convention of Black Professional Fire Fighters had gone out to fire departments in cities around the country. Letters of invitation had also been mailed to Black fire commissioners, Black deputy fire commissioners, Black administrative heads of fire departments, and other high-ranking Black fire service officials around the country.

Press releases were sent to Black newspapers and radio stations, and 122 letters had been mailed to the National Urban League Chapters around the country. The corresponding secretary also planned to send personal letters of invitation to Roy Wilkins, national secretary of the NAACP, and to Whitney Young, president of the National Urban League, urging them to publicize the national convention in their newspaper columns. One of the brothers suggested that a letter be sent to the Southern Christian Leadership Conference in Atlanta. Brown agreed an invitation would be sent to the Reverend Dr. Ralph David Abernathy, president of SCLC. Getting the word out about the national convention was important, and we wanted to make sure that every Black fire fighter in the country got the word. Cecil Alston reported that Black fire fighters from New Haven, Connecticut, would be joining the Phoenix Society, along with the one lone Black fire fighter from Springfield, Massachusetts. Vulcan Society member David Jackson reported that he had contacted Black fire fighters in Baltimore, Maryland, and they too wanted to organize and be part of the national convention. We spent the rest of the meeting discussing and making convention assignments, listing the convention materials that would be needed, and fine-tuning the convention agenda.

The next meeting of the convention committee took place in July 1970 in Philadelphia. The national convention was less than three months away, and the planning was moving along without any real hitches. Phoenix Society member Otis Haywood reported that the Black fire fighters in Savannah, Georgia, who made up 20 percent of that city's fire department, were interested in attending. Haywood also reported that the Brotherhood of United Fire Fighters from Camden, New Jersey, planned to attend. It was agreed, though not without some opposition, to invite the president of the International Association of Fire Fighters, and the president of the International Association of Fire Chiefs to the banquet dinner, both of whom were White.

We then held a drawing to determine which organization would lead which panel at the national convention. The results were that the Name and Structure workshop would be led by the Phoenix Society. The Membership and Dues workshop would be led by Club Valiants. The Bylaws workshop would be led by the Vulcan Society. The Purpose and Aims workshop would be led by the Pioneers of Hudson County, New Jersey, and the Constitution workshop would be led by the Vulcan Pioneers of Newark, New Jersey. Each organization was instructed to develop a plan for presenting its workshop at the national convention.

In August, one month after Hartford's fourth consecutive summer of racial disturbances, the Pioneers of Hudson County, New Jersey, finalized their work on the convention purpose and aims. These all-important purposes and aims would speak to why we felt it necessary for Black fire fighters around the country to come together, and the mission we would undertake once organized. These Purposes and Aims of the National Convention of Black Professional Fire Fighters were as follows:

> To create a liaison between our Black brothers across the nation;
> To compile information concerning the injustices that exist in the working conditions in the fire service, and to implement actions to correct them;

To collect and evaluate data on all deleterious conditions incumbent in all areas where minorities exist;

To see that competent Blacks are recruited and employed as fire fighters, wherever they reside;

To promote interracial progress throughout the fire services; and
To aid in motivating our Black brothers to seek advancement to elevated ranks throughout the fire service.

The convention was less than a month away when I chaired a meeting of the convention committee on September 12, 1970, at Vulcan Hall in Brooklyn. After reviewing the convention agenda and panel discussion materials, I proposed that we add a sixth panel that would focus on the problems of youth in the Black community. This was prompted by the racial disturbance in Hartford two months earlier, and the work we were doing in Special Services. I thought it was important that Black fire fighters have an understanding of the unique points of view that youth have on the problems existing in their communities. After some conversation it was decided we would add a plenary session where adults would talk with young people about their issues and concerns. Two weeks later, on September 26, 1970, I chaired the final meeting of the convention committee in Wethersfield, a suburb of Hartford. At this meeting, which took place at the Horne's Motor Lodge, we went over the convention agenda, finalizing all of the remaining details. When the meeting adjourned, there was a feeling of great excitement and enthusiasm. We were ready to convene what would be an historic event—the first of its kind in this country.

Making final plans for the Black Professional Fire Fighters Convention (left): Nelson K. Carter, Phoenix Society of Hartford, interim national treasurer; David Floyd, Vulcan Society of New York, interim national co-chairman; John B. Stewart, Phoenix Society of Hartford, interim national chairman; Donald Brown, Club Valiant of Philadelphia, interim national secretary; and Howard Rhone, Club Valiant of Philadelphia, interim national corresponding secretary. (Photos by Henry Morris)

Presidents gather at pre-convention conference at Hornes Motor Lodge (l): Cecil Alston, Phoenix Society, Hartford; Joseph Tinsley, Vulcan Pioneers, Hudson County, New Jersey; David Jackson, Vulcan Society, New York City; Howard Rhone, Club Valiants, Philadelphia; and Robert Slaughter, Vulcan Pioneers of New Jersey, East Orange, New Jersey.

Vulcan Society of New York convention delegates – Vinson Julius, Charles Burgess, James Lee, David Floyd, Aiden Spooner

Club Valiant delegates Donald Brown and Howard Rhone.

Vulcan Pioneers delegates – Thomas Taylor, Robert
Slaughter, Alex Miles, Jr., John Sterling, Joseph Tinsley.

Phoenix Society members with convention delegates Cecil Alston, Otis
Haywood, Leonard Wallace, John Stewart, Aaron West, Frank Carter,
Richard Epps, Nelson Carter, Audabon Hill. (Henry Morris Photos)

Finally the day of the national convention arrived. "The National Convention of Black Professional Fire Fighters will now come to order!" Cecil Alston called out over the din of excited voices. With these words and the striking of his gavel on the podium, the Phoenix Society president opened the historic national convention of Black fire fighters. It was 4 p.m., Thursday, October 1, 1970. "On behalf of the Phoenix Society, I welcome all of our brother professional fire fighters from around the country, and their guests, to this first ever National Convention of Black Professional Fire Fighters!" Alston announced. "It is reported that over four-hundred fire fighters have registered today for this conference!" Applause and cheers sounded throughout the room.

Even though most of the fire fighters were meeting one another for the first time, there was an immediate feeling of brotherhood and togetherness. Smiling faces were extending hands of greetings and introductions. Many of the fire fighters brought their wives or girlfriends. Several brought teenagers as spectators. Those of us who had envisioned such a national convention just a year earlier were overjoyed by this response. Not only had we made the national convention happen, but it also confirmed our belief that Black fire fighters felt a common need to come together and address common concerns. The attention of those in the room now focused on Alston.

"One of the reasons for this historic gathering is to establish an ongoing relationship with brother fire fighters throughout the United States!" said Alston. "Our main work of this national convention will be to establish a national organization of Black professional fire fighters, draft a charter, and elect a slate of officers!" Alston then called upon Collin B. Bennett, the city's lone Black city council member, who came and extended words of welcome on behalf of the City of Hartford. Reverend Robert A. Moody, the esteemed pastor of Shiloh Baptist Church on Albany Avenue, came next and gave an opening prayer.

Alston then introduced me as the national convention chair. As I stood at the podium preparing to give my opening remarks, I looked around the room at the brother fire fighters from around the country. I was elated.

"Welcome to Hartford!" I said in a loud voice. "What a great occasion this is! This is a dream come true! This is a moment for the history books! This is something to tell your children and your grandchildren about." After the applause I thanked them for coming and then introduced the other officers of the convention committee, who were sitting with me on the dais. Then I began my opening remarks.

"Let me tell you why we think it is necessary that Black fire fighters from around the country come together. Just as it has been for some of you, the recent summers in Hartford have been something I never thought I would experience as a fire fighter." I then talked about the racial disturbances in Hartford over the past four summers and the toll they had taken on Hartford fire fighters, city government and the minority community. I spoke of the underlying causes of the disturbances in Hartford, and in other cities represented at this national convention. I told how conditions in the inner city perpetuated the notion that fire fighters were outsiders, and not friends of the young people living there.

"We must no longer stand by watching this situation and remain inactive!" I continued. "We must mobilize! We must do something to change this negative perception, while helping to bring about the changes that make for better living conditions in our communities! One of the primary purposes of a national organization of Black professional fire fighters should be the mending of community relations in the poor inner-city areas of this nation." I then shared with them the history of Blacks in the Hartford Fire Department, its segregationist practices, and the fact that I was the lone Black officer. I spoke of the need to open more opportunities for Blacks to advance in fire departments across the country, the necessity to improve relations between

Black and White fire fighters, and the need to recruit Blacks into the fire service.

I concluded my talk by saying, "This national convention is important because we cannot move out into the community and help bring about change until we ourselves are together." I had spoken for nearly twenty minutes without benefit of a written text, just a few thoughts I had scribbled on a piece of paper. I felt good when I returned to my seat. I felt like I had sounded the right theme for the opening of the convention. When the brothers stood and applauded, I knew that my words had been received well.

Announcements that needed to be made from the podium were made, and questions raised by registrants were answered. At 6 p.m. the meeting was adjourned, and the attendees dispersed for dinner. The first-ever National Convention of Black Professional Fire Fighters was off to a great start!

The next day convention participants reconvened at 10 a.m. for a day of work. When the meeting was called to order, David Floyd, who was in charge of registration, reported that with the morning's registration, nearly six- hundred fire fighters had registered. He reported that fire fighters had come from Los Angeles, New Orleans, Chicago, Detroit, Cleveland, Philadelphia, New York City, Syracuse, St. Louis, Indianapolis, Boston, Albany, Buffalo, Savannah, Baltimore, Massachusetts, Connecticut, and several smaller cities and towns around the country. Hearing this, cheers and applause echoed through the Park Hilton ballroom.

After extending words of greeting, I went over the day's agenda, explaining what needed to be accomplished. We then broke into groups for our first set of three morning panel workshops, with participants attending the workshop to which they had been assigned. The workshops, which were held at the hotel and the downtown YWCA included Purpose and Aims, Name and Structure, and Bylaws. Each sponsoring organization charged with leading these workshops shared with the attendees the work they had done prior to the convention. The morning was spent discussing, debating, and when agreed upon modifying language of the proposals to be brought before the body at plenary. In the afternoon the second set of three panel workshops which included Constitution, Membership and Dues, and Community Relations were held. The format for these afternoon panel workshops was the same as those held in the morning.

Following the afternoon workshops, all participants gathered in plenary session, where reports from the six workshops were presented by appointed spokespersons. Questions were raised and answered. Meanings were clarified and choice of language explained. One questioner was concerned about the use of the word *Black* in the organization's name. Would it imply that we were a radical organization, he wanted to know? After some discussion we agreed to keep the word *Black* to indicate by our name that we were an Association of Black Professional Fire Fighters. Another questioner had concerns about the amount of dues each individual organization should pay.

"Should dues be kept low to prevent the payments from larger organizations from becoming vastly disproportionate to those of smaller organizations?" Another brother fire fighter wanted clarification on the voting structure.

"When it comes to voting, how can smaller organizations, with only three members, for example, have parity with larger organizations, say with fifty members?" After these and other questions were answered to everyone's satisfaction, and agreed upon changes made, the plenary session was adjourned.

That evening the fire fighters, many of them accompanied by their wives or other guests, filled the Hilton's grand ballroom for a dinner and keynote address. As master of ceremonies, I welcomed our guests to the National Convention of Black Professional Fire Fighters banquet dinner and then introduced those sitting on the dais. They included my fellow convention committee officers; Connecticut Governor John Dempsey; Hartford's Deputy Mayor Allyn Martin; Fire Chief Edward Curtin; John T. Kelley Jr., president of Local 760 of the International Association of Fire Fighters; and New York Fire Commissioner Robert Lowery and his wife, Marjorie. Governor Dempsey was the first to bring personal greetings and greetings on behalf of the State of Connecticut. Deputy Mayor Martin offered words of welcome on behalf of the City of Hartford. Fire Chief Edward Curtin Jr. and John T. Kelley Jr. also extended words of welcome.

After dinner had been served, I introduced Commissioner Lowery as our keynote speaker for the evening. Commissioner Lowery had the distinction of being the first Black to head the fire department of a major US city. He was one of the organizers of New York's Vulcan Society, and his life story and climb to the top of his profession were an inspiration to Black fire fighters. He was born in 1916 in Buffalo, New York, and moved with his family to Harlem when he was nine. After completing high school he enrolled in City College with plans to become a lawyer. Economic hardship, however, made it necessary for him to leave school and go to work. He found a job as an usher in a Harlem movie theatre. Later, after passing several civil service exams he was hired as a city subway conductor. In 1941, when he was twenty-five, he accepted a job with the city's fire department, making him one of only fifty Blacks in the entire New York City Fire Department. He was assigned to a ladder company in Washington Heights, where he was not allowed to use the kitchen utensils and was made to sleep in an area separated from Whites.

Within five years he had been promoted to the position of fire marshal. While serving as fire marshal, he won a commendation for arresting a man who had committed thirty acts of arson and a number of burglaries. For his actions Lowery was given a citation for the daring capture of an arsonist armed with a gun. His next promotion was in 1961, when he was made acting lieutenant in the Bureau of Fire Investigation. Two years later he was appointed deputy fire commissioner. In 1965, after twenty-four years in the department, he was named New York City fire commissioner by Mayor John Lindsay.

It had been said of Commissioner Lowery that he had a reputation of not being the least bit hesitant about addressing the prevalence of racism within the fire service in mixed company. After my introduction he delivered the keynote address, in which he lived up to his reputation.

"When I joined the New York City Fire Department, it had the vilest kind of segregation. There were Jim Crow beds and kitchens, and Blacks were detailed to the worst janitorial duties in the firehouse. Despite my persistent efforts to improve race relations, the bitter racial tensions that persisted in the newly integrated fire service environment might have been worse than under the earlier segregation," he said.

"Because your careers in the fire department would encompass the most important years of your adult life, you must learn your job well and study for promotion while your mind is still young and receptive. Time spent idly or in unimportant pursuits can never be recaptured. Always remember that America, including many White fire fighters, will never let you forget that you are recognizable because your ancestors were brought to this country in chains and that they believe you are inferior," he continued. "It is up to you to keep proving over and over again that they are wrong." He spoke of how Mayor John Lindsay had put it on the line when he appointed him the twenty-first commissioner of the New York City Fire Department.

"It was inconceivable that a Black man would be put in this position. I became the head of a department of 13,500 people, only 600 were Black. People were watching me, both White and Black, simply because I was Black." He told of how, after being named commissioner, a small group of White fire fighters initiated a racially motivated campaign to discredit him. "They started a false rumor that I was about to be indicted for selling drugs, and that I had sold answers for a promotion examination to Black firemen." He told how the city's investigation commissioner eventually brought before a judge those who had participated in the campaign to defame him. All were disciplined for violating a fire department regulation that stated, "Members shall not perform any act which may be instrumental in arousing religious or racial hatred whether by speech, writing, or dissemination of material designed to bring about ill will against any race or creed."

Lowery talked about the alarming problem of attacks on fire fighters with bricks and other weapons on the mostly White fire fighters who came into Black and Hispanic communities to battle fires. He talked about the need to get better cooperation from the citizenry in these areas, and encouraged Black firefighters to involve themselves in community activities to gain insight into the underlying causes of the problems in those communities. He spoke of the value and need for such a national organization of Black fire fighters, and how pleased he was to be part of this present gathering. He promised to continue his involvement with us in the struggle for justice and equality. When he concluded his address, everyone in the hall stood to their feet and gave the commissioner loud applause in appreciation. Those of us on the convention committee could not have been more pleased with his moving and heart-felt oration. On such a grand occasion as this, no one present at the dinner could have imagined that in less than three years, and at the age of fifty-seven, Lowery would resign as commissioner. Nor could anyone have imagined that Manhattan's Black Borough President Percy Sutton would accuse Mayor Lindsay of forcing Lowery out. On this convention night, we were just encouraged by the words of a man we greatly admired.

Black Fire Fighters Convention Banquet, October 1970, Hartford, Connecticut
In rear seated on dais Lt. John Stewart fourth from right,
Commissioner Lowery seated fifth from right.

On Saturday, October 3rd, the final day of our convention, the atmosphere of excitement that we felt on the first day still permeated the air. None were more excited than those of us on the convention committee, who had done the planning. In the future, we would be referred to by a younger generation of Black fire fighters as the "Founding Fathers." On this last day of the national convention, we knew we had already accomplished something that was meaningful and lasting. While it had been our initial intention at the convention to form a national organization, what we would be voting that morning was the formation of an international organization. Phoenix Society member Aaron West, who chaired the Name and Structure panel, had proposed during the workshop that we become an international organization and proposed the name "International Association of Black Professional Fire Fighters."

While some participants noted that there were no Black fire fighters from other countries present at the national convention, West envisioned that one day there would be. He had in mind fire fighters in the Caribbean, and perhaps countries in Europe and Africa. West' proposal had been adopted during plenary a day earlier. After that vote, I explained that all Black fire fighters would remain members of the International Association of Fire Fighters Union (IAFF), which focused on labor. Our organization would focus on the unification of Black fire fighters both nationally and internationally, and we would be involved in our respective minority communities. Now, as we gathered in plenary session at the Hartford Insurance Plaza on this last day we voted unanimously to adopt the following constitution, which resulted from the work of the five panel workshops and the proposals adopted during plenary.

Black professional fire fighters and their guests seated at banquet tables at National Convention in Hartford, Connecticut, Friday, October 2, 1970.

Constitution

The International Association of Black Professional Firefighters (IABPFF)

Preamble—Whereas we, Black Fire Fighters, aware of the increasing complexity of our problems and those of our Brothers and Sisters within the community, feel called upon to form an organization for the purpose of studying and solving such problems; in order to take our place in the vanguard of civilization, we hereby form ourselves into an organization for the purpose of cultivating and maintaining professional competence among fire fighters, and establishment of unity, also keeping alive the interest among retired members, for the avowed purpose of improving the social status of our RACE, and increasing professional efficiency.

ARTICLE I   *Name:* The name of this organization shall be International Association of Black Professional Fire Fighters.

ARTICLE 11   *Purpose and Aims:*

(1) To create a liaison between our Black Brothers and Sisters throughout the globe.
(2) To collect and evaluate data on all deleterious conditions incumbent in all areas where minorities exist,
(3) To compile information concerning the injustices that exist in the application of working conditions in the Fire Service, and implement action to correct them.
(4) To promote interracial progress throughout the Fire Service.

(5) To see that competent Blacks are recruited and employed as fire fighters, wherever they reside.

(6) To aid in motivating our Black Brothers and Sisters to seek advancement to elevated ranks throughout the Fire Service.

ARTICLE III   *Membership:*

Membership is for those who are members of a bona fide Black Fire Fighting Organization and that organization is a member of the International Association of Black Professional Fire Fighters. In the absence of an organization the International may accept individual memberships.

ARTICLE IV   *International Officers:*

The officers of the International Association of Black Professional Fire Fighters shall be a President, Vice President, six Regional Vice Presidents, Recording Secretary, Corresponding Secretary, Treasurer, Financial Secretary and Sgt-At-Arms, The term of office shall be two (2) years.

ARTICLE V   *Regional Conferences:*

A Regional Conference shall be held on odd number years, in the time period of 15 September to 31 October. The International Convention shall be held on even number years during the time period of 15 September to October 31. A notice of these meetings shall be sent by the Corresponding Secretary to all Regional Organizations at least three (3) months before the meeting.

ARTICLE VI   Regional Vice Presidents:
The Regional Vice Presidents of the International
Association of Black Professional Fire Fighters shall
constitute the Board of Directors. The International
Board of Directors shall have all power and authority
over affairs of the International during the interim
between the International Convention.

ARTICLE VII   *Parliamentary Authority*:
The parliamentary authority governing the
International shall be "Robert's Rules of Order Revised."

ARTICLE VIII   *Constitution Amendments*:
This Constitution may be amended by a two-third
(2/3) vote at any International Convention, pro-
vided a copy of amendment has been sent to the
Regional Officers at least ninety (90) days before
The International Convention

After adopting our constitution in the morning, we reconvened
in plenary session after lunch. It was now time to elect the founding
president of the International Association of Black Professional Fire
Fighters. There had been talk of nominating me to this honored position, but I made it known that I would respectfully decline. I reasoned
that as head of Special Services, I couldn't give this new organization
the time and energy that was needed in its infancy stage. David Floyd
of the Vulcan Society and Shelly Harris of the Vulcan Pioneers Inc.
became the nominees. When the votes were counted, Captain David
J. Floyd had been elected founding president. Floyd was a ten-year veteran of the New York City Fire Department, and current president of
the Vulcan Society. At thirty-three years of age, Floyd was viewed as
a young man of vision. The other founding officers elected included:
vice-president, Robert Paul, from Gary, Indiana; treasurer, Charlie

Hendricks from Philadelphia; and recording secretary, Bill Brogden from Philadelphia. After the founding president received the oath of office, he thanked his brother fire fighters for the honor of serving as president of the International Association of Black Professional Fire Fires. He then said in part:

> …We have common interests. Number one is that we're Black. We know the games Whitey plays. But now we've planted a seed and we'll till the soil with muscle, and water the seeding with sweat, and watch the mighty oak grow. The number one problem facing Black fire fighters is recruiting. Cities are recruiting firemen from outside the city. We feel there should be increased inner-city recruitment. If you don't live within a city, you don't have a feeling for it. Too often, firemen don't live within the city that pays their salary or within the city they protect.
>
> The second biggest problem is that a different kind of discrimination exists in some cities in the form of promotions. We've found that parts of the country promote men on the basis of a written examination, and others on an oral examination, or on performance evaluated by a superior. We feel the oral exam and the evaluation by a superior have built-in problems. Other problems that must be fixed include the attacks on fire fighters in the Black communities, and government neglect of these communities and the people living there, he continued…

When our founding president completed his remarks, we hailed our chief with rousing applause and cheers of joy and delight. After a break we reconvened in a General Session. During this session I spoke of the historic nature of what we had accomplished at this convention, and why establishing the International Association of Black Professional

Fire Fighters was necessary. I talked about the two-day conference in July of the previous year, when John Ruffins and Vincent Julius called us together in New York and stated that something must be done. And how what we had now accomplished was the result. "We should feel proud for what we have done," I told them. After final questions from bother fire fighters had been answered, concerns eased, and expressions of satisfaction offered, I stood with the other convention committee members and thanked all the brothers for their participation, and for making the national convention a great success.

"This has been a great convention, a historic national convention, and you made it happen," I said. "We have a constitution and we have officers. There is much for us to do when we return to our respective communities. Because we are in the right, by the grace of God we will get it done." I then announced that the Second Biennial Convention of the International Association of Black Professional Fire Fighters would convene in October 1972, in a location to be determined. I thanked everyone for coming and wished everyone God's blessings and a safe journey home.

Before adjourning Phoenix Society President Cecil Alston announced: "The Phoenix Society's Women's Auxiliary is hosting a cocktail sip at 8: p. m., at Jonathan Temple, 700 Blue Hills Avenue, with music by "Rockin" Robin of WKND. We hope those of you who are still in town can make it." The Phoenix Society president then brought down his gavel on the podium, "The National Convention of the International Association of Black Professional Fire Fighters is now adjourned!" There was applause, cheers and handshakes, as new friends promised to see each other again in two years. We had organized!

After adjourning, a reporter approached President Floyd and wanted to know "why a Black fire fighter's organization was needed, and whether we would withdraw from the International Fire fighter's Union."

"We met in order to find out areas where common problems exist for Black firemen, and where similar problems existed in the past so we'll know how to resolve them," President Floyd told the reporter. "But we'll work within the framework of the International Association of Fire

Fighters. And we will stress local union participation." The next day an article appeared in the local newspaper with the headline, "A Black Fire Fighter With Clenched Fist." It opened with the following paragraph:

> As the first convention of the International Association of Black Professional Firefighters concluded in Hartford last night, the new president clad in a black shift-like shirt with a huge peace symbol in the center offered a few impromptu comments. David Floyd took his oath of office with a clenched fist, rather than a raised right hand.

The story continued, referring to Floyd's remarks as "seeming militant rhetoric." For whatever reason, the reporter left out of his story that Floyd had called for unity among Black and White firemen.

One controversy that did arise during the convention was the result of an incorrect rumor. Some brothers mistakenly thought that once we formed our own organization, Black fire fighters would resign membership in the International Association of Fire Fighters Union (IAFF). This was not true. We would not segregate ourselves from other organizations within the fire service. Chief Curtin heard the rumor and believing it to be true, had called Phoenix Society President Cecil Alston to his office.

"To leave the International is a violation of city regulations," he said in an angry tone. He then threatened to fire Alston and have him jailed.

When word of Curtin's threat got back to other Phoenix Society members, several of them vowed, "If he goes to jail, we go to jail with him!" So on the last day of the convocation, I went to Chief Curtin and explained that the rumor was untrue. Our organization would have a different focus than that of the International Association of Fire Fighters, I said. All Black fire fighters would continue as members of the IAFF.

Those of us on the convention committee knew that the work we had accomplished was a milestone for Black professional fire fighters in regard to our efforts to improve and advance the standards of the fire service throughout this country. We knew that, as Frederick Douglass had said, "Power concedes nothing without a struggle." If struggling was necessary in order to achieve equality in the fire fighting profession, then we would struggle. Still, our elation over the success of the convention was dampened by our concern for the Black fire fighters in Boston who had not attended. During our planning we had been contacted by that city's Black fire fighters saying they planned to attend. In the end, the White chief did not allow it.

A week after the convention, Gladys and I decided to go to New York City for a few days of rest and relaxation. We checked into a Ramada Inn on Eighth Avenue at 51st Street. The next evening as we were on our way out to dinner, we noticed a large number of police and unmarked cars blocking the street in the front of the Howard Johnson Motor Lodge directly across from where we were staying. When I asked a man standing near-by what was happening, "The F.B. I. just arrested Angela Davis," he answered.

In November, a few of us in the Phoenix Society made plans to go to Boston to meet with the fifteen Black fire fighters there. We were warned by the Black fire fighters that White fire fighters had put out the word that a group of Black troublemakers were coming from Hartford. They threatened us with bodily harm and were trying to find out where the meeting would take place. Knowing the history of racial tensions in Boston, we took the threat seriously. But we went anyway and held our meeting in the home of a Black fire fighter in Cambridge. The fire department there was more progressive in its thinking than Boston, with a Black lieutenant and battalion chief. (Back in 1871 the mayor of Cambridge appointed a Black man, Patrick Raymond, the son of a runaway slave, as chief engineer of the Cambridge Fire Department. Raymond, who is believed to have been the first Black fire chief in the country, held this position until 1875.) Eventually, Black fire fighters in Boston, Cambridge, Medford, and other Massachusetts cities were successful in organizing and today they are the Vulcans of Massachusetts.

As I reflect today, nearly forty-four years after our historic gathering, I am convinced it was the signal event that began a movement to bring equality to the fire service on an international scale. In order to address the lack of substantial access into the fire service and the lack of upward mobility opportunities, it became necessary for Black professional fire fighters to press for reforms both nationally and internationally (internationally, through the work of our chapters in the Caribbean and in England). In the course of dealing with these issues, it was also our desire to reduce the number of fire deaths and property loss in our respective communities, and in society as a whole. We were also convinced that in the Black community, there was an abundance of untapped talent to offer the fire service.

In addition, we expected to improve the economic development and employment opportunities for minorities. As Black fire fighters, we had before us the challenge to make the fire service more relevant to the needs and aspirations of minority citizens. The International Association of Black Professional Fire Fighters (IABPFF) would ensure that Black and other minority fire department officials become full partners in the leadership and decision-making arenas of the fire service. Today the IABPFF can be pointed to as a shining example of what Blacks can accomplish with hard work, discipline, and a sense of organization. I look back with additional pride because I was fortunate enough, and extremely honored to have served as the chair for this historic event.

The IABPFF was not without opposition in its formative years Two years after the Hartford Convention, the Second Biennial Convention of the IABPFF was held in St. Louis, Missouri. Our St. Louis Chapter was experiencing some difficulty with officials of the International Association of Fire Fighters (IAFF), who felt another international fire fighter's organization was unnecessary, regardless of any differences in focus. This prompted IABPFF President David Floyd to hold the biennial in St. Louis, as a show of solidarity and national support for Black fire fighters in that city. When members of the Phoenix Society and our wives flew out of Bradley Airport we occupied a full third of the airplane. To our delight, the attendance at this second convention surpassed that of the first. As we looked from the window of the convention hotel at the arch that announced the Gateway to the West, we knew that IABPFF was on the move.

IABPFF being on the move was not to the liking of some White firefighters. In 1976, the IABPFF was receiving threatening letters warning us not to hold the Fourth Biennial Convention in the city of San Diego, California. As a scare tactic, a picture of a Black man hanging from a tree was mailed to IABPFF President David Floyd. This scare tactic made President Floyd and his executive board even more determined to hold the convention in that city. They thought it was important not to show a weak IABPFF to the public. They also wanted to show support for the brothers in San Diego who were experiencing pressure from White fire fighters. This may have been the reason for a frightening attack that took place on September 28, 1976 on a Brooklyn, New York street. A few days before the opening of the San Diego convention as President Floyd was leaving a men's clothing store he was bumped by two White men. One of the men threw a liquid believed to be toxic into Floyd's face. The men then disappeared around a corner. Fortunately the liquid missed Floyd's eyes. No arrests were made, and no one could say who was behind this attack. But one is left to wonder why President Floyd had been singled out. All we could say was that the IAFF was involved at the time in a lawsuit against the city of San Diego to prevent the IABPFF from holding its convention there.

When President Floyd reported the attack to the IABPFF executive board, they wanted him to have police protection, but he declined. In spite of the attack, the IABPFF convention convened in San Diego as scheduled. In 1980, at the Sixth Biennial Convention in Detroit, David Floyd stepped down as president to make way for new leadership. Since David J. Floyd's election as IABPFF's first presidency in 1970, there have been eight presidents.

David Floyd 1970–1980; Charles Hendricks 1980–1984; Clarence
Williams 1984–1988; Romeo O. Spaulding 1988–1996; Oshiyemi
Adelabu 1996–1998; Theodore O. Holmes 1998–2002; Johnny
Brewington 2002–2008; and Joseph Muhammad 2008 to present.

IABPFF President
James Hill, 2012 -

During his first year as president, David Floyd designed IABPFF's official logo.

Colors

Red, black, and green were the colors used by Marcus Garvey's Black pride or African Movement of the 1930s. Garvey explained that the red is for our blood; the black is for the race, and the green is for our hope.

Hand

The five fingers on the hand represent the five founding organization of the International: The Phoenix Society, Hartford, Connecticut; Valiants Inc., Philadelphia, Pennsylvania; Vulcan Pioneers, Hudson County, New Jersey; Vulcan Pioneers, Newark, New Jersey; and the Vulcan Society Inc., New York, New York.

Clenched Fist

The fist symbolizes strength and power realized when the fingers (organizations) came together.

Outline of Fingers

It was strongly felt by the designer that the Almighty has a guiding hand in bringing Black fire fighters together from across the nation. The outline of the fingers was shaped to form the Arabic word *Allah*, which means God.

Flame

The flame represents the heat that is necessary to take something old (five groups) and forge them into some new (International).

Seventh Biennial Convention of IABPFF

In August 1982, twelve years after our organizing convention in Hartford, I attended the Seventh Biennial Convention of the IABPFF in Lexington, Kentucky. As this convention was underway, we realized that another historic event had occurred in our midst. For the first time ever, a total of five Black fire chiefs were in attendance! Besides me, they included Samuel Golden, chief of the Oakland, California, Fire Department, who made chief in 1981. Golden had been hired by the Oakland Fire Department in 1949 as a hose man in a segregated engine company. When the fire department was integrated in 1955, Golden checked in at his new assignment and was told by the captain he couldn't eat with the White fire fighters. He was also told to bring his own mattress when he was on watch.

Despite the racism, Golden was steadfast and rose through the ranks. He was now the first Black fire chief of the Oakland Fire Department. Also present was Robert E. Osby, chief of the Inglewood, California, Fire Department since 1979. Chief Osby was a sophomore at San Diego State University in 1959 when he noticed a long line of young men applying to become fire fighters. Osby decided to join them. He would later become chief of the San Jose and then the San Diego Fire Departments. In 2011, his son Darryl Osby would become the first Black fire chief of the Los Angeles County Fire Department.

There was Raymond Brooks, chief of the Michigan City, Indiana, Fire Department, since 1979. At 38 years old, he was the youngest of the Black fire chiefs, and would go on to become chief of the Evanston, Illinois; Alhambra, California; San Jose, California; and the Birmingham, Alabama, Fire Departments. There was also Larry Bonnafon, who in 1979 had become the first Black fire chief in Louisville, Kentucky. Bonnafon had joined the Louisville Fire Department in 1955, just twelve days after his nineteenth birthday. This gave him the distinction of being the first teenager to be hired by that city's fire department. Chief Bonnafon had traveled to Hartford in 1980 to serve on the panel of experts that examined me when I was a candidate for chief of the Hartford Fire Department.

Another chief who joined us later at the 1982 convention, bringing the number to six, was Chief Ronald C. Lewis from the Richmond, Virginia, Fire Department. Chief Lewis was appointed in 1978, making him the first Black to hold the position in that Southern city. Prior to assuming this top position, Lewis had spent twenty-two years as a fire fighter in Philadelphia, rising to the rank of battalion chief. The City of Brotherly Love was forced to remove its White-only color bar in 1886 after Blacks there spent more than sixty long years trying to integrate the fire department. Lewis was an active Club Valiants member and had played a key role in a 1974 anti-discrimination suit that brought jobs and promotions to Black fire fighters in that department. Because of his activism, Fire Commissioner Joseph Rizzo, younger brother of Philadelphia Mayor Frank Rizzo, was glad to see Lewis leave for Richmond.

When Lewis was named Richmond's fire chief, Commissioner Rizzo offered no words of congratulations, and when prompted for a statement by reporters, he was "unavailable for comment." Commissioner Rizzo's disdain for Lewis was on display when Lewis sought permission for a local newspaper to photograph him with fire-fighting apparatus at battalion headquarters. The commissioner vetoed the request. Lewis explained to the reporter that "since the suit the commissioner has responded to me as though I don't exist." When Lewis sent another request to the commissioner asking that he be allowed to keep his battalion chief fire helmet as a memento, Rizzo approved the request—provided Lewis reimburse the city $26.50 for the cost of the helmet. Upon his arrival in Richmond, some White fire fighters refused to work under Chief Lewis. At least forty White fire fighters resigned within the next three months. Indeed, for all six of us who were now Black chiefs, it had been a hard climb up the ladder.

It was at this Lexington convention that IABPFF President Charles Hendricks requested that the chiefs sit together as a panel and take questions from the brother fire fighters in attendance. This proved to be a very informative session for everyone. Later that same year, the six Black chiefs were together again, this time at the International Association of Fire Chiefs Convention in Philadelphia, Pennsylvania. It was after that convention that President Hendricks requested that we form an association and offer our experiences to the IABPFF membership. We agreed, and I volunteered to undertake the task of organizing an association of Black fire chiefs. Four years later, at the 1986 IABPFF Convention in Buffalo, New York, the Chief Officers Resource Committee of the IABPFF was officially established.

Even as we formed this committee to provide a means to discuss shared concerns and issues, we determined that we would never separate ourselves from IABPFF, our mother organization. We were still a vital part of the International and committed to its goals, and we would continue to be present at its bi-annual meetings. I was elected committee chair, and the other elected officers included vice chair, Chief Claude Harris; secretary, Chief Robert Osby; corresponding secretary, Assistant Chief John H. Wells Sr.; treasurer, Assistant Fire Prevention Chief Bill Brown from San Diego; and chaplain, Battalion Chief Don Barlow from Anchorage, Alaska. Interestingly, before meeting Chief Barlow, many of us were unaware that we had a Black fire fighter up there in Alaska. Together, we drafted the following mission statement:

CORC Mission Statement

The Chief Officer Resource Committee of the International Association of Black Professional Fire Fighters Inc. was formed to pool and coordinate resources of black chief officers and improve relationships between the IABPFF, fire fighters and other officers around the country by supporting member organizations' events and networking through written communications that enhance the education awareness and employment opportunities for chief officers, officers and fire fighters who desire upward mobility.

The Chief Officers Resource Committee was later renamed Black Chief Officers Committee (BCOC) and today represents more than five-hundred Black Chief officers in emergency response and preparedness services in the United States, Africa, United Kingdom, and the Caribbean. The president of BCOC is Chief J.D. Rice, the first Black fire chief in Valdosta, Georgia. You can visit the BCOC at www.blackchiefofficerscommittee.com.

The Thirty-Second Biennial Convention of IABPFF

Another gathering that stands as a pivotal moment for Black fire fighters was the Thirty-Second IABPFF Biennial Convention convened in Buffalo in 2002. As IABPFF President Theodore Holmes passed the leadership baton to President Johnny Brewington, I saw an organization that continued to be on the move. Fire fighters from the Caribbean attending the conference were so impressed with the way they were hosted and with the history of the IABPFF and what we were doing, they announced that they intended to break their professional ties with England and seek membership in the IABPFF. We enthusiastically invited them to become members of the International. We didn't know what the outcome would be, but it showed us how this movement and the spirit of what we were doing was branching out. Another highlight was the memorable address given by Captain Vincent W. "Vinny" Julius of New York City's Vulcan Society. He spoke with passion about the creation of the IABPFF, and why the birth of such an organization became necessary:

> My brothers and sisters I greet you with love, tenderness, and care. My topic is the creation of the International Association of Black Professional Fire Fighters. As I reviewed the notes that I have put together this morning, I became somewhat emotional. When I look over the room I see so many men that I have known over the course of the years.
>
> I am going back to 1956 up through 1969. The International Association of Black Professional Fire Fighters in effect started in the spring of 1956, when I and my wife and another member of the Vulcan Society in New York and his wife went to Newark, New Jersey, to attend a dance of the Vulcan Pioneers of New Jersey. With that humble meeting, the International Association of Black Professional Fire Fighters, in my mind, started.
>
> It is not possible to discuss or to trace the formation of the IABPFF in its proper perspective without discussing what was going on in African American communities nationwide during those, turbulent, activist, unifying and progressive sixties. The formation of the IABPFF was rooted in the civil rights revolution of the 1960s.
>
> *The Catalyst*—On May 17, 1954, the United States Supreme Court made its landmark decision outlawing the doctrine of separate but equal facilities in our nation's public schools. This was the start of the civil rights revolution. This momentous decision, a ruling of nine in favor

and none opposed, was the inception of the civil rights movement.

The Birth—The Birth of the civil rights revolution took place in Montgomery, Alabama, when a dignified, quiet African American lady with tired feet, Miss. Rosa Parks, refused to give her seat on a municipal bus to a white man. From this action Dr. Martin Luther King Jr. used the balance of his much too short life trying to lead his people out of bondage. "Go down, Moses, way down in Egypt land and tell ole Pharaoh, to let my people go."

At this point many of the segregated firehouses in the north, with black fire fighters who would go along to get along, had to start questioning themselves. We were happy. We had it made. We thought that we had been accepted.

The Awakening—The spring of 1963 in Birmingham, Alabama, put an end to that thought. We saw our so-called brother blue-shirts fire fighters train high-pressure water hoses on African American women and children. So strong was the force that a teenage girl was bowled over by a high-pressure hose. I wonder if this young tender girl, who placed her well-being on the line for me, and by her actions and the force of fire department high pressure hose stream, has lost forever the joy of becoming a mother.

It was then that many Vulcans in the New York City Fire Department began to question our involvement, or lack thereof, in the struggle taking place in the South. Could we, should we, or can we, identify and show our support to our African American fathers, mothers, brothers, sisters, and their children who we saw nightly on television being arrested, humiliated, brutalized and murdered? Were we existing in a vacuum? We in the Vulcan Society of the New York City Fire Department were not existing in a vacuum. We would interact with the leadership of both our fire department unions. We realized we had allies among some, if not many of the white members of the fire department.

I wish to share with you excerpts of a resolution discussed by members of the Vulcan Society and supported by the entire Executive Board of the Uniformed Fire Officers Association Local 854 of the International Fire Fighters AF of L at their regular meeting on July 8, 1963.

> Whereas, we hold these truths to be self evident that all men are endowed by their Creator with certain inalienable rights that amongst these are life, liberty and the pursuit of happiness,

> And Whereas, the liberties of the Negro people of Birmingham, Alabama, have been denied to them and whereas, the protection of life and property are the prime functions of fire fighters and whereas the fire fighters of Birmingham, Alabama, have been misused in being recruited to assist in the denial of fundamental God-given and lawfully guaranteed rights,

> Be it therefore resolved, that this Local Union 854 protests most viciously the City of Birmingham, Alabama, for their debasement of the fire fighters by using them to hurt, rather than to help people.

This was introduced by the entire executive Board Local 854 IAAF John A. Crawford President, Antonio B. Morelli,

Secretary. To my knowledge, never has such a resolution been passed by members of the honorable profession of Firefighters…

When Vincent Julius concluded his remarks everyone under the sound of his voice had been moved emotionally. His heartfelt words served to deepen our resolve that through IABPFF we would make a difference in the fire service, and in the Black community.

Fortieth Anniversary Gathering of IABPFF

On October 30, 2010, in commemoration of its Fortieth Anniversary, the IABPFF returned to Hartford, Connecticut, the city of its founding. The Fortieth Anniversary Dinner and Dance was hosted by the Northeast Region of IABPFF and the Phoenix Society. Captain Patrick Jones, president of the Phoenix Society, welcomed back to Hartford Black fire fighters from around the country and the Caribbean:

> It is my pleasure to welcome everyone to the 40th Anniversary celebration of the International Association of Black Professional Fire Fighters. It has been forty years since the start of the International Association of Black Professional Firefighters in Hartford, Connecticut. Forty years of challenges, fights, blood, sweat, tears and scars, some physical and plenty of mental ones, but with fight and determination also comes success. Just as this country decided that they had enough of the British rule and fought for its independence, these men (no women at the time) also had enough. They had enough of injustices, racism, physical and verbal abuse, enough to where they had to form their own organization to unify and fight against those that opposed them. Members of the IABPFF have served and continue to serve at every level possible in the fire service from privates to chief of fire departments, large and small,

in this country and across the world. We have broken barriers and created history in the forty years of our existence.

Tonight we celebrate forty years of the IABPFF. The Phoenix Society Inc., one of the five founding members of the association, is proud to host this 40th Anniversary Dinner Dance here in Hartford, Connecticut, the birthplace of the IABPFF. Keep the fires burning for Justice!

The president of IABPFF, at the time of our fortieth anniversary was Lt. Joseph B. Muhammad, of the Vulcan Society and White Plains, New York Fire Department. President Muhammad offered these words of welcome:

Dear attendees and supporters, on behalf of the International Association of Black Professional Fire Fighters, I humbly thank you for your participation in the celebration of our 40-year existence. It was here in Hartford, Connecticut, where the Founding Fathers saw fit to officially declare, "Keep the Fire Burning for Justice." It was here where the Phoenix Society saw fit, as they see fit today, the need to host our commemoration. It was here when five local chapters in the Northeast region and members from various parts of the country dared to organize in early October 1970. At the pleasure of Northeast Regional Director Del Coward, and the IABPFF Executive Board, your invaluable contribution to this important and uplifting event is well appreciated.

This weekend is as much a tribute to the freedom fighters of the past, as much as it is a check of intestinal fortitude for Black fire fighters serving in the present. What will be the significance of our organization in the next forty years or the next forty days? Will the poem often times recited by Chief John B. Stewart be written on our hearts? Are we dedicated to activating our will to improve the leadership laid by our founders for future generations? Not to do so would be an injustice and question our celebration. It is my hope all of us will use this time as an opportunity to enrich our personal integrity and passion for social justice. Our extraordinary advocacy and recommitment to the great cause of the IABPFF continues to be an asset to our communities. Our choice of hard work to preserve our essential history, while making our own history today will determine our destiny.

Again, I applaud the Phoenix Society of Hartford and the Northeast Region for your hospitality. I also commend all who have worked together to provide building blocks of compassion, education, insight and foresight. To our friends who have partnered with us across cultural, political and social lines in the midst of adversity, I salute you. To all who have sacrificed tirelessly for the advancement of humanity through the IABPFF, may your efforts be pleasing in the sight of God. Do you know what today is? It's your 40th Anniversary! Enjoy, in hopes to have many, many more and never forget to support those who support us. "All that I am, I owe. I live eternally in the red."

These words from our then IABPFF president, Lt. Joseph B. Muhammad, are a reminder that since our beginning, the ranks of the fire service across the country have been enriched with Black brothers and sisters who were helped by our efforts either by court action, or gentle but convincing persuasion. In 2012 President Muhammad handed over the leadership of the IABPFF to our current president James Hill, of the Dallas Fire -Rescue Department.

At this fortieth anniversary celebration I was honored to be called upon, as one of the Founding Fathers, to give the history of IABPFF. For me, at eighty years old, sharing our history with young Black fire fighters, many of whom were not born when the IABPFF was founded, was a moving and heartfelt experience.

A Look At IABPFF Nationally and Internationally

IABPFF started with five organizations in five locations, Philadelphia, New York, Newark, Hudson County, New Jersey, and Hartford. Today IABPFF is organized into seven regions throughout country and the Caribbean, and has over 90 Chapters representing 5,100 fire service personnel and 200 lifetime members, The IABPFF regions and chapters as of this writing include:

North Central Region (Established 1971)

Indiana, Illinois, Iowa, Michigan, Minnesota, Nebraska, North Dakota, Ohio, South Dakota, Wisconsin.

Chapters

Indiana	Indianapolis	Indianapolis Black Firefighters Association
Illinois	Chicago	African-American Firefighters League/Chicago
	Peoria	African American Firefighter of Peoria
	Robbins	Brotherhood of Black Smoke
Minnesota	Minneapolis	Minneapolis African American Professional Firefighters Association
Michigan	Detroit	
	Flint	Society of Minority Firefighters
Nebraska	Omaha	Omaha Association of Black Professional Firefighters

Northeast Region (Established 1970)

Connecticut, Delaware, Maine, Massachusetts, New Hampshire, New Jersey, New York, Pennsylvania, Rhode Island, Vermont, Nova Scotia, Canada.

Chapters

Connecticut	Hartford	Phoenix Society Inc.
	Bridgeport	Firebird Society of Bridgeport
Delaware	Wilmington	Gallant Blazers
Pennsylvania	Philadelphia	Club Valiants Inc.
New Jersey	Atlantic City	Atlantic City Vulcans
	Englewood	Jabari Society of Bergen County
	Trenton	African American Firefighter Association
	Elizabeth	Vulcan Society of Elizabeth Inc.
	Newark	Vulcan Pioneers of New Jersey
New York	Rochester	Genesis The Alpha
	New York	Vulcan Society of New York

Northwest Region (Established 1976)

Alaska, Idaho, Montana, Oregon, Washington, Wyoming

Chapters

Washington	Seattle	Seattle Black Firefighters Association

South Central Region (Established 1970)

Arkansas, Kansas, Kentucky, Louisiana, Missouri, Oklahoma, Texas, West Virginia.

Chapters

Arkansas	Little Rock	Helping Others to Teach All Responsibility (HOTTAR)

	Pine Bluff	Banishing Racial Animosity Vigorously Everywhere (BRAVE)
Kansas	Kansas City	
Kentucky	Louisville	Louisville Black Professional Firefighters
Louisiana	Baton Rouge	Association of Minority Fire Fighters (BRAMF)
	Brossier City	African American Firefighters (AAFFBC)
	Central Louisiana	Black Professional Firefighters (CLBPFF)
	Lafayette	Southwest Association of Professional Firefighters (SWAPFF)
	Monroe	Twin City Fire Fighters Association
	New Orleans	Black Association of New Orleans Firefighters (BRANOFF)
Missouri	Berkley	Black Firefighters
	St. Louis	Firefighters Institute Racial Equality (FIRE)
	St. Louis	St. Louis Chiefs
Texas	Austin	Austin African American Firefighter Association
	Dallas	Dallas Black Firefighter Association (DBFFA)
	Fort Worth	African American Firefighters Reaching Out (AAFRO)
	Houston	Houston Black Firefighters
	San Antonio	United Black Firefighters of San Antonio (UBFSA)

Southeast Region (Established 1970)

Alabama, District of Columbia, Florida, Georgia, Maryland, Mississippi, North Carolina, South Carolina, Tennessee, Virginia.

Chapters

Alabama	Birmingham	Professional Firefighters Association
	District of Columbia	Progressive Fire Fighters Association of Washington, DC
Florida	St. Petersburg	African American Firefighters Coalition
	Palm Beach	Gold Coast Progressive Firefighter Association
	Jacksonville	Brotherhood of Firefighters
	Pensacola	United Fire Fighters Association
Georgia	Atlanta	Brothers Combined
Maryland	Baltimore	Vulcan Blazers
	Baltimore County Chapel Oaks	Guardian Knights
	Howard County	The Phoenix Sentinels Inc.
N. Carolina	Charlotte Metro	Fraternal Order of Progressive Firefighters
	Raleigh	United Professional Firefighters
Virginia	Fairfax County	Professional Firefighters
	Norfolk	United Benevolent Fire Fighters— Promethean Guardians
	Richmond	Brothers and Sisters Combined Professional Fire Fighters Inc.
	Lynchburg	Progressive Firefighters Association

Southwest Region   (Established) 1972)
Arizona, California, Colorado, Hawaii, Nevada, New Mexico, Utah

Chapters
California

Alameda County Chapter	Berkeley Chapter	Clark County Chapter
Colorado Chapter	Compton Chapter	Contra Costa Chapter
Emeryville Chapter	Fresno Chapter	Los Angeles City
San Diego Chapter	San Francisco Chapter	
Santa Clara County Chapter	United Firefighters of Southern California	
Vallejo Chapter	Oakland Chapter	

Nevada

Phoenix Chapter	Reno Chapter
Richmond Chapter	Southern Nevada Chapter
Las Vegas Chapter	

International
Caribbean (Established 1995)
Barbados, St. Lucia, Trinidad, Antigua, England

Future Regions: Africa, Europe, Central and South America

A TROUBLED CITY

The idea of New England serenity and prosperity was a myth as far of the city of Hartford was concerned. In early 1971, just a few months after the Phoenix Society had been instrumental in helping to establish the IABPFF, I was aware of the continuing exodus of families and businesses out of the city. Four consecutive summers of rioting had proven to be too much for many. Businesses along with many of the city's affluent and middle class residents, both Black and White, were fleeing to the tranquility of suburban life. Even some city government workers were searching for employment in more serene settings. In April City Manager Elisha Freedman submitted his letter of resignation to the mayor. He had accepted a position as chief administrative officer in Montgomery County, Maryland, more than two-hundred miles from Hartford. It seemed only the committed and those who had no other choice remained.

After Freedman's departure, the city council, by a seven-to-two vote, appointed Fire Chief Edward Curtin as interim city manager. Those who voted for him believed the fifty-three-year-old Curtin to be the person whose leadership might ensure a calm summer. The two council members opposed to Curtin believed the city's Public Works Director Bernard Batycki, who had previously served as city manager in New London, or Deputy Corporation Counsel Richard Cosgrove were better qualified. In accepting the interim appointment, Chief Curtin told council members, "I accept only to meet the present need of the city, and I look forward to my return as fire chief."

After being sworn in the following week, to my surprise Curtin asked me to be his interim assistant city manager. I agreed because I wanted to experience how city government worked. Curtin put me in charge of four field offices that functioned as satellite offices of city hall. People could bring their concerns to one of the field offices and not have to travel downtown. Two of the offices were in the North End, on Albany Avenue, and Barbour Street. Another satellite office was on Park Street, a busy commercial street on the south side. This predominantly Hispanic area had been the scene of rioting in the summer of 1970. A fourth office was on Franklin Avenue in the South End. This particular office was established at the prompting of the Equal Employment Opportunities Commission after residents in this Italian neighborhood complained they were being overlooked. While this middle-class neighborhood was ineligible for the federal funds going to poorer neighborhoods, Curtin thought it best to set up an office there. So we established the South End Community Services office and opened for business.

Curtin had given me the responsibility of coordinating city and state services through these four field offices. In each of these offices, I had a desk and administrative support. To these offices community people could come and see city government at work on their behalf. Of course, my new responsibilities were in addition to my duties as head of Special Services.

It wasn't hard for me to guess why Chief Curtin wanted me to be his assistant. He knew my strength was in community organizing, and he knew I had built good relations with the Black and Puerto Rican communities. He simply needed someone with my knowledge and skills. As interim city manager, Curtin now had to manage a ninety-four million dollar budget, 2,400 city employees, and more than enough problems to keep him occupied, and on edge. On the very afternoon Curtin was sworn in, for example, around thirty people had formed a picket line in front of Hartford's police department headquarters on Morgan Street. The picketing was over the firing of a Black policeman.

Officer Clanford Pierce had been fired for refusing his commander's order to get a haircut. Officer Pierce wore his hair in a large Afro, which was a popular hairstyle of the day. The Hartford Chapter of the American Civil Liberties Union had condemned the firing.

"Officer Pierce served through two tours in Vietnam, wearing gas masks and helmets, and was promoted in the field, with his hair twice its present length," the ACLU said in his defense. Two other organizations, the Police Citizens Planning Committee and the Coalition of Citizens for Improved Law Enforcement, also denounced Pierce's firing.

"Is length of hair really the issue?" the protesters who filed into Curtin's office on his first day as city manager wanted to know.

The only response Curtin could give was, "I will look into it."

With my newly added position as interim assistant to the city manager, I thought it best that I move from Bloomfield back into Hartford. Twelve years earlier Gladys and I decided to raise our children in the suburbs. We moved out of the city before the riots, so no one could accuse me, as some later would, of being one of those who abandoned Hartford because of the racial disturbances. We just wanted to move to a quiet neighborhood and a better school system for our children. So I began looking for a house in Hartford. Meanwhile, I took note in early September 1971 that thirty-five candidates from around the country were under consideration for the permanent city manager position. This was the same time much of my attention, and the attention of the nation, was focused on the prisoner riot at the Attica Correctional Facility in Attica, New York. About a thousand Black prisoners, many of them with raised clenched fists, were demanding better living conditions and an end to racist treatment by White prison guards. They had taken over the prison and were holding thirty-three guards hostage. The standoff would end four days later under a fusillade of bullets and tear gas, claiming the lives of twenty-nine prisoners and ten prison employees.

Meanwhile, after looking closely at the thirty-five applicants for city manager, the city council concluded the best man was already doing the job. In the last week of November, Mayor George Athanson and all nine council members approved a resolution making Edward Curtin the permanent city manager. That same day Curtin resigned as fire chief and named Deputy Chief Edward Fennelly as his successor. I liked Fennelly and felt I would have no problems working closely with him. Like me, Fennelly was a Hartford native and graduate of Weaver High. He had joined the department four years before me. He made lieutenant in 1955, captain in 1962, and deputy chief in 1968. Now he was the chief. While it took him only seven years to make lieutenant, it had taken me fifteen years to break the color line in the officer's rank.

After several months of looking, in early 1972 I found what I considered the perfect house. It was a fourteen-room colonial-style house on Canterbury Street in Hartford's North End. The house was on the same block where my mother babysat little Jewish children forty years earlier. This picturesque tree-lined street with its wide driveways, well-manicured lawns, trimmed hedges, and well-kept colonial and ranch-style homes was named after the town in England well-known for its majestic Gothic cathedrals. The city had once used pictures of Canterbury Street for advertisements promoting Hartford as a wonderful place to live and raise children.

Years earlier, when I was a student at Weaver High, I dreamed of one day owning a house on Canterbury Street. I used to walk by the street and say to myself, "One day when I'm rich and making five thousand dollars a year, I'm going to buy one of those big houses on Canterbury Street." It was several years after I graduated from Weaver, in the early 1950s, that a gradual transformation of Canterbury Street from predominantly White and Jewish to predominantly Black began to take place. One of the earliest Black families on Canterbury Street was the Barlow family.

In telling the story of his move to Canterbury Street, Boce Barlow would later say, "I had heard about the single-family house in a quiet neighborhood near Keney Park. Not wanting to attract attention in an all-White neighborhood, I drove by for a glimpse. When I expressed interest in the house, the real estate agent, not wanting to sell to Blacks, dropped the listing. The owner of the house, being open-minded, invited me and my family in to look at the house. Afterward I offered to buy it." When Boce and his wife, Catherine, and their two small children moved into the house, they received an icy reception from many of their Irish, Polish, and Jewish neighbors.

"I knew what to expect," Barlow said later. "I just paid no mind." He would later recall that at the time he bought the house, there were only a few Black teachers in the Hartford public school system, and only one Black employee at city hall. Now, about twenty years after the Barlows, I moved my family into a house on Canterbury Street almost directly across the street from the Barlows. There were only a few other Black families on the block. But as time passed my White and Jewish neighbors began moving off Canterbury Street. Because I was a Realtor, I was able to convince the majority of them to let me serve as broker for their houses. Believing I could get them a quicker sale, they agreed. Of the forty-one houses on Canterbury Street, I would eventually serve as broker for thirty-eight or thirty-nine of them—all of the buyers were Black.

The year I moved back into Hartford, there was an opening in the fire department for the position of line captain. I was advised by City Manager Curtin to take the test. I had been a lieutenant for three years, so I was eligible for promotion to the next level. Other fire fighters were preparing to take the test as well, so Curtin cautioned me.

"Remember, John, the line captain test will have nothing to do with the administrative work you are learning working out of my office, or working with people in the community," he said. "So don't forget to study." Lots of eyes were on me when word got out I was going to take the test for captain. Many expected me to score in the top five, and become the department's first Black captain. One advantage I had when I was assigned to a firehouse was there was always time to study. Working three days on and three off, or pulling three hours of watch duty, made studying possible. Even after I became a lieutenant, I could find time to study. But after becoming head of Special Services and also serving at interim assistant to the city manager, I found myself with very little free time. How could I find time to study when I was in the community working day and night? So I took the test and I failed it. I was embarrassed when the test results were made public.

When I met later with City Manager Curtin, he chided me, "You dummy. You should have studied."

All I could say was, "I let my guard down." I had learned a valuable lesson the hard way. When you finish one test in the department, you immediately begin studying for the next. You don't wait.

After moving the family back into the city and settling into our new home, I began to feel a renewed sense of hope for the future of Hartford. Managing the four field offices gave me the opportunity to talk with people who were committed to staying in the city, and to help them resolve issues they were having with city government. I also believed that the relationship between the fire service and the minority community was getting better. My days and evenings were spent meeting with community organizations, social agencies, city officials and residents, clergy, and business leaders. I attended youth gatherings and spoke at recreation centers. Because I was out of the house all day and most evenings, Gladys was constantly cautioning me to take better care of myself.

"You're a workaholic just like your father...You're going to make yourself sick...You're not taking care of yourself...John, you have a hard head." I heard her, but what could I do? I had to do my job. So I continued with my busy workaholic schedule. This schedule kept me from having dinner at home with my family most nights, so I was eating a lot of takeout, much of it spicy Spanish and West Indian food. This diet gave me quite a scare one November evening in 1973. I was sitting at the counter of a restaurant on Albany Avenue eating a meal of curry chicken when I began feeling dizzy. My head was spinning, my stomach was churning, and I thought I was going to fall off the stool. So I grabbed hold of the counter to steady myself.

As my head dropped I could hear someone asking, "Are you okay? What's wrong?" "Are you alright?" Thinking I was having a heart attack, the man behind the counter dialed the operator and asked for emergency help. The next thing I knew I was in the back of an ambulance. I was taken to Mt. Sinai Hospital and spent the next several days undergoing tests. The doctor told me that my feeling of dizzy and like I was about to pass out was caused by a sudden spike in my blood sugar. Then he told me I had developed Type-2 diabetes. So at the age of forty-three, I began taking insulin, something I would do every day for the remainder of my life.

I spent eight days recuperating at Mt. Sinai and getting my blood sugar under control. During my hospitalization City Manager Curtin told the city council that my illness was due to "five years of working long hours on the battlefield." As a result the city council passed the following resolution:

This is to certify that at a meeting of the Court of Common Council, November 26, 1973, the following resolution was passed.

Whereas, Lieutenant John Stewart of the Hartford Fire Department has been hospitalized for the past week, and,

Whereas, it appears that his many years of dedication to the Hartford Fire Department have caught up with him and fully depleted his seemingly boundless reservoir of energy and stamina; and whereas, Lieutenant Stewart even while hospitalized continues to be concerned over the problems which plague this city; now,

Therefore be it resolved, the Hartford Court of Common Council extends its wishes for a speedy recovery to Lieutenant John B. Stewart Jr., whose presence is sorely

missed by his peers and the citizens whom he has so tirelessly labored to serve.

The day I was discharged from the hospital, I promised Gladys I
would take better care of myself and only eat dinner at home. I knew
that Type-2 diabetes could lead to a lot of other health problems, so
this was a promise I had no choice but to try and keep.

The Hartford Fire and Police Departments are cousins. Both are
charged with public safety, and both have a long tradition of selecting a
new chief from within their respective departments. In early 1974 one
of City Manager Curtin's first decisions was a decision that angered
many of the high-ranking members of Hartford's police department.
He broke tradition and hired an outsider. His choice was Hugo Masini,
a forty-nine-year-old former high-ranking official with the New York
City Police Department. To make matters worse, Masini was Italian,
not Irish. This was the first time in the history of Hartford's Police
Department that it did not have an Irish chief. This was all a delicate
matter because there were Irish officers in the department with both
time and experience that qualified them to be made chief.

I found it interesting that Curtin, who I thought had gone way
out on a limb to make me the fire department's first Black officer,
had asked Black officers in the police department about their level of
interest in becoming the city's next police chief. Curtin found that the
Black officers who were qualified were reticent about accepting the
position. None seemed interested in becoming Hartford's first Black
police chief. In spite of the anger of those who did want the job, in
April 1974 Masini was sworn in as Hartford's new police chief. No one
could have foreseen at the time that within six years, Masini, under
heavy pressure from fellow officers and the city council, would be
forced out.

When Masini began his tenure as Hartford's police chief, he began
with a mandate from the city council to reorganize police operations. To help curb crime, council members felt it best that the police

department move from a centralized form of policing to neighbor-hood team policing. This would move the focus of police operations from police headquarters to the neighborhoods where crimes were taking place. Because this change of focus meant the police would have to spend more time in the community, the city manager assigned me to assist Chief Masini. He wanted me to be his liaison to people in the community. So I had no choice but to take on yet another responsibility.

"I intend to make police-community relations more than window dressing and talk," Police Chief Masini told North End residents at a community meeting we attended together. "I know that police offi-cers are being viewed by many young people in this community as the enemy, and it will not be easy changing that image, but I assure you I will do my best," he promised the north enders. Working with Chief Masini added a different dimension to my community work. I was now trying to convince community people of the value of having a good relationship with not just the fire department, but with the police department as well. As I went about trying to meet all of my responsibilities, I wondered if I was spreading myself too thin. I knew that sometimes when a person tries to do too many things, it's possible that a real and significant impact will not be made with any of them. Plus, I had promised Gladys that I would slow down because of my previous health scare.

Still, taking my own counsel as I usually did, I reasoned that all would be well. With my added assignment, I was able to observe police operations close-up, and how these operations interacted with city government. Following the city council mandate given him, Chief Masini implemented the neighborhood policing concept first in the Asylum Hill neighborhood, and then in the North End.

Since being established six years earlier, the responsibilities of Special Services had steadily increased. The five of us who comprised the Special Services unit were now responsible for all aspects of pub-lic relations, minority recruitment, false alarm and public safety programs, educational programs to prevent Dumpster fires and illegally opening fire hydrants. We also organized and maintained recreational programs for children and youth, and we served as liaison to other city agencies and state and federal community relations divisions. We took care of department and community complaints and any other related concerns as they would arise. As assistant to the city manager, I was also working closely with Police Chief Masini and other city government officials. Because of the nature of my work, I was being called upon to speak at community and civic meetings, and conferences in other cities.

My level of activity prompted the city's personnel department to undertake a study, which resulted in a reclassification of the rank needed to head Special Services. In early 1974, with the approval of the fire fighter's union, the city's personnel department announced that the work of Special Services required someone at the head with the newly created rank of administrative captain. Because this reclassification of rank had union approval, others in the fire department were eligible to take the administrative captain's test. This meant that if I wanted to hold on to my position as head of Special Services, I would have to take and pass the test. But not only that, I had to come out number one if I wanted to keep my job. I recalled that I had failed the line captain's test just a year earlier because I didn't study. I would definitely have to study this time, because my job as head of Special Services was on the line. So I built time into my schedule that allowed me to hit the books for an hour or two every day.

When the day came, I took the test with a number of others and anxiously awaited the results. When the test scores were announced, you can imagine how relieved I was to learn I had come out on top. In August 1974, just over a week after a disgraced Richard Nixon resigned his presidency as a result of the Watergate scandal, I was promoted to the rank of administrative captain. This was my fifth promotion since joining the fire department twenty-two years earlier, and my second promotion as an officer. In the presence of city officials and family members, Fire Chief Fennelly pinned the silver captain's badge onto my jacket.

"Congratulations, Captain Stewart," he said, shaking my hand. Sure, I was proud, and the wide smile on my face evidenced that. Still, I calculated, it had taken 110 years for a Black person to make captain in the Hartford Fire Department.

It was reported by the Federal Emergency Management Agency (FEMA) that approximately one hundred fire fighters are killed each year in this country fighting fires. In September 1974, a month after I made captain, a pall of grief hung over the Hartford Fire Department. The ringing of the fire alarm at Engine Company 8 on Park Street one evening sent fire fighters rushing to fight a fire. In a matter of minutes, they arrived at the scene to find a building ablaze. What gave them cause for concern was that this was the same building where they had extinguished a fire just a day earlier. The line officer in charge made a quick assessment and then sent several fire fighters into the building to fight the fire from the inside. With tools and hose, they made their way into the burning building. Soon after they entered, fire ripped up the walls of the building, engulfing the roof in flames. Sensing danger, the fire fighters began to retreat out of the building. As they were making their way out, the roof collapsed.

Once out on the street, they discovered that one fire fighter, the pump operator, was not among them. As soon as they were able, they quickly went back into the smoldering building to locate him. It didn't take long to find his lifeless body buried beneath the debris. While hoping for the best, they discovered the worst. The death of this fire fighter caused questions to be raised within the fire department, by city officials, by the fire fighter's family, and by the public.

"What went wrong? Should they have even gone inside? Did anyone recognize the danger? Why didn't they retreat sooner? Who's at fault?" As the fire department's public relations coordinator, I had to find answers to these questions. An investigation revealed that all proper procedures had been followed. No one was to blame. This was just one of the unfortunate aspects of being a professional fire fighter. Since this was the second fire at the same location in as many days, there was an arson investigation. I let it be known that if someone had intentionally set this fire and was arrested, that person would be prosecuted for the fire fighter's death.

As the year 1974 was coming to an end, I was still adjusting to my new captain's rank. Special Services now consisted of a captain, a lieutenant (earlier that year Richard Epps had become the second Black fire fighter to be made an officer), two other fire fighters, and two civilian employees. One of our major projects this year had been organizing two midget football teams. The team in the North End of the city was supported by the Stowe Village fire fighters, while the team in the city's West End was supported by fire fighters at the Parkville Firehouse. The football season ran from mid-August to the end of November. We had fire fighters who were volunteering their time to coordinate the two teams and doing whatever else was needed to keep the teams going. We had a total of eighty-six boys, ages nine to thirteen, enrolled in the football program, and twenty girls serving as cheerleaders.

Another program we had established during the year was our summer bowling league. This program generated our most enthusiastic response and citywide support. The number of youngsters we were able take into this program depended on the availability of funds. Fortunately, we were able to get federal funds from the Department of Labor, and several local businesses, which resulted in nearly 250 youngsters' ages nine to thirteen participating in this program. To a large extent, this program was successful because over twenty adult volunteers from the community were serving as supervisors.

Another program we had going was the Explorer Scout Fire Cadet Program. This program operated year-round for boys and girls ages fourteen to twenty-one. Each week the young fire cadets would gather at a different city firehouse. Under the supervision of the officer in charge, these cadets would participate in drills with the entire fire company. They would answer emergency phone calls and distribute educational pamphlets in the neighborhoods on the dangers of false alarms and hydrant abuse. They also assisted in the operation of some of our community programs. Because it was important to me to have total community involvement, for the first time in the history of this fire department, I had girls and not just boys participating in this fire service program. My hope was that this program would become a training ground for future fire fighters. At the end of 1974, I submitted my annual report to Fire Chief Fennelly. In the report I described the accomplishments of the Special Services unit since it had been established six years earlier.

> Special Services is now an integral part of the life of much of the Hartford community.
>
> The football program has grown so much that Dillon Stadium will be the site of its games in the coming season. The move to the stadium has received full backing from the Parks and Recreation Department. As a result of the football program, the eyes of many young men in the community have been opened to career possibilities in the fire service.
>
> Each summer our bowling program proves to be the most popular program in the Hartford community, and it provides Special Services with the opportunity to befriend key youngsters and adults living in various areas of the city. The bowling program is great because it provides a fun activity for youngsters at no cost to them.
>
> Our Explorer Scout Fire Cadet Program now has eighteen male and female participants. It is the first program in our department's history to include women. It is Special

Services' wish that this program become a launching ground for a cadet fire fighter training program, similar to the Hartford Police Department's cadet program. We also feel that the time is fast approaching when positions will open up to young women, positions such as dispatcher, inspector, and possibly even fire fighter.

Besides me, Special Services has one other permanent and two detailed men, plus the assistance of one Spanish-speaking fire cadet. The cadet works with us ten hours per week, from September through June, while going through the cadet training program. Afterward he spends twenty-five hours per week with the Unit.

Our false alarm education program carried us into areas of the city where previously there had been no problems. We were happy to see positive results from this program.

We spoke to fifth and sixth graders, introducing them to the possibility of employment within the fire service when they become adults.

With help from the Fire Department and the Hartford Insurance Group, brochures were created for the Career Opportunities Program (COP). The program includes the Fire Cadet, False Alarm Education and Recruitment programs.

One of the Unit's major achievements in 1974 was the city's purchase, through the Fire Department's budget, of Hydrant Safe-T-Locks. These locks, along with the annual Summer Sprinkler Program, played a major role in bringing hydrant abuse under control.

Respectfully Submitted, Captain John B. Stewart Jr., Special Services Unit

Walking the streets of the city's North End in 1975, my eyes were opened to the reality of the damage done by four summers of rioting and also by government neglect. In a number of the neighborhoods, overgrown, trash-strewn vacant lots and boarded-up buildings stood out like sore thumbs. Even before the riots, many areas in the North End had been crippled by decades of redlining and governmental neglect, which transformed them into underdeveloped zones of large housing projects with an abundance of run-down apartment buildings, whose residents were mostly poor Blacks and Puerto Ricans.

A year earlier, in 1974, the city council had undertaken a study to measure the effectiveness of municipal performance throughout the city. The study revealed that 61 percent of the people living in Hartford lived on incomes below the poverty line established by the Federal Bureau of Labor. The study found that Hartford, which is one of 169 towns and cities in Connecticut, had the ninth lowest per-capita income. A large portion of city residents was either on fixed incomes, or they were the working poor or unemployed. Many of them were in extreme poverty where hunger was a persistent problem. Most of these people, the study said, had little or no expectation of moving into the mainstream culture.

It was the dismal findings of this study that prompted City Council Majority Leader Nicholas "Nick" Carbone, a liberal South End Democrat, to set up a bus tour through the North End. He wanted White suburbanites to see what real poverty and governmental neglect looked like close up. Carbone, viewed by many in the North End as a feisty and sympathetic Italian, loaded three buses in April 1975 with state legislators, small-town officials, businesspeople, and newspaper reporters. Through "Nick's Tour," as he called it, he would show them "the worst of Hartford." He wanted to get these influential people "up close enough to smell the poverty." Then he planned to appeal to them for help in financing the improvement of the area. I thought Nick's Tour could have positive results for the North End, so I agreed when Carbone asked me to be one of the tour guides. I sat in the front seat of the first bus as it slowly made its way through the most run-down and unsightly neighborhoods. The buses lumbered up Albany Avenue, down Garden Street, through Acton Street, over to Clark Street, along Bellevue Street, and up Main Street's Arsenal neighborhood.

Fifty-six percent of the people in the Arsenal neighborhood, which was the area of some of the worst of the summer disturbances, lived on public welfare. The buses rumbled past boarded-up tenements, trash-strewn lots, and ugly scarred buildings. I saw the shocked look on the faces of the people as they peered out the bus windows.

"How could this have happened to a major part of the city?" the White suburbanites wanted to know. When the tour ended, the tourists were taken downtown to the Civic Center for what Carbone called "a welfare luncheon" of chicken wings, rice, bean salad, corn bread, and coffee. In a question-and-answer period, none of Hartford's city officials in attendance accepted blame for the North End's neglect and crumbling infrastructure.

"There's not enough money to correct all of the problems in the city," a city council member said with a shrug of his shoulders.

"The city is falling into a fiscal morass," explained another. As I listened, I interpreted their remarks as meaning there were no immediate plans to do anything to improve the quality of life for people living in these troubled neighborhoods.

A month after Nick's Tour, the Gonzalez family was finally having their day in court. Summer was approaching, so I was paying close attention to the trial. It had been five years since twenty-eight-year-old Efraira Gonzalez had been shot and killed on a North End street. The slain man's brother had filed a $750,000 wrongful death suit against the city. Those named in the suit included former City Manager Elisha Freedman, former Police Chief Thomas Vaughan, and the four police officers present at the shooting. To some city residents and public officials, the circumstances surrounding Gonzalez's death were still uncertain, to others less so.

Even I was experiencing some puzzlement. During the disturbances on the night of July 31, 1970, sometime between seven thirty and eight o'clock, Gonzales was shot and killed. One police officer testified that he had fired, but that his shotgun contained only pellets. The hospital report said Gonzalez had suffered two bullet wounds, one in his arm and the other in his chest. The police contended that Gonzalez had been shot by a hidden sniper. The Gonzalez family maintained that a policeman shot and killed Efaira. Former Police Chief Thomas Vaughan testified that he "wanted the Gonzalez killing solved and had ordered a detective to investigate, leaving no stone unturned." Several people who lived on the street where the incident took place witnessed the fatal shooting. One was a sixteen-year-old girl shot in the arm as she pulled down the shade in her apartment. She was shot about the same time Gonzalez was shot, but testified at the trial that the police never questioned her.

Another witness testified that he had told the police he could pick out the man who shot Gonzalez from a police lineup, but the lineup was never held. A week after the trial ended, an all-White jury cleared everyone named in the lawsuit. When questioned by a reporter about the outcome of the trial, the mother of the slain man replied, "It was never a question of money; it was a question of my blood."

In July 1975 Hartford's economic woes were made even worse by the actions of some off-duty fire fighters who formed a picket line on the sidewalk in front of city hall. Their protest was over the ongoing delay in negotiating a new labor contract. This was a difficult time for the former fire chief, now city manager. As a former fire fighter, Curtin could identify with the fire fighters' concerns. Still, Curtin stated publicly, he would "take his own tough stance regarding city finances." The picketing and extended contract negotiations were not Curtin's only concern at the time. He was also being criticized by the mayor and by Republican council members as being ineffective.

Facing these pressures, Curtin submitted his resignation on the first day in October. This was the same day that many people the North End planned to sit in front of their television and watch the "Thrilla in Manilla" between Muhammad Ali and "Smokin'" Joe Frazier. Curtin said only that he was tired and wanted to be a private citizen again. When his resignation took effect in December 1975, my nearly five years as interim assistant to the city manager came to an end. I was left feeling extremely satisfied with my first taste of working in city government. In August 1976, eight months after Curtin's departure, the city council selected James B. Daken as his successor. This selection was met with great delight by the business and political leaders in Hartford. Even the local newspaper expressed its pleasure with the appointment of the highly praised thirty-four-year-old career administrator from Toledo, Ohio. It cited the fact that Daken had recently been named Innovator of the Year by the Professional City Managers' Association.

In lavishing praise on the new city manager, the *Hartford Courant* in its August 15 edition said, "The appointment of James B. Daken to become city manager is the result of months of search, and—judging from his accomplishments as manager of Toledo—the time was well spent." In October 1976 the new city manager was sworn into office with a promise to help Hartford's poor. No one could have foreseen that an embattled Daken would resign in less than two years.

One of the things I had learned early while working in the public domain was not to be surprised by the things people say and do. This point was brought home during an Urban League Board meeting I was attending in January 1977. Michael Sharp, the League's director of housing, told the following story. A week earlier he had gone to the new regional American Airlines Reservation Center that was soon to open in downtown Hartford. He learned that the airline was in the process of transferring approximately four hundred out-of-state employees to the Hartford area to work in the new center. About a hundred of these out-of-state employees were Black. Sharp said that during his conversation with a Black female airline employee, a certain story about a map kept coming up. She told him that a firm in White Plains, New York, had been hired to help the out-of-state employees find suitable housing. Black airline employees moving into the area, she told Sharpe, were not being given the same level of help as White airline employees moving into the area. She told Sharp that the firm had only mailed her a map of Hartford with written comments suggesting she avoid certain areas in the city.

Sharpe then produced a copy of the map for us to see. The map was a standard Board of Realtors Multiple Listings Service map of the Hartford metropolitan area. Written on this particular map, however, was the notation that most of the city of Hartford was unsuitable to home seekers. And there was a big red "NO" in bold capital letters written across the entire North End. The implication was that this section of the city—which just happened to be inhabited by the majority of Hartford's Black and Hispanic residents—was undesirable. When asked about it, the executive vice president of the Hartford Board of Realtors claimed to have no knowledge of the altered map.

"No way did anyone in my office alter any maps," he stated emphatically. "Whether somebody took them and altered them, I don't know, but we didn't do it."

Reverend George Welles, a member of Hartford's Human Relations Commission, summed up the feelings of those of us on the Urban League Board when he said about the altered map: "As initially shocked as I am, I'm not surprised. It points to business as usual."

Just a month after the altered map issue, another issue with racial overtones brought a large crowd of angry people to the Urban League offices. In February 1977 close to three hundred people gathered in the League's Albany Avenue office for an emergency community meeting. They were vowing to fight as long as it took to keep Hartford's first Black school superintendent in office. The school board was scheduled to meet in executive session the following afternoon to decide whether or not the contract of Superintendent Dr. Edythe Gaines should be renewed. It was public knowledge that board members had already made up their minds to dismiss Dr. Gaines. The crowd of angry protesters felt the school board had not given a justifiable reason for her dismissal.

"It looks to me like a lynching!" one person said in a voice loud enough for many in the crowd to nod in agreement.

"They oppose her because she's Black," said another. Many in the crowd lavished praised on the superintendent for the improvements she had made in the school system since taking the job two years earlier.

"She's responsible for the improvement in the students' ability to read!" one lady spoke out.

"My fear," said Norvell Goff, president of the Hartford Chapter of the NAACP, "is that the city is systematically removing Blacks from positions of power. We've got to look out because it's happening now with Dr. Gaines."

Another voice calling for the retention of Dr. Gaines was the Interdenominational Ministerial Alliance of Greater Hartford. "The Hartford Board of Education members are mistaken if they believe the Black community will stand for anything less than the renewal of Mrs. Gaines's contract," said the Reverend Paul Ritter, president of the alliance. "The renewal of her contract would give the superintendent the authority and the freedom to bring meaningful and quality education to the city." The reason why I was troubled over the board's pending action was because I had sat on the three-person school board panel that interviewed Dr. Gains and recommended her for the job. I had been impressed by her background and her thoughts on how to improve public education in our city schools. But even in the midst of the protesting, when the school board met the following day, Dr. Gaines's contract was not renewed. Protest rallies and marches continued for weeks, but the school board was not swayed, and Dr. Gaines was out. The only conclusion I could draw was that Hartford was not ready for a strong Black woman.

In the spring of 1977, the city was experiencing its usual budgetary shortfalls. Preparing the budget for the next fiscal year, which needed to be approved in July, was proving to be a difficult task for City Manager Daken. Having now had the experience of working in city government, I had what I believed to be a solution to the city's budget woes. I decided to write an opinion piece and mail it to the *Hartford Courant* editorial board, hoping they would publish it. On Thursday morning, April 1, 1977, I was pleased to see my essay on the editorial page for city residents to read. I had written the following:

...Or Is It "Broke"?

Hartford, like many other cities throughout our country, has reached a very critical point in its life—in the midst of its current labor-relations problems, particularly relating to the Fire Department, the Police Department, and the In-School Educational Staff.

It is quite evident that this labor situation has been, and is, continuing to fester to the point of open confrontation, not only with the city's administrators and the general public, but also among the three labor factions—one against another, and also internally within the respective groups themselves.

An in-depth study of the history of labor relations and conditions in the City of Hartford reveals that in the past we have prospered in direct proportion to the growth of our region. However, we—the administrators, residents, businesses, and employees—neglected to heed the warnings and trends which began to develop, and therefore did not even begin to prepare ourselves to adjust to or even cope with the present economic conditions.

As we approached the 1960s and our city began to undergo revolutionary economic, social, and ethnic changes, there began a mass exodus of whites and middle-class blacks to areas outside the city limits (thus creating a reduction in city income during a time when existing services costs were on a steady annual incline) and new services had to be created to assist a city which was now becoming more and more heavily populated with low-income residents.

As a result of increased costs and reduced income, the city, in an attempt to meet its obligations, had to raise its tax structure, thus driving more residents and businesses and their income out of the city and over burdening, even more, those who chose or were forced to stay.

City employees drifted to the suburbs. Hiring for vacancies within city departments drifted not only from our city to the suburbs, but also encompassed nation-wide recruiting. The city also failed to mandate that the top department heads live within the limits of the City of Hartford. Thus allowing incomes paid to city employees to support the suburbs instead of helping the city's cycle of expense and income cash flow.

Secondarily, larger numbers of persons unfamiliar with the changes taking place in the City of Hartford began taking their places in the daily operation of the city. Here, again, our city failed when sufficient emphasis was not placed on training for our employees in human relations, communication, and the understanding of the ethnic make-up of our city. This should have been a top priority for the Fire Department, Police Department and teachers, all of whom directly service all the residents and taxpayers of the City of Hartford.

Presently, Hartford has a minority population of approximately 71 percent. Further, only 21 percent of the Fire Department, 22 percent of the Police Department, and 35 percent of the Teachers employed by the city live within the limits of the city. All these circumstances have led to an overall and general insensitivity toward the plight of the City of Hartford.

City employees who still reside within the city are now feeling the sting of fellow employees residing in suburbia, who do not care in the least about the social and economic plight of Hartford, therefore bringing us closer, daily, to open confrontation of city employee vs. city employee.

Finally, compounding all the above-mentioned factors, Hartford also happens to be the Capital City of the State of Connecticut. This fact simply translated into dollars and cents means that approximately 55 percent of all the property in the city is either federal, state or city and therefore non-taxable. Also, as a Capital City, Hartford must provide more services of all kinds, increasing its problems in relation to the "average American city."

Perhaps the solution to our plight is to follow the example of New York and countless other cities by layoffs now—with federally funded rehiring giving preference to our city's residents in these critical times.

My point in this essay was that Hartford would be better off financially by hiring people who lived and paid taxes here, and who greatly cared about the condition and the future of the city. I knew that those who worked for the city and lived in the suburbs would take exception with my point of view, but so be it. Sure enough, several responses appeared in the newspaper a few days later. What I found interesting was that many of those disagreeing with me were city fire fighters. One fire fighter living in the suburbs wrote:

> It seems the general gist of Captain Stewart's article is that residency should be the sole criteria for employment by the City of Hartford. To quote from the article: "Hiring for vacancies within city departments drifted not only from our city to the suburbs, but also encompassed nation-wide recruiting." Captain Stewart knows as well as I do the reason for this happening. In the late sixties and early seventies nobody in this fair city seemed to want to be a policeman.
>
> This particular time was also a critical time for Hartford. It was the time of major civil disturbances. If it were not for the courage shown by city fire fighters and police officers, Hartford would have simply ceased to exist, reduced to ashes and ruled by anarchists. Shortly after this crisis the politicians of the city could not say enough about the "wonderful courage and devotion" of its civil servants—even though I might add, the majority of them resided in the suburbs.
>
> Nowhere in the article does Captain Stewart mention that he too was one of the "whites and middle-class blacks exiting to the suburbs." Only recently did he move back to the city, for a reason known only to him. A guilty conscience perhaps?

He was correct on one point. I did move my family to the Bloomfield suburb. The reason was because Gladys and I believed they could get a better education in the Bloomfield public schools. This was in 1960, seven years before Hartford's first racial disturbance.

Another fire fighter living in the suburbs wrote:

> Captain Stewart's desire is that only residents of Hartford proper be hired as city employees. I would like to remind Captain Stewart that when life-threatening riots and strife were taking place, the city was not able to fulfill its obligations to supply sufficient fire and police protection from within, and was forced to turn to the suburbs and a nationwide recruiting program to meet this obligation. Now that economic conditions have changed, the people that met the need in hazardous times are to be replaced by proposed federally funded inner-city people.

Still another fire fighter living in the suburbs had this to say:

> Regarding the comments of Captain John B. Stewart…it would seem that the employees who live outside the City of Hartford are the villains and the sole reason for Hartford's demise. He would have us believe that his fellow employees do not care about Hartford and its financial problems. This, I say, is absolutely ridiculous. To the contrary, we, the city employees—whether firemen, policemen or teachers—do care what happens to the city.
>
> I care. I do want to keep my job, but I don't want anyone to throw it in my face by telling me that I shouldn't be working here because I am not a city resident. While Captain Stewart has been involved for the past eight years or so in the plight of the city, I find it a little hypocritical that a man

who only moved back into the city two years ago can now stand so high on the "Residency Bandwagon."

The only thing I could say after reading their responses was that they had a right to their opinion, just as I had a right to mine. I believed what I said was an accurate assessment and solution to the city's budget woes. Whether any members of the city council agreed with me or not, the fact is nothing changed.

Even though he was asked by her supporters to do so, during the protracted controversy prior to the school board's failure to renew Dr. Gaines's contract, City Manager James Daken said little. In early August, as the protests over her dismissal continued, Daken left Hartford for a three-week European vacation. While he was vacationing abroad, an issue surfaced in Hartford that cost over a thousand people their jobs. The issue had to do with the city-run Comprehensive Employment and Training Act (CETA) program. An audit revealed that an anticipated $400,000 deficit was actually closer to $1.6 million.

With a deficit more than double what was anticipated, the city ordered the layoffs of close to twelve hundred CETA workers. The layoffs included workers in Hartford as well as the twenty-four surrounding towns. Added to this, the US Labor Department, which funded the CETA program, was preparing to do its own full-scale audit, and the FBI was investigating the possibility of fraud. As city manager, Daken had the responsibility for managing the program. Some elected officials, including Councilwoman Barbara Kennelly, felt that Daken, being aware of a deficit problem, should not have gone away on a vacation.

"Daken knew the four hundred thousand CETA deficit was in danger of escalating, but still left on a European vacation," Kennelly told her council colleagues - this according to the *Hartford Courant*. Daken, the recipient of accolades upon his arrival in Hartford almost two years earlier, was now being perceived by some elected officials as a weak and ineffective leader. Shortly after his return, an embattled

Daken, believing the CETA matter could be better resolved without his presence, submitted his resignation. In September 1978 Daken's staff presented him a framed line drawing of Hartford's skyline and a decanter of twenty-one-year-old scotch as a farewell gift. Just as those before him, Daken's successor would discover that being appointed city manager in Hartford was no assurance of long-term employment.

Becoming administrative captain meant I had to take on more responsibility as head of Special Services. Not long after my promotion, I became the department's civil preparedness officer. This meant I not only had to have regular communications with the city's civil preparedness director, but I also had to keep Chief Fennelly informed of the developments in national, state, and city civil preparedness programs. Another new responsibility was that I was now the department's affirmative action officer. In preparation for this job, I attended several workshops, where I learned techniques for establishing meaningful affirmative action programs. I also gathered materials for the structuring and maintenance of an effective fire department affirmative action program, and later began conducting my own workshops. I had now spent almost ten years as head of Special Services, and had worked with and come to know people in just about every neighborhood in the city. Along the way I had experienced a gradual transformation. That is to say, what started for me as a job to be done, I now viewed as a calling. I truly desired to make a real difference in the lives of all the people of Hartford, but more especially in the lives of our residents who were marginalized.

A large portion of my time was spent talking with school-age children and youth. I believed that education was the key to these young people becoming productive adults. And it was a way to get those involved in criminal activity on the right path. For these reasons, when Assistant School Superintendent John Shea asked me to chair a committee on quality education, I gladly accepted. The formal name of the committee was the Council for Quality Education, which had been established to study discipline problems in the city's public schools. Shea explained to me that the committee would have a three-fold objective. First, it was to analyze legal aspects of school discipline; second, it would study the dynamics of the student-school relationship, and why it produces disciplinary problems; and third, the committee would devise a standard system for reporting disciplinary actions. My feeling was that if by chairing this committee, I could help the city to better educate its public school students, then I would gladly serve. So I began chairing weekly committee meetings at the board of education office on High Street. By now I had become somewhat well-known as a community activist and organizer, and someone who wanted to help those in Hartford who needed help the most.

One cold, gray, and snowy afternoon in January 1978, I made my way downtown to a luncheon sponsored by the Greater Hartford Jaycees. I was to be recognized at the luncheon for my work in the community. When I stood beside the president of the Jaycees to receive the award, he called me an outstanding civil employee, and presented me with their Community Service Award. This award especially pleased me because the Jaycees was an organization that was also working for the betterment of Hartford. I thanked the Jaycees, saying it was an honor to be recognized by such an organization with so long a history of community service in Hartford.

Another reason why I remember this award is that I received it a day or so before Hartford escaped a near disaster that could have cost thousands of people their lives. It was Wednesday, January 8, and the region was in the midst of one of its most severe snowstorms in recent years. Snow and ice had accumulated on the roof of the downtown Civic Center, and in the early hours of the morning, the roof collapsed onto the floor below. People later said they heard the bending and crashing of metal. An eyewitness said he heard a low rumble that ended in a loud boom.

"Suddenly pieces of roof were falling to the ground with the snow," the man said. In that instant the 1,400-ton roof became a twisted wreck of tons of steel and wet snow, now covering the very seats where nearly 5,000 cheering college students watched the men's basketball team from UConn defeat the University of Massachusetts only four hours earlier. If the students had been there at the moment of the collapse, many of them would surely have lost their lives. Later in the day, this same space was to be filled with hundreds of city high school kids. Public safety was a responsibility of the fire department, so when the call came in, Chief Fennelly rushed to the scene.

Sitting in his study on the day of the roof collapse, the Reverend Robert Edwards, pastor of Immanuel Congregational Church, changed his sermon topic. In his Sunday sermon, he said to his congregation, "I'm thankful the Civic Center wasn't filled with thousands of people. Disasters like the roof collapse take our self-sufficiency down a peg and remind us where our real trust has to be." He compared the collapse to other disasters such as the sinking of the *Titanic*, which showed the frailty of man-made structures when compared to natural forces.

At nearby First Presbyterian Church, Reverend Frank Hoffman was telling his congregation that the absence of any deaths "was providential."

I was kept busy throughout the winter and into the spring and summer months of 1978 by an ever-increasing number of community people and organizations seeking my participation in this or that program. Besides my community work, there were also yearly fire and education conferences and management seminars in various locations in Connecticut that I had to attend. In September I added another activity to my schedule. I enrolled in a degree program at the University of Massachusetts in its School Without Walls. So two evenings a week, I drove the fifty-two miles to the University of Massachusetts campus in Amherst.

NEARING THE TOP

One warm afternoon in the summer of 1979, I was standing on Magnolia Street near the Crown Gardens Housing Project talking through a bullhorn to a group of state legislators who were touring the North End. I was giving them a close-up view of what a blighted neighborhood looked like.

While I was telling them about the problems, a street-wise bystander remarked, "They ain't gonna do nothing. They just wanna look."

Another man standing beside him made a wide sweeping gesture with his arm. "This here is bad. It needs work on the inside and out." Then he gave me a plaintive look and asked, "Are they going to fix it up?" Like many other North End residents, these men had become cynical of politicians walking through their neighborhoods and talking about the problems, but doing nothing to fix them.

Near the end of July, I was trying not to pay too much attention to what seemed to be the hottest topic in the Black community: *Would Hartford's next fire chief be black?* A week earlier Chief Edward Fennelly had announced his intention to resign, and a few politicians and community leaders were quietly pushing to have a Black person named to replace him. While Chief Fennelly had not yet submitted his letter of resignation, he let it be known he would be out by the beginning of October, just over two months away. Because the city manager had not yet received Fennelly's letter of resignation, the search for his successor had not begun.

I knew my name had come up repeatedly in some circles, where I was being promoted as one of the most qualified persons in the fire department. While there was a certain amount of inner excitement on my part at the thought of becoming fire chief, I kept quiet about it, deciding not to engage in any self promotion. I did calculate that Fennelly had been with the department twenty-three years when he made chief and Curtin twenty-one years. Both Fennelly and Curtin had been promoted to chief while serving as deputy chief. I now had twenty-seven years with the department, but up to this point, deputy chief was a rank no Black fire fighter had achieved.

With the resignation and departure of City Manager James B. Daken a year earlier, the city council had appointed Deputy City Manager John A. Sulik as interim city manager. Then in May 1979, the council named Glastonbury Town Manager Donald C. Peach as Hartford's new city manager. Near the end of September, Peach sent a letter to officers in the department saying that in anticipation of Chief Fennelly's announced retirement in October, recruitment for the next fire chief had begun both inside and outside the department. Officers eligible for promotion to fire chief were invited to submit applications and compete for the position. After receiving a copy of the letter, I submitted my application. As announced, Chief Edward Fennelly retired the first week in October, and Peach appointed Deputy Chief Charles Gallon as acting chief.

At that year's Phoenix Society Annual Banquet, James G. Harris Jr., executive director of the Community Renewal Team of Greater Hartford, likened the appointment of a Black fire chief to the legendary Phoenix rising from the ashes.

"Captain John Stewart is probably one of the best qualified persons," he told the circle of people standing around him. "As chief he could do more than he is now doing to improve the fire department's relations with the community."

State Representative A. Boyd Hinds Jr., who was also supporting my appointment, said, "In the next decade, in a time of dwindling resources and increasing need, the fire chief has to be in touch and have good relations with the community."

One of the strongest voices calling for my appointment was State Representative Thirman L. Milner, who stated publicly that it was "not necessary to look outside the city for a chief."

Arthur Johnson, head of Hartford's Human Relations Commission, said in support of me, "He has the respect of the fire fighters, and he has strong leadership qualities. I believe that on the basis of the educational background of the fire chiefs I've known, he has strong educational qualifications and has shown a great deal of personal growth. Community groundswell is rising in favor of Stewart. It's the current talk of the day in a number of places." Support for me was also coming from other Black community leaders, including former State Senator Wilber Smith, State Central Committeewoman Ella Cromwell, and former Charter Revision Commissioner Trudy Mero. For some in the Black community, a comment by State Representative Abraham Giles sounded a more cautionary note.

"People in the fire department that I've talked to, mostly White, think he's the best man," Giles said. Then he added, "I know it's going to be a political decision in the end, and I have a feeling there are some political entities who have decided he's gone as far as he's going to go."

This was primary season in Hartford, and no one knew at the time the impact the race for mayor would have on the selection of the next fire chief. Incumbent Mayor George Athanson was being challenged by Deputy Mayor Nicholas R. Carbone. "Little Nick," as Carbone was known among his supporters, had won the endorsement of the Democratic Town Committee. He had picked Rudy Arnold, a young Black attorney, to be his running mate, but Athanson, who claimed to be "for the little people," still remained widely popular in the Black and Hispanic community. He was able to get the 1,700 petition signatures needed to have his name placed on the primary ballot. It was a bitterly fought campaign that highlighted the difference in perspectives in the Black North End and the White South End.

"Because I'm White, people in the North End think I funnel all the city money into the South End," Carbone said. "And because I am viewed as a liberal by Whites in the South End, they conclude that I'm spending all the city money on the North End." In the end a campaign chaired by Sanford Cloud Jr., a knowledgeable and well-respected Black lawyer, a radio announcement by UN Ambassador Andrew Young, and a visit by Washington, DC, Mayor Marion Barry to lead a rally was not enough for Carbone to pull off a victory. While Carbone acknowledged defeat, Arnold was successful in winning a seat on the city council.

Meanwhile, I had quietly submitted applications for several high-ranking positions outside of Connecticut. I had applied for the position of fire chief in Seattle, Washington, and Hampton, Virginia. I had also applied to the US Fire Administration in Washington, DC, for a teaching position at the National Fire Academy. A reply had come from the selection committee in Seattle informing me they had over a hundred applicants, and invited me to participate in the next stage of the selection process. I was asked to give a written response to four questions, which I did and mailed back to the committee. Then, in early December 1979, I went to Hampton, Virginia, for an interview before that Fire Chief Selection Board. It was a good interview, and I left feeling hopeful about my chances. Of course, my first choice was to remain in Hartford. As I told a reporter, "I filed the applications just to give myself other options, just in case because one never knows. But my preference still is for Hartford. My roots are here. This is my home."

A few days after returning from my job interview in Hampton, a story appeared on December 14 in the *Hartford Courant* with the headline, "Athanson Opposes Stewart for Chief; Cites Carbone Ties." In the story Mayor Athanson said I had been too closely allied with Nicholas Carbone in the campaign to unseat him.

He claimed in the story to have told me repeatedly, "We don't mind if you're for Nick, but don't undermine your professionalism by thinking politically you can become chief." I had gone "overboard" when I "chose the political ground to fight the battle to become fire chief," he said in the story. When a reporter later asked if I had a response to the mayor, I simply replied, "No comment." I liked Mayor Athanson and enjoyed a good relationship with him. I had gotten to know him when I served as City Manager Curtin's interim assistant. Athanson had helped my son Jeffrey gain admission to Amherst College, and later seemed to take sole credit for my son's college education. He felt I was indebted to him and to his way of thinking had double-crossed him by supporting Carbone. He was reacting to an untrue rumor started by State Representative Paul LaRosa that I had campaigned for Carbone. I knew that LaRosa and a number of other leaders in the South End had opposed Carbone. Actually, my wife Gladys and my father did campaign for Carbone, but I had not. The only campaigning I did was for several candidates for the school board. But in the end, I did quietly cast my vote for "Little Nick."

The story in the newspaper also quoted Rudolph Fiorillo, president of the fire fighters union, as saying the chief should be appointed on the basis of competence and merit, not color.

"I don't know if he's competent," he said, referring to me. Leaders in the Black community were quick to respond to the newspaper story.

"So he sided with Nick," said State Representative Thirman L. Milner. "That was his decision during the primary. Nick doesn't own him or control him. I don't think he should be penalized for his political alliances."

Novel Goff, Democratic Town Committee member and former president of the local chapter of the NAACP, responded angrily. "The North End gave its support to Athanson, but now it appears that the mayor is ignoring the Black community when the time comes for supporting candidates for professional jobs," he said. "Anthanson told Town Committee members that he had no opposition to making Stewart the next fire chief."

State Representative Abraham Giles also spoke out. "Stewart would be a good candidate not just because he's qualified but because he is

Black. We need a symbol for our young men and women. Because of the impact of the Black vote in the last election, Blacks have earned a prestigious appointment." On street corners and in houses, Blacks in the North End who had voted for Anthanson were voicing their anger after reading or hearing about what the mayor had to say in the newspaper story.

I was trying not to pay any attention to politics. I was busy coordinating what I felt was the most important recruitment drive since becoming head of Special Services. There were forty openings in the fire department that needed to be filled in the next class of fire fighters. I had set a goal of hiring twenty Hispanics, ten Whites, and ten Blacks to fill these openings. I was determined that some of these new recruits would be women. They would become the first women ever hired by the Hartford Fire Department. I did, however, take note of the advertisement that City Manager Peach had placed in national fire fighting magazines and other publications.

FIRE CHIEF
HARTFORD, CONNECTICUT

The City of Hartford seeks applications from well-qualified, progressive and dynamic fire professionals to head this capital city's fire department.

The City of Hartford operates under a Council/Manager form of government with the City Manager appointing the Fire Chief within a salary range of $27,495 to $38,493.

Hartford is located midway between Boston and New York City, has an area of 18 square miles, a population of 156,000 and is noted for its insurance and banking industries.

In addition, to fire fighting units, the 483 authorized fire fighting and support personnel are organized into units providing management services, special services, fire prevention and investigation, alarm, signal and apparatus maintenance, training and civil preparedness. The department's annual budget is 9.6 million dollars.

Applicants should have extensive fire command experience and proven leadership ability, as well as substantial administrative experience in such areas as budgeting, resource management, personnel management, community relations and the application of technological and organizational advances.

Applicants should send a detailed resume to the Personnel Department, City of Hartford, 550 Main Street, Hartford, CT 06103. All responses will be acknowledged and held in confidence.

An Equal Opportunity Employer

I also noted that this was the first time in the history of the Hartford Fire Department that such an announcement had been placed. In the past every single chief had been chosen from within the department. Why the change now? I had my suspicions, but I kept them to myself. One of the persons I had supported during the election was board of education member Wayne Casey. After reading the newspaper story, he called Mayor Anthanson racially biased, then sent a strongly worded open letter to the mayor.

"How can you, as mayor of this city, deny a man of Mr. Stewart's leadership and many years of experience in the fire department, equal and fair Justice?" he wrote. "I don't view this as a political issue, I see it clearly as racial discrimination against a man who had lived and worked his entire life protecting all of Hartford's people. You are spending too much time talking about Carbone and not enough time judging Stewart on his qualifications."

The mayor's public opposition to me becoming fire chief and the responses from Black political and community leaders prompted this opinion piece, titled "Politics in Fire Fighting," in the *Hartford Courant* the next day.

> The selection of a new fire chief for Hartford should not get mired in politics.
>
> The city administration has begun a national recruitment drive to fill the position. Advertisements have been run in fire fighting publications, and about a dozen applications have been received so far. Under the city charter, the city manager appoints the chief.
>
> One of the applications is from Capt. John Stewart Jr., a veteran in the Fire Department. Mayor Athanson has said he would oppose his appointment because Mr. Stewart was allied with former Deputy Mayor Nicholas Carbone.
>
> Coming from a mayor who bitterly complained at election time about the politicalization of the city manager's office, Mr. Athanson's meddling in the selection of a new fire chief is unfortunate.
>
> Perhaps Capt. Stewart did not use good judgment in supporting Mr. Carbone in the Democratic mayoral primary. Although a city employee should not be forced to lose his political rights by virtue of being on the city payroll. But that is all behind us, and Mr. Athanson should turn a new leaf. The decision whether to hire Capt. Stewart should not be based on which candidate he has supported, but on his capabilities as a professional fire fighter.

As if the mayor's interference was not enough, fire union president Rudolph Fiorillo has joined the fray by saying Capt. Stewart was too political. And it has further become a racial issue. Some black leaders and groups believe that Capt. Stewart, a black, should be appointed because it is time that a black assumes a high position in city government.

If this harmful debate continues, it will mean that the next fire chief will not be given full credit for being the best choice of all the applicants. Selection of the chief should not be based on who is the most politically acceptable. We urge the politicians to leave the city manager alone in this important task so that he and the new chief will not be compromised from the first day on the job.

The following day, the same newspaper published an open letter to the city manager from Thomas Wright, president of the Greater Hartford Branch of the NAACP:

Dear Mr. Peach:

The Executive Board and Membership of the Greater Hartford Branch NAACP would like to express our support for Mr. John Stewart Jr., for the position of Hartford's Fire Chief. Mr. Stewart has served with the fire department for twenty-seven years, and is eminently qualified for the position both by experience and education. We differ with Mayor Anthanson's position because it violates the law, which states no one can be denied employment opportunities because of his/her political affiliation or belief.

The NAACP will not stand by and watch this new administration repeat history and pay lip service to affirmative action. The Black and Hispanic voters of Hartford are now a significant voice in this city, and we intend to see affirmative action become a reality.

If John Stewart Jr. is not selected for the position of Fire Chief, this is a clear example of institutional racism. The two previous Fire Chiefs, both men with less experience in the Fire Department, were selected in spite of minimal educational background. One was a high school graduate, the other held a high school diploma, and attended a Junior College. Both were white. Now we have a black man who is qualified both by his twenty-seven years of experience, and a college degree. Affirmative Action in this city has always been, and continues to be a political issue. Where white males are selected without the need for meeting all selection criteria, Blacks, Hispanics, and women need to meet all selection criteria, and even then, are passed over.

In this city where 50 percent of its citizens are minorities, only 13 percent of our fire fighters are Black. This substantiates that institutional racism is alive and well in this city. Previous statements made by State representative La Rosa, and the President of the firemen's Union that Mr. Stewart is too political for the job is only the tip of the iceberg as to their real racial feelings.

We hope that your position as Manager under the new City Council will take our concern into consideration, and appoint Mr. John Stewart Jr., as our next Fire Chief.

January 1980 began with raging fire in the North End that gutted an apartment building and claimed the lives of four people. Other tenants in the building, which was adjacent to my old firehouse at Main and Belden Streets, were left homeless. As head of Special Services, I had to find emergency shelter for the people who now had no place to live. Following an investigation Fire Marshal Ralph Marone announced that the fire resulted from an act of arson. The police, who were experiencing their own internal problems at the time, would now seek to identify and arrest the arsonist. The problems within the police department, which in a few months would leave it without a chief, stemmed from the community approach to policing that Chief Masini had instituted five years earlier as a city council mandate. I was still serving as liaison to Police Chief Masini and knew he was experiencing resistance from some police officers.

During this first week of January, the *North End Agents* and the *Inquirer*, both weekly publications whose readership was mostly Black, ran editorials calling for me to be named fire chief. Television station WFSB/TV3 also editorialized for my promotion to chief. About the time of these editorials, I had decided to call the mayor's office to ask if I could meet with him. A lot was being said about us, even though the two of us had not sat down together to talk. The mayor agreed and we had a brief meeting in his office. Meanwhile, an organized effort to have me named as fire chief had been initiated by a coalition of Black and Hispanic Democratic leaders. A thirty-two-member committee with four co-chairmen, including State Representative Abraham Giles, Wilber Smith, Jose Mendez, and Miguel Hernandez, had been formed.

Following a meeting with Democratic Town Chairwoman Dorothy Quirk at Hartford's Signature Restaurant, Giles made a public announcement of the committee's support for my appointment. "The purpose of the coalition," he stated, "is to have complete and unquestionable involvement in the decision-making process of our city government." Another group that formed in support of me was the Concerned Citizens Club of the Seventh Assembly District. This group cited my urban education and community involvement as qualifying me for the position of fire chief. There was also the Committee of 24, a Hispanic activist group, that came out in my support. The majority of the Blacks and Hispanics in these groups had supported Athanson's reelection, so as the political pressure mounted, Athanson withdrew his opposition to me becoming chief.

"I have no comment on my current position," he told a reporter. "I'm not going to say anything on it." Then he added, "Everybody should be considered. It's up to the manager." When the city manager was informed of the mayor's comment, he responded that he had not been pressured by the mayor to install me. "What he did say," Peach said, "was that Stewart would be acceptable as the new chief."

Meanwhile, Deputy Mayor Robert Ludgin was now publicly criticizing his fellow Democrats for trying to "exercise influence" on the selection process. Objecting to the "political interference" that was mounting against hiring someone from outside Hartford, he stated, "We've got a charter that says the city manager makes that selection. I took an oath to support that charter."

When it became known that I had met with the mayor, I was asked by a reporter what we talked about. "I believe at this time that whether I met with the mayor is irrelevant to the issue which is before this community," I told the reporter. "That issue is the selection of a fire chief based solely on whether I have the qualifications to serve the city." This response brought me a sharp rebuke the next day in a *Hartford Courant* editorial:

> …This is not the sole issue. If he is found to be qualified for the post, he must be a better candidate than all others who apply for the job. The best candidate should get the job. This point seems to be missed by Greater Hartford NAACP President Thomas Wright, who recently said: "If John Stewart Jr. is not selected for the position of fire chief, this is a clear example of institutional racism." If Mr. Stewart believes he is without question the best person for the job, he will be selected on the basis of merit; then he should make a strong public effort to

discourage those people and groups politicking to get him the appointment.

At the end of the week, the city's personnel director, Elias Pealer, made a rather surprising announcement.

"Unlike the last time a fire chief was chosen, all candidates for the current vacancy will be required to pass a written test," he said. "They will also stand before a panel of experts for an oral test before being considered for the appointment." In explaining the change in procedures, Pealer said, "In the past there hasn't been this type of publicity." Then he added, "Of the forty persons who have applied for the fire chief's job, most live outside Hartford. The tests will provide the city manager with a better measure of how the applicants would function on the job."

On hearing of this change in procedure, some Black elected officials and community leaders became suspicious. "The city had never used a test for selecting a fire chief," they complained. "City residents should be considered for the position first."

"Why is Hartford changing the rules when for the first time, a qualified Black man is a leading candidate for the job?" Council Majority Leader Rudolph Arnold wanted to know. Arnold then placed the matter on the city council agenda. When questioned about the change in hiring procedures at a council meeting in January, Peach explained that in the past, the merit system was rarely used when department heads were chosen, and appointments made without the so-called merit process being followed.

"I'm trying to keep it nonpolitical, because it's highly controversial," he continued. "I'm trying to be as objective and evenhanded as I can." While many Blacks in Hartford were criticizing the new procedure, city council members agreed they would not violate the current policy of not interfering with the city manager's selection of a department head. My thinking at the time was that no one could question my qualifications, but if I had to take a test, I would do so. I would do this, even though no one previously appointed to the chief's position had done so. And all of them had been promoted from within the department. Meanwhile, I received word that I had been passed over for the fire chief's job in Hampton, Virginia.

Throughout the rest of January, tension mounted over who would be named the next fire chief. It seemed as if everyone in Hartford had an opinion. Politicians, businesspeople, ordinary citizens, and organizations were taking one side or the other. Everyday there were stories on television and radio news and in the newspapers. During the last week of January Dr. Frederick G. Adams, president of The Urban League of Greater Hartford, and the League's Executive Director William J. Brown send a letter to Peach expressing the League's support of my promotion to chief.

"There is no need to search nationwide for a chief because Captain John Stewart Jr. has the proper qualification, knows the city, and has the respect of the Hartford community and of firemen throughout the country," the letter read in part. It was during this last week in January that the question being asked by a lot people in Hartford was, "Who made the calls?" Someone had made several phone calls to the US Justice Department asking for assistance, and the department sent one of its men to Hartford to "measure the level of racial tension." Joshua Liburb, a community relations specialist from the Justice Department's New England Region office in Boston, was meeting with city government officials and community leaders.

"It has come to our attention through telephone calls and previous work in Connecticut that there was some unease in the minority community regarding the selection process of a new fire chief," Liburb told them. No one seemed to know who had made the calls to Martin Walsh, director of the Justice Departments' Community Relations Service for the New England Region. The caller had criticized the testing procedures for the fire chief's position, and said it had created precarious racial tension in the city. The caller also told Walsh that he himself had received several telephone calls where racial slurs were made because of his public support of Captain John Stewart. When Liburd asked the city manager how the selection process would be carried out, Peach told him it would be based on merit. When their conversation ended, Peach confided to others that his impression was that Liburd was pushing for Stewart's appointment.

"I got the feeling that we ought to be putting Stewart in there," he told them. Deputy Mayor Robert Ludgin said Liburd urged him to get involved in the fire chief appointment and instruct the city manager to appoint Captain John Stewart. Ludgin said he told Liburd that "selecting a new fire chief should not be a political issue and should be left solely to the city manager." After Liburd left Hartford, everyone's curiosity was satisfied when State Representative Thirman Milner let it be known he placed the calls.

Before the month was out, the city manager announced a change in the testing procedure. Now there would be no written test for the fire chief position, but only an oral examination before a panel of experts. The oral exam, he said, would be given to both in-house applicants and applicants from around the country. In February I received a letter from the personnel director inviting my participation in the selection procedure. The letter stated that I was scheduled to meet with the panel on Tuesday, March 4, 1980, at 2:45 p.m., and I should be prepared to spend about three hours. I later learned I was one of sixty-three applicants scheduled to sit before the panel. A consulting firm in Philadelphia had been hired to develop the test questions that were to be asked by panel members. The firm would then grade the answers and provide a list of qualified applicants to the city manager. That same week four organizations met together and drafted a joint resolution supporting my candidacy. They included the Greater Hartford Branch of the NAACP, the Ministerial Alliance of Greater Hartford, Operation PUSH, and the Urban League of Greater Hartford. The resolution was forwarded to City Council Majority Leader Rudolph Arnold, who distributed it to the full council.

On the day of the test, I reported to the function room at city hall, and sat before the oral testing panel and answered questions for nearly three hours. I was pleased to see on the panel Chief Larry Bonnafon, who a year earlier had become the first Black fire chief in Louisville, Kentucky. After the test it seemed everyone wanted to know how I did. My answer was, I thought I had done very well. As the days passed, it seemed most of Hartford was anxiously waiting for the test results. During the third week in March, Peach announced he had received the test results of eleven candidates who were ranked the highest qualifiers, and would select a chief from among the top three. He refused to give names of the eleven, or to say if any of the top three were local.

Then, in the last week in March, something unexpected was happening in Hartford that shifted the focus of people's attention. It was reported that Deputy Mayor Robert Ludgin was leading an effort to oust City Manager Peach from office. To the surprise of just about everyone, Ludgin and four Democrats on the city council, Olga Thompson, Antoinette Leone, Mary Martin, and Antonio Gonzalez, were calling for Peach's resignation and had scheduled a vote on the matter. When asked by reporters why the council majority was dissatisfied with Peach, Ludgin responded that Peach was "unable to establish a working relationship with the new council."

"The city manager was uncommunicative and failed to consult with the council," Ludgin added. Republicans on the council saw it differently. They saw it as a power grab by the deputy mayor. Some also felt it was an attempt to prevent Peach from naming a new fire chief. It was also reported that Ludgin wanted to make Peach's assistant city manager, W. Wilson Gaitor, the city manager. Gaitor presently was manager of the Northside City Service Center, which provided social services to people living in the North End. Making Gaitor city manager was a cause for some concern among Black leaders who believed that the appointment of Gaitor would reduce the pressure to appoint me fire chief. This was because Gaitor was Black. State Representative Abraham Giles and State Central Committeewoman Ella Cromwell prevailed upon Councilwoman Olga Thompson to delay the resignation vote. While Representative Thirman Milner, Wilber Smith, Novel Goff, and Council Majority Leader Rudolph Arnold were opposed to Peach's process of naming a new fire chief, they reportedly viewed Lugdin's move as a power grab.

At a specially called council session on Friday, March 28, the Democratic council majority voted to request Peach's resignation. But Peach, who had said he would resign if such a vote passed, had changed his mind. Instead, he said he would fight the attempt to oust him. The change of mind came about because of the support he was receiving from his staff and from a large segment of the community. Two days later Peach announced it would take him at least a week to appoint a new fire chief. He said he had not been able to interview the top candidates for the job because of the uncertainty of his own future. While the city manager did not identify the top three candidates, he had told the council a week earlier that the highest scoring candidates were not Hartford residents.

"I will interview the top three candidates and then decide which of the three to appoint," Peach said. Although the names of the three top finishers were a closely guarded secret, I just knew my name had to be one of them.

The word going around Hartford was that both Acting Chief Charles Gallon and I were among the top six finalists, but not among the top three. On Thursday morning, April 3, Art Johnson, director of the Department of Human Relations, called me on the phone and asked me to come to his city hall office. This call was unexpected, and on my way, I wondered what he wanted to meet with me about. When I arrived, Johnson asked me to have a seat. I sat down in the chair facing his desk. When he looked over his desk at me, I noticed the rather serious look on his face and the deep furrows that had formed in his brow. I thought to myself, that's not a good sign. I certainly wasn't prepared for what Johnson said next.

"John, I hate being the one who has to tell you this, but you are not among the top three finishers." I stared straight ahead at Johnson, not saying a word. Then he said, "You finished seventh." I sat still, trying to process what I had just heard. My mind was racing. Did I hear him right? Did he say I finished seventh? That's what I thought I just heard him say. But how could that be? I looked over at Johnson. He was still talking. "Therefore you will not be interviewed for the position of fire chief. I'm sorry, John." I looked at Johnson. There was an anguished stare looking back at me. I sat there for a few more moments in stunned silence. Then I stood up. I uttered words of acknowledgement and walked out of Johnson's office. Seventh, I said to myself. How could that be? I felt good during the test. I was so confident as I answered the panel's questions. I was thinking to myself, this test was designed for me. I just knew I scored at the top. But seventh! How could that be? Something just wasn't right. Then my mind went to all the people in the city who had supported me. People who had publicly spoken out in my defense. People who had put themselves out on a limb for me. I had let them all down. I had failed them. I sighed deeply. In my entire life, I had never felt more miserable than I did at that moment. Oblivious of everyone and everything around me, I made my way home.

Just over an hour later, City Manager Peach announced that the top three finishers were from out of state. "If any one of them accepted the job," he added, "that person would be my first choice." When reporters asked about local candidates, Peach responded: "Deputy Chief Salvatore Visconti finished fourth; Acting Fire Chief Charles Gallon finished sixth; and Captain John Stewart finished seventh." I was thankful that evening for the love of my family and the support of friends. A number of people called or came by the house and offered words of encouragement. Still, I was embarrassed and felt miserable. The next day, March 5, the story appeared in the *Hartford Courant*.

"The chances of a Hartford man winning the Hartford fire chief's post were dealt a heavy blow Thursday when it was disclosed that the top three qualifiers for that position are all from outside the city," the story read. "Acting Chief Charles Gallon and Capt. John B. Stewart Jr., both of whom had received city support for the position, finished sixth and seventh in the testing, respectively." A few days later, I left Hartford to attend a national meeting of fire education experts and community leaders in Chicago.

After being out of the city for two days, I came back to Hartford to find that the city's Black leaders and ordinary citizens were still supporting my candidacy. In the next few days, letters of support from a man in Hartford and a lady in Rocky Hill were printed in the *Hartford Courant*. The Greater Hartford Black Democratic Club still sought to have me "secure the city fire chief's position." And the city's Human Relations Commission voted to ask the city manager how affirmative action had been used in selecting city department heads. Meanwhile, City Manager Peach announced that he planned to interview the top three candidates the following week. At the same time, his own job remained in jeopardy. Ludgin was still calling for his resignation.

As Peach tried to quietly observe his forty-ninth birthday on Thursday, April 10, he was hoping he could work out his differences with the five council Democrats. The next day he held a nonpublicized meeting with Councilwoman Olga Thompson at Mount Olive Baptist Church in the North End. The meeting was arranged by the church's pastor, Rev. Richard A. Battles Jr., and several other Black leaders who wanted Thompson to withdraw her opposition to Peach. But the councilwoman was unmoved.

"They wanted to change the rules in the middle of the game," she said in reference to the procedures for appointing a new fire chief. She saw this as a process to avoid naming me. "It had consistently been the other way," she added. A few days later, Peach announced that he planned to interview the top three candidates the following week. In response, the *Hartford Courant,* in an April 19 editorial, advised him to hold off:

> Hartford City Manager Donald C. Peach, whose own job is in jeopardy, is in no position to offer key jobs to anyone else, especially to a new fire chief.

Mr. Peach plans to interview top candidates for the chief's job next week. He may even offer one the job, explaining first, of course, that the manager (and also the chief) could lose his job any day.

Filling the chief's job has become controversial. Black community groups and politicians have been pressing for the appointment of Capt. John B. Stewart Jr., a department veteran who is black. Mr. Peach, for the first time in Hartford's history, has engaged in a national search for a new chief. None of the top three, out-of-town candidates is black.

Selection of the chief has become politicized. It is one of the issues dividing Mr. Peach and the five City Council members who want to oust him as manager.

The fire chief will have to work closely with the city manager, and the City Council, to reorganize and modernize the department. He should not be appointed by a man whose tenure is uncertain and whose every move is being criticized, albeit unfairly, by a majority of the City Council.

As long as the division between the manager and Deputy Mayor Robert F. Ludgin remains, no useful purpose would be served by going through the motions of choosing a fire chief.

Mr. Peach may want to establish his professional independence, but he should not make an appointment so crucial to the future of the city until his own future is assured.

Each of the five city council members who wanted Peach out submitted separate resolutions calling for his resignation. Peach was determined to stay, at least until the city budget was passed during the third week of May. He also planned to go ahead and interviewed the top three candidates for fire chief. By the end of April, two of the candidates, one from Michigan and the other from Ohio, were expressing reservations about accepting the position.

"They're concerned about the political instability in the city and the controversy surrounding the appointment," Peach explained. "They feel that whoever the city manager appoints as fire chief may not have full council support." Peach said that if the top candidates dropped out, he would interview the remaining eleven candidates certified by the consulting firm. This would include me. At the same time, Union President Rudolph Fiorillo was accusing Peach of "unnecessarily delaying the appointment of a new fire chief because of the political turmoil."

At the city council meeting on Monday, May 12, the council majority did something that caught everyone in Hartford by surprise. Without any prior notice, the city council majority imposed an immediate freeze on all hiring by the city. Since this matter had not been on the council agenda, the city manager told reporters that the intent appeared to be to freeze all appointments unless approved by the city council.

"To fill any vacancies, I've got to ask for permission," he told them. People weren't sure if this included the appointment of a fire chief.

"The measure wasn't intended to halt appointment of the fire chief," Deputy Mayor Ludgin explained to reporters. "But my expectation is that the man would have a hell of a lot of nerve in filling that position anyway."

In opposing the freeze, the Republican minority on the city council complained that "Despite the repeated claims of the Democratic majority that they would not interfere with the selection process, the imposing of a freeze was to prevent Peach from filling key jobs that they want to fill themselves after the manager leaves."

One suspicious insider questioning the motives of the Democrats stated, "Everything they do has a public reason and a real reason." While the implication was that the freeze was put in place to keep the city manager from filling patronage jobs that Democrats wanted to fill, it actually seemed to have resulted from a report concerning the CETA (Comprehensive Employment and Training Act) fund deficit. At the conclusion of a report by Councilwoman Antionette Leone on the severity of the present deficit, the council majority voted on her resolution and imposed an immediate freeze on all city hiring.

"We are in a tight budgetary period," Leone said in response to reporters' questions. Like others in the city, I wondered if the city manager would ignore the freeze and fill the fire chief position. But Peach chose not to defy a city council resolution. After two weeks Peach asked the council majority to reconsider the freeze, but to no avail. On Friday, June 6, Peach submitted his resignation, saying, "It has proved impossible to develop a good working relationship with the Hartford City Council."

At its next meeting, the council majority voted to remove Peach from office. This prompted lawyers for Mayor Athanason and the council Republicans to challenge this action in court. However the court refused to intervene. Then at its meeting on Monday, June 23, the city council approved a financial settlement with Peach, and he was out. While the naming of a fire chief was in limbo, Police Chief Hugo Masini announced his own resignation effective in just seven days. At the end of June, the City of Hartford found itself in a strange place. It was at the same time without a city manager, a fire chief, and a police chief.

Before leaving office, Police Chief Masini had encouraged Major Theodore Napper, the police department's highest ranking Black, to seek the vacant police chief position. Napper, now nearing sixty, had a long and distinguished career in the Hartford Police Department. Besides being the department's first Black sergeant, Napper was the first Black lieutenant, and the first Black captain. But because of his loyalty to Assistant Chief Jimmy Heslin, who he knew desired the chief's position, Napper choose not to become a candidate. To the surprise of many, what Major Napper did was announce his own retirement.

With Peach out, the city council held a confirmation hearing on W. Wilson Gaitor as the new city manager. In its history, Hartford had never had a Black city manager. Gaitor had served as supervisor of the city's Northside Service Center for the previous five city managers. The center was located on Westland Street in the North End of Hartford. Working out of his second-floor office, Gaitor was responsible for overseeing housing code inspections, welfare programs, youth services, and employment programs. Once the word got out that Gaitor would be the next city manager, it was met with mixed reviews in the Black community.

"The choice of Gaitor is an excellent one," said Francisco Borges, president of the Greater Hartford Black Democratic Club.

State Representative Abraham Giles said of Gaitor: "He knows the community here. He's been through the good times and the bad." Still, there were those who weren't so sure.

"Gaitor hasn't been a forceful enough advocate for the North End at city hall," said one.

"He's been sitting up there for ten years as that part of the city deteriorated around him," said another.

State Representative Thirman Milner offered yet another perspective. "My fear is that it may be a token movement to pacify the Black community. I hope he's not being used." Some were concerned that appointing a Black city manager would make it more difficult for me to be appointed fire chief. Others, however, believed that Gaitor's appointment would likely improve my chances. It could be they heard Gaitor's earlier statement that I would be good for the job. In an effort to sidetrack a Gaitor appointment, Republican Councilman Sidney Gardner released a list naming other possible Black candidates for the job as city manager. His list included Dr. Frederick Adams, president of the Urban League of Greater Hartford; Dr. Edythe Gaines, the former Hartford school superintendent; and Ben Andrews, the director of the Upper Albany Community Organization. My name also was on the list. No one took this list seriously.

On July 1, 1980, history was made in the city of Hartford when Woodrow Wilson Gaitor was sworn in as the city's first Black city manager. With his quiet dignified manner and strong religious beliefs, Gaitor was a man for whom I had developed a great respect. He had come to Hartford some twenty years earlier to work as supervisor of Parks and Recreation, and now as city manager, he was the city's top executive. This was a long way from the neighborhood in East St. Louis, Illinois, where he was born in 1918. Back then, his father was so elated over President Woodrow Wilson's order that no new fathers be drafted into the army, that he named his newborn son after the president. At the time of Woodrow's birth, his father, Shelly Gaitor, owned a small restaurant and an adjacent poultry store where he sold live chickens. During the Depression both businesses suffered and eventually had to shut down. Woodrow was ten when his father sat him and his older brother down and told them in his most solemn voice, "We've got to tighten up." So the brothers no longer received their one-dollar weekly allowance. For lunch each day, little Woodrow's mother prepared bread slices smeared with butter and dipped in boiled prunes or peaches.

"There was nothing you could compare it with," Gaitor later recalled. "Everybody was poor."

As the Great Depression continued, Shelly Gaitor moved his family to Cincinnati, Ohio, where he found work. There Woodrow Gaitor attended integrated public schools, where he frequently experienced racial discrimination. In high school, for example, swimming classes for Black students were scheduled on Friday, the day the pool was scheduled to be drained and cleaned. This prevented White students from having to swim in the same water that Blacks had swum in. Neither did being the school's star basketball player prevent Woodrow from being left behind when his team played White schools in nearby Kentucky. After graduating high school, Woodrow found a job working at a grocery store. The fact that this store had never had a Black employee didn't bother Woodrow, or any of the store's customers.

"Customers would just come in for a product, they didn't see your face, you're just waiting on them," he recalled. "The staff was where I would have the problem. They would say, 'Hey, Woodrow, you don't use that towel, that's the towel everyone else is using. You take this separate one.' I didn't think about it during the day, but later when I was home reflecting on the day, it kind of got to me."

After completing four years of study at Florida A&M University in Tallahassee, Gaitor was drafted into the US Army. One of his recollections during World War II was of fighting German soldiers in a field in France, with bombs exploding close by. One bomb exploded twenty feet from where he was huddled with other soldiers. Several of the soldiers, including Gaitor, were injured by flying shrapnel. One soldier had both his legs blown off. For acts of bravery under fire, Gaitor was promoted to first sergeant and awarded three Battle Stars and a Purple Heart. He would later reflect on the irony of fighting for democracy on foreign soil while in a segregated army. He had hoped that serving his country would help end injustices against Blacks back home. But after being discharged in 1943 and returning to the United States, he found that fighting for his country had not made any difference. He still faced the same racial prejudice he had experienced all his life.

He returned to Cincinnati and played several years of basketball for a semiprofessional all-Black team. Then in 1946 he moved to Roanoke, Virginia, where he broke the color barrier by being hired as that city's first Black policeman. It was during this time that Gaitor was involved in an incident that shook him deeply and later caused him to pursue a different career. One Halloween night while patrolling a Black neighborhood, Gaitor was attacked by three youths. One stabbed Gaitor in the shoulder while another swung at him with a blackjack. During the struggle Gaitor fired his gun, killing one of his attackers. He later learned that the boy he had shot was just fifteen. This prompted Gaitor to resign from the police force and take a job as that city's director of Negro Recreation. After eleven years on the job, he applied and was hired by the City of Hartford as supervisor of Parks and Recreation. Gaitor later studied municipal administration at the International City Manager's Association. When he completed his study, he was appointed special assistant to Hartford's city manager. Now he was Hartford's chief executive.

Some of his critics believed the new city manager had "been programmed for failure."

"He will not survive," one of them predicted.

"Not only was he part of the old line of management which had departed in the past year from city hall, but the fact is the developments that will take place in this city do not contemplate a Black man in that vital position," intoned another. For the Republican members of the city council, their present gripe was that Gaitor did not live in Hartford.

"An East Hartford resident should not be allowed to hold a position in Hartford's government," they exclaimed. Despite these predictions and objections, Gaitor was the city manager. He immediately turned his attention to the most pressing tasks before him—the naming of a fire chief and a police chief. City Manager Gaitor was aware that different groups had different expectations about who should fill these top positions.

"Rather than leave the screening process to subordinates, I will screen the applicants myself," he announced, "because my head is on the block." The city manager promised city residents that he would fill the two positions within the next fifteen to twenty days. During the next two weeks, he screened the applicants—fourteen for police chief, and the six top finishers of the fire chief exam. I tried not to dwell upon the fact that I had come in seventh.

Sometimes when you finish taking a test and you do well, you just know it. That's how I had felt after completing the oral test for fire chief. And that's why I couldn't help but continue to have an uneasy feeling in my gut about my seventh-place finish. As he sat behind his desk one morning, City Manager Gaitor began going through some folders left behind by the former city manager. Noticing one of the folders was labeled "Fire Chief Test Results," Gaitor opened the folder and began reading. As he read, he noticed that on the test results of Captain John B. Stewart Jr., the original score had been crossed over with a large X, and another score inserted in its place. Upon closer inspection, and to his amazement, the test scores revealed that Captain Stewart had finished not number seven, but number one. Someone had crossed out my first-place finish and moved me down to number seven.

After realizing what had taken place, City Manager Gaitor immediately sent for me. When I arrived at his office and took a seat, a stern-faced Gaitor shared with me what he had discovered in the "Fire Chief Test Results" folder.

"Well, I'll be darn." This was all I could think of to say, and so I repeated it, this time shaking my head in disbelief that someone would have done such a thing. "I'll be darn." Then I became angry and wondered why the former city manager had done this. Did he dislike me that much? Was it because I was Black? He had made a promise to the Black community that if I placed among the top three, I would be strongly considered for the position. Why did he lie? Why did he move me from number one to number seven?

"Son of a gun." I shook my head in disbelief and disgust. My mind went back to the day Art Johnson called me into his office and told me I had finished seventh. I remembered the pain of hearing his words. Had Johnson not seen the test results? Why did City Manager Peach ask Art to be the bearer of bad news? Had Art just taken the city manager's word about my seventh-place finish? Thinking back on our long friendship, I couldn't believe that Art would knowingly be involved in something like this. Before leaving his office, Gaitor assured me that I would be interviewed for the position. I could only thank the good Lord when City Manager Gaitor made the announcement that he would "stand by his commitment to promote from within."

My mother, Mattie Baker

L) Teenage Mattie Baker, her
mother Lela Baker, and her sister.

My godfather Walter Murray

Me at age six or seven

My graduation picture from
Weaver High—1948

Me as a naval reservist,
1950 or 1951

Gladys's mother, Florence Strong

Faith Congregational Church

Me and Gladys on our honeymoon   John B. Stewart Sr.

Family photo taken after I made lieutenant in 1967.
From left, Wendy, Gregory, Jeffrey,
me, Holly, Gladys, Donald, John III.

254

The christening of Jeffrey. From left, Florence Strong, Rev. James Wright, Gladys, Tottie, me, and Henry Times

Me and Tweet celebrating my promotion to lieutenant in 1967.

Me at opening of Black Fire Fighter's Convention, October 1970, Hartford, Connecticut.

Me working in Special Services

Me with neighborhood youth
neighborhood satellite office.

Me after receiving captain's
badge from Chief Fennelly.

Me and W. Wilson Gaitor at
Gaitor's retirement celebration.

Me being interviewed   Me at press conference with   John B. Stewart Jr.
    at scene of fire   Police Chief Bernard Sullivan   Firehouse

TOP OF THE LADDER

The names of the two men selected to be Hartford's next fire chief and police chief were a closely guarded secret. They were to be released to the public at a press conference scheduled for one o'clock in the afternoon, Saturday, August 2, 1980. Only Mayor Anthanson, members of the city council, and the two selectees had been told in advance. City Manager Gaitor had sat at his marble-topped desk the night before and wrote two names on a sheet of paper. He then made nine copies and placed one copy in nine separate envelopes. A police officer then delivered a sealed envelope to the home of the mayor and to each member of the city council.

As the press conference was about to get underway, city and state elected and appointed officials, community leaders, family members, reporters, friends, and curious onlookers crowded into city hall's large function room. Feelings were running high, and many expected history to be made in Hartford on this day. Not only was the city manager to name both a police chief and fire chief on the same day, but there also was a strong feeling that the fire chief would be Black. While City Manager Gaitor was a person who kept his personal thoughts concerning race mainly to himself, he very much wanted to open doors of city government that had been closed to Blacks. Presently, only two of the eight city department heads were Black: Art Johnson at the Department of Human Resources, and John Wardlaw at the Hartford Housing Authority.

At one o'clock the crowded room fell silent as the city manager entered, followed by Mayor Athanson, Deputy Mayor Ludgin, and

City Clerk Robert Galivan. Before naming the appointees, Gaitor told the gathering that during his interviews, he was impressed with the amount of talent within both the police and fire departments.

"That bodes well for those not chosen today," he said. "It means they still have a shot at it the next time around." He asked that the two appointees he was about to name be given the support of second-level people and cooperation from the fire and police union officials. When he concluded his remarks, he said, "Today I am naming Lieutenant George W. Sicaras to the position of chief of the Hartford Police Department." Sicaras came forward and stood beside the city manager. Gaitor thanked Sicaras for his twenty-one years of dedicated service to the Hartford Police Department, and his splendid record of leadership. Gaitor pinned the gold chief's badge to Sicaras' jacket and shook his hand. Sicaras then raised his right hand and received the oath of office from the city clerk. There were words of congratulations, handshakes and applause. The room fell silent.

Gaitor began speaking. "I would like to leave with a record that says to the community, 'Don't be afraid to put a Black in here if he's qualified. Don't be afraid to put any individual in a position because of color. The color angle, throw it out the window! It's been proven that we can do it.' Today I'm naming Captain John B. Stewart Jr. as chief of the Hartford Fire Department." Even though I had been informed earlier of my selection, it is still hard to describe the feeling that came over me when I heard my name called. There was applause and cheers as I went and stood beside the city manager. "Congratulations," Gaitor said, shaking my hand. I shook hands with the mayor and deputy mayor. "I'm not appointing you because we know each other," the city manager said. "I'm appointing you because I believe you have the skills and the knowledge to surround yourself with the best, and for you to turn the Hartford Fire Department around." He then called Gladys forward, and she pinned the gold fire chief's badge to my jacket. Then with my right hand raised, I received the oath of office.

I needed a moment to let it sink. I was chief of the Hartford Fire Department. It had been a long hard climb, but I was at the top. Thoughts began swirling around in my head. The black beds, the segregated kitchens, the unfriendly looks, the courage of the six Black fire fighters hired in 1948, it had not all been in vain. No, my climb to the top was for every Black Hartford fire fighter who had faced discrimination. Then the sound of the city manager's voice brought me back to the present.

"We intend to give the people of Hartford first-class delivery of police and fire services," he was telling the audience. When my turn came to speak, I put on my most confident face as I thanked the city manager for the honor of being named chief of the Hartford Fire Department.

"I am both humbled and proud at being selected," I said. "This is what America is all about. For those who think the city manager appointed me because I am his friend, I know in my mind he appointed me because he has faith in me. And because I was number one on the test."

Standing in the crowd, a smiling Francisco Borges, president of the Greater Hartford Black Democratic Club, said to a reporter, "This naturally restores my faith. This is an American dream come true. There couldn't be a better person for this job."

When the press conference ended, I shook hands and accepted the congratulations of well-wishers. Two months earlier I had turned fifty years old. Now I was the twenty-seventh fire chief in the history of the Hartford Fire Department. This was what the civil rights movement was about. This was the cause for which Martin Luther King and others in the civil rights movement had dedicated their lives. I knew that lots of eyes would be watching me, and I would have to prove myself. I was now in command. I was responsible for the entire operation of the city's fire department, charged with protecting life and property from fire. I was responsible for the enforcement of all laws, ordinances, and regulations relating to fire prevention and fire safety. As an educated fire manager, I would have to draw upon all the experience I had been fortunate enough to acquire, and I would perform my job well.

When asked to comment on my appointment after the press conference Thomas Wright, president of the Hartford Chapter of the NAACP responded, "The city is now moving in the right direction."

When asked to comment Union President Rudolph Fiorillo, responded, "I'll just wait and see."

A few hours later, I was sitting behind my desk at fire department headquarters preparing to hold my first staff meeting as fire chief. This would only be a brief meeting with my assistant and deputy chiefs to talk about reassignments I wanted to make. The reassignments involved twenty-four Hispanic fire fighters who had graduated from the fire training school the day before I was appointed chief. I had personally recruited these men. They were the first Hispanics hired by the fire department. I was determined to recruit them after an unfortunate incident between the fire service and the Hispanic community. A twelve-year-old Hispanic boy was playing in a vacant garage when the roof collapsed, burying him beneath the rubble. The fire fighters searching for the boy could not speak Spanish, and were accused by Hispanics at the scene of being insensitive to their anguish. In what seemed to the parents like an unbearable amount of time, the fire fighters found the boy's lifeless body. A local Hispanic social agency filed a lawsuit calling for the city to hire Hispanic fire fighters.

After recruiting them, I intended to place them in firehouses in Hispanic neighborhoods. Acting Chief Gallon, however, assigned them to various firehouses around the city. Now that I was chief, I would go ahead with my original plans. I also planned to reassign two lieutenants to the training academy. After we drew up the reassignment list, I went home. That evening neighbors and friends called and came by to offer congratulations. With the many thoughts and emotions I was experiencing, it took awhile for me to fall asleep that night.

The next morning I was back at fire headquarters. It was my usual habit to be at Faith Congregational Church on Sunday, but I wanted to go over the list of reassignments again before circulating it on Monday. As I sat there, I could feel the weight of the chief's badge pinned to my jacket. With it came the responsibility of appointing and removing officers and employees of the department; assigning people to their posts, shifts, details, and duties; the responsibility for making rules and regulations concerning the operation of the department and the conduct of all officers and employees; the efficiency, discipline, and good conduct of the department; and the care and custody of all property used by the department. I would handle all of these responsibilities, and in addition I would make the department more community-oriented.

At the Monday morning roll call, fire fighters were notified of the reassignments I had made. In less than one hour, I received a phone call from the union president. This would be the first of many run-ins between Rudolph Fiorillo and me.

"What kind of relationship do you expect to have with Fiorillo?" a reporter had asked me after my appointment.

"We'll have a happy marriage," I had replied.

"Chief Stewart," I said, after picking up the phone. "With these illegal transfers, you have circumvented civil service requirements that provide all fire fighters with the opportunity to compete for new jobs," Fiorillo said angrily. So much for a happy marriage, I thought. His reference was to the two lieutenants I had transferred to the training academy. I had done so because I wanted to emphasize the importance of training and fire preventions activities. The problem, I was to learn later, was that there were no job classifications for the job I wanted the two lieutenants to do. Nor was there a provision in the city budget for training academy lieutenants. "According to the union contract," Fiorillo continued in a stern, slightly raised voice, "such transfers would have to be negotiated." After he hung up I received a phone call from William Darcy, the city's assistant corporation counsel. He too had heard from an irate Fiorillo.

"The problem," Darcy explained to me, "is that the two lieutenants were assigned to positions which really don't exist." I realized then I had made a mistake.

"I hope it was an honest mistake," Fiorillo said, when I informed him that the transfers would be canceled. Several days later the *Hartford Courant* ran an article with the headline, "Chief Gets Burned on Changes." This was the first of many occasions that the union president and I would face-off over the issue of labor relations.

In September, a month after I was appointed chief, a reporter from the *New York Times* came to Hartford to interview me. He was planning to write a story about my appointment as Hartford's first Black fire chief, and the fire department's relationship with the minority community.

"This was probably the touchiest summer I've witnessed, inclusive of 1968," I told the reporter. "Not only with the tension surrounding the appointment of a fire chief, but there were also several occasions where firemen were pelted with rocks and bottles." While the tension has eased, I told him, the city is now faced with a serious arson problem in some neighborhoods with little capacity to investigate them. This is because the streets are crime-ridden and not safe for our plain-clothes arson investigators to be out there in unmarked cars. So now they wear uniforms and are clearly identified as firemen, which could conceivably make them targets, I said.

When I made chief, the city of Hartford was having serious money problems. City officials were scrambling to find ways to reduce spending. I was called to meet with the city council's Operations, Management, and Budget Committee, whose members wanted to reduce the fire department budget. One cost-cutting measure that came up at the meeting was the possibility of closing a firehouse. This was not the first time this idea had been mentioned as a way to help bring the city budget in line. I also knew how unpopular this idea was with the union and with many community people.

"I don't like the idea of closing any company," I said, "because the effect on response time would be serious. It may be feasible in the future, but the need now is to beef up what we have." Jacob Ukeles, who a month earlier had directed a study for the Citizens Committee for Effective Government, was present at this meeting and disagreed with me.

"According to our study, the response time in the city of Hartford would still be considered a reasonable range," he said. "My committee also has ideas concerning technological advances in false alarms and smoke detectors. We would like the fire department to rethink the technology of fire protection and devote more of its resources to new and better equipment and a program to control false alarms and to promote use of smoke detectors. The city should consider either requiring property owners to install smoke detectors or buying detectors to supply to residents," he continued. "A major program of smoke detectors can have a major impact on the loss of property and loss of life. Also, changing the current system of box alarms to a system of voice or phone alarms probably would help solve the city's serious false alarm problem."

Ukeles was right about the false alarm problem. False alarms now plagued the fire department. In the 1979–1980 fiscal year, there were 8,724 false alarms, representing over 57 percent of the fire department's calls for services. In certain neighborhoods the false alarms were almost constant. This was especially true in the public housing projects. We could count on people pulling alarms in Rice Heights and Nelton Court, in Bellevue Square and Charter Oak Terrace, in Dutch Point and Stowe Village. A few years earlier, Special Services had started a public relations patrol with the goal of reducing false alarms. Working with the police department's juvenile division, we put ultraviolet paste on a firebox handle and then sat in our car waiting to see if any kids would pull the handle and set off the alarm. When we witnessed a kid pulling the handle, we apprehended him, took his name, and then took him home to talk with his parents. We called for a member of the police department's juvenile division to meet us at the home. If the kid denied pulling the alarm, we would shine a light on his hand, revealing the ultraviolet paste. In 50 percent of the cases, embarrassed parents took care of the situation right then and there. If the kid had a police record, he was arrested and lectured about the dangers of such actions.

Special Services, now under the leadership of Captain Richard Epps, continued to educate the public, especially youngsters, on the dangers and consequences of false alarms. They continued going to schools and recreation centers, and putting up posters explaining that pulling a false alarm was against the law, and could cause loss of life

Because most fires in the city were called in by people using their telephone, we also began removing neighborhood fire alarm boxes. We did leave fire alarm boxes in neighborhoods where fewer people tended to have telephones in their homes. Still, the number of false alarms was too high. When Ukeles finished speaking, I told them that the fire department had already begun a pilot program replacing about one hundred box alarms with seventy-five voice alarms, using money from a federal grant. I also told them I would discuss all these matters with my chiefs, but that I still thought closing a fire station was not something we should pursue. When I left the meeting, I realized that as fire chief, I was now the first line of defense against any government cost-cutting measures at the expense of the fire department.

Since the fire department and police department are both charged with the public safety, I met with Police Chief Sicaras to explore ways that our departments might be able to work together. This led to a second meeting at the fire department training academy in October 1980. This time we included members of our staff. This first-of-a-kind meeting was for the purpose of getting acquainted and opening lines of communication between the two departments.

"This is the first of what Chief Sicaras and I hope will be regular joint staff meetings to identify, discuss, and solve mutual problems," I said. "We want to get back to basics. We want to achieve good communication at the top levels of the departments so that we will be able to improve delivery of services at the bottom levels." During the meeting we decided to assign members of both departments to various sub-committees to deal with specific areas of mutual concern. These areas included eliminating police response to some fire calls, providing emergency medical service, and knowing whom to contact in the other department in critical situations. Other concerns were arson investigations, false alarms and accidental lockouts from houses. Before ending the meeting, we decided to meet together every two months. Chief Sicaras and I were both pleased that the two departments were breaking new ground together.

Even though Gladys was urging me to do so, there was a matter I choose not to bring up with Police Chief Sicaras. This had to do with assigning me police protection. Since becoming fire chief, I had been receiving threatening letters at the fire station, and hate-filled phone calls at home. One thing the letters and phone calls had in common was the reference to me as a so-and-so "nigger unqualified to be Hartford's fire chief." The calls were so racist and profanity-laced that my wife stopped answering the phone at home. When I began receiving the death threats, Phoenix Society members volunteered to serve as my bodyguards, but I declined their offer.

Chief Sicaras knew about the calls and letters, and the police were quietly conducting their own investigation. I just didn't think police protection was necessary. What was more of a concern to me was the growing rift between me and the union president, which had come to the attention of the city manager. The *Hartford Courant* was also aware of the confrontations and carried an article with the headline, "Honeymoon Looks Over for Chief." While reading the article, I thought to myself, what honeymoon. The union president had his mind set against me from the start. In the newspaper article, he was demanding that the city bargain with the union before I be allowed to make any changes in the fire department. This demand resulted from my decision to establish several committees to address reoccurring problems.

"Appointing union members to committees puts them in management positions and undermines their connection to the union," decried Fiorillo. This matter would eventually be settled by the State Labor Relations Board.

Another matter had to do with the chief's aide. Just prior to my appointment as chief, Chief Fennelly had promoted Nelson Carter to the rank of lieutenant. Carter began serving a three-month probationary period as chief's aide. He was the first Black fire fighter in the department to hold this position. The chief's aide was responsible for picking up the chief at his home in the morning, driving the chief to his various appointments throughout the day, and taking the chief back home. While this was a detailed position, when Lieutenant Carter's three-month probationary period was over, I decided to keep him as my aide. Besides being the chief's driver, I gave him other assignments, including taking care of clothing orders, maintaining the level of supplies, and making sure I kept my appointments with my administrative assistant.

When Fiorillo learned I had kept Lieutenant Carter beyond his probationary period, he filed a complaint with the State Labor Relations Board. In his complaint, Fiorillo stated that I had violated the union contract by keeping a detailed person out of position for over six months. While this matter was still before the Labor Relations Board, I decided to create a new permanent executive officer position. After getting this new position included in the fire department budget, I moved Lieutenant Carter from the chief's aide position to the newly created executive officer position. Then I brought on Lieutenant Thomas Jacobucci as chief's aide and rotated him and two other lieutenants as chief's aide every three months.

Later, when Lieutenant Carter was elevated to the rank of deputy chief, I made Lieutenant Jacobucci my executive officer. One reason for making Jacobucci executive officer was because he and Fiorillo were close friends. I could then send messages through Jacobucci to Fiorillo, and Fiorillo would send messages to me. With Jacobucci working close to me and serving as my unofficial liaison to the union, I was hoping I had found a way to ease the tension between me and the union president.

As far as I knew, the fire department had never done its own administrative work. The administrative work had always been done by staff people in the municipal building. This included preparation of the department's budget. I wanted to change this. I felt we could do the needed administrative functions at department headquarters. The only operation on the third floor at the Pearl Street headquarters was the dispatch center, which occupied only a third of the space. So I had the third floor remodeled and moved my office and the assistant chief's office from the second to the third floor. I also moved my secretary, the administrative office, and the operations and civil preparedness offices to the third floor. Once these moves were all completed, we had a better flow of communication and a more efficient headquarters.

We then began doing our own administrative work, including preparing our budget. This was a change I hoped the Citizens Committee for Effective Government would appreciate. In February 1981, seven months after I became chief, I prepared and submitted my first budget report to the city council budget committee. At the time money for the fire department came from two sources: the capital budget and the operations budget. The capital budget was allocated for capital improvements, like purchasing new apparatus and equipment. From this budget source, there was a projected overrun of $193,840. The operating budget, which funded the day-to-day operations, had an overrun of $560,000. In total, my budget showed a projected overrun of $753,840.

After studying the capital budget section, John Eichner, the fire department's management services officer, question the accuracy of my figures. "The projected overrun contains $85,000 that had been deferred from the 1979–80 fiscal year," he said. After looking, City Budget Director Lee Erdman agreed.

"The report fails to show that the fire department deferred spending $85,000 in the last fiscal year, and included that money in this budget. This is not an overrun," Eichner said.

"The real overrun," said Eichner, was from the purchase of an aerial ladder obtained last fall that exceeded its projected cost by $63,000. There was also the purchase of a van for $1,000 more than what was projected. So "sixty-four thousand dollars is the real overrun," he concluded.

We then looked at the operations budget. I explained the projected overrun there resulted from an increase in overtime—specifically from raising staff levels for platoons on two aerial ladders and an engine company in Frog Hollow.

"It will cost sixty thousand dollars per company to have those extra men on every shift. Other overtime costs result from the transfer of some personnel from fire fighting positions to fire prevention, signal and alarm, and training units," I continued. "When I became chief, the overtime budget had been over expended by more than one-hundred thousand dollars because of a delay in training forty-seven new men. Another reason for the overtime costs was the high percentage of fire fighters who get three or four weeks paid vacation a year. Also, the failure of the forty-seven additional men to substantially reduce overtime, as was predicted when they finished training in August, led the city manager to allow me to train sixteen more men. They graduated this past December, and these additions have produced reductions in overtime. In fact, overtime was down last week to about four thousand dollars," I concluded.

The committee received my report with the hope that I could further reduce the operating budget during the year. I thought it ironic that at the very moment I was in this budget meeting trying to find cost reductions, the city was negotiating a new contract with union officials who were demanding they give more money to fire fighters.

The union president seemed always to be looking to engage me in a confrontation. At the end of February, the battle lines were clearly drawn around another issue. What I thought was a routine appointment had now become a clash of wills. This latest issue had to do with my appointment of a new fire marshal. Fire Marshal Ralph Marone, who had been instrumental in organizing the fire fighters union and was closely aligned with the union president, retired the previous September. I planned to appoint Captain Carl Booker to the vacant position. Booker had worked in the fire prevention bureau for more than ten years, and was presently serving as acting fire marshal. In terms of hierarchy, this was the number three position in the fire department.

When the job announcement was issued the union objected to its wording, claiming it favored Booker. The announcement called for the applicant to have already been certified by the state fire marshal and city clerk as able to perform the job. The union's objection forced the city personnel department to issue a second job announcement in place of the first. The second announcement stated that the applicant must be able to obtain state certification by taking a course or passing a test. When I was questioned by a reporter, I explained that when the first announcement came out some people were upset because it appeared to be locked in for Captain Booker.

"I had no intention of restricting the field of applicants," I told the reporter. "So we made the changes in order to make more people eligible." Captain Booker and four other fire fighters applied for the position and took the oral examination.

When the examinations were graded, Captain Booker came out on top. As a result, I intended to offer him the fire marshal position. He would be the first Black fire marshal in the history of the Hartford Fire Department. On the day I planned to make the appointment, two Republicans on the city council asked that I not make it until an investigation could be conducted. They had received a letter from Union President Fiorillo asking the council and the city attorneys to investigate how the civil service system was being interpreted in the fire department.

Fiorillo also stated in his letter that "the only consistent actions of the Personnel Department of the city of Hartford are their total inconsistencies." He complained that Carl Booker and I were close friends and even lived on the same block. The inference was that I was favoring a close personal friend. Nonetheless, my position was that I had offered the job to Captain Booker, and he had accepted. As far as I was concerned that settled it. If the union president wanted to take the matter to the State Labor Board, he was free to do so.

Ten months after becoming fire chief, I was ready to begin work on another one of the Citizen's Committee for Effective Government cost-cutting recommendations. The committee had recommended that the fire department take measures to improve both its technology and its equipment. So I had on my priority list the need to update some of the older fire stations, and some of the older apparatus. The ladder and pumper trucks were at least twenty years old and outdated. On occasion one of them would break down on the way to a fire. While these pieces needed to be replaced, other apparatus just needed to be refurbished.

Before purchasing any new apparatus, I thought it wise to find out what apparatus fire departments in cities the size of Hartford had purchased in recent years. The fire department in Syracuse, New York, was the one I decided to give a closer look. Syracuse's fire department had reorganized in the 1970s, reducing the number of fire companies while increasing the manpower and apparatus levels. Syracuse's size in square miles and population, as well as the size of its fire department, was similar to Hartford. Syracuse had 190,000 residents and covered twenty-six square miles. Hartford had 140,000 residents and covered eighteen square miles. While Syracuse had eighty-seven fire fighters per shift, Hartford had eighty-one.

Because of these similarities and the success of their reorganization, I arranged to lead a six-man study team to Syracuse. The Hartford team members included John Eichner, the fire department's management service officer; Deputy Chief Salvatore Visconti; Fire Equipment Superintendent Arthur Hanson; Acting Training Officer Captain Raymond McTeague; and City Budget Director Lee Erdman. For two days in June 1981, we studied how the Syracuse reorganization had been done, how effective it was, and whether or not we could do something similar in Hartford. We learned that Syracuse had been successful in raising $2.8 million through bonding measures. The city had erected seven new fire stations and purchased thirteen new fire engines and seven new hundred-foot aerial ladders.

There were a number of other changes initiated by the Syracuse Fire Department that I found interesting. For example, the Syracuse Fire Department has its two seven-man units housed in one central station, and sends them to all building fires. They also used automatic light controls that enable responding apparatus to always go through intersections on the green light, reducing the chance of accidents and providing faster response times. Most interesting was that the Syracuse Fire Department was doing with four men what it took the Hartford Fire Department seven men to accomplish.

When we returned to Hartford, I formed a redeployment task force to study what we could do in our department to improve deployment. I wanted to have input from neighborhood people, from members of the Committee for Effective City Government, and the union. When the union president heard I was looking at the possibility of reorganizing the fire department, his response, as expected, was negative.

"Stewart is a puppet of those people at city hall who want to reduce manning," he griped, "and this union wants no part of his redeployment task force." What apparently did not matter to him was that if redeployment happened, it would mean additional resources for the fire department. The redeployment task force went to work developing a four-year apparatus replacement program and looking at redeployment possibilities.

It was all smiles in August 1981, as I stood in a circle of about fifty people drinking punch and making small talk. Family members, friends, and fellow fire fighters had gathered at headquarters to celebrate my first year as chief. I was especially pleased to have members of my fire department Chaplain Corps at the gathering. The Chaplain Corps was an organization I really wanted to get up and running because I understood its value. It had declined and gone out of existence five years earlier. One of my goals when I became chief was to revive the Chaplain Corps. I first recruited Reverend Joseph Zezzo, a Congregational minister, and then Father Stephen Foley, a Catholic priest. They were present, along with Rabbi Hans Godenheimer, Reverend Charles Blake, my minister at Faith Church, and Father Robert Grace, the priest at St. Michael's.

These chaplains represented the three major religious groups in Hartford— Catholic, Protestant, and Jewish. If a fire fighter was injured or killed, the chaplains would be there to offer emotional or religious support to their families. If a fire fighter felt the need for pastoral counseling, a chaplain would provide it. This was why having fire department chaplains was important to me. The chaplains also regularly visited the firehouses and encouraged fire fighters to contact them to discuss any job-related problems. Each chaplain was issued a dress-blue uniform with cap, a shield that read "Chaplain," and a radio to listen for emergency calls. The chaplains were not paid; they volunteered their services and posted their phone numbers where they could be reached day or night. Despite the skeptics, I felt my first year as Hartford's fire chief had been very productive.

For several months I had been working with my deputy chiefs on a restructuring plan to improve the communication flow between companies, and between all department levels. The plan we were devising would also improve operations and decentralize the decision-making process within the department. I saw this restructuring as necessary after the city experienced several serious fires the previous April, May, and June. The three-alarm fire in April ripped through several apartment buildings at Judson and Clark Streets in the North End, displacing a large number of families. In May seventy-five people were rescued at a three-alarm fire in a four-story brick apartment house in the West End. Fire fighters arriving at the scene early in the morning had discovered two separate fires in the building stairwells, in what was determined to be an act of arson. Ten people were taken to the hospital, and about one hundred people were left homeless. In June a fire engulfed a building on Belden Street, resulting in permanent injuries to several fire fighters.

In all, there would be 834 fires in the city during my first year as chief, representing a 19 percent increase from the year before. Three hundred and ninety-nine of them were incendiary building fires, representing an increase of 29 percent. The dollar loss to fire was over $4 million—a new record for the city. At the time the Hartford Fire Department had twenty fire companies divided into three districts, with 454 fire fighters. The need for better communications throughout the entire fire department had long been a concern of previous fire chiefs. So I called together my deputy chiefs to study how we could establish a better flow of communications.

Once our study was complete, it revealed that in order to have better communications, there needed to be a restructuring of fire department operations. So we developed a restructuring plan that would not only improve communication between companies, but also improve the communication flow between all department levels. It would also improve operations and decentralize the decision-making process, and make for a more efficient and effective fire department. Once implemented, our plan restructured the Hartford Fire Department into the following configuration:

HARTFORD FIRE DEPARTMENT
TABLE OF ORGANIZATION: 1981–1982

Management Services Unit   (3-person unit)

Fire Suppression Bureau   (Under command of assistant fire chief)
Fire Fighting Division
Training Division
      Engine Company Response Districts
      Ladder Company Response Districts
      Deputy Chief Response Districts

Fire Prevention Bureau   (Supervised by fire prevention chief)
Inspectional Services Unit
Fire & Arson Investigation Unit
Records Unit

Support Services Bureau
Communications Division
Building Maintenance Division
Equipment Maintenance Division
Special Services Division
Civil Preparedness Division

Synopsis of Responsibilities of Units, Bureaus & Divisions
The Management Services Unit: This Unit assists the Fire Chief and
Bureau and Division heads in managing the delivery of fire services.
The general duties of this three-person unit include planning, budget-
ing, operations analyses, grantsmanship, financial administration and
report preparation.

The Fire Suppression Bureau: This Bureau is under the command of
the Assistant Fire Chief. The department's largest division is under
this Bureau: the Fire Fighting Division. In this Division there are four
groups of fire fighters manning twenty fire companies. There are three
district deputy chiefs per shift. There are fourteen engine companies
and six ladder companies located at thirteen fire stations.

The Training Division: This Division trains recruits, gives classroom
instruction to line fire fighters, provides instruction to private indus-
try and businesses, and schedules event days at the Training Academy.

The Fire Prevention Bureau: This Bureau is supervised by the Fire
Prevention Chief, who also serves as Fire Marshal. Within this Bureau
is the Inspectional Services Unit with a primary function of State Fire

Code Enforcer. The Unit inspects all city structures once a year, and ensures facilities are operating with the proper permits and licenses.

The Fire and Arson Investigation Unit: This Unit is responsible for the investigation of all fires in the City of Hartford, particularly those determined to be incendiary.

The Communications Division: This Division is responsible for the maintenance of all the emergency and administrative communications systems, plus all 280 city traffic signals.

The Building Maintenance Division: This Division is charged with the operation, maintenance and general repair of the fifteen fire department buildings.

The Equipment Maintenance Division: This Division is responsible for the repair and upkeep of the department's 60 vehicles (apparatus, maintenance trucks and department cars) and all other equipment including seven stationary generators.

The Special Services Division: This Division is responsible for fire safety for the public through preventive fire education. It is also charged with the tasks of keeping abreast of current national and local trends in the fire service, and dissemination of such information to top management.

The Civil Preparedness Division: is responsible for the upkeep of the city's emergency and disaster plans, annexes, and for the emergency shelters.

Reorganizing the fire department did result in one exasperating incident that I would rather sooner forget. The reorganization meant I had to move some people around and assign them different duties.

One of the deputy chiefs I brought downtown and made a shift commander was constantly giving me guff about his new responsibilities with no accompanying pay increase. He accused me of using him. Because he felt he should have been made fire chief instead of me, it made him miserable to have to look at me every day. After a while I grew tired of his bad attitude and his attempts at intimidating me and others.

One day he made the mistake of walking into my office uninvited and closing the door behind him. He immediately started giving me guff about some aspect of his present assignment. As he continued talking, I guess I lost my cool. I've never admitted to having put my hands on him. When people ask, I say that when I opened my office door, he lost his balance.

When my secretary was questioned about it, she said, "I was concerned about him being in the chief's office with the door shut." Then she added, "I didn't see anything. I saw him fall out. I thought maybe he tripped." But the truth is, I opened the door and shoved him out. That incident did straighten him out, and he stopped speaking to me. He later bypassed me and submitted his retirement papers to my assistant chief.

"He doesn't want to see you," the assistant chief told me.

Well, I didn't want to see him either. All I could say was, "He's gone, good."

In November 1981 Hartford experienced another groundbreaking event. Using "Why Not Milner for Mayor?" as his campaign theme, Thirman L Milner beat out Mayor George Athanson to become the city's first Black mayor. Except for Milner himself, no one could have imagined a year earlier the possibility of a Black man sitting in the mayor's seat. Milner had been cautioned by the local NAACP leadership not to run.

"You'll be wasting the Black vote," he was told. "You would do better to run for city council." It was this reaction, rather than a show of support, that made Milner more determined to run. At first it appeared Milner had lost the primary when the votes were counted and Athanson came out ninety-four votes ahead. However, Milner believed some absentee ballots had not been counted and called for an investigation. Sure enough, an investigation by election officials revealed that Milner had a legitimate reason for concern. Irregularities had taken place in the absentee ballot count. Election officials gave Milner the choice of either taking the matter to court and having a judge make a ruling, or requesting a new primary election. Milner did not want to become Hartford's mayor by a court ruling. He wanted to win by popular vote, so he chose to take part in a second primary.

This time when the primary votes were counted, Milner came out on top by more than two thousand votes. In November Milner won the general election. I was so elated by Milner's election that I had the city's public works department paint the word "Mayor" in large letters, and a replica of the city crest on his official car.

After I had it delivered, he sent me a note saying, "Chief, it's an excellent job, but it's a little too flashy for me." I thought it was official looking, and as he rode through the city, everyone would know that the distinguished-looking Black man sitting in the back seat was the Mayor of Hartford. But at Mayor Milner's request, I had the word *mayor* and the city crest removed.

Like everyone else in the Black community, and many in the White and Hispanic communities, I had great respect for our new mayor. As a state legislator, he had a fine record of service to the people of Hartford, and I knew it would be the same as mayor. Like me, Milner grew up in Hartford's North End. His family's roots in Connecticut soil were eight generations deep, all the way back to his Native American ancestry. As a college student in New York City studying to become a pharmacist, he became active in the civil rights movement and marched with Martin Luther King Jr. In Hartford he was an outspoken community activist, and eventually won a seat on the Connecticut State Legislature. He was one of the earliest in the city to speak out publicly in support of me for fire chief. Now he was mayor.

When Thirman L. Milner became mayor, downtown Hartford was in the midst of a building boom. Eight skyscrapers were scheduled to go up, and several were well on their way toward completion. From my office window on Pearl Street, I could see the huge cranes at work on what was to be the tallest building in Connecticut. City Place would be a thirty-nine-story skyscraper, 537 feet high. At present, the fire department's tallest aerial ladder was one hundred feet, and any building taller than that, we considered it a high-rise.

My concern was how we would fight a fire in a building that tall when it was filled with hundreds of people. We had already experienced fighting a high-rise fire the previous year, when a blaze broke out at the downtown One Corporate Center. This fire could not be fought effectively from the outside, so the fire fighters went into the building but had a difficult time carrying their hoses up the stairs. Thankfully, the building was unoccupied at the time. While state law now required a new building of more than four floors to have water sprinkler systems, I felt it was a life-and-death matter that tenants know what to do in a fire emergency. I knew the fire department would have to establish a training program to educate tenants on fire prevention and building evacuation procedures. So I had Assistant Chief Charles Gallon and Assistant Chief John Kehoe chair a committee to study what we could do to prevent high-rise fires, and what we would do if a fire broke out. When their study was completed, one of the findings was that if a major fire broke out, the department would need to commit as many as two hundred fire fighters to battle the fire. That was more than double the number of fire fighters we had on a normal shift.

Nineteen months had passed since Police Chief George W. Sicaras and I were appointed chief of our respective departments. In that time an unfortunate schism had developed between the city manager and the police chief. This resulted in the city manager suspending the police chief for five days. The schism between Gaitor and Sicaras developed the previous December when the city council directed Sicaras to place three members of the city's Human Relations Commission on his department's internal disciplinary board. This was the board that reviewed cases of police misconduct.

Stating that he "should be held solely accountable for his department," Sicaras refused to accept the three onto the board. After receiving an order from the city manager to comply with the council's directive, Chief Sicaras still refused. Then, following some unfavorable comments the police chief made about the city manager at a city council meeting, he was suspended. This suspension happened in February 1982. The next day the city manager rescinded the suspension, but a strained relationship ensued between the city manager and the police chief. It worsened in May when Gaitor ordered Sicaras to put more officers in uniform and "get them on the street."

Sicaras refused to follow the order, saying it amounted to a reorganization of the police department. "Being the police chief is like the Dow Jones average with all of its peaks and valleys," he was said to have remarked.

I was concerned about the rift between the city manager and the police chief, and thought maybe I could help. I decided to talk to Sicaras about his management style. In managing the police department, the forty-one-year-old Sicaras had what he referred to as an "educated management style." Sicaras had the distinction of being the first Hartford police chief to hold a masters degree. This degree in public administration heavily influenced his leadership style. The way I saw it, just using plain old common sense in handling some issues was preferable to his educated, "by the book" approach. Several times a week, I would drive to his house in Newington to talk with him about leadership issues. After a few weeks, I could sense some resistance, so I stopped my visits. While this was taking place, the Guardians, an organization of Black city police officers, were calling on Sicaras to resign.

To this the chief responded, "It's going to be a cold day in hell when I resign due to pressure from anybody." Then, a few weeks later, Chief Sicaras announced that he was the top candidate for police chief in Pompano Beach, Florida, and was going for an interview.

Gaitor gave the police chief the following ultimatum: "Quit, retire, or be fired, before leaving for the interview." Sicaras remained police chief for five more months. In June he accepted a settlement and announced his retirement effective August 1, 1982, one day short of his two-year anniversary. Sicaras would announce two years later, in July 1984, that his "firing followed attempts by top black city officials to get him to take illegal actions and was racially motivated," and that he planned to filed a $5 million lawsuit. He named Wilson Gaitor, Mayor Thirman Milner, Rudolph Arnold, Frank Borges, the city conciliator at the time, and Henry Langley, an assistant city manager, as the defendants. When notified of the lawsuit, they all denied the charges.

"George was always good at making baseless charges he couldn't substantiate," Arnold would say. "This is another one of those allegations."

It was during this rift between City Manager Gaitor and Police Chief Sicaras that my family was torn with anguish. For me personally it amounted one of the worst periods of my adult life. It began when Chief Sicaras called the city manager and told him they were looking for my son John Stewart III, and planned to arrest him on a charge of murder.

"What happened?" Gaitor asked

"A man died after being beaten and robbed," replied Sicaras.

"Are you sure Chief Stewart's son was involved?" asked Gaitor.

"We have eyewitnesses," replied Sicaras.

"Have you told Chief Stewart about this?" Gaitor asked.

"No, I wanted to notify you first," Sicaras answered. "I thought you might want to tell him."

"Call the chief and let him know," Gaitor said. At the same time the city manager and police chief were having this conversation, I was holding a staff meeting in my office. My secretary interrupted the meeting to tell me I had an important phone call. I listened in disbelief as Chief Sicaras told me what he had told the city manager.

He told me that a fifty-one-year-old man had died. According to witnesses, he said, the man was assaulted and robbed by my son and one other person. He had warrants, he said, for their arrest. I was having trouble believing what I had just heard. Visibly shaken, I hung up the telephone. I adjourned the meeting and went home to inform Tweet. My 27-year-old son John had his own apartment and talked with my father more than he talked with me. So I called my father and told him what Chief Sicaras had told me, and asked him to get in touch with John.

Later that evening my father called me, and I went to meet with him and John. My son told me that he was unaware that the police were looking for him. Yes, he was at the a bar on Albany Avenue and had seen the man lying on the ground, but he had not been involved in any crime. I reassured him that the truth would come out and that he would be exonerated. That night, accompanied by my father, I drove my son to police headquarters over on Morgan Street. There my son John surrendered himself and was locked in a jail cell. Then I went home and told Gladys. That was a night I will never forget. It was March 10, 1982.

When the reporters learned that my son had been arrested, charged with murder and jailed, it became both front-page news and the lead story on evening television news. When questioned by reporters about how I felt, and what I planned to do, all I could say was, "I have never been in a situation like this. What do you do? You raise him; you do the best you can. Hopefully, it isn't true." As the news circulated around the community, people who knew my son voiced their disbelief.

"I've always known him as a bright, ambitious, and polite young man," a neighbor told a reporter. Family members, relatives, and friends were shocked at the news, but remained supportive of John and his claim of innocence. City Manager Gaitor, sensing my distress, tried to reassure me and give his support.

"Hold your head up, Chief, and go about doing your job," he told me. "Don't worry about public gossip because people in Hartford have great respect for you." I tried to take his advice and went about doing my job. I believed my son when he told me he was innocent, and I needed to find out what happened. After conferring with my father, we hired a private investigator who was asked to question people and find out what happened. In April a grand jury indicted my son on a charge of felony murder. If he was found guilty, the newspaper reported, he could be sentenced from twenty-five years to life in prison.

State's Attorney Jack Bailey offered my son a plea bargain. "Plead guilty and serve a reduced prison sentence," he was told. My son's defense attorney, Richard Brown, a thirty-seven-year-old lawyer recommended by my wife's brother Edward, refused the plea deal and requested a trial by jury. Gladys and I did not want our son to plead guilty and serve time in jail for a crime he did not commit. As the trial got underway, it seemed all of Hartford was paying close attention. Newspaper and television news were covering the story and the trial from every possible angle, including the defendant being the son of the fire chief. The trial lasted three months. My duties at the fire department meant I couldn't be in the courtroom every day, but Gladys and other family members were always there. In testimony the story came out that the man who had died was drinking that night in the same bar where John and another man were having a drink.

"The victim may have been drunk when he stumbled outside the bar and struck his head on the sidewalk," my son's attorney argued. "The fall apparently left him unconscious. No one saw my client assault the man." It was learned that when my son John and the other man left the bar, the man with John did go through the pockets of the unconscious man. Naturally, people passing by who did not witness the man falling assumed that he had been beaten by the two men who were now in the process of robbing him. The man later died as a result of striking his head on the sidewalk. After three months of testimony, the case went to the jury. The jury's verdict rightly declared John and the other defendant innocent of murder. The other defendant, however, was found guilty of robbery.

After the trial my son took the reporters to task for the way they sensationalized the story. "My father was taking a beating in the media for something his son might have done," he said. "I had totally negative coverage. No reporter asked for my side of the story, yet they printed and reported what the police said about me having a record of convictions for muggings and other such crimes. And that's not true." Afterward, this experience became a life-defining experience for my son John. He shared with the family that this had been for him what he called "a life-altering experience."

"I've lost time," he said. "What remains is to try to resume my life." Indeed, time has proven that John words to us were not idle words. As I write this, I have never been more proud of my son than I am today. John is a happily married husband and father living in Upstate New York. Both he and his wife, Anita, are highly respected senior officers in the Salvation Army Corps. He is a much-sought-after speaker and preacher, and his life has been an inspiration for hundreds of others. In his ministry he is helping people become more productive by finding positive direction and meaning in their lives, and by establishing a closer relationship with God.

When the trial was over, I was back giving full attention to my work. One issue I had wanted to address since my days as head of Special Services was the disproportionate number of Blacks and Hispanics in the fire department. Blacks and Hispanics in Hartford needed to know about the benefits of a career in the fire service. I was now placing a priority on implementing a recruitment program that reached out to these two groups. Special Services had developed a recruitment brochure explaining that running into burning buildings was not the total picture of what it meant to be a fire fighter. Sure, there was some danger associated with being a professional fire fighter, probably more than most professions, but barring the possibility of injury, a person could have a good career with many benefits. For example, if a fire fighter wanted to enroll in school, there were educational benefits. A reimbursement of up to 80 percent of tuition was allotted if the fire fighter maintained at least a C average. If a fire fighter earned sixty credits, there would be an automatic 2.5 percent pay increase. For earning 120 credits, there was an added 5 percent pay increase.

The fire department also had excellent vacation, health, and retirement benefits. When members of Special Services were in the community recruiting, they didn't just say, "Join up and put out fires." There was more to being a fire fighter than just that. As they placed the brochures in stores, libraries, and recreation centers, they stressed to people the great benefits of becoming a career fire fighter.

The fact that there were no women fire fighters in the Hartford Fire Department was a bias I knew had to be corrected. I never forgot the vow I had made years earlier that if I was ever in a position where I could hire women, I would do so. So Special Services was placing and emphasis on recruiting women. When I hired Zandra Clay Watley and Maria Ortiz in August 1982, it was groundbreaking. Neither of these women had ever considered becoming a fire fighter, but became interested when reading material placed in the community by Special Services. The city newspapers heralded the event, and I took great pride as the two became the first women ever to enter the training academy. Eight weeks later over a hundred of their relatives and friends were on hand at their graduation. I presented the two new female rookies with their graduation diplomas, and my wife, Gladys, added a touch of femininity by handing each a bouquet of flowers.

"What was the eight weeks of training like?" a reporter asked Ortiz when the ceremony was over.

"It was rough, kind of hard," she answered. "It was a challenge. I just went for it."

When Clay was asked the same question, she answered, "The training program was very intensive. It called for a lot of determination and positive thinking." I assigned rookie fire fighter Clay to Engine Company 4 at Headquarters, and rookie fire fighter Ortiz to Engine Company 7 at Clark and Westland Streets. With women now present in each firehouse, the men had to make the necessary adjustments to accommodate the female fire fighters. The following spring the new training class would include another female recruit. In the class after that one, there would be yet another female recruit. Hartford would then have more women fire fighters than any other large New England city. I still experience feelings of great satisfaction at having fulfilled my vow. Thirty years later, in June 2012, I would attend an awards luncheon celebrating women in the fire service. Fire fighter Maria Ortiz and Captain Zandra Watley, both having had successful careers and now retired, were honored by the City of Hartford as trailblazers.

I greeted the year 1983 with great enthusiasm, looking forward to what the fire department could accomplish in this new year. Before January was out, however, I received a big dose of reality.

"Even though you had been warned, you performed an illegal act!" the union president railed as he placed his burly five-foot-nine, 250-pound frame in my path. While I tried to portray an outward demeanor of being unruffled, and had been warned that the union president liked to use language that unnerved his opponents, inwardly I was angry. But I knew how to hold my anger in check.

My so-called "illegal act" was promoting Deputy Chief Salvatore Visconti to assistant chief. At the time we already had an assistant chief. By promoting Visconti I had created a second assistant chief position, but I had my rationale for doing this. One of my first projects as chief had been to reorganize the fire department. In the reorganization I created the Support Bureau, and I planned to put Deputy Chief Visconti in charge. The newly created Support Bureau included three divisions: the communications division, the equipment maintenance division, and the building maintenance division. Such an important responsibility, I concluded, called for the rank of assistant chief. So I promoted Deputy Chief Visconti and issued a notice of appointment that read in part:

> …As the junior assistant chief, he becomes the third-ranking officer of the department and will assume the duties of acting fire chief in the absence of both the fire chief and the assistant fire chief for operations…

In all truthfulness Assistant Corporation Counsel William R. Darcy had said to me prior to the appointment that "It can't be done." But later, after receiving the approval of City Manager Gaitor and Personnel Director, E.B. Pealer, I proceeded with the promotion. I did later receive a written opinion from Corporation Counsel stating that Visconti's promotion violated city procedures for the following reasons:

> The city Personnel Board did not approve the new position. The City Council did not adopt an ordinance setting the pay for the position. Visconti was selected from a 1980 certification list for the existing assistant chief position, even though Chief Stewart had said the second assistant chief's position would have different responsibilities, thereby, requiring a different test.

Since becoming chief I had learned that every decision I made that was questioned by the union president found its way into the *Hartford Courant*. When questioned by a reporter about the promotion, I held my ground.

"I have no plans to remove Visconti from the position," I stated. "I take my instructions from the city manager. At the time of the promotion, it was cleared by the personnel director and the city manager. I can't do a thing until they sign off. That was the end of it as far as I know." However, this would not be the end of it. The union lawyers filed a complaint with the State Labor Relations Board. The labor board would later rule in the department's favor, causing the union lawyers to take the case to State Superior Court. The court would also rule in the department's favor.

The Hartford Fire Department was in desperate need of more self-contained oxygen masks. We had such a limited supply of air-compressed backpacks, referred to as "Scott Packs," that we could only issue two per ladder truck. My desire was to have a self-contained oxygen mask issued to every fire fighter. This would make it a lot easier, and more importantly, safer, for a fire fighter to search a smoke-filled building. Since the fire department already had projected over-runs in its current capital budget, it was unlikely I would get the masks anytime soon. So you can imagine my great joy when a local multimillionaire businessman and philanthropist named David T. Chase gave the department thirty- thousand dollars to purchase the needed gas masks. He also gave the department an added gift of thirty- thousand dollars to cover the expense of establishing a high-rise building safety program. This benefactor was no stranger to me. The two of us were classmates at Weaver High and had graduated together in 1948. After graduating we would meet every five years as members of our high school reunion planning committee.

When we were students at Weaver, Chase gave no hint of how one of the largest mass murders in the history of the world had touched his life. When Hitler's army invaded Poland in 1939, David and his family were forced from their home in the city of Sosnowiec, and into a Jewish ghetto. He was just twelve years old when his family, along with thousands of other Jews, began the long death march to Auschwitz. At the concentration camp, sixty of David's family members, including his mother and younger sister, were among the one million Jews put to death. David was later moved to the Mauthausen Concentration Camp. While on another death march from Mauthausen, David escaped and went into hiding. On May 5, 1945, he and thousands of other Jews were liberated by the US Third Army under the command of General George S. Patton. David had escaped death at the hands of the Nazis, but in all, six million Jews, one and a half million of them children, had died in the Holocaust.

David arrived in the United States in 1946 and settled with relatives in Hartford. He was seventeen-years-old when he enrolled in Weaver High, graduating two years later. Over the years the highly motivated and enterprising David Chase built a financial empire. The holdings of Chase Enterprises included hotels, television stations, and real estate. Thirteen years earlier, during our 1970 Black Professional Fire Fighters Convention, our rooms at the Park Hilton Hotel were given to us at half price. David Chase owned the hotel.

The Redevelopment Task Force I had organized back in 1981 had now developed a four-year apparatus replacement program. This resulted in the department taking ownership of a state-of-the-art fire pumper in March 1983. One of our fire chaplains said a prayer of blessing as we dedicated the 1,500-gallons-per-minute Peter Pirsch & Sons Fire Pumper, which I assigned to Engine Company 7 on Clark Street. In May we took delivery of a Sutphen hundred-foot Tower Ladder Truck. This top-of-the-line ladder truck was equipped with a 1,500-gallons-per-minute pump. After prayerfully dedicating this ladder truck, I assigned it to Ladder Company 5 on Sisson Avenue. These two deliveries marked the completion of the "catch-up phase" of the department's replacement program, and reduced the average age of first line fire apparatus from 18.7 years to 7.1 years. We also continued to refurbish and repower our older apparatus. As a result of these new purchases and the refurbishing, I was able to report to the Committee for Effective City Government that the effectiveness and the efficiency of the fire department had been greatly improved.

In August 1983, as I observed my third year as fire chief, the Hartford Fire Department honored the thirteen fire fighters from the 125-member class of 1948 who were still active. This was the class that included six Black men, the first Blacks to be hired since William Henry Jacklyn was offered a job in 1898. Three of the six, Ben Laury, George Hayes, and James Lewis, were among the thirteen being honored. After the ceremony a reporter questioned Laury about what it was like back then.

"Being among the first Blacks in the fire department was not difficult for me," Laury answered. "Oh, there were bound to be incidents, but Fire Chief Henry Thomas was a good man and very tough. They knew better than to go against him. We used to say you'd rather meet your maker than meet Chief Thomas. If you were wrong, look out."

Laury also told the reporter that he never thought he would work under a Black fire chief when he and five others became the first full-time fire fighters in the Hartford Fire Department. "It never came to mind," he said. Nationally, the fire service had come a long way since 1948. In 1983 I counted sixteen Black fire chiefs in cities around the country. These included chiefs of department, deputy chiefs and battalion chiefs.

In the spring of 1984, I decided to undertake a comparative study, looking at the state of the Hartford Fire Department in 1974 and in 1984. When the study was completed several weeks later, one interesting revelation was that the department had 20 percent less manpower in 1984 than it had in 1974. At present there were 434 on-line fire fighters, compared to 569 in 1974. This was because as equipment and training improved, the department needed fewer people. Even with this reduction in manpower, the department was at full strength, and the city was better protected than it had ever been before. The seventeen recruits scheduled to graduate in June from the training academy were better trained than any previous class.

Under my command the training of new recruits increased from two weeks to ten weeks. The average age for a fire truck when I became chief was sixteen years, it was now seven years. In 1983 we dedicated a new rear-mount aerial ladder truck to replace a 1963 model. The old pumper truck required six men to operate and was not as efficient as the new one, which only required four men. We also purchased two new tactical unit trucks, replacing two thirty-year-old trucks, and I created five-man tactical units for more efficient use of manpower for both rescue work and fire fighting. Members of our tactical units were rescue specialists and were present at every fire where lives were at stake. After making sure there were no lives in danger, members of the tactical unit would then help fight the fire.

The department also purchased a rescue boat, which was the first in the history of the Hartford Fire Department. The police department had its own boat, but due to its old age, the boat was retired in

1978. This forced the city to rely on surrounding towns to provide a rescue boat when needed. To my way of thinking, the savings in manpower more than offset what the department spent on new equipment. The results of this comparative study were satisfying, showing that I was leading the department in the right direction.

In July 1984 City Manager Woodrow Wilson Gaitor announced his upcoming retirement. Taking the helm at a tumultuous time, he had brought to the city a period of relative calm and had changed for the better the way the city governed. I was truly sorry to hear he was about to leave, not just because he had supported me, but because he had set a tone that was more business-like and showed more integrity. When his staff formed a committee to plan his farewell testimonial dinner, I volunteered to serve as chair. In August 1984 more than nine hundred people crowded into the Governor's Ballroom at the Parkview Hilton Hotel to pay tribute to W. Wilson Gaitor and to say good-bye. Although his tenure as city manager had not been long, it had been successful. All the naysayers who had doubted his ability to manage the city had been proven wrong. Now, at age 65, Gaitor and his wife, Blanche, were preparing to move to their new home in Petersburg, Virginia. Once again the City of Hartford was without a city manager.

By May 1985 the city council had received over 260 applications for the city manager's position. They had come from around the country, including Alaska, with one applicant describing the position as "the best such opening in the country." The field of finalists had been narrowed down to fifteen by the middle of June, and down to five by mid-August. Since a year had now passed and no new city manager had been named, some community leaders were growing weary of waiting. Because the council had issued no statements, they complained the council was choosing the next city manager in secret. In every section of the city, rumors spread of private political deals, special interest lobbying, and hints of front-runners. As community leaders began calling for a more transparent selection process, two disgruntled council members charged the selection was being influenced by politics and other factors besides the applicants' qualifications. This prompted Councilman Ben Andrews Jr. to call for the council to open the remainder of the selection process to the public.

When the number of finalists was down to four, two of them for unknown reasons dropped out of consideration. Now there were only two applicants left to choose from. Complaining by community leaders grew louder.

"The council is taking too long to make its selection," they complained. It was then leaked that council members who supported one of the remaining two, Alfred A. Gatta, were threatening to force a vote. After what was described as an "often ferocious argument," a bitterly divided council voted five to four to appoint Alfred A. Gatta as Hartford's city manager. Former Deputy Mayor Robert Ludgin attempted to explain what had taken place.

"The conflict over selecting Hartford's new city manager was a struggle for power and control of the city government by those on the council," he said. The present deputy mayor, Francisco L. Borges, who had opposed Gatta's appointment, now offered him a pledge of allegiance. This he did only after Gatta signed an employment contract with the city. The man who was to be the new city manager was no stranger to city residents. He had served for the past two years as the executive director of Hartford's Riverfront Recapture Inc, a nonprofit group that was revitalizing the city's riverbanks. Prior to this, he was director of the city's Parks and Recreation Department, and later an assistant city manager to Donald Peach. In August 1985, forty-four-year-old Alfred A. Gatta was sworn in as Hartford's latest city manager. What was ironic about the whole selection process was that the city had spent $11,000 in a nationwide search that ended with the selection of someone who worked just three blocks from city hall.

There were just two places in the city where I could go to find refuge from the pressing and often stressful matters that confronted me daily, home and church. At home I received family encouragement, and at church I received spiritual encouragement. On Sunday mornings I could still be found at Faith Congregational Church sitting next to Gladys, and being inspired by the preaching and singing. Just as it had been during my childhood, this church continued to hold a central place in my life. I was a church trustee, a member of the men's fellowship group, and when needed I served as an usher. Presently, I had the added responsibility of serving on the church's pastoral search committee. The previous pastor, Reverend Charles Blake, had retired and moved with his wife back to their Kentucky home.

In August 1985 our new minister, Reverend Rubin Tendai, a graduate of Temple University and Howard University Divinity School, arrived from Philadelphia. The minister, his wife, Alana, and their two sons, Jelani, seven, and Kofi, five, settled into a rented house on Litchfield Street, just off Blue Hills Avenue. Alana, who had a law degree from George Washington University, was hired as a law clerk at the courthouse on Washington Street. Their sons were enrolled in Sarah J. Rawson Elementary School on Holcomb Street, in the city's North End.

A few days after their arrival in Hartford, I sat at their kitchen table and over coffee shared with the new minister and his wife some of the realities of the city they now called home.

"Hartford is an urban paradox," I began. "White-collar high-salaried employees of more than a half-dozen banks and insurance companies coexist with the unemployed and the working poor. If you stand at the intersection of Albany Avenue and Main Street, you can see the wealth of downtown and the want of the North End at the same time. Just a mile from downtown, you will find blighted neighborhoods with hundreds of families in a day-to-day struggle to exist. In this city, which was the wealthiest in the nation following the Civil War, we have 25 percent of the people living below the poverty level. Five years ago the Census Bureau named Hartford the fourth poorest city in the nation. An encouraging sign," I told them," was that a number of the larger insurance companies in Hartford, like Aetna, Travelers, Cigna, and the Hartford Insurance Group, are committing large amounts of money to help address our social problems. The insurance companies are playing a role in housing, education, and employment of Hartford's poorest residents. And we have many community leaders and elected officials in both the Black and White communities who have dedicated themselves to making life better for all who live here. So you see, there is hope for the city you now call home."

In February 1986, while the nation was still in shock over the explosion of the space shuttle Challenger killing seven, including the country's second Black astronaut, Ronald E. McNair, I held a swearing-in ceremony for two new chaplains.

"What are your duties?" a reporter asked Reverend Tendai after the ceremony.

"Fire fighters have many problems related to the peculiarities of their job," he said. "We see our role as being available to them and their families just to talk and listen."

"It's a life-threatening job with irregular hours and a lot of stress," added Father Grace. "The chaplains will also participate in the training program," I told the reporter. "I want new fire fighters to know that our chaplains are available to them."

A few weeks later, Governor William O'Neill did something that was the cause of great pride in Black communities throughout the state. He appointed Attorney Howard Brown Jr. to the position of State Banking Commissioner. The Morehouse College and University of Connecticut Law School graduate now had all the banks and credit unions chartered in the state of Connecticut under his supervision. A personal friend and fellow Faith Church member, Brown became the first Black person in the history of Connecticut to hold this high office. "Good Morning Commissioner," I said, when I saw him with his family at church the following Sunday.

As the year progressed, a fair amount of my time was spent testifying before the Labor Relations Board in response to some complaint the board had received from the union president. In August, when the summer was at its hottest, I had to make the unfortunate decision not to attach sprinklers to city fire hydrants, thus denying the children a way to cool off during hot spells. This was a painful decision, because I had initiated the sprinkler program when I was head of Special Services. But I made the decision based on the department's experience the previous summer when sprinklers were placed in various neighborhoods. We gave keys to neighborhood adult leaders so they could turn on the spray when kids wanted relief from the heat. Soon people began complaining to police that they were intentionally sprayed with water as they walked by. Drivers with their car windows rolled down also complained of being sprayed inside their vehicles. At the same time, kids in neighborhoods that had not been given a sprinkler were complaining of being treated unfairly. Added to this, I was being told by my officers that the sprinklers were hurting our ability to fight fires.

When my decision was made public, young people began turning on the fire hydrants themselves. When we turned a fire hydrant off, they would turn it back on as soon as we left. We were turning off as many as forty hydrants a day, only to have most of them turned right back on.

"Why is it the law you can't open them up?" young people wanted to know. "It's hot outside."

"We turn them off to protect you," the fire fighter answered. He explained that open fire hydrants jeopardized the safety of their neighbors. "Small children playing in the powerful stream of water could be knocked in front of a passing car. And fire fighters responding to a fire," he told them, "may be held up for up to five minutes turning off the hydrant so they can connect their hose."

Even with this explanation, after the fire fighter left, the young people would turn the hydrant on again. Fire hydrants being turned on illegally in both the South and North Ends of the city had become a serious problem. Sometimes teenagers would hassle a neighbor who called and requested that a hydrant be turned off. There were so many being turned on we were hampered in fighting fires because of low water pressure. In some cases when arriving at the scene of a fire, we lost precious time because we had to unlock hydrants or turn them on at underground mains. Turning on fire hydrants was a criminal offense, and the police arrested those they caught in the act. Sometimes it was an adult turning on the hydrant, and that person was charged with disorderly conduct. A person under eighteen was turned over to juvenile authorities.

As chief, the responsibility for solving this problem rest with me. I knew there were special hydrant caps that made opening hydrants more difficult because these caps called for a special wrench. I requested that the city purchase these special caps, and the department eventually received four hundred of them. Hartford had 2,500 hydrants throughout the city, so we strategically placed the four hundred caps in neighborhoods where we had experienced the most problems. I then made the public announcement that "the days of permissiveness were over." By this, I meant I was sorry to say that the days of the summer sprinkler program had come to an end.

In January 1987 another historic first occurred in Connecticut. Francisco L. Borges, Hartford's former deputy mayor, was elected to the office of state treasurer. The story of Borges' rise to one of this state's loftiest position is a story of achievement that inspires both Blacks and Whites. When Borges, who was born in Cape Verde, an island off the coast of Africa, arrived in New Haven at eight years of age, he spoke only Portuguese. The highly motivated young Francisco would graduate from Trinity College in Hartford and go on to earn a law degree from the University of Connecticut. In his first attempt at electoral politics, Borges would be elected to the Hartford City Council in 1981. He would then go on to serve as Hartford's deputy mayor from 1983 to 1985. Now, as state treasurer, he was Connecticut's highest elected Black official. In one of his earliest statements, the thirty-five-year-old state treasurer said that in this position, he would exercise his social consciousness. In a move that drew praise from many quarters of the Black and the White communities, State Treasurer Borges divested

Connecticut's pension portfolio of companies doing business in racist South Africa.

In November 1987, there was another first in Hartford. After a tough campaign, Democrat Carrie Saxon Perry was elected Hartford's first Black female mayor. When Mayor Thirman L. Milner decided not to seek a third term, he encouraged Perry to seek the office. Perry, who had served four terms as a state legislator, agreed to run. Now she had become the first Black woman popularly elected mayor of major northeastern city. Perry was a Hartford native, born and raised in the city's North End. As a child she was encouraged by her perceptive mother and grandmother to follow her dreams. While in high school, young Carrie's dream was to help people by becoming a social worker. She entered Howard University, and after earning her degree in social work, she returned to Hartford. After working several years at the Community Renewal Team (CRT), an antipoverty agency located in the city's North End, Perry was promoted to the position of administrator. At CRT Perry interacted with many of the city's politicians on behalf of the city's neediest residents.

As a result of these interactions, she came to believe she could help people more if she held political office. So in 1980 she won a seat in the Connecticut General Assembly. Now, in December 1987, wearing her trademark big hat, the fifty-six-year-old Perry was sworn in as mayor of Hartford. In her inaugural remarks, Mayor Perry downplayed the fact that she was a Black woman. She believed that both Blacks and women should naturally have a voice in all levels of city government. After concluding her inaugural remarks, Perry gave what would become her trademark signoff.

"Have a mellow day," she told her listeners.

After almost nine years as fire chief, I had learned to enjoy the high moments, because I knew from experience that low moments were sure to follow. It was a high moment in the spring of 1989 when I walked onto the stage in cap and gown at the University of Connecticut and was awarded my bachelor's degree. I had never given up my goal of completing my education, and now after eight years of evening classes, I had achieved this goal. My graduation was reported in the newspaper, and my hope was that I would be an inspiration to others. At fifty-nine I was proof you're never too old to realize a dream.

The low moment came when I was notified by police that before escaping from a local institution, a fire fighter threatened to kill me. This particular fire fighter was having personal problems, which caused him to abuse alcohol. On one occasion when he reported to duty seemingly under the influence, I had no choice but to send him home. Another time he was engaged in erratic behavior while on duty, so I had him taken to the Institute of Living for psychiatric evaluation. While there he apparently left the facility on his own, but was overheard to say, "I am going to kill Chief Stewart." This was not the first time a threat had been made against my life. The police didn't know if this latest one was serious, but they wanted to provide me with protection. When I was informed a few hours later that the individual had been taken back into custody, I gave the matter no further thought.

When City Manager Gatta announced his resignation in November 1989, it came as a surprise to most of Hartford's residents. By the end of December, he told council members, he would be gone. Gatta had accepted a position as city manager of Ann Arbor, Michigan, a city thirty-five miles from Detroit and the home of the University of Michigan. When the new year, 1990 began, Hartford was once again without a city manager. The city would again have to undertake a national search. In September 1990, nine months after Gatta's departure, the city council named Eugene Shipman as the new city manager. At the time of his appointment, Shipman, who was fifty-years-old, held a high administrative position in Kansas City, Missouri, and before that he held a high city government position in Chapel Hill, North Carolina.

"I know Hartford is this nation's fourth poorest city of more than 100,000 people," he reportedly told friends, "but beyond the numerous challenges, I see an opportunity to make a difference." He was now

Hartford's second Black city manager. After only a few months on the job, some community leaders in the North End were expressing their displeasure with Shipman. He would often express himself in ways that offended listeners. For instance, in December 1990, two months after his arrival in Hartford, he met with a number of city clergy in the North End to get their support for a plan that would move poor Blacks and Hispanics out of the city.

"I would like to demolish some of the city's public housing developments and move the residents to subsidized housing in the suburbs," he told them. "We cannot survive unless we divest ourselves of many of our less fortunate. It sounds hard and mean, but it's fair. Hartford has for too long had a too liberal welfare policy. Government cannot be all things to all people." This plan caused a stir in the minority community and was strongly opposed by many of the clergy and community leaders. The new city manager was not off to a good start.

As fire chief, I had the unpleasant responsibility of having from time-to-time fire people. I did not look forward to this responsibility, and found it to be one of my more painful duties. Telling a person he no longer had a job meant I was taking away his source of financial livelihood. When a fire fighter I had to fire had a family and a mortgage, I felt even worse. As chief this was a responsibility I needed to come to terms with. I once told City Manager Gaitor of the tremendous feelings of remorse I experienced after firing someone. He told me how he was able to fire a person and not experience any feelings of remorse at all.

"When I had to fire people, I didn't worry about it," he told me. "You don't fire them. They fire themselves when they violate the rules." I thought about this and concluded that it did make sense, and was helped by Gaitor's response. Not too long after this conversation with the city manager, Assistant Chief John Kehoe was doing his morning roll call and inspection when he noticed a fire fighter who appeared to be intoxicated. The assistant chief called me and several other officers to come and see if his suspicion was correct. When I looked at the fire fighter, I saw that his eyes were red and he was walking unevenly and slurring his speech.

So I asked him, "Were you drinking this morning?" He looked at me but didn't answer. So I asked him again. "Were you drinking last night?" He still gave no answer. This wasn't the first time this particular fire fighter had committed this type of infraction. I had, in fact, fired this same fire fighter back in 1981 for drinking on the job, but the union had him reinstated. He claimed at the time that his condition was the result of taking prescribed medication. After this present infraction, I again fired him for reporting to work intoxicated. Even remembering what the city manager had said to me, that they fire themselves, I still felt some remorse. Again, the union filed a complaint with the Labor Relations Board. After the fire fighter testified before the board, it ruled that he be reinstated because I had failed to order him to undergo a medical examination. This particular complaint by the union and my appearance before the State Labor Relations Board was just the tip of a huge iceberg.

UNION TROUBLES

My poor relationship with Local 760 and its president is a matter of record. It is well documented in the minutes of the Connecticut State Board of Labor Relations, city records, and newspaper accounts. Local 760 of the International Association of Fire Fighters, AFL-CIO, is the union that represents the interest of Hartford's fire fighters. According to the men who organized the union in 1943, there was "a need to protect the safety, rights, and benefits of fire fighters." The union currently represented 370 Hartford fire fighters. For twenty-eight years I was a dues-paying, card-carrying union member supporting the union's actions. Now, as fire chief I was barred from membership. And quite naturally, as chief my perspective on union activities had changed. I was aware, of course, that the larger number of union members did not favor me being made chief.

"I'll just wait and see," the union president remarked, while questioning whether I was competent enough to lead the fire department. On hearing this I promised myself that I would leave the fire department in better shape than I found it.

Barely a month after I made fire chief, the union president and his lawyers filed the first of many complaints they would lodge against me with the State Board of Labor Relations. In this initial complaint the union alleged that I had engaged in a number of prohibited practices. One of these prohibited practices was having only certain captains attending weekly staff meetings and receiving overtime pay. Holding such meetings, union officials complained, resulted in an unjust overtime situation for all captains who weren't present at these meetings. The union wanted me to "cease and desist from the creation of patronage by allowing only special captains the ability to earn overtime money." The union also wanted me to "pay all other captains in the bargaining unit the same amount of overtime money earned by the special captains." The second prohibited practice had to do with my transferring a number of Hispanic fire fighters to fire stations near their homes.

"Resident fire fighters being assigned to stations in areas where they lived, discriminates against non-residence fire fighters by not affording them the opportunity to work where they want," the complaint read. The union wanted the labor board to order me to "cease and desist from job assignments according to residence and reverse assignments which have already taken place."

As a result of the complaint, I appeared at a hearing before the State Labor Relations Board in Wethersfield on Friday morning, September 5, 1980. This was just one month after my appointment as chief. My assistant chief and several city representatives accompanied me to the hearing. I explained to labor board officials that the purpose of the meetings was to address the various problems that were always reoccurring within the department.

"Such meetings have not been held regularly in the past, and the union objects to your right to call them," the union president interjected. "Having union members attend such meetings puts them in management positions and undermines their connection to the union." After some discussion I agreed to make the meetings available to all captains who wanted to attend. Their presence, I added, would be voluntary. This seemed to satisfy the union president who then asked, "How long will you continue to hold such meetings?"

"Indefinitely," I said. As soon as I said this, I realized that holding the meetings indefinitely was financially impractical. So I quickly amended my statement. "The meetings will end when I feel the work of the committee has been completed."

The labor board then took up the matter of the transfers I had made. "Transferring minority recruits to stations in their neighborhoods discriminates against non-residence fire fighters by not affording them the opportunity of working where they want," the union president said. "The union is asking that the city cease and desist from job assignments according to residence and reverse assignments that have already taken place. The union president then added, "This can be resolved by automatically granting all requests for transfers from one station to another."

"To resolve as you propose would create insoluble practical problems," I replied. "Suppose two people requested the same position."

"This could be solved by seniority," he answered.

The union president said he would not want the city to be compelled to grant every request for transfer. He then said he would draft language that would justify denial of a transfer request if the city or an individual might be harmed unduly by the transfer. He began writing and handed me the following to which I agreed.

Official Notice
Policy on Transfers

It shall be the policy of this department to honor all transfers upon request. Transfer request shall be honored for vacancies based upon seniority. Transfer request shall be honored where mutual request are submitted. This policy shall be implemented in all cases except where undo harm to the individual or department would be experienced.

This ended the hearing. Two weeks later I sent the union president the following letter, which in effect cancelled the agreement.

Subject: Residence Clause

Sir: After a meeting on September 5, 1980 on the subject grievance, a thorough evaluation and discussion was held regarding the (residence grievance). The department has always allowed personnel to request transfers to various stations and will continue to do so, as in the past. It is also our understanding that the intent of the residence clause takes on a different connotation than was previously discussed.

The above grievance is denied.

I also sent this second letter.

Subject: Staff Meetings with Captains Present

Sir: In the office of the Chief on September 5, 1980, a meeting was held to discuss the above subject grievance.

It is an established practice that individuals in various acting capacities: Deputy Chief, Division Head, etc., be included at any staff meeting being held in the department. This practice will continue in order to effectively coordinate the various functions of the department.

The above grievance is denied.

On receipt of these letters, the union president forwarded a complaint to the labor board. Eight months later the labor board contacted me, ordering that I rescind my letters. Two years later the board reversed this order and dismissed this initial complaint.

Another instance where it became evident the union president was questioning my every decision, whether large or small, can seen in the following. I issued an order instructing firemen to wear their blue hats in the summer instead of changing to their white hats. This order effectively ended seasonal changes in the color of hats. The union president viewed this change as a reduction in benefits, and filed a complaint. I viewed this complaint as frivolous, and I was getting fed up with the union president's interferences. I decided to talk this situation over with City Manager Wilson Gaitor and Assistant Corporation Counsel William Darcy. They both handled city personnel matters, and I wanted to talk with them about my worsening relations with the union president. Gaitor and Darcy acknowledged they were aware of the growing tension between the two of us.

"I blame Fiorillo for the tension," said a frustrated Darcy. "He's filing unnecessary demands. Everything Chief Stewart does, he objects. He's really getting petty. Some people in city government are viewing Fiorillo's actions with suspicion." Gaitor asked if I thought the union president's actions might have racial overtones.

"I can't say for sure," I answered. The union president had earlier denied that race was an issue.

"My only problem with Stewart," he was reported to have said, "is that he has never been a strong union man." The meeting ended with Darcy saying he would call Fiorillo in for a meeting. After being notified to meet with the head of personnel to discuss his disagreements with me, Fiorillo refused to meet. "I don't want to respond to anything Mr. Darcy says," he said, "except in front of a tribunal."

In September 1981 the seven-month-long contract negotiations between the city and the union collapsed. City fire fighters had been without a binding contract since July. The deep lines of division separating the city and the union looked to be unbridgeable.

"The city is trying to weaken the union by reducing the size of the bargaining unit and by denying the fire fighters a bill of rights," an angry union president told reporters. "The city is allowing the fire chief to revise department conduct and discipline regulations without union approval. Too many fire fighters are being temporarily appointed to positions that should have been established as permanent civil services posts," he added. "The city is trying to bust the union!

I'm just trying to protect our position, which is what a union is supposed to do!"

When Darcy was informed of Fiorillo's remarks, his response was, "The city is not trying to break the union! The main problem is that the union is trying to dictate how the fire department will be run. This is something the city would never tolerate. We also have a problem with some union proposals, including those to establish minimum manning levels, abolish overnight watch, and full payment of retirees' insurance premiums."

But union officials were demanding even more. They were demanding language in the new contract that they said would "protect a fire fighter when he is unfairly accused of wrongdoing by citizens, or superiors." The union wanted a provision saying a fire fighter cannot be penalized for most conduct while off duty, or for his personal beliefs. The union also wanted the city to commit to keeping all firehouses open at a minimum staffing level of eighty-one fire fighters per shift throughout the department. This, the union contended, was necessary for the safe operation of the department.

"What Fiorillo is asking for amounts to a bill of rights," responded Darcy. He felt the union was going too far in asking for rights that modified existing guidelines for fire fighter discipline and conduct. "The rights of fire fighters are already adequately protected," he said. Darcy was committed to properly staffing each firehouse, but he refused to allow the union to set the terms on how to achieve this. "A contract that set staffing levels would take away the flexibility needed by the city council to staff firehouses according to shifting populations and budgetary restraints. The city is committed to properly staffing each firehouse," Darcy stated.

The union was also asking that the new contract contain what was being called a "silent night" provision. This provision would allow all fire fighters to go to bed after 9:00 p.m. instead of having one of them stay awake to staff an overnight watch. The union contended that such a provision would cut down on fire fighter fatigue.

"It has worked in fire departments in other cities and wouldn't cause problems if alarm boxes were installed outside the firehouses to wake sleeping men," the union argued. To this Darcy was adamantly opposed.

"Allowing fire fighters to go to sleep after 9:00 p.m. instead of staffing an overnight watch is a safety hazard," he contended. "People coming to the firehouses for first aid would have a hard time reaching fire fighters. It would also make for increased response time as groggy fire fighters tried to get to calls." Darcy summed up his feelings about the overall negotiations by stating, "The union is really trying to take the basic decision-making power over what happens in the department away from the city council, the city manager, and fire chief. We really can't run the fire department at the sufferance of the employees."

Another sticking point in the negotiations was money. The city had offered a contract that some city officials were calling too generous. In the contract the city would increase salaries and fringe benefits for fire fighters by 26.5 percent over three years, plus a 6 percent increase in the first six months. This would be followed by a 2 percent increase in the second six months of the first year. The same increase would be repeated in the second year, followed by an 8 percent increase in the third year. This was not the city's final offer; the city was willing to go as high as 33 percent. This caused the union president to tell negotiators that he thought they were very close on money.

"The sticking point," said the union president, "is that the union wants the city to maintain longevity pay." Longevity pay was a bonus given employees based on their years of service. The city wanted to eliminate such bonuses. Darcy explained that fire fighters would be compensated for this with such improvements as a dental plan, improvements to the pension fund, and elimination of a pension penalty for early retirement. But this did not satisfy the union. Nor was the union satisfied with what it saw happening to employee insurance benefits.

"The city is trying to cut corners by not paying full insurance benefits for retirees," the union president argued, "and presenting the union with a pension plan that does not provide sufficient survivor-ship benefits for the spouses of deceased fire fighters." Neither the city nor the union could find a suitable way to close the gap that divided them.

In September 1981, I was back testifying before the labor board. This complaint claimed that I had performed five illegal acts. My first illegal act, the union claimed, was establishing an arson task force. The second was that I had appointed bargaining unit members to various committees. The third had to do with the wearing of civilian clothes. The fourth had to do with discontinuing the practice of having police detectives work with members of the bargaining unit. The fifth had to do with the wearing of uniform caps. It took three additional hearings before the labor board dismissed this complaint.

In November 1981, I did something that left Phoenix Society members puzzled. I promoted the man who was my chief antagonist.

"Why would you promote Rudy Fiorillo," they asked. He does his best to block everything you do." They were right. But you would have to sit in the chief's chair to better understand my reasoning. Outside of the union president challenging my every decision, and trying to make me look like nothing before the labor board, he really didn't do anything to warrant me not promoting him. Plus, he was on the list. I believed that if I didn't promote him, and he took me to the labor board or to court, I would have no valid reason except that he acted like a labor person. Sure, he did things to antagonize me, but I wanted him to see that between the two of us, I was the bigger person. When I advise Blacks who may want to follow me, I tell them that you've got to be careful when you're sitting in that seat, because they expect you to do what they would do to you if they had the job. You can't afford to do what they would do. They would get away with it, but you're being scrutinized. Whatever you do, somebody's watching you.

After scheduling Fiorillo's promotion ceremony, I received word that he would not accept the promotion to lieutenant. He said he didn't believe I would really promote him. He knew he was a thorn in my side, so why would I reward him. But I wouldn't let spite prevent me from going forward with the promotion. I had a good relationship with Fiorillo's father, a former deputy chief in the Bristol, Connecticut, Fire Department. On occasions I would call him to talk about how to handle his son. This time I told him his son was not going to accept the promotion, and maybe he could convince him to change his mind. I also invited his father to the ceremony and encouraged him to bring Rudy's ten-year-old son.

On the day of his promotion Fiorillo was present and so were his father and son. At the ceremony I watched as the union president's son pinned the lieutenant's badge on his father. As I saw it, I was the chief, and had no valid reason not to promote him. I still say to this day that I saw a difference in Rudy after I promoted him. And I could look him in the face and see a man who did not measure up to me. It was department policy that when a fire fighter was promoted to lieutenant that he serve a three-month probationary period. At the promotion ceremony, I informed him that because he was on detached duty as the union president, his probationary period would be delayed. I didn't think at the time that this would prompt the new lieutenant to file a complaint against me, but this is what he did two weeks later.

On Wednesday, December 29, 1982 I was back testifying before the labor board in response to a complaint that I failed to provide information the union needed in order to conduct contract negotiations with the city in an intelligent and meaningful manner.

On this complaint the labor board ruled in favor of the union stating that in future negotiations, the city will "promptly provide the union, upon request, with access to sick leave experience records of bargaining unit employees if either part had made or intends to make proposals to which such information is relevant."

In September 1983, I testified before the labor board because of a complaint filed by Fiorillo after I promoted him. He complained that delaying his probationary period until he was no longer on detached duty was a unilateral change of practice. After the finding of facts, the labor board dismissed this complaint. The union president appealed to the State Superior Court, but the labor board's ruling was upheld.

The following month, October 1983, I testified before the labor board in response to a complaint that I failed to comply with a previous labor board decision. The complaint said that I had denied certain request for voluntary transfer, and made involuntary transfers. Here, the labor board ruled in favor of the union.

On Tuesday, October 16, 1984, I testified before the labor board in response to a complaint that I had engaged and was engaging in prohibited practices. The so-called prohibited practice was my plan to have each fire fighter have a self-contained breathing mask. The union claimed that wearing gas masks meant changes in the condition of employment that constituted mandatory subjects of bargaining and should have been negotiated before the mandatory mask rule was implemented.

In its ruling the labor board responded to each of the union's concerns.

The question of communicable diseases was not substantial. While at the site of a fire, each fire fighter was supposed to use only one mask. In between fires, the masks were supposed to be sanitized by appropriate cleaning before being used again. The question of a false sense of security strikes us as an inherent potential resulting from use of the masks, but that appropriate training should effectively deal with that problem. As the record showed, training in the use of the masks was part of the City's mask program. Insofar as exhaustion resulting from additional weight from the masks and accompanying apparatus is concerned, there was no evidence introduced showing that the weight of the apparatus was such that it would create exhaustion problems. The emergency incidents referred to in finding of fact are case by case situations that should be handled as such and we believe the City's masks policy appropriately recognized that. The question of "claustrophobic" fire fighters, so far as the record shows, is speculative. No such problems were shown to exist. Finally, the duties of Deputy Chiefs at the site of a fire are in most respects different from those of other fire fighters at the scene of a fire. In any event, the Union's expressed concern here seemed to concern perceptions of equality and equal treatment in the eyes of the fire fighters. Although the Deputy Chiefs are part of the bargaining unit, the Union has not shown to us that a difference in when masks are required to be worn by such higher ranking officers creates an arbitrary inequality that would impact in any substantial way on working conditions. As we stated in Town of Hamden, before we can find that an employer has failed to bargain over impacts on conditions of employment in an alleged unilateral change situation, the union must show that such impacts do in fact exists. As is discussed above, the Union has not met that burden in this case.

Therefore, we find no refusal to bargain and, accordingly, dismiss the Union's complaint.

Now for a matter that really did get under my skin. The union president refused to address me as "Chief." In a defiant and disrespectful manner, he would call me "John" or "Mr. Stewart," but never "Chief." He maintained that his attitude toward me was not racially motivated. I, on the other hand, felt that he could not bring himself to call a Black man "Chief." Believing that I was seeking some reprisal against him because of his attitude toward me, he filed a complaint with the labor board in April 1983. In this complaint Fiorillo alleged that the City of Hartford had violated the Municipal Employee Relations Act by threatening the union president with reprisals for carrying out his union functions, and by threatening the above labor organization and preventing it from carrying out its duties as the collective bargaining representative of fire fighters and officers in the City of Hartford. A month later a second complaint was filed alleging that the City had threatened the union president with demotion and other discipline because of his union activity in violation of Connecticut General Statutes.

On both these matters, I testified before the labor board on Tuesday, June 24, 1986, and on Monday, March 2, 1987. More specifically, the complaints charged that the City of Hartford, through the city manager and fire chief, had engaged in a designed pattern of threatening Union President Rudolph Fiorillo Jr. for his union activities over several years, and that the threats of demotion in 1983 and a suspension in 1985 were part of that pattern. Here, for the first time, race would become part of the testimony. The findings of facts included:

> There were several conflicts in 1981 between then City Manager Woodrow W. Gaitor and Fiorillo presented by the Union as background in support of its claim of a pattern of illegal threats.

> Specifically, on July 3, 1981, Fiorillo sent a letter to Gaitor concerning a dispute over work assignments of fire fighters. In his letter, Fiorillo stated among other things that if members were "not returned to their normal duties, this union will seek relief through the court."

> In response, Gaitor sent two separate letters to Fiorillo dated July 8, 1981. In one letter Gaitor stated:

> > In your letter dated July 3, 1981 you did not state specifics (Names, positions, etc., etc.). For me to take actions on some general statement is not

proper unless I have some evidence to back up that action.

I must also inform you that you are an employee of the city first; then Union President. You are not the reverse. I would advise you to consider your position as an employee in the future, before you write me any more threatening letters. In the first place they do not frighten me or intimidate me.

I will not allow any employee, department head, citizen or citizens; union official or officials to disrespect the office of the City Manager or the chair of the City Manager. I hope that this is very clear.

This office will always carry out the wishes and mandates of the Court of Common Council, and I do not need a letter from the Union President every other day threatening to take me or the city to court. I still believe that men of good will can reason together.

Gaitor's other letter, whose context is unclear, stated:

Your letter dated July 3, 1981, was copied to the Mayor, Court of Common Council, Messrs. Gagne, Pealer and Stewart, and because of this I feel I must respond in kind.

I do accept your apology and trust that reasonable men can reason together.

On July 10, 1981, Fiorillo wrote a letter to Gaitor, which, among other things, advised Gaitor that he had learned

Gaitor had been working on the work assignments issue referenced in Fiorillo's July 3 letter, apologized to Gaitor for the July 3 letter, and advised Gaitor that the Union would not seek court relief concerning the work assignments issue.

About two years later, on March 9, 1983, Fiorillo again wrote to Gaitor reiterating a previous Union request for information on assignment of "work fare" personnel, complaining that "work fare" personnel were "still" doing bargaining unit work and concluding: "We are hereby demanding that all workfare personnel assigned to the Fire Department be removed until such time as you meet and negotiate with us."

On March 17, Gaitor replied to Fiorillo in a letter, stating:

> Your letter dated 9 March 1983 in which you demand something from the City Manager or this office is quite out of order.

> You may be president of the Union; but first of all you are an *employee of the City of Hartford, paid by the City of Hartford* and a *representative* of employees of the City of Hartford.

> You have a right to request, but you have no authority to demand anything from this office. May I suggest that in the future you refrain from using the "demanding" terms that have been expressed in many of your past communications.

Soon thereafter, Gaitor and Fiorillo encountered each other at a function at City Hall. Gaitor grabbed Fiorillo by the belt and told Fiorillo that it would be better if Fiorillo never again sent him letters of "demand."

This case remained unsettled, then on March 8, 1985, Fiorillo became involved in a loud, heated verbal exchange with Fire Chief John Stewart Jr. at a disciplinary hearing concerning a bargaining unit member.

Fiorillo was present at that hearing in his capacity as a Union officer.

The disciplinary hearing involved a claim that the bargaining unit member had made improper use of leave, and at the hearing management concluded that he should receive a four-day suspension.

Fiorillo believed that due to the complexities of fire fighters' schedules and pay system, the suspension would result in him working but not being paid.

Fiorillo testified that he told Stewart: "Goddamn it, John, this is Hartford, Connecticut, not a cotton plantation. People have to get paid when they work. You are violating state law here and it is a real inhumane way to treat employees."

According to Fiorillo, "Stewart then insisted that I start addressing him as 'Chief' and I told him that he start addressing me as 'Lieutenant Fiorillo' and I told him that I wasn't Lieutenant Fiorillo that day. I told him that I was the President of the Union and that I wasn't going to participate in the scenario that would make me subject(ed) to his whims."

(On an earlier occasion Stewart had told Fiorillo he wished to be called Chief. Stewart claims that the parties had an understanding that he would be so referred to at disciplinary hearings.)

Fiorillo testified that Stewart's reply was as follows: "He told me I won't be a lieutenant much longer. He told me that effective immediately I have a reprimand in my file. He told me that I will receive it in the mail. He ordered me to leave his office, and he ordered me, calling me his subordinate, Lieutenant Fiorillo."

Stewart testified that during the above exchange Fiorillo had stated: "Goddamn, John, this is like picking cotton in the days of slavery."

Stewart further testified that he had cautioned Fiorillo not to continue, and Fiorillo had responded: "John, John, John." Stewart testified that he had replied: "It is Chief," and that Fiorillo had then said: "It is John, John, John until you learn your job and when you learn to respect that office, at that time I will address you as Chief."

Stewart terminated the hearing after this exchange.

On March 11, 1985, Fiorillo sent Stewart a letter referring to the events at the above-described disciplinary meeting of March 8, 1985, stating in part:

> ...When I raised objection to your inhumane actions, you told me to watch my demeanor, address you as Chief, or you would adjourn the hearing. At that point you addressed me by my rank, which I

earned, and when I objected, you told me I had a reprimand in my file and I would be demoted if I kept it up.

I don't feel I have to address you as Chief while I'm in my capacity as Union President on Union Business, especially when you are treating our members as indentured servants. You appear to be more interested in form than substance and although I expect that from you, I still feel it is unfortunate for everyone involved.

In my opinion, an apology is in order, and until I receive same, I intend to limit all lines of communication with you to strictly business matters.

On or about March 13, 1985, Fiorillo was instructed by Assistant Chief Gallon to attend a disciplinary hearing on March 15, 1985, for having engaged in conduct unbecoming an officer.

The hearing was rescheduled to March 20, 1985 and resulted in Fiorillo's receiving a one-day suspension.

The suspension was explained in a March 22, 1985, letter from Stewart to Fiorillo, which stated in part:

You are being charged with violating the following rules and regulations of this department:

Rule No. 23—Officers in their intercourse with each other shall observe a courteous demeanor. Officers and members in addressing each other will do so in a respectful manner.

Rule No. 25—Discourtesy of Officers shall be liable to disciplinary action by the Chief.

Rule No. 36—Chief or Acting Chief will have the power to suspend for cause any member of the department...

The above rules encompass the overall charge of 'Conduct unbecoming an Officer of this department.'

During a disciplinary hearing in the office of the Chief for the unit bargaining member on March 8, you became highly belligerent and made the following remarks. 'Goddamn, John, what are you doing? This is like picking cotton in the field in the slavery days.' This remark of picking cotton suggests a racial overtone since I am a black Fire Chief. Your constant reference to me as 'John' and also the statement that you have no respect for this office along with threat of 'I will not stop calling you John' cannot and will not be condoned by this office. You are first and foremost an officer of this department and secondly, Union President. In that regard, your conduct shall reflect what is expected of an officer of this department.

At this time you are hereby notified that you shall be suspended for one (1) day from duty on Monday, March 25, and you are further warned that any future violations of this department's rules and regulations will necessitate a more severe penalty being assessed.

Fiorillo filed a grievance concerning the suspension. A second grievance hearing was held before Personnel Administrator Skaba, who with the concurrence of then Acting Personnel Director Jennifer Smith, sustained the grievance and overturned the one-day suspension. Skaba and Smith's reasons were set forth in the written April 29, 1985 grievance decision:

Per Article VI, section 6.7 of the collective bargaining agreement, the union president is on union business leave for the purpose of conducting union business. During the disciplinary hearing of March 8, 1985, the grievant was representing the union in his capacity as union president. Union officials are guaranteed certain labor relations freedoms without fear of reprisal as long as—the union official is pursuing an activity protected by labor law and such activity is not pursued in bad faith for unlawful ulterior purposed or is not an illegal activity.

During the hearing of March 8, 1985, the grievant did say some things which could be construed as belligerent, disagreeable and perhaps offensive. However, it is difficult for this writer to read the mind of the grievant to determine his motive for his actions at the hearing of March 8, 1985 and it was not proven that the intent was racially motivated or insubordinate. Being offensive may be in poor taste but is protected under the law in this instance.

In conclusion, the grievant is union president, was acting on union business and was pursuing an activity protected by labor law, thus truculence and disagreeableness of his manner in doing so is not a basis for a one-day suspension in this case.

Therefore, this grievance is sustained.

By the time of the March 8, 1985, incident, Wilson Gaitor was no longer City Manager. He had been replaced by Alfred Gatta.

There is no evidence that Stewart's decision to impose discipline on Fiorillo was prompted by recommendations of anyone else, including Gatta.

Stewart testified that he had imposed the discipline because Fiorillo's conduct demonstrated disrespect for the office of fire chief and because Fiorillo had made a racial comment. Stewart's specific testimony on this score was:

"I felt that this particular incident was way beyond the realm of what is in the scope of what is Unionism and Union rights. I think it infringed and caused great disrespect in this office of the Chief…

> Very candidly, as a black chief I felt it reflected the days that the blacks were in slavery in the field…

In its discussions, the labor board, in part, stated the following:

> We do not believe Fiorillo's remarks were intended to be racially discriminatory in the sense that Fiorillo intended to degrade or humiliate Stewart … Fiorillo's argument was that because Stewart is black, he should have a special sensitivity to the injustice of requiring people to work against their will without pay. The argument is fallacious because it

had no tendency to prove whether the unit bargaining member would have been required to work without pay under the terms of the suspension; on the other hand, the argument was not designed to degrade, humiliate or cast negative aspersion on Stewart's racial background as would be the case in the "abusive for of Argumentum ad Hominem… Accordingly, only the most flagrant or egregious conduct or speech will deprive a union representative of protection when he is engaged in otherwise protected union activity." Fiorillo's statements did not reach such a level.

The result of this hearing was that one complaint was sustained, ordering the City to cease and desist from threatening employees with discipline or otherwise discriminating against employees for engaging in protected union activity. The complaint of a designed pattern of threats and intimidation was dismissed. Still, I can say without reservation that no previous fire chief had been subjected to such obstruction and disrespect by a union president.

There was no question in my mind that this union president was attempting to do what he could to make my job more difficult. It seemed his sole purpose was to obstruct, nullify, and attack my every decision. In one instance he complained that for two consecutive years, I had fired recruits from the training class without notifying the union, as required by contract. In each instance I was told by the city to rehire and give back pay to the fired recruits and to notify the union. Since whether or not the recruits should be fired was not at issue, only the process, I proceeded to fire them again. I knew the union president delighted in criticizing me in the press.

"Is it my fault he can't learn?" Fiorillo told a reporter for the *Hartford Courant*.

The only response I could give in my defense in this instance was, "I forgot. I'm human." A different union president might have said, "Hey, you forgot to notify us." But not this union president. He used this instance to say publicly, "Hey, that stupid Stewart, he doesn't know what he's doing."

On another occasion I had scheduled the fire department's annual awards ceremony to honor twenty-two fire fighters and five civilians. Each of the honorees had performed some life-saving service or other honorable deeds. Under the union president's orders, the fire fighters to be honored planned to boycott the ceremony. Other fire fighters planned to form a picket line if I proceeded with the ceremony. This, they said, would be their way of protesting that they had been working without a contract for almost a year.

"It appears to some people that it's been a long time," I told a reporter for the *Hartford Courant* when he questioned me about the contract negotiations and the planned picketing of the ceremony. "If they don't want to show up for their own ceremony, it's up to them. Who am I to tell them what to do on their off-duty time?" On the day before the ceremony, we began getting calls from the honorees saying they would not cross the picket line. Nearly all of the twenty-two fire fighters to be honored said they would not attend. Two hours before the ceremony was scheduled to begin, I decided to cancel it. Meanwhile, at least two hundred fire fighters had gathered to form a picket line, only to learn the event was canceled. Undaunted, they decided to march in front of the Old State House to let people know of their grievance.

In my mind the most outrageous act committed by union members was releasing three live rats at a city council meeting. This despicable act was their way of expressing dissatisfaction with the council's lack of response to their contract grievances. Outraged council members immediately denounced the act. But a council angry over the release of rats in their chamber was not sufficient to stop the determined fire fighters. On another occasion when the council was in session, a fire fighter set off a loud firecracker.

City Manager Alfred Gatta felt some progress was being made in the contract negotiations. One sticking point had to do with a requirement reached in the earlier 1981 contract settlement. The city had agreed then to maintain twenty fire companies at all times, with each company having a minimum crew of four fire fighters. Now, after six years, the city wanted to have the option of using three fire fighters on each truck instead of four. The union president objected, believing that a three-person crew could cause injury and death to fire fighters, as well as to city residents. City officials now maintained that four-person companies were not always necessary, and meeting that earlier contract requirement had pushed the fire department's overtime pay to $2.3 million in 1986–87.

The city was also attempting in these negotiations to recover management rights it had given away in past contract settlements. The union president contended that the current talk of "management rights" was a smokescreen for a return to the days before there was a strong union. Back to the days, he said, when a fire chief ruled like a military commander.

"Mr. Stewart's interpretation of management rights is he can do anything he wants, at any time," Fiorillo fumed.

By August 1987 no contract settlement had been reached, and a panel of arbitrators was selected to find a solution to the impasse. One evening while I was relaxing at home with my family, a large number of fire fighters entered my block and set up a picket line in front of my house. They paraded back and forth and with loud voices read their picket signs. "Support Your Life Savers! Gatta Gotta Go!" I estimated their number to be nearly one hundred. This loud demonstration brought my neighbors out of their houses. Seeing their dismay, the fire fighters grew even louder. This was the first time in my thirty-seven years with the fire department that fire fighters had picketed the home of their chief.

I knew most of them and went outside and said, "Welcome to Canterbury Street." A reporter came up to me wanting to know why I didn't display any anger over the demonstration in front of my house. "Hey, it's a free country," I said, "It's their right." At the same time, a group of fire fighters were parading in front of the city manager's house. I suspected rightly, that the union president was behind these demonstrations.

Another tactic being used by the union during the contract negotiations was absenteeism. The rate of fire fighters absent from their shift was at an all-time high of 25 percent. When Deputy City Manager Michael Brown was asked at a city council meeting if the fire fighters' absenteeism rate was high for Connecticut, he responded, "We will demonstrate conclusively that our absences are high when judged against anywhere in Western civilization." Brown also explained that the overtime expenses resulting from absenteeism made up a large part of the $1 million deficit projection in the fire department's operations budget.

"It is projected that the fire department will have a crushing deficit by the end of the fiscal year," Brown added. Because of the absenteeism and a previous agreement that called for a reduction in staffing, I had no choice but to offer overtime in order to properly man the fire-suppression division. The contract agreement signed between the city and the union in 1980 required that a minimum eighty-six fire fighters be available for firefighting at all times. This minimum staffing was one of the aspects the city was now seeking to change through binding arbitration. Of course, the no-shows during these negotiations caught the attention of the *Hartford Courant*. An editorial on Wednesday, November 16, 1988 said in part:

> Listening to Hartford officials complain about the high absenteeism rate of fire fighters, one might think that a mysterious virus had invaded the firehouses and infected the crews with laziness and a predisposition to commit extortion. The fire fighters union says high absenteeism is the result of an understaffed and demoralized department's being forced to protect a city full of tinder-box housing.

The city and Local 760 of the International Association of Fire Fighters are negotiating a new contract, which is in arbitration, so the hyperbole is expected. Hostility prevails and sometimes it has become childish. As when someone exploded a firecracker during a union protest Monday at City Hall.

Finally, after nearly three years of contract negotiations, the panel of arbitrators was able to resolve the issues that separated the city and the union. No one in city government was happier than I was to see the negotiations come to an end. In all, a total of sixty disputed issues had been settled, and a new four-year contract had been signed. I was pleased with some of the city administration's gains, and was relieved to have a new contract in place. These contract negotiations had been the most difficult and prolonged in the history of the fire department, and the first decided by arbitration since 1976.

One issue that the union had to concede was the matter of "management rights." I now had the power as chief to make temporary staffing assignments. I was given the authority to change the current staffing requirement of eighty-six fire fighters per shift to seventy-eight fire fighters. This decision would result in a budget savings of approximately $700,000. The bottom line was that I could now manage the department with fewer challenges from the union. I had the authority to make assignments and also to discipline fire fighters when necessary, without interference from the union president.

As expected, some of the fire fighters were dissatisfied with the contract and still bitter over the lengthy negotiations.

"We're glad it's over with, but it's going to take more than that to heal the wounds that have been inflicted on us by the city administration," one lieutenant told a reporter. "The union did not get what it wanted," he added. "It was half-and-half, and we were looking for the whole thing." One of the things that angered him was that for the first time, fire fighters would not earn as much as city police officers.

Another fire fighter put a different spin on the final contract. "We didn't lose anything as I see it. The chief always had management rights. It was just how you exercise them."

Still another said angrily, "If they think they're going to break the union, they're wrong. We're actually stronger." None of these fire fighters would give their names to the reporter, fearing I might seek some form of retribution. That was the farthest thing from my mind. I felt the arbitrators had treated the rank and file fairly. They had received pay raises amounting to 31 percent over a four-year period. The weekly pay of a fire fighter was immediately raised from $538.50 to $666.75 and would increase to $707. They would receive $12,000 retroactive pay. Retroactive pay for lieutenants amounted to $13,000, $16,000 for captains, and $19,000 for deputy chiefs. Fire fighters would still pay $1.15 per week for health insurance, and not the $5 the city wanted. Annual pension payments would be based on the average of the best three years of pay during a fire fighter's last five year of service. The pension was currently based on the best five salary years of the final ten. The union had sought to have the pensions based on a final paycheck, with a portion of unused sick days factored into the computation. They didn't get this. It was my hope that the relationship between management and the union would improve as a result of the contract.

As a result of the contract agreement, the following editorial appeared in the *Hartford Courant* in May 1990:

Reality Comes to the Firehouse

After a nasty three-year struggle, City Hall and the Hartford fire fighter's union have a contract that brings reality to the firehouse. The contract paves the way toward letting the chief be chief, grants generous pay raises and may even plug the dollar drain from the city treasury. And it lets everyone know that juvenile antics, such as exploding firecrackers and setting rats loose at City Hall, won't score points.

Supervisors will have more control over assignments, discipline, pension and overtime costs. For example, Fire Chief John B. Stewart Jr. may take up to eight fire fighters off regular duty for three months to perform special projects, such as turning off fire hydrants during summer or helping to teach the public about fire prevention. He didn't have authority to do even that before. By reducing the work force in the slow summer months, City Hall could save $700,000 in overtime pay. The city won lower pension contributions that will save millions of dollars in the long run. Also the chief gains more power to suspend fire fighters accused of serious crimes.

The union did well, too. Members only have to look at Springfield, Mass., where about 75 fire fighters are losing their jobs, or at New Haven, which may close a few fire companies to bring the municipal deficit under control. The base pay of Hartford fire fighters will go from about $29,000 to $39,000 in July. They will continue to enjoy excellent health benefits for a contribution of only $1.15 per week. Most of them will receive $12,000 in back pay. That's because the contract actually covers the past three years. It expires in June 1991.

Alas, both sides will be at it again in February. There's much to set right before the public gets what it pays for. Overtime costs must be further reduced. So long as every supervisor except the chief and two assistants have to belong to the same union as the rank and file, oversight and discipline will suffer. This settlement was expensive for taxpayers, but at least it puts some curbs in the union's renowned omnipotence.

As the editorial stated, I now had more control over assignments and discipline. I was more than pleased with this outcome. During the contract negotiations, I observed my tenth anniversary as fire chief, and made the comment to a fire fighter that I would soon be looking toward retirement.

When word of this comment reached Fiorillo, his response was, "I've been with the department twenty years, and I'm already eligible for retirement. But I'm going to try to stay as long as John Stewart is here."

KEEPING IT REAL

In March 1991 City Manager Gene Shipman requested that I assist him in his effort to become better acquainted with the relationship between city residents and city government. I had been recommended to him as a person who understood the dynamics of the city and the minority community in particular. Shipman was also told that I had served as assistant to City Manager Ed Curtin. So I made Assistant Chief John Kehoe acting fire chief and took a leave of absence from the fire department. I was now back serving the city manager, this time as his acting deputy. Instead of going to my office at department headquarters, I reported to work each morning at city hall. During the week Shipman and I worked closely together on city business, but almost every weekend, Shipman would disappear to some unknown destination. He never bothered to inform me of his whereabouts. On these weekends he just left me in charge to run the city. When Deputy Mayor I. Charles Matthews or another city official would ask me, "Where's the city manager?" I simply answered, "He's out of town."

Shipman may have seen the handwriting on the wall when Democratic council members who supported him were voted out of office in the September 1991 primary. Before leaving office they planned to extend Shipman's contract for two years, thus making it harder for the incoming council to oust him. They also planned to give him a pay raise, from $100,000 to $107,000 per year. But they were not able to get the measures passed in time.

"Had we been reelected, we would have extended his contract," Deputy Mayor Matthews told a reporter. Even as the incoming council members were preparing to take office, they were questioning Shipman's loyalty to them and his leadership style. Councilwoman and Green Party member Elizabeth Horton Sheff was one of Shipman's most vocal critics.

"We had the opportunity to interact with Mr. Shipman all through the orientation process, and there were instances that demonstrated the difference in leadership style," she told a reporter. It took only eleven days for the beleaguered Shipman, under pressure from Mayor-elect Perry, Sheff, and other incoming council members, to submit his letter of resignation.

"It is my firm belief that in order to give you the opportunity to provide leadership and policy direction for the city, you need the opportunity to fill my position with a person of your own choosing," he wrote in his resignation letter. On the last day in December 1991, Shipman was in Philadelphia accepting a top government position in the City of Brotherly Love.

"I had fun," Shipman told a reporter when reflecting on his time in Hartford. "Quite frankly," he added, "it had been a manager's dream." Shipman's time as Hartford's city manager had been one of the shortest. It lasted just fourteen months.

With Shipman no longer the city manager, I was back working full-time as fire chief. To my way of thinking, it was to my credit that I had now had the opportunity to work as interim assistant and as deputy city manager to two city managers. These experiences added to my growing fascination of how city government worked. I was now looking more closely at how the elected officials were handling the many challenges facing the City of Hartford. I took note of the issues that were causes for concern among elected officials, government workers, and community leaders. For example, Hartford's population over the past five years had increased from 136,000 to 140,000 residents. Just over 25 percent of these residents were living below the poverty line. The average monthly welfare payment for a mother and her three children was $625, and no less than 40,000 children in the city were dependent on food stamps.

Forty-eight percent of the city's schoolchildren lived in poor families, and over 40 percent of these children under twelve years old went to school hungry every day. Added to this, 35 percent of these children were at risk. In response to these staggering statistics, Mayor Perry established a task force on hunger with a mandate to formulate strategies to combat hunger in the city. Part of the task force's strategy was to mobilize citizens, churches, businesses, and government to work for the sustained elimination of hunger. Another major concern was the city's failing educational system. T. Josiah Haig, the new school superintendent, had recently called this his major concern. He called for school board members to "forget about ideology and concentrate on educating the children."

Still another concern I saw was the growing problem of drugs, gangs, and drive-by shootings. The police and neighborhood groups were desperately trying to find ways to end the violence. The National Institute of Justice had developed and funded a Drug Market Analysis Program, and city officials in Hartford were attempting to implement it. Its basic premise was that street-level drug sales were a key factor in the declining quality of life in inner-city neighborhoods. The program involved neighborhood revitalization through community policing, and was now in place in the North End. City officials were hoping this program would curb, if not end, the city's drug and gang problem.

In order for it to be successful, the program needed a joint effort from police, city agencies, and community groups. The program employed what was called "a reclamation and stabilization approach." The way it worked, police would reclaim the Stowe Village housing project target area by employing a variety of high visibility and anti-drug tactics over a period of several months. Once this area was reclaimed, the stabilization phase would attempt to maintain the area in its reclaimed state over the long term through a partnership involving the community, the city, and the police.

The city had implemented this program in four target areas, but it wasn't working as hoped. Unfortunately, it had become largely a police-only project with mixed short-term results. I can say, however, that in the future, the program would be refined and implemented with some measure of success in the Stowe Village Public Housing as the "Weed and Seed" program. Another concern for the segment of the population that enjoyed hockey, was a threat by owners of the city's professional hockey team, the Hartford Whalers, to move the team to another city. City officials were taking the team owners at their word and joined by loyal fans had organized a "Save the Whalers Campaign."

With Gene Shipman gone and the city now without a city manager, I begin to envision myself in that position. After thirty-nine years with the fire department, I had climbed to the top position, and I was only sixty-one years old. I reasoned that being appointed city manager would be a great way for me to top off my career. I knew I could do the job. I had served as interim assistant to City Manager Edward Curtin for nearly five years, and for eight months as interim acting deputy city manager to Gene Shipman. The current procedure was that in the absence of a city manager, the corporation counsel would become interim city manager until a successor was appointed. The corporation counsel at the time was Richard Cosgrove, a twenty-seven-year veteran of city government.

Excited over the prospect of becoming the next city manager, I prepared a cover letter, and along with my resume, mailed it to Mayor Perry. I also mailed it to each member of the city council. In my letter I detailed the experience I had acquired while serving the city over the past thirty-nine years. I reminded them of the five years I had served as interim assistant to City Manager Curtin, my work with the last city manager, and my familiarity with the position's responsibilities. I wrote of my dedication to the City of Hartford and of my desire to continue playing a part in its future. I reminded them that they all knew me and knew of my work on behalf of the city. Why conduct a time-consuming and costly nationwide search, I told them, when I was right here, ready, willing, and able to do the job? I was encouraged about my chances when I learned later that a number of council members wanted to find someone local to fill the position, or someone with Hartford roots.

"We want someone who really knows where this city is today and where it's going in the future," said Councilman Anthony DiPentima. The way I figured, who better than me?

Word began spreading throughout the city that I wanted to be the next city manager. At the end of February 1992, an editorial appeared in the *Hartford Courant* that I thought might hurt my chances. Anyone reading the story might get the impression that I had unwittingly opened the city vaults to the fire fighter's union. The story said in part:

> Fire Chief John B. Stewart is a contender for the position of city manager, vacated by Gene Shipment late last year. He has not enhanced his image as a leader with his handling of the fire fighters' contract...

> Tying the city to an unaffordable agreement reached without the approval of the city manager is no way to do this. The council must reject the agreement.

When people began questioning me about the editorial, I explained to them that Interim City Manager Richard Cosgrove had given me authorization to meet with the union president and to resolve a disagreement about private-duty jobs. At that meeting we discussed this matter, and also a number of other issues. I told them I had met with the union president in order to avoid a repeat of the last lengthy and acrimonious contract negotiations. When we concluded our discussion, the union president and I signed a memorandum of agreement. Again I stressed to my questioners that I had prior authorization to do so. Still, the editorial gave me cause to reflect on my actions and what had followed. The agreement I had signed with the union president included pay increases of almost 25 percent over three years, generous improvement in pensions, and fully paid medical benefits for fire fighters retiring after 1993.

After learning of the agreement, Interim City Manager Cosgrove contacted the union president, informing him that he had not approved the agreement. Cosgrove then wrote a letter to the city council saying that the city could not afford to be so generous. Disregarding what Cosgrove said, the union president called a meeting of union members and ratified the agreement. At the next city council meeting, Cosgrove told council members to reject the agreement.

"I fear that if thirty days elapse, the statutory amount of time after which the contract would go into effect by default, the city would be legally bound by it," he told them. I was called by the council to meet with them in a closed executive session to explain why I had entered into such an agreement.

"It was my understanding that before going into effect, the agreement would go back to the city manager for review," I explained to the council. "I never thought it was a done deal." In the end the council rejected the agreement.

As pleased as I was when on occasion my name was mentioned as Shipman's possible successor, you can imagine my great disappointment when I learned that the city council was now undertaking a national search for the next city manager.

"We want to make sure we appoint the best person available," a council member announced. By March 1992 I was more hopeful when I later learned that I was one of eight semifinalists for the position. Only three of the eight were local. Besides me, the others were Alan J. Greenwald, the former executive director of the Hartford Redevelopment Agency, and George B. "Pete" Kinsella, the former city treasurer. Word had it that Kinsella was the early favorite. However, I continued to believe that my chances of becoming city manager were good. The letdown came in May when it was announced that the city council voted unanimously to offer the position to Howard J. Stanback. Talk about hopes rising and waning, that's what I had experienced over the past several months. Now my hopes of becoming city manager had faded. The council had selected an aviation consultant from Chicago who had once managed O'Hare International Airport. That ended my hopes.

Several other cities, including New York and Atlanta, were interested in Stanback for a top administrative position, but he chose to accept the city manager position in Hartford. The announcement by Deputy Mayor Fernando Comulada was that "Mr. Stanback showed some experience in the problems that we face here in the city of Hartford." Another council member stressed that Stanback being African American played no part in his selection. Because he had been recommended by his former college classmate and now Councilwoman Louise Simmons, there were some feelings both inside and outside city government that Stanback had the inside track.

It was hurtful to know that the mayor and those on the city council who knew me well did not believe I was the right person for the job. Who more than me had experience in helping to solve the tough problems confronting Hartford? I knew the city inside and out. I could have hit the ground running, while Stanback would have to be brought up to speed. But these were moot points now. Howard J. Stanback was the council's choice. The same day that the announcement of Stanback's appointment was made, I sat at my desk and prepared my retirement papers, and had them delivered to the city's personnel director. I had allowed myself two months to finalize my work at the fire department.

Even as I was doing this, I was aware of some tension in the Black community. People who had been victims of police brutality and their sympathizers were planning a public demonstration. I was paying close attention to the potential for violence and the destruction of property. As a precaution some store owners closed their doors and sent their workers home. I was contemplating whether or not to put the fire department on standby. The demonstration was to protest the not guilty verdict for four White police officers in Los Angeles who had beaten Black motorist Rodney King. Seeing this as injustice, mobs of people in that city viciously beat motorists, set fires, and looted stores.

During the demonstration Mayor Perry addressed the nearly one-hundred people who had gathered for a rally in front of the Old State House, "Today there were 5 million rumors going around! None of them are true! We are together as a city and we are going to see this through! We will not tolerate violence from anyone!" she continued. "We are going to fool them by Hartford being the peaceful city of the country!" Even so, a White man driving on Granby Street in the North End had his car window shattered and some attackers tried to pull him from his vehicle. When police arrived at the scene the youths dispersed.

This took place as Rodney King uttered this plaintive plea: "Can't we all just get along."

When word got out that I was planning to retire, Andrew Julien, a writer for the *Hartford Courant*, came to interview me. In May the following story ran in the newspaper.

Fire Chief to Retire; Broke Racial Barriers

John B. Stewart Jr., who broke racial barriers to become Hartford's first black fire chief 12 years ago, announced Tuesday he is retiring in June.

Stewart, a third-generation Hartford native from a prominent local family, joined the department as a fire fighter in 1952. At a time when blacks in many cities are struggling against disappointment and despair, Stewart said he is proof that the promise of America is still alive.

"When I graduated from Weaver High School in 1948, I looked at the world and the world told me, 'Why did you go to high school? There's no place for African-Americans in this world,'" Stewart said.

"When I started in the fire department, they told me I was lucky to get on the job and I'd never become an officer," he said. "I am proof that Hartford, Connecticut, represents the American dream."

Stewart was the first black to be promoted in the department and its first black captain. He said he was the first black in New England to become chief of a professional department.

Stewart, 61, will work in real estate and economic development, primarily in Hartford's North End—a section of the city he saw damaged by race riots in the late 1960s.

Stewart had hoped to become city manager, but was not one of the three finalists selected earlier this month by the city council. Monday the council selected Howard J. Stanback, a labor economist and former city resident, to be the new city manager.

Stewart said he had planned to retire at the beginning of this year but held off to apply for the manager's job. He had a brief stint as deputy city manager last year, and was among the leading local contenders for the position. But when the council chose Stanback, Stewart decided to retire.

"I competed," Stewart said, "that's all I asked for."

City officials said Tuesday it was too early to discuss possible successors.

Mayor Carrie Saxon Perry said Stewart has been a source of stability in the city and worked hard to maintain the fire department as a professional and responsible organization. "He's a fine man. I'm going to miss him dreadfully," Perry said. "You just could count on him in this chaotic world; there are not too many people you could say that about."

Middletown Fire Chief George P. Dunn, president of the Connecticut Fire Chiefs Association, described Stewart as a quiet, sincere person who was always easy to work with. "He's a true professional in the true sense of the word," Dunn said. "His consideration for the fire service and community protection is always at the top of his list."

Stewart has guided the department through periods of change and unrest. He has had stormy relations with union officials—capped by a bitter contract dispute that dragged on for three years in the late 1980s and was brought to an end in 1990.

A bid by Stewart earlier this year to avoid a similar showdown backfired. Union members voted on a tentative accord reached with Stewart, but on the advice of interim City Manager Richard M. Cosgrove, the council rejected the pact.

But along with the problems, Stewart said, there have been accomplishments: a modern fire fighting force, increased awareness of fire safety in the community and a more diverse department. Under Stewart, the department hired its first women, promoted its first Hispanic fire fighters and greatly increased the number of blacks.

But the time Stewart remembers most clearly was the late 1960s—when race riots erupted in cities across the nation.

Stewart was appointed to a special community relations team that went into Hartford's troubled neighborhoods and tried to stem the violence. It was a time of destruction and devastation, he said, but also historic changes.

"People felt they didn't have part of the American dream— they rioted, they tore up and they burned," Stewart said. "I'll never forget those years; those years were historic and memorable in this city."

Council member Eugenio Caro, a former police officer— worked with Stewart on the community relations team. Over the years, Caro said, Stewart had proved his devotion and dedication to the city.

"We've known each other a long, long time," Caro said. "Personally I think he's a very fine person, very dedicated individual—not only dedicated to his job and the city of Hartford, but to his family and his fire fighters."

Stewart is active in many civic and community organizations, including the Urban League, the NAACP and the board of education. He is a member of Faith Congregational Church, and lives on Canterbury Street in Hartford's Blue Hills neighborhood.

After his retirement from his $77,000-a-year post becomes final June 7, Stewart said he would like to work on economic development in the city's North End.

"You have to look hard to find a drugstore. You look at empty lots—there used to be buildings there," Stewart said.

"I believe that there is a place in this community for the former fire chief to become more active."

He says he's looking forward to the change, but admits to some nostalgia already. "I will miss the interaction, the excitement and the challenge," he said. "On the other hand, it's going to be nice to take the beeper off."

It had been awhile since a story about me in the *Hartford Courant* struck a positive note. For the longest time, it seemed every story about me had to do with my union troubles. So I was pleased with this story. It implied that my nearly twelve years as fire chief had been years of effective leadership. The story made it clear that being passed over for the city manager's job didn't hasten my retirement; I had originally planned to retire at the beginning of the year anyway. It also said I was leaving the department because I wanted to experience new challenges. As a result of the story, my upcoming retirement became public knowledge. So as I traveled around the city, I was receiving questions, comments, and words of congratulations from people I knew and some I didn't know.

"Congratulations, Chief." "You're too young to retire, Chief". "Why are you retiring, Chief?" "Are you being forced out?" "What are you going to do now, Chief?" Most people, however, just offered congratulations and thanked me for my service to the city.

My last two weeks as a member of the Hartford Fire Department seemed to pass very quickly. Maybe it was because I was feeling a sense of release from the pressures of being fire chief. When I awoke to my last day on the job, I thought to myself, had it really been forty years since my cousin Frank Davis caught my eye as he strolled up Martin Street in his uniform, and planted the first seeds in my mind of becoming a fire fighter?

Friday, June 12, 1992, was my last day as fire chief. I planned to spend the day finalizing some things and tying up loose ends. Then I would say my good-byes and that would be it. As I looked through that morning's *Hartford Courant*, I noticed an editorial with the headline "Hail to Chief Stewart and Farewell." After reading the editorial, I read again the last two sentences:

> ...In retirement Mr. John B. Stewart Jr. will work on economic development in the city's North End. Despite these hard economic times, Mr. Stewart will make a difference once again.

I had faced some real challenges, and I had surely taken my lumps over the past forty years, but according to the editorial, I had made a difference for the good of Hartford. That's really all I wanted to do as head of Special Services and then as chief of the fire department. I wanted to make a difference for the betterment of Hartford. When I joined the fire department in 1952, I had no idea what the future would hold for me. When I became an officer and was put in charge of Special Services, I tried to make a difference for the citizens of Hartford who were marginalized. As chief, I appointed Blacks to the officer's ranks, and I broke barriers of racism and sexism by hiring Hispanics and women. In taking these steps, I brought to an end the "traditionalism" and the entrenched racism that had long defined the culture of the city's fire department. I truly did believe, as the editorial stated, that I had made a difference.

It was customary that on the last day on the job, a department head would attend a farewell reception at city hall. When I walked into the function room the people in the room broke into applause. I saw city administrators, politicians, community leaders, city workers, fire fighters and well-wishers standing in clusters around the room. When Mayor Perry beckoned to me, I moved to stand beside her. The room became silent as the mayor spoke.

"Chief Stewart, on behalf of the citizens of Hartford, I thank you and congratulate you for your forty years of dedicated service to this city. Your service to the City of Hartford has been exemplary and it will be missed. We wish you God's speed and all the best in your retirement." City Manager Stanback then offered words of congratulations, followed by several other city officials.

"Today marks the end of forty years on the Hartford Fire Department," I said when it was my turn to speak. "They were years filled with many challenges and rewards. Twelve years ago I broke racial barriers when I was appointed Hartford's first Black fire chief. I accomplished many of the goals I had set for myself and for the fire department. I restructured the department, allowing for better communication. We purchased new apparatus, brought women and Hispanics into the fire service, overhauled the training program, and increased the number of fire chaplains. This I did for the purpose of giving the best protection possible to the life and property of the citizens of Hartford. There's faith and hope in this world," I said. "That's what you see here today. The good of Hartford. Thank you and God bless." Applause sounded throughout the room.

"What do you intend to do now, Chief?" someone asked.

"Gladys wants me to stay at home," I said with a half smile. When the reception ended, I went back to headquarters. After saying my final good-byes and collecting personal papers and articles, the chief's aide drove me home. True to his word that he would outlast me, Union President Fiorillo would remain another three years with the department before retiring.

Climbing to the very top of the promotional ladder had been hard, but I had made it. Once there, I found my footing. All of the misguided efforts of the union president had not kept me from being a successful fire chief. From 1980 to 1992, the Hartford Fire Department was one of a select few in the country to receive a top rating. Now that I was stepping down by my own choice, I planned to "keep it real." Keeping it real for me meant the old practice of traditionalism, where only those of a certain ancestry ascended to the chief's office, was now unrealistic. The reality was that people of color had come much too far and sacrificed too much for things to revert back to what they once were. Keeping it real meant that anyone who met the qualifications, regardless of race or gender, would have an equal chance at climbing to the very top of the promotional ladder.

A few weeks before retiring, I had met with City Manager Stanback and recommended to him that Assistant Chief Nelson Carter be named acting fire chief until a new chief was named. I had great confidence in the ability of Assistant Chief Carter to lead the fire department. He had worked his way up through every rank in the department. He was the department's first Black dispatcher and first line chief's aide. After making captain he was appointed head of Special Services, and later executive officer. Because of his excellent administrative skills, Assistant Chief Carter was situated in an office at headquarters next to mine. One of the things I liked about my relationship with Nelson Carter was that the two of us did not think alike. In many instances his opinion would differ from mine. This would always give me pause to reflect and think more deeply and consider other possibilities. On the day of my retirement, I was pleased to learn that the city manager had named Assistant Chief Carter as the acting fire chief.

In recognition of my service to the City of Hartford, a testimonial dinner was held in my honor on a Saturday afternoon in September 1992. I sat on the dais in the ballroom of the La Renaissance Ballroom in East Windsor, looking out as city and state officials, community leaders, colleagues, family members, and friends were welcomed by Chief Nelson Carter, who had been named as my successor. I saw Chief Claude Harris, of the Seattle Fire Department, and Chief Ronald Lewis, of the Richmond Fire Department. My former minister at Faith Church, Reverend Rubin Tendai, and his wife, Alana, had driven up from Maryland. The presence of all these people, I thought, was a testament to my time in public service and the people I had met and friends I had made over the years. Following his words of welcome, Chief Carter introduced local television personality Lew Brown as master of ceremony. Brown then introduced a representative from Governor Lowell Weicker's office, who read the governor's statement:

Dear Chief Stewart:

Congratulations on your fine, groundbreaking career at the Hartford Fire Department. I am proud that a man with your integrity became the department's first black chief 12 years ago.

You are a symbol to all Hartford residents—men, women and children of all colors—for the courageous and graceful ways you overcame prejudice and discrimination to reach the top of your profession. I realize it was not easy. But I also realize that you chose a job that helps others—friends and strangers alike—by protecting them from fire and educating them about fire safety. That is indeed the highest form of public service.

Please enjoy your retirement. I know even in retirement you will always find ways to help the Hartford community and the state. Your family will enjoy having you around more. Of course, your son Jeff has joined my staff, so don't expect him to visit too much on weekdays. Good luck.

Sincerely, Lowell P. Weicker Jr., Governor

Lew Brown then introduced Congresswoman Barbara Kennelly, who came forward and offered remarks:

John, all through our nation each one of our communities has been graced by very special people. People who by the strength of their spirit and ideals, are able to have a profound effect on the community in which they live and the people who live there. John, you are one such person.

In private and professional life, you have represented the best there is in the proud tradition of public service and civic responsibility. While it would be almost impossible to name the countless number of civic accomplishments that are yours, I can personally attest to your warmth, integrity and love of community and family. Your pioneering work on behalf of the NAACP, the City of Hartford, and its Fire Department has contributed immensely to uplifting our community's way of life. Our region is truly indebted to you for your outstanding fortitude and leadership in this role.

Congratulations and best wishes as you mark this occasion with family and friends. I am quite sure that Hartford will continue to benefit from your many talents and generosity. God Bless you.

Hartford Mayor Carrie Saxon Perry was next to offer remarks:

As Mayor of Hartford, it is my special pleasure to acknowledge the 40 years of distinguished service, including 12 years as Fire Chief, delivered to our city by Chief John B. Stewart Jr.

Chief Stewart has had a marked influence on Hartford and its communities far beyond his professional life as the city's chief fire fighter. He has taken a long and continued interest in the development of the city's educational, business and religious life, serving the Hartford community on many panels and advisory groups.

His service to the city has included times of conflict, periods of growth and contraction. In a variety of appointments

Chief Stewart sought to bring about harmony and better understanding between the community, the city's administration and the city's employees.

John B. Stewart Jr. has long been—and continues to be—a major asset and credit to Hartford. I am proud to have known him professionally and I am glad to have you as a friend.

Esther Bush, president and CEO of the Urban League of Greater Hartford Inc., made the following statement:

Congratulations to Fire Chief John B. Stewart Jr., on his retirement. Chief Stewart broke the stereotype barrier when he became the first African American Fire Chief in Hartford. We know that even though he will no longer hold the position of Fire Chief, he will continue to be an agent of change and leadership in the Greater Hartford community.

Chief Stewart has demonstrated an unsurpassed dedication to the citizens of Hartford through community service. He has provided Hartford with an exceptional example of achievement through such roles as his tenure as the Urban League's Board Chairman.

What a pleasant surprise it was when I saw Mary Turley, my fourth grade teacher at Brackett Elementary School, and now deputy mayor of the town of Windsor, make her way to the dais. After remarking about the good nature of her ten-year-old student of fifty years earlier, she offered me congratulations on a successful career of public service. The statements by Governor Weicker and Congresswoman Kennelly, the remarks of other dignitaries, and the presence of my family and so many people made me feel that thus far my life had been purposeful and meanindful.

As you might imagine, when it was my time to speak, I was filled with emotion. I spoke of my forty years of experience as a member of the Hartford Fire Department, and the many joys and the challenges. I thanked everyone for their belief in me and their support over the years. And as usual, I gave thanks to the good Lord for a blessed life. When I finished the people stood and applauded. This was an afternoon I knew I would not forget.

What was ironic was that at the time of this testimonial dinner, City Manager Stanback was wondering if he had made a big mistake in coming to Hartford.

"You have to ask yourself sometimes: What am I doing here," he opined several days earlier to a reporter. "I had a nice existence in Chicago. I gave up income. I don't have my family here with me. My daughter started playschool and I wasn't there," he said. Not long after my testimonial dinner, the city manager met with a group of local clergy and asked them to talk with council members in an effort to end their disputes and political infighting that were now a regular occurrence within the council.

"Whose side are you on?" a council member had asked the city manager.

"I'm committed to the mayor," he answered.

"That's a problem for us," the council member replied.

"I admit I am disappointed," Standback told the reporter. "But it's way too soon to make a judgment about my future." He had only been city manager four months, but as in the case of Gene Shipman's brief tenure, I again saw the handwriting on the wall.

FROM FIRE FIGHTER TO POLITICIAN

After retiring from the fire department I was faced with another one of those life-defining moments. What would I do with the remainder of my life? I was only sixty-one years old. Too young, as far as I was concerned, to just sit at home. I would have to redefine myself. At the farewell reception at city hall, I told those gathered that my retirement didn't mean I would not be active in Hartford anymore. What I didn't tell them was that I was already poised to take a seat on the Democratic Town Committee. Having been passed over for city manager, my goal now was to eventually take a seat on the city council. The day I retired, the council was in a state of confusion. Mayor Carrie Saxon Perry and six other Democrats, and three People for Change party members had taken office in January. I thought that with a Democratic majority, the council would be able to work together and get things done for the betterment of the residents of Hartford. But by June some of the Democrats elected with Perry were questioning the council's direction, while the other council members were wondering if they could even work together.

There were initial signs that the council members were working together and achieving results that advanced the city's interest. In February 1992 five of them had sponsored an ordinance restricting what Hartford buys from companies doing business in South Africa. The ordinance would force the city to reconsider future purchases of hundreds of items, from computers to fuel oil.

Council members (standing from left) Sandra Little, Elizabeth Horton Sheff, Fernando Comulada, Eugenio Caro, Anthony DiPentima. Seated from left Louise Simmons, Nick Fusco, Mayor Perry, Henrietta Milward, and Yolanda Castillo.

"What this ordinance does," Councilwoman Louise Simmons explained, "is that given a choice, we will do business with companies that aren't involved in South Africa." Another sponsor, Green Party member Elizabeth Horton Sheff, said she was mad that Hartford had not passed the ordinance in 1986 when it was first offered.

"The poverty in South Africa is still there!" she exclaimed. "The racial oppression is still there! Nelson Mandela still cannot vote!" Nonetheless, the council still had before it an ambitious agenda, and I felt they had a responsibility to work together for the good of Hartford. The Hartford Federation of Teachers' proposed contract still needed council action. There was the proposal by Police Chief Ronald J. Loranger to involve community residents through "community service warranties." These warranties were supposed to make police more accountable if residents helped fight crime in their communities. The council had yet to act on the proposal. And there was the important matter of charter revision. This had been the main theme of Perry's reelection platform. The coalition that came into office on Perry's coattails also supported charter revision and a strong mayor form of governance. But by July the coalition had fallen apart, and bickering seemed to be the main activity of council members.

Power on the council had shifted from Mayor Perry to a five-member Democratic majority apparently frustrated with the direction of city government. The five included Yolanda Castilo, Henrietta S. Milward, Eugenio Caro, Anthony DiPentima, and Fernado Comulada At a special meeting, they appointed Milward as deputy mayor, and Castillo as council majority leader. This new alliance had been formed without Perry's input or her blessing. The five were playing down the shift in power, saying it was not a break from the mayor, while at the same time now favoring retention of the council-manager form of government.

This was a slap in the face to the mayor as she witnessed the five, who were a part of her slate, switch their support away from charter revision. Apparently in the months since the election, the five had become convinced that Perry "did not possess the leadership traits" to be a strong mayor. Still, it was the Charter Revision Commission that had the responsibility of proposing what charter changes would be on the next ballot. In Perry's favor was the fact that the majority of commission members handpicked by her, still favored charter change. As I watched the bickering and confusion within the council, I felt that with my years of experience working as a city department head and in the city manager's office, I could make the council into a more effective body.

Meanwhile, editorial writers at the *Hartford Courant* had suggested to Howard J. Stanback that he step out of the corner office and from behind his marble-topped desk, away from the inexperienced city council and department heads who communicate poorly with one another, and take a look around. In the neighborhoods that lie in almost any direction—the North End, the South End, downtown, the Park Street area, and the West End, the editorial said, are residents and community groups that will be looking to him for solutions to their problems. Even though my attempt to be appointed city manager had not been successful, I held no animosity toward the new city manager and hoped for his success. However, with a divided city council, I knew this was easier said than done.

I had decided to begin my political career in my own backyard. My son Jeffrey was giving up his seat on the Blue Hills Town Committee, and I planned to assume that seat. Once this happened I would represent the nearly fifteen thousand residents of the Blue Hills neighborhood. Of these fifteen thousand who would be my constituents, 56 percent were Black (many of Caribbean descent), 20 percent were White, and 6 percent from other minority groups. The Blue Hills Town Committee was one of three Town Committees in the North End. Each committee represented a different assembly district—the First, Fifth, and Seventh. The Blues Hills Town Committee, which consisted of about eight or nine members, was in the Seventh District.

This Town Committee had once been a real power base in the North End. But the leadership was diluted when redistricting divided up the old Seventh District, giving parts of it to the First and Fifth Districts. After the reapportioning, the First District and the Fifth District formed a meandering pattern across Blue Hills, Upper Albany, Asylum Hill, and the West End. In all, there were a total of seven Town Committees that together made up Hartford's Democratic Town Committee. When I was selected to fill the remainder of my son's term, the Democratic Town Chair was Edwin Vargas Jr. He was a member of Perry's Democrats for Leadership Coalition and with her support, had been elected chair the previous March. His election was a stunning turnaround for Vargas, who a week earlier had lost his bid for a seat on the Town Committee from a district in the South End. He became the first Puerto Rican to chair the fifty-six-member Democratic Town Committee.

Because the Democratic Town Committee had the responsibility of endorsing the official Democratic slate of candidates for elective office, Vargas's election caused some initial fear that a "Puerto Rican takeover" would ensue. Those who voted against Vargas had voted for Trude Johnson to assume that position. Johnson's strongest supporter had been North End power broker Abraham A. Giles, an iconic leader of the Fifth District. While supporting Johnson, Giles was seeking to be endorsed for a seat in the General Assembly. After serving sixteen years in the General Assembly, Giles had lost in 1988 to Maria Sanchez. When Sanchez died in office, Giles tried to regain his seat but lost in a special election to Edna Negron. In the September 1992 primary, Giles was successful in becoming the endorsed candidate for the Fifth District seat in the General Assembly, only to lose in the general election to Marie Kirkley-Bey. This was the fourth consecutive lost for Giles, who, if the *Hartford Courant* is to be believed, "ranked as one of the worst lawmakers during his sixteen years in the House."

While Giles's overall record in the State Assembly from 1972 to 1988 may have been questionable to some, to be fair I felt he had developed some meaningful legislation for his North End constituents. This included legislation for job training, day care centers, and Head Start. He had also played a role in passing legislation for affordable housing, and legislation enabling senior citizens to receive proper Medicaid and property tax relief. He also assisted in passing the Enterprise Zone legislation, which did attract some needed business to the North End. Also, to the delight of many city Blacks, Giles introduced Connecticut's first anti-apartheid bill and led the fight for divestiture of state funds in South Africa. He also helped in the fight to make Martin Luther King's birthday a state holiday.

So whether Giles was, or was not, to be viewed as an effective legislator was in the eye of the beholder. Even though Kirkley-Bey had defeated him in his bid to return to the State Assembly, Giles still had a substantial power bloc in the North End. I viewed the sixty-six-year-old Giles as the quintessential old-school politician. If a constituent needed a streetlight, that person would get a streetlight; if a stop sign was desired; Giles would see to it that a stop sign was put in place; if a family member was sick, the family would receive a call from Giles; if you needed a few dollars, he would give you a few dollars. On occasion he would pay rent for a constituent, buy food, or stave off an eviction. Once when I was having financial issues, I borrowed money from Giles, but first I had to kiss his ring. Then he hounded me until I paid back every cent.

Abraham Lincoln Giles was born on June 21, 1926, in Jenkins County, Georgia, and raised in Savannah, Georgia. His father, Frank Giles, was a carpenter who helped build houses for a living, while his mother had a job peeling shrimp. One story had it that the elder Giles cared more about preaching and politics than he did about carpentry. He took his young son Abraham with him on the long walk each year to pay his poll tax. This, it was said, was how Abraham Giles got his start in politics. In 1956 Giles and his wife, Juanita, relocated from Georgia to Hartford. Giles would often boast of his strong work ethic, which could be seen in the types of jobs he had, including hotel clerk, bowling alley manager, computer operator, busboy, lawn man, laundry worker, laundry owner, carpenter, real estate broker, state marshal, supermarket owner, novelty license plate maker, parking lot operator, and furniture mover. While Giles attributed his business success to his work ethic, his critics attributed it to plain old politicking. Many who knew Giles feared that his wheeling and dealing would one day land him in serious trouble.

By July 1992 Town Chairman Edwin Vargas had not held a Town Committee meeting or a spokesperson committee meeting. For this reason I was becoming disappointed with his performance. There had been talk among committee members of taking a no-confidence vote, but I thought we should give Vargas a chance to pull things together before taking any action. After completing my son's term on the Blue Hills Town Committee, I began serving my own two-year term after securing signatures from 5 percent of the Seventh District registered voters. Each area Town Committee had a spokesperson, and I was elected to be the spokesperson for my district. As spokesperson, I decided to reach out to the other Town Committee spokespersons and try to form an alliance of

Town Committees. Since council members benefit from a Democratic Town Committee endorsement, it was my belief that a unified committee majority could have influence over city council members. My hope was to use this body as a base for building a coalition to knock some sense back into our present council members and the mayor. Their continuous bickering was hurting Hartford at a time when the city was suffering. I planned to use every skill I had to build an alliance that would work for the benefit of the whole city. I wanted to build an alliance that would have people with differing beliefs working together to stabilize the city's economic, business, and employment situations.

While all this was taking place, Thirman L. Milner, who had stepped down as Hartford's mayor, announced his candidacy for the state senate. Former State Senator Wilbur Smith had planned to run and regain his seat in the Second Legislative District, but having been diagnosed with cancer, Smith was too sick to run. From his deathbed Smith asked Milner to run in his place. Milner promised his friend that he would. The seat was currently held by State Senator Frank Barrows. Barrows had won the seat from Smith in 1985 and was well liked by his constituents. He now chaired the Senate's Public Safety Committee and Select Housing Committee. Seeking the endorsement of the Democratic Town Committee, Milner accused Barrows of not having "taken a pro-active leadership position in the senate, even though he's on some important committees." When Milner became the endorsed candidate, Barrows ran on the "A Connecticut Party" line, seeking to retain his seat. This resulted in a September 1992 primary battle, which Milner won. In the November general election, Milner was victorious over his Republican opponent, as well as Barrows, who had kept his promise to run against Milner twice.

I had made it a point during this time not to publicly voice my disappointment with the ineffectiveness of the city council. I was spokesperson for the Blue Hills Town Committee, but I was keeping a low profile. I was aware that City Manager Stanback was really having problems with the infighting among council members. At times the bickering was so disruptive that the city manager was again voicing second thoughts about having accepted the position. The council majority, that is the five former mayoral allies, had drawn Stanback into the conflict, accusing him of showing favoritism toward the mayor. It was this favoritism, they said, that was behind Stanback's decision to give a consulting contact to a company owned by one of Mayor Perry's financial donors. The contract called for W&R Associates to study ways to improve the city's computer system and make it easier for Stanback to supervise city departments and prepare budgets. After learning of the contract, the council majority rescinded it, leaving Stanback to do the study himself.

On another occasion, when Stanback spoke out publicly about the bickering between the two factions, he was chastised by Councilman Anthony DiPentima, who said Stanback was wrong to speak publicly about the council's disputes, especially since he seemed to be taking Mayor Perry's side. DiPentima viewed Stanback's public speaking as lobbying on behalf of the mayor.

"Stanback should stick with city management and not speak publicly about the council's performance," he told a reporter. Because I had worked in the city manager's office, I understood how the infighting could not only prevent the city manager from doing his job in the most efficient way, but could also keep the council from concentrating on important issues like the looming budget deficit, erosion of the city's tax base, and loss of jobs in the private sector. Indeed, Hartford officials were still reeling from the announcement by G. Fox & Company that it intended to close its large downtown department store. This would result in hundreds of people losing their jobs, as well as the elimination of a significant tax base. Added to this, there was the large number of layoffs now taking place at the Travelers Insurance Company.

When the G. Fox Department Store did close its doors, I answered the call when the city council named me to a downtown development task force. We were given the responsibility of determining what to do with the now empty eleven-story building on Main Street. I was pleased to have been asked to help formulate plans for developing the downtown area. At a task force meeting, I suggested the building be used to house discount and midrange retail, with entertainment options that included a casino.

"We would have to take great care in planning the entertainment center," I said, "but we could do it." I envisioned the best parts of Las Vegas, like great shows and reasonably priced food, while avoiding the mistakes of Atlantic City. My thoughts on this were not too different from what had been proposed by the five-member city council majority. They had proposed discount outlet stores that would attract tourists to downtown. They wanted the State Assembly to approve a casino hotel complex that would draw the kind of tourists that are drawn to Las Vegas. A major stumbling block was that Connecticut Governor Lowell Weicker Jr. had already vowed to veto a gambling bill if proposed by the General Assembly.

Mayor Perry and her council minority had yet a different vision for developing downtown. They wanted to bring an arena football team to Hartford and build a new convention center and hotel. They also wanted large well-known retail stores to anchor the downtown retail district. And they wanted to increase attendance at Hartford Whalers games by having fine restaurants for fans. This, they hoped, would keep the Hartford Whalers from leaving the city.

While these developmental plans were being debated by city officials, the financial situation in Hartford grew even more dire. The city's projected budget shortfall of $5.4 million for 1993 was projected to be even greater in 1994. To try to head off such large shortfalls, the council majority ordered Stanback to freeze the hiring of any new city employees. They also discussed whether they should call in financial experts from outside the city for fiscal advice. They were aware that such a move would send a message to the city manager that they lacked confidence in his ability to get city finances under control. The thought of the council taking such a step caused considerable discomfort for the city manager, leaving him to wonder if his authority was being questioned, and if the city council was now making decisions for him.

When Carrie Perry began her third term as mayor in January 1992, her political advisers could envision five defining events that would lead to her reelection for a fourth term—this time as a strong mayor. They included a victory in the charter referendum, renewal of the city manager's contract, passage of the new fiscal budget, a successful primary campaign for the official nomination, and a winning campaign in the general election. The mayor and her advisors were confident that all five could be achieved. In the middle of January, a wrinkle appeared in their plan that needed to be quickly ironed out. Howard Stanback, who had been Hartford's city manager for only seven months, confirmed that he had been contacted about a high-ranking position by a member of the Clinton administration in Washington, DC.

Learning of this, some council members were first surprised and then angered. They were angry over the fact that they had found out about Stanback's interview with Frederico Pena, secretary of transportation, not from the city manager, but by reading about it in the newspaper.

"I think he caught everyone off guard," Councilman Anthony DiPentima said. "If he wants to use his position as Hartford's city manager as a stepping-stone, then he should just use it and we'll go on." While Stanback would not reveal what position he was being considered for, speculation was that it was either as chief of the Federal Aviation Administration, or some deputy secretary position. Councilwoman Louise Simmons, who was Stanback's classmate at the University of Connecticut School of Social Work, and the one who had recommended Stanback for the city manager's job, rose to his defense.

"If he does not get a federal job," Simmons told her council colleagues, "the council should get the message that the city is lucky to have him." After a meeting with Perry, Stanback confided in her that he was not interested in a federal position, but wanted his name to remain on the candidacy list to be able to talk with influential people in Washington in order to help Hartford. So for the time being, it appeared this wrinkle had been ironed out.

The vote on the charter change was less than a month away when another wrinkle appeared. Democratic Town Committee Chair Edwin Vargas, who owed his chairmanship position to Perry, had done an about-face. He was now opposing charter change. He argued that charter change would give too much power to one person. Vargas went even further by announcing that he planned to form a special committee that would raise money for an anti-charter-revision effort. Of course, this left Perry and her advisors fuming. They knew this wrinkle would be more difficult to iron out, because charter change had become a hot-button issue throughout the city. A solid block of South End Town Committee members and many in the North End were opposed to revising the city charter.

Opposition to charter change was also growing in the West End, Frog Hollow, and Asylum Hill neighborhoods. I had initially thought charter change was likely to happen. I had even considered running for one of the two at-large city council seats that would result from the charter change. Given my citywide recognition, I felt I was well suited for an at-large seat. My support base was not only the North End, but it also included the South End and West End, as well as the Hispanic community. But with the council shift and the increasing numbers voicing opposition to charter change, I was no longer sure of its passage.

The high-spirited Perry, however, was not one to give in without first putting up a good fight. She and her supporters began organizing to do battle with the charter change opponents. After several unsuccessful attempts, Perry managed to get the signatures of ten-percent of the city's registered voters, forcing a citywide referendum as proposed by the Charter Revision Committee. Perry took great pleasure in the fact that she had bested her council rivals, who had already voted against having such a referendum. The mayor's loyal supporters then conducted a telephone poll to gauge the level of charter revision interest among city voters.

A professional poll to gauge voter attitudes toward charter revision was also commissioned by Perry. This poll revealed that charter revision was favored in the Blue Hills area and some of the other North End neighborhoods, but it was being rejected in the West End, Parkville, and Frog Hollow neighborhoods. This poll also revealed that charter revision was favored in only a third of the city's twenty-seven voting districts. Undaunted by the unfavorable poll numbers, Perry called on her 1991 campaign manager to organize voter turnout in support of charter revision. Meanwhile, her council opponents, confident they would defeat charter revision, organized a coalition to work against it. The coalition included White voters in the South End and West End, Puerto Rican voters in the central districts and part of the South End, and some Black voters in the North End.

The council majority, having been forced by the mayor's success at getting the needed signatures, set the referendum vote on charter change for the first Tuesday in February 1993. They knew that a February vote, which was unusual, would result in low voter turnout. What the council majority could not have foreseen, and what surely must have brought them much delight, was that on the day of the vote the city was in the midst of a heavy winter snowstorm. By mid-afternoon things were not looking good for the mayor, who was still hopeful she could garnish the needed votes. By evening her team expected it would fall short of the 15 percent affirmative votes needed to adopt the revision, but hoped to carry most of the city's twenty-seven voting districts. At the end of the day the charter revision proposal was defeated.

"We had a sweet victory," the Reverend Paul Ritter, a local minister and one of those leading the anti-charter revision campaign, told a reporter. "We had gotten bogged down in personalities, but people were saying let's get down to business. We have a system that works."

The next day Mayor Perry told a reporter that she did not regret going through with the referendum. "I blamed the defeat on a bitter city council majority that had scheduled the special referendum in the middle of winter," she bemoaned. The *Hartford Courant* at least agreed with the mayor's assessment.

"Tuesday's voting followed a long weekend," stated the newspaper article. "City hall was closed Monday, hindering last-minute efforts to register voters and file absentee ballots. Voters aren't accustomed to going to the polls in mid-February, and Tuesday's winter storm, cutting down the turnout, was a predictable possibility." I personally liked Mayor Perry, but seriously questioned whether she would make for a strong mayor. So in the end, I voted against charter change. With the charter referendum defeated, my thoughts of holding an at-large seat on the city council vanished. I decided to focus my efforts on the next primary and on becoming an endorsed candidate for a regular council seat on the Democratic slate.

The most pressing challenge facing City Manager Stanback at the time was the 1993–1994 fiscal budget that he was scheduled to present to the city council in April. Council members had hoped the state legislature would do as Governor Weicker proposed and divide among towns and cities all of the $130 million he had received for allowing Mashantucket Pequots video slot machines at their Ledyard casino. Legislators, however, used a third of the money to balance the state budget, and were still arguing over how to divide the remaining $85 million. Unless new revenues could be found or spending cut, Stanback estimated the city faced a shortfall of up to $35 million. The city manager did, however, have a plan for reducing this projected shortfall. One aspect of his plan included collecting grants for housing renovation, school construction, job training, street repairs, and façade improvement on retail stores. The grant money would be combined with money from private business and then be directed to struggling neighborhoods. Council members were especially receptive to the long-term initiatives of the overall plan.

As the budget deadline neared, the city council adopted the city manager's proposed 1993–94 budget of $431 million, even though it was $27 million less than what the council wanted. It was also $10 million short of what the schools had received in the last budget. This meant that city workers would have to be laid off in order to bring the budget in line. Besides teacher layoffs, the city manager was proposing layoffs in some city departments. Using her line-item veto, Perry cut twenty-seven city jobs, further reducing the budget by $1.7 million.

Stanback's close working relationship with Perry continued to present a problem for the council majority, in particular Deputy Mayor Henrietta Milward. This was evidenced at a council session in March 1993, when Milward called Stanback "defiant" and "unprofessional." This may have been in response to an earlier memo from Stanback accusing Milward of trying to discredit him, and his refusal "to be a lackey" to the five-member council majority.

On another occasion Stanback said he was "disgusted by the council majority's attempt to undermine him." He may have been referring to his proposed recommendation to lend a Bloomfield woman $60,000 to open a health center. The council majority feared the health center would really be a massage parlor in the North Meadows. Stanback later withdrew the recommendation and apologized to the council, which was prepared to reject the proposal, citing the woman's criminal past and bad credit rating.

In July 1993, members of the Democratic Town Committee gathered at Hartford Public High School for its nominating convention. At the convention, committee members planned to put together their slate of endorsed candidates for the upcoming September primary. At the time I was being encouraged by some of my supporters to run for a city council seat. While I had been planning such a run for some time, several things were happening that made me question whether this was the right time. I was feeling a little uneasy over the unsettled mood in the North End. The Black community was split politically between the mayor and her council rivals. Tensions were also running high over the lack of progress in improving their quality of life.

Should I now toss my hat into the ring? I asked myself. Were the people ready for me at this present time? Was I assured a victory? Another reason for my hesitancy and perhaps even the biggest reason was my wife, Gladys. She frowned upon the idea.

Every time I mentioned running for city council, she always gave the same response. "You're crazy to get mixed up with those people," she would tell me. "They don't know what they're doing. Forget about it. You need to stop running around and stay at home." With all of these thoughts going around in my head, I was feeling that now was not the time to put my name out there as a candidate.

"I have decided at this time not to run for a seat on the city council." This was the announcement I made to the delegates who had gathered that evening for the nominating convention. "As one of the fifty-six Democratic Town Committee members, I will help decide who will be on the next slate," I said. Mayor Perry, of course, was eager for the Democratic Town Committee to nominate her to serve a fourth term. Meanwhile, Deputy Mayor Henrietta Milward had announced her own candidacy for mayor and was seeking the Town Committee's endorsement. Except for Abraham Giles, Milward had little support among committee members. Giles had originally supported Mayor Perry, but had switched his support to Milward. In the end, because many on the Town Committee who had been Perry allies had now abandoned her, Perry's name was not placed in nomination.

The two names placed in nomination for mayor were John D. Wardlaw and Michael "Mike" Peters. For the past fifteen years, Wardlaw had served as the executive director of the Hartford Housing Authority. The fifty-six-year-old former professional football player had been credited with reforming public housing and was now a powerful voice in Hartford. When the committee votes were counted, Wardlaw had a total of sixteen votes. Peters, a forty-four-year-old fire fighter and former chairman of the Hartford Civic Center Authority, received fourteen votes. Both, however, had fallen well short of the twenty-nine votes needed to secure the nomination.

By the end of August, Perry, Milward, Peters, and Council Majority Leader Yolanda Castillo had enough signatures to have their names placed on the September primary ballot. On the day of the primary, Perry surprised many. With thirty-five- percent of the votes casted in her favor, the triumphant candidate claimed her victory. Just as Perry had hoped, a large majority of the Black community turned out to support her. That night a jubilant Perry and her supporters celebrated her primary victory at City's Edge, a popular downtown eatery favored by politicians and government workers. The next day, at a city hall press conference, an ebullient Mayor Perry spoke to reporters.

"The things that people criticize me for are my strengths," she said in a defiant tone. "The definition of leadership is defined by men. They determine leadership qualities by what is not important anymore." The mayor was clearly in her element. Mike Peters had finished the race a close second, and after conferring with supporters, announced from his Franklin Avenue headquarters that despite his loss in the primary, he planned to run as an independent in the general election. The Black community was not pleased that Peters had been coaxed to run by North End resident Bob Jackson. Jackson lived on my block and was presently chair of the Democratic Town Committee, the first Black person to hold that position.

While campaigning for her reelection, Mayor Perry and her team of seven were referring to themselves as the "real Democrats"—an apparent slight to her five Democratic detractors. The mayor's slate included Nicholas J. Fusco, Elizabeth Horton Sheff, Susan E. Hyde, Noel F. McGregor Jr., and the People for Change candidates, Louise B. Simmons, Sandra E. Little, and Herminia Cruz Resto. On the day of the election, Perry's name and the names of three independent candidates for mayor appeared on the ballot. The independents included Michael Peters, Kenneth Mink, and Reverend Nora Wyatt. As the day went on, the poll numbers across the city were not looking good for the mayor. Peters was leading sixty-four-percent, to the mayor's thirty-five-percent.

When the polls closed and the votes were counted, the results this time was not a repeat of the primary held just two months earlier. The tables had turned, and it was Peters and his supporters who were now celebrating. Bob Jackson was being given credit by some and blame by others for orchestrating Peters's campaign and bringing him a stunning victory. His strategy had included going after independent voters and convincing Democrats and Republicans, many who had not voted in the primary, to support Peters. Disenchanted Blacks held Jackson largely responsible for Perry's defeat. An angry Perry called foul, claiming racism had played a part in her losing campaign, but she could identify no specific instances.

As I looked at the election, I didn't believe racism had been involved. But what else was an incumbent with the mayor's temperament to say? Could she say, "People didn't vote for me because I was incompetent?" Or "People didn't vote for me because they didn't want me anymore, or because I almost went to jail?" I felt Perry had lost her credibility, and I cast my vote for Peters. So after six years as Hartford's mayor, Perry was out of office. It would be a long time before she would forgive Jackson.

Two weeks after the election, Mayor-elect Peters and the incoming council members attended the regular Monday night meeting of the city council. As they sat in the council chamber, they couldn't believe what they were hearing. Outgoing Mayor Perry was recommending to outgoing council members that City Manager Stanback be given $150,000 in return for submitting to them his resignation. Just a month earlier, Perry and her council allies had extended the city manager's contract for one year. At this meeting, Mayor Perry and her council supporters were also recommending that Deputy City Manager Henry Langley be appointed the new city manager with a one-year contract and a salary of $105,000.

"What you're doing is outrageous," shouted an angry Mayor-elect Peters, in a voice that carried over the more than two hundred people crowded into the council chamber. "The city cannot afford such a buy-out; I plead with you not to take these measures tonight."

His pleading, and a warning from Corporation Counsel Pedro Segarra that a vote on these two recommendations would be illegal, fell mostly on deaf ears. The five-member council majority, including Elizabeth Horton Sheff, Nicholas Fusco, Louise Simmons, Sandra Little, and Yolanda Castillo, approved both recommendations.

An angry Councilman Anthony DiPentima, who spoke out prior to the vote, saying to the mayor, "Madam Mayor, this is an absolute disgrace. You should be ashamed of yourself," had also been ignored.

"I feel ashamed to serve with some of these people tonight," said Councilman Fernando Comulada. "I just want to leave this room immediately." Then, tearing the Stanback resolution in half, he walked out of the chamber.

Peters, who had already told reporters he wanted Stanback out, stormed out of the council chambers, followed by the incoming council members. The mayor, however, who was not yet finished with her power play, then filled nearly sixty city vacancies with people who had supported her. The next day Corporation Counsel Segarra announced his refusal to sign the agreement, which meant the Director of Finance William Cohran would not process the voucher for payment to Stanback. This move by Segarra drew the ire of Councilman Nicholas Fusco, who fumed that Segarra worked for the city council and had no right to disregard a vote it had taken.

"He talks about morals and ethics, and he disregards our vote," Fusco was reported to have said. Stanback's response was to issue a memo suspending Finance Director Cohran without pay for insubordination—a memo that was later rescinded. Things in city government were a mess, and as an onlooker, I could only hope that the incoming mayor and council would be better servants of the people of Hartford.

Meanwhile, Peters said he would do all he could to keep Stanback from receiving the windfall buyout, and to keep Langley from being hired. On Monday, December 6, Mayor Peters and the new council, made up of five Peters supporters and four Perry supporters, were sworn into office.

"I am a free man, free at last, thank God Almighty, I'm free at last!" This was the cry a city hall worker heard coming from the office of a jubilant city manager.

Stanback was reacting to the news that the incoming council had approved his severance package, which had been negotiated down to $75,000. Dropping his threat to sue the city, Stanback resigned as city manager, and was on a plane the very next day heading for Chicago. Recognizing that the hiring of Langley was illegal and invalid, the council majority voted Senior Assistant Corporation Counsel Saundra Kee Borges as the interim city manager.

"Henry Langley should sit in that chair," Councilwoman Elizabeth Horton Sheff said while abstaining from the vote. Langley also felt that he should sit in the city manager's chair. In an attempt to prevent Mayor Peters from filling the position with someone else, Langley hired a lawyer who petitioned the court for a temporary restraining order. With sixteen years as a city employee, the forty-nine-year-old Langley, claimed he was removed because he was Black, a claim to which Perry and a number of her allies agreed.

"The decision to replace Langley was based on politics and not race," responded Mayor Peters, who noted that Borges was Black. After a three-month wait, the court ruled against Langley in March 1994. He then filed suit for a permanent injunction.

As Mayor Peters and the city council got down to work, they faced what seemed a mountain of issues. High unemployment, under-resourced schools, deteriorating housing, downtown revitalization, a shrinking tax base, a toxic waste problem in the North Meadows, and violent street gangs, just to name a few. It was the problem of the growing number of violent street gangs that had become most troublesome. As they battled each other for drug turf drive-by shootings had become commonplace. The number of gang-related murders had now surpassed the previous year's number.

"Whenever anything happens now, people think of gangs first," Hartford Police Chief Joseph F. Croughwell Jr. said. As the city council got down to work I noted that they were having difficulty reaching consensus around many of the pressing issues. I was still biding my time as to when I would make my run for a council seat. I now had a solid core group of supporters waiting for me to give the word. In November 1994, I felt my time had come. The Democratic Town Committee nominating convention would be held in July. This time I wanted my name on the endorsed slate. I called a group of my supporters and we began planning my campaign strategy. I had now taken my first step to becoming a member of the Hartford Court of Common Council. Several weeks later I took my message for more effective government out to the public. I figured I had a number of things working in my favor. I had over forty years of experience working in city government, twelve years as a department head, nearly six years as assistant to two city managers, and I had citywide name recognition.

On the campaign trail, I told listeners of the city council's inability to resolve key issues facing the city, as well as its their inability to appoint a permanent city manager. Assistant Corporation Council Saundra Kee Borges had been appointed interim city manager a year earlier, following the resignation of Howard Stanback. Mayor Peters had then referred to Borges as a "caretaker" while a national search was undertaken. The report was that the resumes received during the yearlong national search were "gathering dust in a box under the mayor's desk." My mention of this prompted the mayor to say that a pending lawsuit was the reason for not selecting a city manager from the thirty finalists. The court had yet to settle Henry Langley's second lawsuit against the city. However, as December was coming to an end, Peters named Borges as the permanent city manager.

"We're not in the mood for a change right now," explained Councilman Michael McGarry.

A few months after I retired from the fire department, I had been offered a consultancy and vice president position with Professional and L & M Ambulance Services. I knew the West Hartford-based company had offered me the position because it needed some color in order to renew a contract with the City of Hartford. I had accepted the position because it called for limited responsibility and an annual salary of thirty-thousand dollars. Now that I was officially in the race for a city council seat I resigned this position, because I needed to focus on my campaign.

At the same time, I was giving some attention to troubling news coming from the fire department. A number of racially inspired events had caused Assistant Fire Chief Bill Smith to resign as president of the Phoenix Society. He did this after receiving racially charged telephones calls and having his locker in the firehouse vandalized. This harassment started after the Phoenix Society sent a letter to city hall criticizing the fire department's minority recruitment efforts. The letter was prompted by an article in the *Hartford Courant* that said ten out of thirty-three recently hired fire fighters had received bonus points for living in the city, despite evidence showing they lived outside Hartford. The Phoenix Society letter said in part:

> We the members of the Phoenix Society are appalled at the total disregard for the laws governing our city and the negative impact this behavior has had on our bona fide city residents. We ask the governing body to take all the necessary steps to correct this practice so all Hartford residents are given a fair chance at the jobs.

After the Phoenix Society letter appeared in the newspaper, Assistant Chief Smith began receiving racial slurs over the telephone. Then someone broke into his locker and put glue into the lock, and filled his boots with a soapy substance. Ben Andrews, president of the Connecticut chapter of the NAACP, was now looking into the matter. Edward Casares Jr., president of the Society of Latin American Fire Fighters, had also sent a letter to the *Courant* criticizing the department's lack of residency verification. I was pleased to see this response from the Hispanic fire fighters. To make sure their voice was heard, they had formed the Society of Latin American Fire Fighters in 1982, two years after Special Services recruited the first Hispanic into the department.

With an eye on these troubling events, I continued my campaign by speaking at political and community gatherings around the city. I was also handing out literature that outlined what I called my "extensive record of accomplishments toward making Hartford a better city in which to live and work." Gladys wasn't happy about my being out of the house most days and evenings, but she gave my efforts her full support. Just over seven months after I had announced my candidacy, delegates from nine districts around the city came together during the last week of July at Sanchez School on Park Street for the Democratic nominating convention. I was excited because this was the gathering where the sixty-six delegates would identify those who would be on the endorsed slate. I attended this convention confident that I would be one of those selected.

When the votes were tallied, Mayor Peters had received more than enough to win the endorsement for a second term. I was one of seven candidates getting the most support for one of the six available city council seats. The other candidates included Anthony DiPentima and Frances Sanchez, both of whom were incumbents, and first-timers Arthur Feltman, Steven Park, Luis Ayala, and Louis Watkins. When a second vote was taken, Steven Park was eliminated. I was now an endorsed candidate. I left the convention feeling a sense of accomplishment: My name would be on the ballot in the November 1995 general election.

Endorsed Democratic Slate includes (back row, from left) Denise L. Nappier, Luis Ayala, John B. Stewart Jr., Arthur Feltman, (front row, from left) Louis Watkins, Mayor Mike Peters, Frances Sanchez, Anthony DiPentima.

None of us on the endorsed slate for mayor and city council left the convention anticipating a primary battle, since we had no opposition. Then, during the first week in August, Councilwoman Elizabeth Horton Sheff declared her candidacy for mayor. (This was the Elizabeth Sheff whose son Milo, while a fourth grader at Mark Twain Elementary School in the North End, became the lead plaintiff in *Sheff v. O'Neill*, the lawsuit against the State of Connecticut for inequities in the public school system.) Horton-Sheff and her slate of Democratic candidates for city council were intent on forcing a primary election in September.

"This is not an anti-initiative, this is a pro-Hartford, for-Hartford campaign," she announced. "We hope to unite the city, north and south, east and west." Later, at a press conference held at the Polish Veterans Association Hall, she introduced her slate, referring to them as the "Democrats for Justice." They included Councilman Noel F. McGregor Jr., Ida Colon, Ralph Carucci, Carmen Torres, Ken Kennedy, and Zenon Kolakowski. When the primary was held in September, the endorsed slate outpolled the Horton-Sheff slate by a four-to-one margin. Primary results also revealed that on the state level, Representative Eric Coleman had won over Carrie Saxon Perry for the Senate seat vacated by State Senator Thirman L. Milner.

It had been less than three years since my retirement as fire chief, and now I was on the endorsed slate for a seat on the city council. Besides those already mentioned, Denise L. Nappier was also on the endorsed slate. Nappier was Hartford city treasurer and was seeking reelection to that position.

Out on the campaign trail, Mayor Peters was telling voters that "Our council candidates are experienced, effective, and committed community leaders who are eager to bring their combined experience to city hall for the good of our whole community." He told the voters that for Hartford to keep moving forward, "We need a unified team that will find common ground in our diversity to develop programs that will make our entire city a better place to live and work." I felt we had a strong slate and expected that we would win easily over our opponents. On the other side, the candidate for mayor was Edward V. Conran, a low-key Republican soldier. On the slate with him were incumbents John O'Connell, Veronica Airey-Wilson, and Michael T. McGarry. Three lesser-known Town Committee members, Aldo Provera, Michael Lupo, and Joe Salvo, made up the rest of the slate.

During the third week of September, I welcomed the International Association of Black Professional Fire Fighters (IABPFF) to Hartford for its Twenty-Fifth Anniversary Convention. More than three hundred Black professional fire fighters converged on the city where the IABPFF was born twenty-five years earlier. The fire fighters had come to rededicate themselves to racially integrating the nation's firehouses. I served on an oral panel and as one of the so-called Founding Fathers, I gave a talk on the historical events that had brought the International into being.

In October I stopped campaigning long enough to sit in front of my television and watch an historic event unfold. Hundreds of thousands of Black men and boys from all over the nation, including Hartford, gathered in front of the US Capitol Building in Washington, DC, for the Million Man March. This was one of the largest gatherings ever to take place on the Mall. They had answered the call from the Muslim Minister Louis Farrakhan to take responsibility for their lives and families, and commit to stopping the scourges of drugs, violence, and unemployment in their communities.

"We must atone for the destruction that's going on: the fratricide, the death-dealing drugs, and the violence that plagues us," Minister Farrakhan said.

THE MAJORITY LEADER

Being defeated in the primary election did not end Elizabeth Horton Sheff's attempt at becoming Hartford's mayor. Running now as an Independent on the Pro Hartford Party ticket, her name appeared on the ballot on the day of the general election. I voted early along with Gladys and then waited anxiously while voters went to the polls to decide who would lead city government for the next two years. When the polls closed and the final votes were counted, Mayor Peters had beaten Horton Sheff by an 86–14 percent voter margin. Edward Conran, Peters's Republican opponent, had earlier dropped out of the race. Many felt correctly that his heart was not in it.

What left me feeling an enormous sense of gratitude was the announcement that I was top vote getter in the entire general election with 6,981 votes. I could only say that the people of Hartford knew my good reputation. Poll watchers said the reason why Peters won so convincingly in the mostly Black districts was because my name was on his ticket.

When the makeup of the next city council became clear, the *Hartford Courant* editorialized, "Not since then-Mayor Carrie Saxon Perry won a third term in 1991 has the city council started a new term so seemingly unified in philosophical outlook and purpose." Reading this, I could only say I would do my best to see it stayed that way.

With the campaigning over and the incoming council not set to begin its work until January, I was able to spend some quality time at home with Gladys and other family members. As Christmas drew near, city hall workers and department heads gathered in the second-floor function room for their annual Christmas party. Since I was no longer the fire chief, I was not present, and I'm glad I wasn't. Approximately fifty fire fighters protesting the lack of a new contract crashed the party.

Carrying protest signs they chanted, "John O, where did our contract go?" and "Taxpayer Alert: Arbitration could cost you your shirt!" The fire fighters were angry that Minority Leader John O'Connell and the rest of the council had rejected a three-year contract that would have given them a three-percent raise in the third year. I also took note that the protest was being led by Carmine Zitani, the new union president. My hope was that the newly appointed Fire Chief Robert Dobson, who had succeeded Chief Nelson Carter when he retired the previous year, would have a better experience with the union president than I had.

In tux and gown, Gladys and I went to Trinity College at the end of December to attend the Mayor's Inaugural Ball. In January 1996 I took the oath of office and became one of six Democrats and three Republicans that made up the new city council. Initially we differed over who would chair which council committee, and who would be deputy mayor. The highest vote getter traditionally became deputy mayor, but because this position was largely ceremonial, I didn't want it. When my name was placed in nomination for council majority leader, I accepted the nomination, feeling it would give me the leverage I needed to get things done. As majority leader I would set the council's monthly agenda, choosing what issues would be placed before the body at our regular Monday evening council session. In this position I felt I could be a constructive force on a city council where members approached every issue from a partisan party line perspective. Both Councilwoman Francis Sanchez and her Hispanic constituents were pleased to see her voted as deputy mayor. It was not the $15,000 annual salary that motivated any one of us on the council, since this was considered only a part-time job; we were all just ready to get to work for the good of Hartford.

In some ways being the council majority leader was similar to being the fire chief. At the start of the council term, I was confronted with one challenge after another, with each one said to be the most urgent. This was no surprise given the many challenges facing the city. One of the council's immediate challenges involved the education of the city's public schoolchildren. A week after being sworn in, I was in a meeting with City Manager Borges and Minority Leader O'Connell when a secretary walked in and handed the city manager a fax. After reading it Borges shared with us part of its content:

> The City of Hartford is in breach of contract. The city of Hartford has violated its contract with Education Alternatives Inc. (EAI) in 16 areas and EAI is preparing a lawsuit against the city.

It was in its desperation to turn the city's failing schools around that the school board in 1994 had entered into a five-year contract with EAI. This was after the Minnesota-based educational firm convinced board members it would transform the city's public schools "from top to bottom." This made Hartford the first city in the nation to have all of its public schools taken over by a private management company.

The school board had entered into the contract with EAI against the advice of many concerned onlookers, including Acting School Superintendent Eddie Davis, the former principal of Weaver High School.

"Education Alternatives Inc.'s ability to work in our schools has major barriers," he wrote in a private letter to the school board prior to the agreement. "Hiring an outside company," he cautioned, "will not solve the system's complex problems." Unfortunately, Davis's advice went unheeded by board members. The teacher's union also opposed the hiring of EAI, fearing an EAI takeover of the school system. The union sued the school board to prevent the bidding process, claiming the school board had given EAI inside information ensuring its selection. The court, however, dismissed the suit, disallowing the union from interfering with the bidding process. Even members of the city council had voiced reservations about hiring EAI. One point of concern for council members was how much authority to give EAI. Would EAI have control over the school's $171 million budget and the $66 million employee benefits plan?

Unfortunately, these questions were not answered before the school board entered into the contract with EAI. Thomas Cox, the acting deputy corporation counsel, had negotiated the agreement, which became a sixty-three-page contract proposal between the school board and EAI. For this Cox was fired by the city, but later rehired. The contract allowed EAI to take control of the school system's budget of $200 million and the city's thirty-two public schools. The school board was now ordering EAI out of city schools after only two years, and denying EAI's allegation that they had breached the contract. EAI was demanding the $11 million it claimed to have invested in the school system, or else it would file suit against the city. As majority leader I immediately put this matter on the council agenda.

Whether or not to privatize Hartford's public schools had been a hot-button issue during the election campaign. Mayor Peters had publicly endorsed privatization. Now his endorsement had come back to haunt him. Elizabeth Horton-Sheff, with her in-your-face style, told Peters during the campaign that she was going to "work hard to send EAI back to Minnesota." Four candidates seeking seats on the board of education had also vowed to oust EAI from city schools.

"With this slate we will be waking Hartford up," Stephen Founier, one of the four candidates for a seat on the school board, told an audience of listeners. "EAI is a scourge and its representatives are vultures," Founier had said, "and the school board is pathetically gullible for hiring EAI." Over the next month, I sat in on several meetings with Mayor Peters and Council Minority Leader John O'Connell, trying to find a solution to the EAI problem. We eventually devised a plan that called for EAI to agree to settle its claims for less than the $11 million it said it was owed. The plan also called for EAI to oversee the school board's finances until they were untangled and some administrative problems were addressed. In effect EAI would be working for city hall. EAI was quick to reject this plan, saying it would sue unless it was rehired to manage the school's finances. When informed of EAI's rejection, I was annoyed.

"I don't think EAI is acting very professional," I told council members. "I personally feel that they should not get anything. There is no point in holding the citizens of Hartford up with a shotgun." Negotiations with EAI would go on for six months before a settlement would be reached for just over $3 million.

On Sunday, March 31, 1996, I received the painful news that my father, John Bradley Stewart Sr., had died. Since I was an only child, my father and I were extremely close. His death was a great loss for me. I no longer had my father's physical presence in my life, and I had also lost a good friend and valued counselor. For months my father had put up a valiant fight against prostate cancer, and it pained me to see him in such a weakened condition. Now, finally, on his eighty-ninth birthday, the disease had claimed his life. The following week hundreds of people crowded into Faith Congregational Church to celebrate his life. During the service government officials and community leaders spoke of the positive contributions my father had made to the city of Hartford. He was then laid to rest alongside his mother and father and his sisters at Center Cemetery in East Hartford. A week later the *Hartford Courant* ran a story that had me doing a double take. The newspaper had placed "Jr." instead of "Sr." after my father's name. The lead into the story read:

> In a week that saw the loss of three strong African American leaders—former Cleveland Mayor Carl B. Stokes, Commerce Secretary Ron Brown, and civic leader John B. Stewart Jr. in Hartford…

Indeed, former Cleveland mayor Carl B. Stokes, the first Black mayor of a major US city, had died of cancer the previous week. And Ronald Brown, the first Black secretary of commerce, had died in a plane crash in Croatia the previous week. I was pleased with the intent to include my father with such notable Black Americans, but the story had stated I was the one who had died. I called the reporter and assured him that I was still alive and serving on the city council.

Meanwhile, I found the best way to get through my grief was to stay busy. I immersed myself in my city council work. It was during this time that I was criticized in the newspaper for joining with Minority Leader O'Connell in rejecting a proposed new three-year contract with the Hartford Federation of Teachers. To my way of thinking, why increase teacher benefits when our public schoolchildren were not receiving the education they needed? I had no confidence in the school board and wanted to hold a hammer over the heads of board members as a way of pressuring them to fix the chronically low-performing schools. As chair of the council's education committee, I held a hearing during which council members were moved by parents pleading with us to do something that would turn the failing schools around.

Student performance in Hartford lagged behind the rest of the state. I knew that for kids from our city's poor and low-income families, getting a good education was their best hope for a better life. Councilman Louis Watkins wanted to form a committee to investigate the city's ailing school system. Watkins, my Blue Hills neighbor and a friend, cared as deeply as I did about the education of the city's schoolchildren. But I did not support the idea of forming yet another council committee.

"This does not reflect the desire of the council and is not the direction in which we are going right now," I told Watkins. Plus, I was waiting for the results of the top-to-bottom inquiry into the city's failing school system presently being conducted by state legislators.

Council members were so upset over the school board's failure to properly educate students that at a May 1996 council meeting, the mayor was asked to declare an emergency in the city's public schools. Minority Leader and Budget Committee Chair John O'Connell called for city hall to take over "the damn school board."

I told council members that "An emergency declaration would be a hammer over the head of the school board as we try to make this system work." Mayor Peters said that he was inclined to declare the 24,000-student school system to be in a state of emergency, but a day later had changed his mind. While the newspaper accused us of "grandstanding," I truly wanted some drastic action to be taken if we were to rescue city schools.

The council also needed to find ways to bring more funding to the schools. We were holding public hearings on bonds as a possible funding source when the State Supreme Court handed down the ruling in *Sheff v. O'Neill*. I called the education committee together to see if there was anything in this ruling that could be parlayed into increased capital spending for the city's public schools. The state's highest court ruled that "the state has an affirmative obligation to provide Connecticut's schoolchildren with a substantially equal educational opportunity and that this constitutionally guaranteed right encompasses the access to a public education which is not substantially and materially impaired by racial and ethnic isolation." The ruling only confirmed what I already believed, that Hartford public schoolchildren were not getting the education to which they were entitled. Meanwhile, we continued holding hearings and eventually came up with a slate of bond proposals to repair and renovate city schools. I was moving very cautiously because I knew that prudence was necessary whenever one was contemplating spending city money.

Our bonding proposals were based on a variety of city factors related to city finances. But I also wanted to find out if other city and state funding options existed. When the report of the state's inquiry into the city's failing school system was finally issued by state legislators, it declared the Hartford public schools to be "in a state of crisis." It stated that "the continued existence of this crisis and the threatened loss of accreditation of schools are detrimental to the children of the city." State legislators also took the dramatic step of calling for the dissolution of the Hartford Board of Education for a period of at least three years and for the creation of a state board of trustees.

These state trustees, the legislators announced, "would be responsible for governance, management and fiscal operations of the Hartford school district all in order to increase student achievement, enhance the adequacy and equality of educational opportunities, and allocate and manage resources efficiently and effectively." I thought this was a great plan and was eager to see it put into effect.

The City of Hartford was financially strapped. So as chair of the education committee, I was continually looking for ways to fund the city's public schools. In September 1996 I saw a way to put some desperately needed money into our school system. The city council had begun considering a proposal by City Manager Saundra Kee Borges to sell a portion of a city park to a movie-theater company. The company was offering the city $8 million for seventy-five acres of Batterson Park. Because other prospective buyers were also enquiring about the purchase of this same portion of parkland, the council directed the city manager to formally put the wooded acreage up for sale. In doing so Council Minority Leader O'Connell stated that the city had an obligation to get the most value that we could. At the time I was already thinking ahead about what the council could do with the proceeds.

"If we can get a few million more than the eight million, there are many areas of the city where we can put the money to use," I told council members, "including directing some toward fixing our public schools." Meanwhile, local park advocates who had heard about the council's plan to sell parkland came to a council meeting and raised their objection. As their numbers increased, the *Hartford Courant* joined their cause, convincing the majority of council members to vote against the sale.

In my frustration over this turn of events, I wrote an open letter to the *Hartford Courant,* explaining that "this was an opportunity to get an excellent price for a less than perfect lot and to invest city resources closer to home. This warranted serious consideration," I wrote. When Democratic Town Chairman Robert Jackson and other Democratic leaders urged me to drop the Batterson Park issue, I reluctantly did so. It was an election year, and they felt the issue had become too political and would be used against the Democrats. In my way of thinking, politically expediency had trumped the need to help the city's school children.

In October 1996 a local developer filed a human rights complaint against the city, naming Mayor Peters and council members Michael McGarry and Anthony DiPentima. The developer, Dana Wright, accused them of corruption and malicious interference with his downtown development project. Their response to the complaint was that Wright was handed the city-owned land on a platter, but failed to raise the necessary money to move his project forward. Now, they said, he was pointing the blame at them. Wright later added two more names to what was now a lawsuit, John B. O'Connell and John B. Stewart Jr. I didn't give it a whole lot of thought at the time because as a councilman I felt these kinds of things came with the territory. Little did I know that this matter would in the future cause me a considerable amount of distress.

Meanwhile, I was giving attention to another problem with racial overtones that had surfaced at the fire department. The union president was calling for the city manager to fire Assistant Fire Chief Billy Smith. Over a hundred fire fighters had disrupted a council meeting by jamming noisily into the council chamber. During the council session, they coughed loudly, and one called out to me "Thanks, Chief!" I suspect he was sarcastically thanking me because all fire chiefs after me had been Black. Another fire fighter shouted to Mayor Peters, a former fire fighter and union supporter himself, "Good to see you, Mayor!" At the same time, other fire fighters picketed on the sidewalk outside city hall, passing out fliers.

This protest started after some unnamed person tapped into Assistant Chief Smith's telephone and overheard him making racially charged comments. When his phone conversation, which had been illegally taped, was made public, Smith became the subject of controversy. As a result Fire Chief Dobson removed Smith as commander of operations and reassigned him to desk duties. At the disrupted council session, I told council members that "the comments made by Assistant Chief Smith, who was Black, pointed to the need for a broad response." I suggested to the council that we pass a resolution directing the city manager to make sensitivity training mandatory. Soon after I co-authored the resolution, which stated that all departments that had not had such training in the previous year would hold training that promotes an awareness of race, ethnicity, and gender issues in the work environment, and that reinforces positive interaction in city government.

As chair of the education committee, the continuing problems of low performance prompted me to call for an investigation into how money for public schools was being spent. To this end, the council voted in March 1997 to hire a law and accounting firm to undertake an investigation. The cost of the investigation was $250,000, but for the sake of the city's public schoolchildren, I thought it was city money well spent. During this time word came that Edward Curtin, the former fire chief and city manager, had died at a hospital in New Britain, Connecticut. When I read the newspaper article announcing his death, I could only agree with his younger brother Jim, who commented, "He was a leader with a tough moral fiber and a big heart who believed in the city. He did what he thought was right." To this I could give like testimony. Chief Curtin was the man who had gone out on a limb to make me the first Black officer in the history of the Hartford Fire Department. He was the man who had established the Special Services unit because he wanted to do something about the underlying causes of the anger in the minority community. And he was the man who had selected me to work as his assistant when he was city manager. I had nothing but high praise and fond memories of Chief Ed Curtin. Had it not been for him, my life may well have taken a different track.

Every day as I encountered constituents, I was reminded of the reason I had become a member of the city council. In the spring I joined with Councilman O'Connell, who co-chaired the budget committee, in a plan to give Hartford residents a 1-mill property tax cut. However small, this would still be of some help to people who were struggling financially. Once instituted, this plan would make Hartford the only major city in Connecticut to cut property taxes for three consecutive years without destroying city services. State lawmakers had already taken over the administration of the city's general assistance welfare program, saving the city $13.5 million. O'Connell and I wanted to give city taxpayers yet another break.

In October 1997, I took note that Mayor Peters, who had spoken earlier of the possibility of running for a seat in the US Congress, had not ruled it out. If Peters choose to run and was elected, the city charter called for Deputy Mayor Francis Sanchez to become mayor. Bob Jackson and other Democratic leaders, however, let it be known to us that Sanchez would remain deputy mayor and I would remain majority leader. This left me wondering just who Jackson and the other Democratic leaders had in mind for mayor. However, this became a moot point when Peters decided not to seek a congressional seat.

A month later, in the November 1997 general election, I was elected to my second term. Even though the voter turnout was a low twenty-eight percent, my 7,256 votes again made me the highest vote getter on the Democratic slate. Anticipating that our Democratic majority would remain intact, we had already assigned leadership positions. I continued as majority leader, and Frances Sanchez continued as deputy mayor. Council Democrats did, however, strip three Republican council members of their position as committee chairs. This was done to diminish their power. Following his election to a third term, Mayor Peters set public expectations high.

"The next two years will be dynamic for our city," he promised city residents who were celebrating with him at his victory party. One issue that was most pressing for those of us in city leadership positions was the need to attract businesses downtown, which would translate into jobs. Naturally, people living in poorer sections of the city were of a different mindset as to what issues were the most pressing. They wanted city government to pay less attention to downtown and focus more on neighborhoods and providing for their own pressing needs. Those of us on the city council wanted to do both. So we planned to lobby state officials for financial help with major projects such as the construction of a downtown convention center, and the improvement of basic services to city residents.

But the way of politics is to take care of first things first. At the council's first meeting of the new term, we voted to extend City Manager Saundra Kee Borges's contract for only one year, instead of the usual two. We also did not take a vote on the city manager's expected pay raise. The *Hartford Courant* claimed the council was playing "petty politics" and that I was the orchestrator. This, the newspaper said, was because I didn't think I had enough access to the city manager, and because she kowtowed to the mayor. This was true. I was not only irritated that as council majority leader, I had to go through the mayor to get to the city manager, but it also irritated me that she kept the council in the dark on city hall decisions. It also troubled me that she didn't give priority to projects that were most important to the council. While I understood the job of the city manager to be that of managing and giving direction to department heads, nonetheless, her goals and objectives seemed out of sync with council priorities.

"I want to fine-tune the way city agencies operate, and the manager's office is the place to start," I told my council colleagues. I pointed out that a consultant whose services the council had employed earlier in the year found fault with the city in the way it provided services to the public. The majority of council members tied this problem to the city manager's office.

Because we had questions about the city manager's communications, administration, and managerial skills, I wanted to start this council term with a system of accountability in place. I personally liked

Saundra Kee Borges and admired her intellect and accomplishments. The East Orange, New Jersey, native had come to Hartford twenty years earlier. After graduating from Trinity College, she earned a law degree at the University of Connecticut. After serving for ten years as assistant corporation council, the thirty-eight-year-old Borges was appointed as the interim city manager, and made permanent a year later. It was my present frustration over our lack of communication that left me no choice but to exercise my power over the city manager position.

The Republican Minority Leader John O'Connell, who at first supported the one-year contract, withdrew his support because "as chair of the budget committee did not want to jeopardize" his considerable access to the city manager. Republican Councilman Michael McGarry, who was hoping to win back a staff position taken from him, also withdrew his support. Still, I had enough votes to carry the measure, and did so. I never used what power I had as majority leader for power's sake, but only to help me do the council work I felt was necessary for the good of Hartford. After all, wasn't that the reason the people of Hartford voted for me?

The work of the city council was not what I would describe as very exciting, but it was both interesting and educational. As council members we performed the necessary and sometimes unpopular duties to keep the city solvent and moving forward, and we looked for solutions to the multitude of problems that daily confront city residents. For instance, two months into the new council term, in March 1998, the city council was planning to take an important vote on a revitalization plan for the downtown Civic Center Mall. The three-level enclosed shopping mall and office complex was the commercial portion of a four-square-block structure called the Hartford Civic Center. The entire complex was a downtown urban redevelopment project that opened in 1974. But the mall was losing money and something had to be done. Aetna Inc. owned the mall, but the city owned the land beneath the building, making it necessary for council members to vote on any plan for development. The mall had approximately fifty small shops opening on a central atrium, a design that was intended to compete with the suburban-style shopping mall.

At a council hearing, we learned from city planners that such a design was incompatible with an urban setting because it cut the shops off from pedestrians out on the sidewalk. Aetna wanted to redevelop the ailing mall and had sent out sixty requests for proposals, but received only two responses. The one response I favored was a proposal from LaSalle Partners, the company that currently managed the mall. This proposal called for consolidating all mall shops on the first and lower levels and making them open to the street. A few days before the council was to vote, Mayor Peters held a meeting with Democratic council members to discuss the LaSalle proposal.

Because Democrats were the only ones attending this meeting in the council caucus room, the *Hartford Courant* was quick to accuse the council of "reverting to its old ways." It wasn't a caucus meeting, the paper said, it was an "illegal meeting." This didn't bother me. I was anxious to get something done. I was tired of watching a downtown cornerstone hang in limbo. I just wanted to get at least one important downtown development project started as soon as possible. It didn't matter to me that a fellow council member on the Republican side was now publicly referring to the LaSalle Partners plan as being "lame."

We voted to go forward with the development plan offered by LaSalle Partners, but held off giving LaSalle the okay to proceed with its work. This was because of the lingering concern by a number of council members that unlike the one other proposal, the LaSalle plan lacked a major new entertainment draw. The proposal submitted by the other developer included a sports technology museum and movie theaters. Meanwhile, seeing no movement from the council, Aetna was preparing in October 1998 to put the mall up for sale. In order to speed things up, I decided to join forces with Minority Leader O'Connell. We proposed to extend a $30,000 contract to Richard Goldstein, the former corporation counsel, to advise the city on the sale of the mall.

No input on this proposal was sought from other council members or from the mayor. When Mayor Peters and Deputy Mayor Sanchez returned from an out-of-town trip, they quickly squashed the proposal.

"I'm troubled by the secretive nature of the proposal," Sanchez stated. O'Connell explained that we were looking for a lawyer to aggressively represent the city, and the corporation counsel's office was stretched too thin for the job. Since Goldstein had earlier informed O'Connell he was looking for some city work, O'Connell recommended him. Seeing nothing improper, I went along with the recommendation. At the time I was unaware that Goldstein, whom the newspaper called "politically connected," had contributed two hundred dollars to O'Connell's election campaign. Feeling some pressure, we went back to Aetna and were successful in convincing them to reach out once more to developers. This time request for proposals were sent out to approximately a hundred developers around the country. The council was now right back where it started months earlier. The only positive step toward fixing the mall problem would not take place until six years later, in 2004, when the mall would be demolished.

While the council was busy trying to decide the future of the Civic Center mall, we were also trying to resolve an issue that had come before the council during the previous term. This was the Pope Park billboards issue. The park, which sits on 175 acres of land bequeathed to the city in 1895 by industrialist Colonel Albert A. Pope, was located in the city's Parkville neighborhood. I voted in 1996 with other council members to approve a lease agreement between the City of Hartford and Martin Media, a national billboard company based in California. In part, the lease granted Martin Media a zoning variance allowing it to erect four two-sided billboards inside Pope Park. The billboards, each fourteen feet wide by forty-eight feet high, would be placed on sections of the park on the other side of Interstate 84. The signs, which would face the interstate, would be cut off from the park's recreational area by this highway.

Martin Media, which would make $500,000 a year from the billboards advertisements, pledged to the City of Hartford $1.2 million over twenty years. These funds would go toward improvements to the park. When Connecticut's Department of Transportation, which monitors projects near state highways, raised zoning questions about the billboards, Martin Media applied to Hartford's Zoning Commission for hearings on a zoning change. A zoning change was better suited for Martin Media's purposes, because it was more binding and lasting than the variance it had received from the council. A zoning change would change the eleven acres from recreational to industrial.

In November 1997 the council held a hearing on the zoning change. When Parkville residents and area merchants heard about the hearing, they reacted angrily over not having been invited to participate.

"Once zoning is changed, what's going to stop more billboards," the president of the Parkville Business Association wanted to know. His feeling, like many of the other protesters, was that a zoning change would add to further decline in the area. Since there was such strong public opposition, the council held a second hearing, this time opening it to the public. At this hearing, held the second week of January 1998, Parkville residents presented the council with two petitions protesting the rezoning and the erecting of any billboards.

I listened closely as Parkville Business Association Treasurer Bill Howard angrily told the council, "We don't want their money. We don't want them and we don't need them, and we will do everything to keep them out." I also heard from other city residents who took an opposing view. The city needed the $1.2 million, they argued.

Albert Pope, Colonel Pope's great-grandson, had been notified about the hearings and came up from New York City to testify. Speaking in favor of the lease agreement, he said, "The small parcel of land where the signs will be erected isn't suitable for recreation because of the highway. Martin Media will improve the park with its pledge of one-point-two million over twenty years."

Another Pope descendant at the hearing, William Pope, who lived in Rocky Hill, Connecticut, and grandson of the colonel, took a position opposite that of his cousin. "My grandfather wanted people to enjoy the land. He employed three thousand in his factory and was concerned for their well-being," he told the council. "I don't see any place for billboards."

Some of the protesters were suspicious and raised questions about special influence by Martin Media at city hall. "Is Martin Media receiving favored treatment?" they wanted to know. "Why was there no competitive bidding?" The *Hartford Courant* had raised suspicions when it ran a story reporting that Martin Media had given money to several council candidates during the campaign. It reported that Martin Media had put up a promotional billboard with a picture of Deputy Mayor Francis Sanchez. While Sanchez maintained the billboard had nothing to do with the Pope Park lease agreement, some pointed out that the billboard with her picture went up just before the elections and that it was Sanchez who introduced Martin Media's proposal to the council.

I couldn't recall if Martin Media was listed among my contributors, but I didn't think so. Councilman Steven Park, chair of the zoning committee, raised the concern that a zone change from park to industrial might leave the door open to having to widen the I-84 highway. He said the committee wanted to postpone any action until more research was done on zoning regulations. When State Senator John Fonfara spoke in favor of the zoning change, some protesters complained of a possible conflict of interest. The senator acknowledged that he had done work for Martin Media and had earlier lobbied Parkville's business leaders. He said he had also met with the corporation counsel to discuss the law that forbids billboards within one hundred feet of public parks.

Two months later, in February 1998, the city council still had not made a decision on the zoning change. Before making a decision, we wanted to study the city's overall policy on outdoor advertising. We also wanted to further gauge public sentiment about the Pope Park zoning change. Toward the end of April, I shared with the council my lingering concern about Martin Media. I was particularly concerned about their refusal to pay past rent for three billboards it already had standing on city-owned land. I accused Martin Media of not paying the $30,000 it owed because it was playing games. It was stalling for time to see how the Pope Park issue would play out.

Two months later, in June 1998, the council voted to approve the zoning change. Aware that State Attorney General Richard Blumenthal had informed the council that the Pope family deed did not allow nonrecreational uses in the park and that only a superior court judge could approve a change, Parkville residents filed suit. They wanted the court to stop the billboards from going up. In all, the billboards issue extended over a period of two years, before they finally were erected in a portion of the park that is now zoned industrial. Today the billboard advertisements are there, money is going toward park improvements, and the Parkville neighborhood has not suffered. As I stated, council work may not be exciting, but it's interesting and educational.

In the fall of 1998, an issue came before the council that was much closer to my heart than billboards. The Greater Hartford Adult Literacy Coalition, an umbrella group of adult-education providers, released a study on the high incidence of adult illiteracy among city residents. The study called attention to the problem the coalition was having in its attempt to raise the level of adult literacy. During a council meeting, coalition members voiced their concern over the lack of coordination between various agencies dealing with literacy. They wanted the council to create a task force to take a look at the prevalence of adult literacy in Hartford. As chair of the council's education committee, and a supporter of quality education for the city's minority population, I cosponsored a resolution requesting the creation of a Hartford Task Force on Adult Literacy. After approving the resolution, the council identified twenty people to serve on the task force. Their mandate was to identify gaps in current services to illiterate adults and to recommend remedies. The illiterate were primarily poor people of color, and I felt the city needed to look at ways to help them become better educated so they could hold jobs and climb out of poverty.

As majority leader one of my major responsibilities was moving the city's budget for the next fiscal year through the council. I considered it a major accomplishment when the budget for fiscal year 1999–2000 was adopted before the July 1998 deadline. What stood out in this budget was that for the fifth straight year, the city lowered property taxes with no lessening of the services provided city residents. Because the issue of poor performing schools was still on the council agenda. I joined with council members John O'Connell, Michael McGarry, Veronica Airey-Wilson, and Louis Watkins Jr. in approving a resolution calling for an extension of the tenure of state Board of Trustees. The state board had taken over the city's failing school system the previous year. It was the Hartford School Board's failure to improve city schools that had prompted the state to dissolve the board in 1997 and to appoint state trustees to manage the city's schools. The schools were in such bad shape that more than five hundred students had left the previous year, reducing the student population in the state's largest school district to below 24,000.

With many of the students transferring to schools in East Hartford, Manchester, and other surrounding communities, city schools had seen the steepest student decline in four years. Since the trustee takeover, there had been a noticeable improvement in operations and the implementation of policies intended to increase student achievement. Encouraged by this, I applauded the trustees and joined with others in recommending they remain until June 30, 2002.

In September 1998 Connecticut Governor John Rowland announced the creation of a program aimed at developing downtown Hartford. The program would be managed by the newly created Capital City Economic Development Authority (CCEDA). The governor named his friend Arthur T. Anderson, a developer and West Hartford resident, as chair of the CCEDA board. Of the six others named to the board, only one, Miguel Jose Matos, lived in Hartford. This caused questions about linkage of downtown development to the needs of city neighborhoods. Matos, who was chair of the Hartford chapter of the Local Initiatives Support Corporation, pledged not to forget the city's neighborhoods.

The charge given CCEDA by Governor Rowland and state legislators was to stimulate Hartford's economy by the development of what they called the "six pillars." The six pillars included building a convention center, a downtown University of Connecticut campus, renovation of the Civic Center, one thousand units of housing, revitalization of the riverfront, and new parking facilities. Although it was not one of the "six pillars," a stadium would also be built for the New England Patriots. Owners of the professional football team were considering a move from Massachusetts, and both state and city officials in Connecticut were trying to convince the owners to move the team to Hartford. Three hundred million dollars had been set aside by the state legislature to finance CCEDA's work.

"If CCEDA is successful, in forty years there will be a lot more people living downtown and throughout the city," Anderson told those gathered at Burns Elementary School for the annual Hartford Areas Rally Together Community Congress. Two weeks later, in October 1998, some of Hartford's Black leaders met with the CCEDA board. They included Muhammad Ansari, president of the Greater Hartford African-American Alliance, and a number of others from the North End.

"I've been here most of my life, and I've seen North Hartford get shortchanged like everyone else," Ansari said.

In reply, Anderson promised that "CCEDA would work hard to make sure city residents benefit from jobs created by downtown development." As news of CCEDA became front-page news, some city leaders complained that it looked as though Hartford's elected officials were being pushed aside.

Hearing these complaints, I stated publicly that "downtown Hartford was in need of revitalization, and CCEDA and the city council would work together." At the conclusion of the first joint meeting between the city council and the CCEDA board in November, my expectations were high. I felt the city was finally moving toward developing downtown. Who could have known at the time that within a year, a scandal would bring CCEDA's work to a halt and force Anderson to resign as board chair?

In early February 1999, my attention turned to yet another disturbing occurrence at Fire Department Headquarters. Fire Chief Robert E.J. Dobson had been given three weeks unpaid suspension by City Manager Borges. She also ordered him to reimburse the city more than $3,500 for the compensatory, sick, and regular time he was accused of misusing. For some reason unknown to me, the *Hartford Courant* had been tracking the chief's movements. The newspaper reported that it had observed Dobson spending time at his family business in Bloomfield during periods when he reported on his city time card that he was working. Dobson, who became the city's third Black fire chief after Chief Nelson Carter's retirement, was appointed in 1995. But this was not the only matter giving me cause for concern. Events surrounding a yearlong lawsuit had now become a personal irritation. I had been accused of "interfering with, and preventing" the plaintiff, Dana J. Wright of Lewis Street Holding Company, from purchasing and developing property in downtown Hartford because he was Black. Mayor Peters and three other council members were also named in the suit. What I was beginning to realize at the time was that this issue, which became known as the "Cutter Site issue," was turning me off politics.

The so-called Cutter Site issue began almost four years earlier, in May 1995, prior to my election to the city council. The council voted then to allow Lewis Street Holding Company to purchase a parcel of land downtown called the Cutter Site. On this site, the holding company planned to develop a pedestrian-oriented urban square with boutiques, galleries, cafes, and a bed and breakfast. There would also be a simulated rain forest on a rooftop that would serve as an aviary for rare, tropical species and exotic butterflies. The new development, which would be called Olde Town Square, was estimated to cost $25 million. The contract which was signed in July 1995, called for the holding company to pay $4 million for the purchase of the city-owned land. It stipulated that the company had six months to close on the sale. Dana J. Wright, one of the Lewis Street Holding Company's principals, estimated that the development would create at least four hundred jobs and bring families into the city.

In early January 1996, when the $4 million was due, Wright asked the city to lend back to the company $1.5 million to help leverage the cost of financing the construction. I listened as Wright explained that the city loan would expedite the project and allow them to avoid raising the money privately over the next several months.

"The Lewis Holding Company has raised five million dollars to buy the site and to do the initial demolition and environmental work and an additional two-point-five million," Wright explained. "By adding the city's one-point-five million, we would have enough equity to borrow sixteen million more from area banks for construction." When Wright finished speaking, some council members raised concern over the city lending back $1.5 million to the company, saying they never anticipated any city funding of the project. The session ended with the council asking Wright to provide more detailed information about the source of construction funds. City Manager Borges told Wright she wanted letters from the banks showing their level of commitment. When questioned by a reporter about Wright's request, I responded that I would remain undecided until the city manager had all the necessary information.

"We're in the trenches trying to fine-tune everything," I said. At the February council meeting, it was voted only to extend the closing date of the sale of the property. No action was taken on the request for the city to lend $1.5 million back to the Lewis Holding Company. The company now had until noon Friday, March 1, 1996, just under two weeks, to show it had financial backing for the project.

Meanwhile, Wright had filed an ethics complaint in late January with the Commission on Human Rights and Opportunities against

Mayor Peters and council members O'Connell and McGary, claiming they were conspiring against him. He also claimed they privately favored another developer who had bid on the property. In his complaint Wright told the commission that he was being treated differently than White businessmen. On March 1 the city manager announced that the noon deadline had expired, and she had not received the requested financial information from Wright. When questioned as to what the city would do now, the city manager replied that the city would again seek bids from those interested in developing the site. Wright objected, claiming that the city council had ignored the financial backing he had obtained from Memcorp, a financial consulting firm based in Dallas, Texas. Wright said he was confused by the council's actions.

"We walked in with a bona fide party that has assets and the ability to finance the project one hundred percent," he told a reporter. "With the game they're playing, I could walk in there with twenty million dollars in cash, and they still wouldn't sell me the property." Wright claimed that city officials were undermining his efforts. "The city violated its contract to sell the property by not providing me with key documents, and by placing additional conditions on Lewis Holding Company," he said. Meanwhile, after reading Wright's complaint, the Commission on Human Rights and Opportunities announced that it merited further investigation. Hearing this, Wright felt somewhat vindicated.

"It's a small victory," he said, "but to get to closure on this, we are going to need a lot of small victories." While all of this was happening, I knew Wright believed I was part of a conspiracy against him. I actually wanted his company to develop the property. But as city council majority leader, I had to be sure all matters leading to that end were done in proper order.

While City Manager Borges was preparing to put out the call for new bids on the Cutter Site, council members responded with jubilation when news came that Hartford had been selected to host a presidential debate between President Bill Clinton and Senator Bob Dole. Four years earlier Connecticut had submitted a bid to the Commission on Presidential Debates to host one of the four nationally televised debates.

"If Hartford is selected," Governor Rowland said at the time, "the debate would bring in two thousand journalists and generate an estimated two million dollars in local revenue. Now that Hartford had been selected, members of the state's congressional delegation responded with enthusiasm.

"This is without a doubt a major league victory for our state," said an elated Connecticut Senator Christopher Dodd.

Speaking to reporters at a press conference in the Civic Center, a joyful US Representative Barbara Kennelly said, "This is one of the most important events in the city's three hundred year history. I never wanted a vice presidential debate." This remark was in reference to an earlier notification that the state had been awarded one of the vice presidential debates between Vice President Al Gore and candidate Jack Kemp. "I always wanted a presidential debate and I am absolutely ecstatic," the congresswoman said. "This should put Hartford on the map," the *Hartford Courant* said the next day.

The presidential debate was set for Sunday, October 6, 1996. While this gave those of us on the council a welcome relief from city politics, we had just two weeks to prepare Hartford for the national stage. Cleaning crews began working overtime, sprucing up city streets. Abandon buildings were boarded up, so as not to offend any sensibilities, and planters with chrysanthemums were placed along downtown streets. Banners reading "Welcome to the Home of the Presidential Debate" were hung along the highways leading into the city. At the downtown Bushnell Theatre, where the debate was to take place, employees were at work painting and polishing brass.

"The brass is shining like it never has in sixty-six years," Bushnell's associate managing director, Deidre Tavera, said with obvious enthusiasm. Even with all of the excitement, Hartford's ills were not far from the minds of some city residents.

Retired Fire Department Captain Steven Harris was hoping the problems facing Hartford would be discussed during the debate. "I think both parties are getting away from cities to attract those angry White suburban men," he said in response to a reporter's question.

Dan Papermaster, the thirty-two-year-old lawyer who was first with the idea of bringing a presidential debate to Hartford, was upbeat. "What happens at the debate could be critical to the success of Hartford," he told a reporter. For Papermaster, the debate was "a chance to show that tremendous things are going on in Hartford."

Having voted for Clinton in the last election and intending to vote for him again, I was hoping the candidates would say something about the problems facing our nation's cities. When the debate began, I was sitting near the front in a seat reserved for city council members. Jim Lehrer of the *PBS News Hour* introduced President William Jefferson Clinton and invited him to give a two-minute opening statement. The president thanked the City of Hartford for hosting the debate. He highlighted his record, which included putting more police officers on the street; tackling juvenile gangs; and moving people from welfare to work. He talked about his desire to make education a high priority in his second term. During the debate I listened intently as the president spoke about his effort to help families impart values to their own children; about his support of safe and drug-free school programs; and his effort to get marijuana and cocaine off city streets. I was pleased with what President Clinton had to say, and after the debate, I was honored to shake his hand and introduce myself as a city council member and supporter.

The presidential debate was a positive distraction from the frustration I had felt three days earlier when I learned that I was named in a lawsuit. I was now being accused of conspiring to damage Dana Wright's credibility because he was Black. How ironic, I thought. Throughout my career I had fought against racism and for the elimination racial and gender barriers. I knew firsthand how it felt to be the object of discrimination. Skin color was a factor in my experience as a rookie fire fighter and during my time as fire chief. I knew of Wright's social activism in the city, and admired him for what he was trying to accomplish. He had been one of the leaders of the local Black Labor Committee that picketed St. Francis Hospital for not having sufficient numbers of Black and Hispanic workers on their construction site. When I was chief of the fire department, one of my priorities had been to advance the cause of women, Blacks, and Hispanics.

During the protests at St Frances, the State Commission on Human Rights and Opportunity called for separate hiring goals for women and ethnic minorities. And as the well-respected civil rights lawyer John Brittan took up Wright's cause, I quietly sided with him on this issue. But now Wright had included me, along with Mayor Peters, John O'Connell, Anthony DiPentima, and Michael McGarry, in his lawsuit against the city. His suit alleged I was a co-conspirator in breach of contract, and racial discrimination. This lawsuit would hang over my head for the next two years.

Politics, someone said, is the art of making good compromises. I had grown weary of making compromises and the contentiousness of politics. In a few months, the Democratic Town Committee would meet to identify its slate of candidates for the next election. I had already decided not to seek reelection. I was sixty-eight and wanted no more of politics.

"After a life dedicated to public service, it is time for my family and, particularly my cherished wife, to enjoy the autumn of our life together," I told a reporter. Not far from my thinking were the recent deaths of two friends, former Councilman Collin Bennett and former Deputy City Manager Henry Langley. I was having thoughts about my own mortality, and how I could best use whatever time I had left on this earth. I knew my record as city council majority leader over the past four years would show I had made a successful transition from the fire chief to an effective city council member. Sure, I had to become political. I learned that one has to be a political in order to get things done.

At the end of April 1998, a story ran in the *Hartford Courant* with the headline, "3ʳᵈ Term For Stewart Not Likely."

"Council Majority Leader John B. Stewart Jr. is expected to announce that he will not run for a third term this year," the article began. "Stewart, 68, said that after more than 40 years of service to the city, including 12 as the city's first African American fire chief, it may be time to spend more time with his family."

As I told the reporter, "I had other roles to play and you don't know how long the good Lord is going to keep you here." At the opening of the city council session on Monday, May 24, 1999, I announced my retirement.

> After 47 years of public service, I have come to a decision that it is time to make way for a new generation of leaders. It is time to pass the challenge and opportunity of leadership to the next generation. You're looking at one of the most blessed persons in the world. I have been blessed with a wonderful wife, children and family. I have been blessed with good health and a strong faith in God. All of which have provided meaning and direction in my life. Most would say that this is enough for anyone to be grateful for. Who could ask or expect more out of life? And yet, I have been blessed with much more. I have been blessed with the additional fulfillment of having the opportunity to serve the community I love most, the City of Hartford, for more than forty-seven years.

> When I became a fire fighter in 1952, Hartford was a different city. I was the seventh African American fire fighter in the Hartford Fire Department. Who at that time, including myself, would have dreamt that I would rise through the ranks to become the department's first African American Fire chief? But that did happen. Dreams do come true. And

dedicating my life in service to the people of Hartford has been a dream come true for me. Yes, Hartford has changed. Many today seem to dwell on the negative, to see only the cracks and faults in our city. But I challenge everyone to stop for one moment and reflect. We've had bad times in the past, and we have always overcome them.

I'm sure many of my colleagues seated around me today, and viewers at home, remember the riots of the '60s, the collapse of the civic center roof, the tragic circus fire, and floods which devastated the people of Hartford in the earlier part of this century. The good old days were not always that good. But we overcame these adversities. Today, African Americans and Latinos hold positions of power, authority, and leadership, not only in our great city, but also in our state and nation. This is a legacy I am proud to have been a part of for my entire adult life. God bless the City of Hartford! God bless us all.

Before taking my seat, I offered my council colleagues some words of caution. "There are some strong candidates in the upcoming election. This will make it very interesting. I would caution my fellow council members to be alert." Then I made my pitch for Steve Harris, a Vietnam veteran and retired fire department captain, as the person I was supporting to replace me on the city council.

"I urge my city council colleagues to support him. It is my firm belief that Steve Harris will bring the kind of leadership skills and abilities that will carry the city of Hartford into a new era of prosperity. I am placing my full support behind him. He's a guy who can go anywhere, work with anyone, from corporate boardrooms to any neighborhood in the city." When I completed these remarks, the people in the council chamber stood and applauded. As I sat down, I thought to myself, this is my second and my last retirement from city government.

Some people in Hartford city government had thought that I had been in contention with Mayor Peters to see which of us had the most clout with the voters. To be honest, I did feel as though I had considerable power, but it was the power given to me by the people of Hartford. So I was pleased to read in the newspaper that Mayor Peters agreed with my selection of Steve Harris as my replacement on the Democratic slate.

"I think Steve would be a wonderful addition," said the mayor. "He's been in Hartford all his life. He cares about the city. He's someone you can trust." When the November 1999 general election results were counted, fifty-two-year-old Steve Harris had easily won the council seat I had left empty. I was now back at home with Gladys. In February of 2000 I learned of the death of my cousin Frank Davis, one of the first six Black fire fighters hired in 1948. I was glad he had lived long enough to see the department go through a positive transformation. For the remainder of the year, I concentrated on my real estate business, *Stewart and Associates*. On occasion Gladys and I would take our bag of quarters and drive over to Foxwoods Casino in Mashantucket, Connecticut. Then in December came the news came of the death of former City Manager Woodrow Wilson Gaitor.

JOHN B. STEWART JR. FOR MAYOR

In January of 2001, I let it be known in certain political circles that I might be interested in running for mayor. I would only do so, I said, if the present mayor chose not to run. Sure, I had given my farewell speech over a year ago. I said it was time to hand the leadership over to a new generation of leaders. And yes, I had said that I was done with politics and wanted to spend more time with my family. So you can imagine how surprised people were when they read Stan Simpson's column in the *Hartford Courant* in February.

> I thought the 70-year-old Stewart, adamant about enjoying life in semi-retirement, was simply blowing smoke about his mayoral intentions. Plus, I figured his wife, Gladys, would clobber him if he even thought about getting actively involved in politics again. But Stewart is already recruiting.

Well, Simpson was partly right. My mind wasn't completely made up, but I was very close. Gladys didn't "clobber" me. But even at the thought of running for mayor, she did tell me I needed to have my head examined.

At city hall I saw only gridlock and political infighting. It had been more than a year since Mayor Peters had been able to get a majority council vote, and his lack of effectiveness made him look vulnerable. He had lost the battle over who would be the city's new corporation counsel, and he was defeated in a special charter reform election. After his charter defeat, he had spoken publicly of possibly not seeking reelection. If I chose to run for mayor, I knew I could take that office back to where it belonged. I decided to make the rounds of friends, community, and political leaders to seek their counsel. A number of them felt that if Peters didn't run, I would be the natural successor. Others remained loyal to the mayor.

At the same time, some elected officials were accusing me of causing trouble during a difficult time in city government. Then there were those who saw me as an old political veteran and the last person to be considered as "an agent of change." But by now I had made up my mind. I had decided that if Peters rejected the endorsed Democratic slate and formed his own slate, I would run against him. Simpson had already written of such a matchup in his column.

This would set the stage for the most contested city mayoral race in 10 years. It would feature retired fire fighters: John B. Stewart Jr., the stalwart Northender and twice the top council vote getter, vs. Peters, the still-popular but fading South Ender.

In March, I decided to have a sit-down with Eddie A. Perez, who many believed was planning to enter the race and attempt to become Hartford's first Hispanic mayor. The forty-three-year old community activist was president of the Southside Institutions Neighborhood Alliances. He had also served as director of community relations for Trinity College. If Perez entered the race, I knew he would be a strong candidate. Hartford was 40 percent Hispanic, one-third Black, and 27 percent White. He was assured the Hispanic vote and would probably win a percentage of the Black and White vote as well. I knew I had my own powerful voting bloc, even though my support in the Black community was not unanimous. I also knew, as one reporter put it, I was still regarded as "a hero in many parts of the city."

At my meeting with Perez, we spent the time feeling each other out and sizing each other up. While he didn't come out and say it, I left with the feeling that Perez was likely to run. The following month, Peters announced he would not seek reelection to a fifth term. Some observers believed Peters decided not to run because he thought I was going to enter the race. Peters knew of my meeting with Eddie Perez, and I wondered if this had something to do with his decision. Was he trying to send me a message? Was he saying, I can't beat Eddie Perez, but I believe you can? Was it that Peters knew that if I ran against him, he would lose? After giving it more thought, I concluded this was the real reason he decided not to run. He knew I could beat him at the polls. For that matter, I also believed I could beat Perez. After being fire chief and majority leader of the city council, I was now envisioning me capping my career as the sixty-fifth mayor of the City of Hartford.

In May I was still somewhat undecided when Perez went to city hall and completed the paperwork that would formally make him a candidate for mayor. Speaking to reporters who had been notified in advance, Perez told them, "In two weeks I will officially announce my candidacy; and I'm going to lay out my vision and hope to unify the city behind that vision." I knew the Democratic Town Committee would announce its endorsed slate in less than two months. This meant that if I wanted to be the endorsed candidate for mayor, I had to make up my mind in a hurry.

In June the Reverend Nora Wyatt and Janice Ford Rossetti, a journalist, both Democrats, announced they were entering the race for mayor. In early July, John Wardlaw the executive director of Hartford's Housing Authority, announced he was in the race. Wardlaw's announcement was followed by one from the Reverend Paul Ritter, a sixty-five-year-old Congregational minister. In his announcement Ritter said he would not seek the official Democratic endorsement, but was setting his sights on winning the September primary. If elected, he promised to follow in Mayor Michael Peters' footsteps and be a cheerleader for the city.

"I'm tired of people saying everything is bad in Hartford," he told reporters. "There is more excitement in Hartford now than in the past twenty years." Ritter had no illusions about the uphill nature of his candidacy. "I'm a survivor," he said. "The Lord kept me here for a reason, and one of them is to be mayor of Hartford." Ritter may have been making reference to a fire at his Tower Avenue home in 1995 that left him severely burned and in critical condition.

Then, a week later, in a sudden about-face, Wardlaw withdrew from the race. This was the result of fallout from negative comments he made when announcing his candidacy. Wardlaw had stated to reporters that he was running because he wanted to ease racial tensions and the possibility of a race riot in Hartford. He called Hartford a "racial tinderbox" and voiced concern that a campaign against Perez could increase racial tension. He said he would reach out to Perez and ask him to pledge not to engage in a race-based campaign. Throughout the week people were dismissing Wardlaw's dire predictions. The lack of support from residents, he was now saying, had caused him to change his mind about running for mayor.

"I'm very, very disappointed that anyone who walks the streets, who goes into the neighborhoods, would just flat-out deny its existence," he said. "Racial and economic tensions are a sleeping monster in Hartford that must be addressed. I would be the wrong man for the job if city leaders and residents did not want to acknowledge obvious problems." Wardlaw ended his announcement by calling for the formation of a commission to study racial division in Hartford. This call was quickly rejected by Wyatt.

"I think we have problems, but not to the extent that there could be race riots," he said. He then added, "Wardlaw's withdrawal leaves just two legitimate candidates in the race, me and Mr. Perez." The following day three more people entered the mayor's race. They included Robert Ludgin, the former councilman and deputy mayor; Adam Cloud, a member of Hartford's Economic Development Commission; and Kenneth Mink, a North End community activist. This brought the total number of Democrats in the race to six. If I announced my candidacy, I would be number seven.

At the time, I was giving serious thought to something Stan Simpson had written in a recent column:

> Hartford's first Black fire chief is a living legend. He's a mentor for a host of political wannabes. But the man who turns 71 in June also represents the same sort of old-guard leadership and petty politics that have stymied progress.

Could Simpson be right? Did I really represent the old-guard leadership and petty politics that stymied progress? If that were truly the case, then it was time for me to "hang them up," as Simpson suggested. Gladys also thought it was time. In July 2001, as a noncandidate, I attended the Town Committee meeting and watched Eddie Perez become the endorsed candidate for mayor. The primary was held on September 11, 2001, when the country was trying to recover from the terrorist attack on the World Trade Center eleven days earlier. Perez received more than 70 percent of the primary votes, far outdistancing Robert Ludgin. When the general election votes were counted, Eddie Perez became the mayor-elect. He had come a long way since 1954, when he came to the United States from Puerto Rico, unable to speak a word of English. Now he was set to become the first Hispanic mayor in Hartford's history. I have never regretted not running for mayor, but I still believe that if I had run, I would have won.

Twenty-two months later, on the morning of May 16, 2003, I was honored by the City of Hartford in a way that it had not honored any person before. Over a hundred people gathered outside Engine Company 14 on Blue Hills Avenue. The gathering was not in celebration of my seventy-third birthday, which happened to be that very day, but to witness a firehouse being named in honor of a living person. I sat between Mayor Perez and Fire Chief Charles Teale, on a stage that had been erected in front of the firehouse. The several dozen chairs in front of the stage were occupied by family members and friends. Mayor Perez stood at the podium and read the city's official proclamation:

> Whereas John B. Stewart has received many honors and awards because of his stellar career over the years, today, Hartford wants to honor you for your exceptional public service, now be it resolved that I, Eddie Perez, Mayor of the City of Hartford, alongside the City Council, your loving family, residents of this city and your many friends, hereby name engine Company 14 firehouse after you and declare today, Friday, May 16, 2003 as John B. Stewart day in the City of Hartford.

When Mayor Perez finished reading the proclamation, the cover was pulled away from the top entrance to the firehouse, revealing in large letters the words "Chief John B. Stewart Jr. Fire Station." I stood looking up at my name carved deep into the red brick. While such an honor is not rare in some cities, I knew this was a first for Hartford. There was no precedent in the city for naming a fire station—a public building that the city controls—after a living person. Added to this, May 16, 2003, was being proclaimed John B. Stewart Jr. Day in the city of Hartford. Then the cover over the bronze plague affixed to the front of the building was pulled away. The Chief John B. Stewart Jr. Fire Station, it read. On the wall inside the firehouse was an image of me etched in bronze. Beneath my image it read:

> To Commemorate John B. Stewart Jr. who has demonstrated by his many actions and has created an exemplary long record of services and accomplishments that have added to the quality of life of our communities by which he has become a recognized leader internationally, nationally and locally as both a fire professional and humanitarian.

The Hartford Court of Common Council hereby wishes to commend and recognize John B. Stewart Jr. for his years of faithful service to our city, its communities and the fire service, and therefore names and dedicates this building the John B. Stewart Jr. Fire Station.

When the applause ended, I stood at the podium to speak.

I am reminded today why it was so important for me to select a black person to succeed me as fire chief. It has to do with history. Unfortunately, too often and too quickly, we forget our history. I grew up in a Jewish community and they never let me forget the Holocaust. I always admired the Jewish people because they never let you forget their history. Blacks in the fire service from around the country made history when we came together in 1970 and organized the International Association of Black Professional Fire Fighters. We were fighting for equality in the fire service.

In August of 1982 we held our Biannual Convention in Lexington, Kentucky. In attendance were five Black Chief Officers. This was the first time that we'd had a conference where chief officers were assembled. There was Stan Golden, the first African American Chief in Oakland, California. Also present were Ray Brooks, the first African American chief in Indiana City, Indiana, Colonel Keith Larry Bonnafon, the first African American Chief in Lexington, Kentucky, and Robert Osby, the first African American Chief in San Jose, California... We were later joined by Ron Lewis, who left Philadelphia to go to Richmond and become the first African American chief. He'd been told by Philadelphia Mayor Frank Rizzo's machine that "you're not going any further."

The late Charles Hendricks, a fire fighter out of Philadelphia, Pennsylvania, who didn't want to take the time to fight the system in Philadelphia, was there. One of the challenges he gave those of us who were chiefs was to reach back and help others in our organizations. "Now that you chief officers have made it to the top," he said to us, "you must be role models to ensure others to follow your path, to be encouraged, to move up through the ranks." I feel honored that I can see my name up here before I close my eyes, that someone doesn't have to come up to heaven and say, Chief Stewart, they finally put your name up.

As I reflect on this special day, I give thanks to the good Lord. Even now when I drive by this firehouse, I am left feeling very humbled and blessed. It was a hard climb up the ladder, but I made it to the top.

EPILOGUE

"HEY, BLACK MAN!"

One Sunday after worship had ended, I was standing in front of Faith Congregational Church talking with several friends. My daughter Holly, a little four-year-old at the time, was holding tight to my hand. Having grown tired of waiting for our conversation to end, she called out to me in a soft voice, "Dad, Dad." I heard her calling out, but I continued talking with my friends. After a few seconds had passed she called out again, this time a little louder while tugging on my arm, "Dad, Dad." Still I continued in conversation. Now, having grown angry at being ignored, little four-year-old Holly tilted her head up in my direction and yelled-out in a loud voice, "Hey, Black man!" Well, that was enough to stop our conversation. We all looked down at little Holly in surprise and then broke into smiles. As Holly looked up at me with pleading eyes, I couldn't help but wonder how this child knew these words would grab our attention? I gently squeezed Holly's hand to let her know I had heard her. Then looking over in the distance, I could see Gladys and several others of our children. Holding on to Holly's hand, we walked toward them. Yes indeed, I thought to myself as a scooped Holly up into my arms, I am indeed one proud Black man.

Being married to Gladys was like a dream come true. If it had not been for her, I would not have achieved all that I did. You had to have a wife like I had to truly understand what I mean. God brought us together, and we had never been separated. I was the only man she was ever with. When our children were young, Gladys provided for them a home atmosphere of family love, nurture, and togetherness.

She participated in all of their activities, helping out at their school, with the scouts, and being a baseball coach. I looked forward to coming home in the evening and checking on Gladys and the children, making sure they were okay. Our evenings at home together were to be family time, free of the worries and the stresses of the day. Even as my responsibilities in the fire department increased, if I started talking about how the day went, Gladys got the family to cut me off and change the subject.

"Leave those headaches downtown," she would tell me. "When you come home, you have a wife and a family that you have to think about." On some occasions she would ask me how my day went, but not if it was obvious and she could see it on my face or in my attitude.

Gladys also had a very busy life. Besides being a wife and mother she served on the usher board and was chairperson of the flower committee at Faith Congregational Church. She was a member of the Eastern Star, Daughters of Isis-Prince Hall Masons, and she was designated a Silver Star Mother by the Salvation Army. She loved to restore furniture, decorate our home, and entertain relatives and friends. On my days off, I would help around the house by washing windows, mopping floors, washing dishes, and helping Gladys with other household chores. Sometimes the children would help me as I did repairs around the house. Like the time Wendy was on the roof helping me replace broken tiles. She seemed so happy working with me. On weekends when I wasn't on duty at the firehouse, I would make breakfast for the family. We would have pancakes, eggs, bacon, and cereal. I enjoyed doing this, plus I wanted to give Gladys a break. I watched cartoons with the children, and then took them to the grocery store, where they would pick out the cereals they saw advertised on the television. I never hollered much at the kids. I didn't believe in hollering. I thought if you screamed at the kids, it didn't make for a happy home. At Christmas I was like a big generous kid. I would buy the children lots of toys.

"Stop spoiling the children," Gladys would tell me. "You give them everything they want." But I didn't spoil the kids. Gladys wouldn't let me—although I did give the kids whatever they wanted. For example, when Wendy and Gregory wanted bicycles, Gladys said, "Don't buy them brand new bikes. We can't afford it. Get used ones." But I didn't listen to her. I brought two brand-new bikes. The owner of the bike store let me have them on credit when he saw me in my uniform. He didn't ask any questions. I was simply to pay him $2.50 a week. I thought that would be easy enough. But when I didn't have the money and couldn't pay, he came down to the firehouse looking for me. Maybe I should have listened to Gladys, but I felt my kids had to have new bikes. When our other children wanted bikes, they got rehabbed ones.

At times I could be stubborn. At least, that's what Gladys would tell people. "He's stubborn just like the rest of the Stewart clan," she would say. Once I was taking the family to Yankee Stadium in the Bronx to see a New York Yankees baseball game. Tweet, as we affectionately called Gladys, was a Yankees fan. At the time Jeffery was a baby, so he was to stay with his Aunt Dottie. Wendy, who was a tomboy, wanted to wear pants to the game. Feeling she ought to dress up, I told her to put on a dress or a skirt. But Wendy could be stubborn too. She refused to change clothes, so I made her stay with her Aunt Dottie as well.

At times I could also be a real prankster. Once when the family was getting ready for bed, Wendy came and told me there was a spider on her pillow. I pretended to pay her no mind, and told her to go to sleep. After Wendy came back several times complaining about a spider on her pillow, her brothers Gregory and Donald began to laugh. Only then did Wendy realize who had placed a rubber spider on her pillow.

In those early days when the children were young, I had a green 1969 station wagon. Green was my favorite color. I loved taking the family on day trips. We went to Lake George, Fort Ticonderoga, the Catskill Game Farm, a Native American village in Upstate New York, and many other places. Sometimes we would go on overnight trips, like the time we went to Quebec and slept in a log cabin. Two times

I drove the family down to Disney World in Orlando, Florida. Each time we stopped over in Hampton, Virginia, to visit relatives. The children had so much fun. The family would tease me because wherever we went on a road trip, I would strike up conversations with strangers while they waited patiently—and sometimes not so patiently. We attended family and company picnics, and we went to the ocean, to lakes, and to beaches. We regularly went on Sunday drives through the New England countryside, especially when the foliage was changing colors.

But it was Gladys who made us a family circle. She was my loving partner and our children's patient and understanding mother. She didn't let things bother her. Most of her strength came from her faithful reading of her Bible, and the verses she would quote. You couldn't put anything over on her. She could see through things, when people were using you and not being true. It was in 2004 that Gladys was diagnosed with a breathing disorder. As her condition worsened, she rarely left the house except for scheduled visits to her doctor. This was a difficult time for the family. After more than seven years of trouble breathing and growing weaker and more tired, Gladys, who loved the Lord dearly, began to say she was ready for the Lord to take her home. On Sunday, April 17, 2011, God did take our beloved wife and mother to be with Him.

That Sunday morning Gladys had been taken by ambulance to St. Francis Hospital because her breathing had become very shallow and faint. We had rushed her to the hospital several times before, but this time she appeared to be in more distress. She was seventy-eight years old, and had been my companion and loving wife for sixty-one wonderful years. Now Gladys was gone from me. The following week, on Thursday, April 21, the family gathered at Faith Congregational Church to celebrate her life. Our son John, a major in the Salvation Army, spoke for the family. Reverend Rubin Tendai, a former pastor of Faith Church, delivered the eulogy. His text was chapter fourteen, verses seven through nine, of Paul's Epistle to the Romans which reads: